# ECONOMY-WIDE MODELS
# AND DEVELOPMENT PLANNING

## Contributors

CHARLES R. BLITZER  is an Economist at the Development Research Center of the World Bank.

MICHAEL BRUNO  is Professor of Economics at the Hebrew University in Jerusalem and Director of the Maurice Falk Institute for Economic Research.

HOLLIS CHENERY  is Vice President, Development Policy, of the World Bank.

PETER B. CLARK  is Staff Director, New England Energy Policy Council, and at the time this volume was prepared was a Senior Economist at the Development Research Center of the World Bank.

MRINAL K. DATTA-CHAUDHURI  is Professor of Economics at the Delhi School of Economics.

JOHN H. DULOY  is Director of the Development Research Center of the World Bank.

PETER B. R. HAZELL  is an Economist at the Development Research Center of the World Bank.

JANOS KORNAI  is Professor of Economics at the Institute of Economics of the Hungarian Academy of Sciences.

DANIEL P. LOUCKS  is Associate Professor of Environmental Engineering at Cornell University.

T. N. SRINIVASAN  is Professor of Economics at the Indian Statistical Institute and head of its Planning Unit.

LANCE TAYLOR  is Professor of Economics and Nutrition at the Massachusetts Institute of Technology.

TSUNEHIKO WATANABE  is Professor of Economics at Osaka University.

LARRY E. WESTPHAL  is Chief of the Economics of Industry Division of the World Bank, and at the time this volume was prepared was Associate Professor of Economics at Northwestern University.

# Economy-Wide Models
# and
# Development Planning

*edited by*

CHARLES R. BLITZER
PETER B. CLARK
LANCE TAYLOR

*Published for the*
**WORLD BANK**
*by*
OXFORD UNIVERSITY PRESS
1975

*Oxford University Press, Ely House, London W.1*

GLASGOW   NEW YORK   TORONTO   MELBOURNE   WELLINGTON
CAPE TOWN   IBADAN   NAIROBI   DAR ES SALAAM   LUSAKA   ADDIS ABABA
DELHI   BOMBAY   CALCUTTA   MADRAS   KARACHI   LAHORE   DACCA
KUALA LUMPUR   SINGAPORE   HONG KONG   TOKYO

CASEBOUND ISBN 0 19 920073 4
PAPERBACK ISBN 0 19 920074 2

*Library of Congress Catalog Card Number 74–29171*

*Printed in Great Britain*
*by William Clowes & Sons, Limited, London, Beccles and Colchester*

# CONTENTS

# PREFACE

This volume amounts to a rather comprehensive survey of the specification and uses of economy-wide planning models for developing countries. These models focus mainly on medium-term and perspective planning, and in practice must be used with tools more adapted to other concerns of planning offices, i.e., short-term stabilization policy, on the one hand, and evaluation of possible industrialization strategies and even specific investment projects, on the other.

Why, then, have we all collaborated on a book with this particular focus? First, most (if not all) developing country governments are attempting at least some economy-wide modelling. Fairly large resources, in terms of skilled manpower and computational facilities, have been committed to building, estimating, and solving all the types of models discussed in this book—from Harrod–Domar forecasts to dynamic multisectoral optimizing models. Second (and more importantly), there is a strong learning-by-doing phenomenon in model building. Data are forced into a consistent framework, with obvious implicit suggestions for improvement, and the models themselves often shed considerable light on the workings of the economy. Our hope here is to aid both practical planners and potential model builders by providing a summary of best-practice techniques and extensive discussion of what models can and cannot do in practice. Since putting together an economy-wide model is time-consuming and laborious, such guidelines as are laid out here may prove to be useful in the field.

There are a dozen essays written by as many authors in this volume. As editors, we have not sought to impose full uniformity of style or opinion; indeed, several chapters reach opposite conclusions regarding the same issue. But we have tried to minimize duplication of effort by dividing the volume into differentiated parts and chapters. Chapters I–IV are concerned with general planning issues, data collection and estimation, and the theoretical bases of economy-wide planning models. The next four chapters deal with how these models are applied to specific policy problems such as investment planning, income distribution, and foreign trade. Finally, Chapters IX–XII cover methodological problems, such as how to model economies of scale, factor substitution, and regional interactions in the national economy.

In order to coordinate and discuss among ourselves the succeeding drafts of the chapters in this volume, the authors met three times between September 1972 and September 1973, twice at the Development Research Center of the World Bank and once at the Institute for Development Studies at the University of Sussex in Brighton, England. The project as a whole was financed by the World Bank and organized through the Bank's Development Research Center. However, all views expressed are those of the individual authors,

they should not be taken as representing either official World Bank policy or the viewpoints of other contributors.

On behalf of all the authors, we wish to thank the following individuals for the many constructive comments and suggestions they have made on drafts of various chapters: Clive Bell, University of Sussex; Jorge Cauas, Development Research Center, World Bank; Hollis Chenery, Vice-President, World Bank; Richard Eckaus, Massachusetts Institute of Technology; Donald Erlenkotter, University of California, Los Angeles; Leif Johansen, University of Oslo; Dharma Kumar, Indian Statistical Institute; Alan Manne, Stanford University; Graham Pyatt, University of Warwick; Ardy Stoutjesdijk, Development Research Center, World Bank; and Suresh Tendulkar, Indian Statistical Institute.

The authors wish to thank each of their respective institutions for providing logistical and secretarial support. We are also grateful to the Institute of Development Studies at Sussex for the use of its facilities. Frank Lysy of the Development Research Center has kept our references and bibliographies both coherent and up-to-date. He has also prepared a list of additional readings, not cited by the chapter authors, to provide further background or alternative treatments of the topics covered in this book. We are also indebted to Nina Michajliczenko of the Development Research Center who provided most of the logistical support for regular meetings of economists from several continents and did a remarkably efficient job of typing, cataloging and circulating the various chapter drafts.

Finally we thank our girl friends, wives and children, who have gracefully accepted our preoccupations and absences during this period.

*Brasilia*  
*December 1973*

CHARLES R. BLITZER  
PETER B. CLARK  
LANCE TAYLOR

# FOREWORD

HOLLIS CHENERY

In the past quarter century the field of development planning has evolved from the first crude attempts to formulate development policies into an established branch of economics with an extensive literature and widespread practice. As countries have developed and their experience has increased, approaches to policy making have become more complex. Although debate continues over the role of formal planning and the relations between planning and implementation, there is widespread acceptance of the usefulness of some form of systematic economic analysis as a basis for government policy.

The models of developing countries that are used as a basis for policy making reflect economists' changing perceptions of the basic characteristics of developing countries. For example, the existence of a surplus of unskilled labor, while a debatable hypothesis in the 1950s, is all too apparent in the 1970s as a result of the accelerated growth of population. On the other hand, models of closed economies, despite their pedagogical usefulness, have been of little value for development policy because of the crucial role of international trade in the process of development.

The analytical tools that were initially applied to the study of development were borrowed with little modification from advanced countries. The result of twenty years of empirical experimentation and theoretical refinement has been to produce a second generation of planning models that have been tested in empirical applications and redesigned to fit the data and policy instruments available. As a way of introducing the subject matter of this volume, it may be useful to view some of the central problems of planning today against the perspective of the evolution of this methodology over the past fifteen years.

First of all, there is a widespread acceptance of planning techniques that were largely experimental ten or fifteen years ago. These planning techniques have centered on the multisector input-output framework and its extensions into linear programming. In the course of this development, data have been collected specifically for use with these techniques. As a result, interindustry, foreign trade, consumer demand, and employment data are now compiled regularly in many developing countries. Since time series of these statistics are accumulating, future estimates can be based increasingly on econometric techniques rather than on single-point observations.

Ten years ago, few countries took any objective seriously other than that to maximize economic growth. Now, the modification of social objectives and the introduction of new constraints, particularly in the areas of improved

income distribution and employment possibilities, are close to the top of the planners' agenda.[1] Since aggregate income is so low in developing countries, these other objectives become meaningful only when adequate overall economic growth can be attained. Therefore, the recent shift in emphasis does not necessarily imply that planners misjudged priorities in the past. Rather, the success of policies for accelerating aggregate growth now permits the planner to deal with income distribution in an effective way.

Another major development of the past decade has been the widespread acceptance of shadow pricing or its equivalent as a practical tool for the appraisal of investment projects. While one should not exaggerate the extent to which investment decisions are influenced by shadow pricing today, understanding of this approach is sufficiently widespread to have produced several volumes written especially for the practical planner. The acceptance of shadow pricing provides an essential link between macroeconomic plans and decentralized decisions on investment projects.

Increasing sophistication requires greater use of the computer. This is no longer a serious obstacle in most countries. Until quite recently, multisectoral models of developing countries often had to be sent to the United States or Europe for solutions, which greatly limited their usefulness. As large-scale digital computers have become more widespread and solution algorithms more efficient, planning agencies have come to perform more of their own calculations. It is now possible to do a number of model experiments with alternative options at reasonable cost. Among countries that have followed this procedure in their planning process are Korea, India, Turkey, Mexico, and Chile.

With the development of planning methods has come a shift in planning administration—decentralization is becoming increasingly popular. Since the techniques required for decentralized planning are still experimental, they receive considerable attention in this volume. Much of the research effort of the next decade will probably be at the sectoral and regional level and on the relations to national plans.

In reflecting on the effect planning models have had on policy, it would be wrong to think of the numerical elaboration of plans as the main result of these exercises. Far more important has been the effect on the planners' way of thinking about development problems. To use the shadow pricing example, the ability to choose among projects has probably been improved greatly by a more sophisticated perception of social opportunity costs and benefits derived from an optimizing model, even without the full-scale application of such a model in a given country.

Perhaps more important than the development of planning models is the increased ability of decision makers to utilize them. In many developing

1. This aspect of planning is examined in a companion volume on *Redistribution with Growth* (Chenery and Associates, 1974).

countries, the economic leadership is increasingly drawn from professionals with sufficient education and ability to conceptualize problems, so that they can use the options provided them by technical planners and model builders. For methodological improvements to be of practical use, this evolution must also continue.

The present volume is aimed primarily at narrowing the gap between theoretical analysis and its practical applications in developing countries. As a development institution, the World Bank has a vital interest in shortening the lag between fundamental research and its application to policy making. In planning the present volume we invited contributors with experience of both kinds to survey the existing literature and promising new techniques for development planning at the national level. Hopefully both the theoretical insights and the distilled experience of applications will be useful to practitioners and students of this field.

Chapter I

# THE STATUS OF PLANNING: AN OVERVIEW

### Charles R. Blitzer

---

## 1. Introduction

Development planning is a complex process involving many different organizations and individual agents interacting in the formulation and execution of a country's economic and social policies. This volume deals with one aspect in this process—the use of economy-wide planning models. Before beginning this review of technique and practice, it is important to put this subject matter into its proper perspective, by examining where our topics fit into the wider and more general field of development planning.

Among the principal agents in the planning process are: policy makers, planners, statisticians, and researchers. Although in the real world there is considerable overlap in their activities and responsibilities, it is useful for our purposes to visualize each agent as being involved in different tasks, typically communicating with each other along the lines outlined in Figure 1. Effective planning, to a great extent, involves developing an efficient flow of information along this chain. This flow is not generally one-way but is multilateral, involving important feedback at all levels.

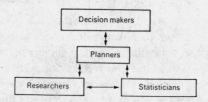

Figure 1.   Information Flows in Planning

These agents need not be identified with any particular organizational set-up; indeed, these same information flows occur in any planning framework—centralized or decentralized, private sector or government. Neither agents designated "planners" nor a central planning office is necessary to the process. Throughout this volume, the use of these terms should be interpreted as suggestive of one common style of organization.

Economy-wide planning models are intended to be a practical tool for investigating certain development problems. As such, their proper operational usage involves all of the chains shown in Figure 1. However, as we shall

emphasize later, because the usage of these models is still largely experimental, we are most concerned in this volume with the planner–researcher linkage. To date, the techniques of formal modelling represent attempts by researchers to respond to the needs of planners to learn more about the aggregate problems and intersectoral relations of the growth and development process.

As more countries gain experience with these techniques, more attempts will be made to use model results as part of the information flow between planners and policy makers. This part of the process is the principal subject of Chapter II. At the same time, much data of good quality are required if these models are to evolve beyond the experimental stage. The necessary linkages with the statistician are discussed at length in Chapter IV.

In this chapter, we address the relationship between economy-wide planning models and the whole of development planning from two perspectives. The first involves the conceptual view of models and the planning process, while the second focuses on past experiences and the types of countries for which these methodologies seem most appropriate.

Section 2 begins with a discussion of various organizational frameworks for planning which have been adopted in developing countries. The basic characteristics and uses of formal models are presented in section 3, with special emphasis on the role of economy-wide models. In section 4, we become more specific and address the relationship between the choice of models and particular economic problems and strategies.

## 2. THE FRAMEWORK OF PLANNING

Planning represents an attempt to coordinate economic decision making over the long run, in order to give direction to and accelerate a country's development. This process involves choosing social objectives, setting various targets, disseminating information, as well as organizing a framework for the implementation, coordination, and monitoring of the plan. For the time being, leaving aside economic aspects (such as criteria for project selection or techniques of forecasting national income), we shall concentrate on the structure of planning—the organization of the decision making process, relationships between various decision makers and planners, and strategies for plan implementation.[1]

The countries with which we are concerned all have mixed economies with important public and private sectors producing goods and services. These

---

1. There is voluminous literature on development planning which cannot be adequately summarized in only a few pages. Most of our discussion is based on Tinbergen [1958] and Lewis [1966]. Other important references include Waterston [1965], Hagen [1968], Higgins [1968], Tinbergen [1964], and Meier and Baldwin [1957].

economies are mixed not only in terms of ownership of the means of production but also in terms of interdependence of decision making. For example, the government influences private sector decision making only indirectly through its manipulation of prices, taxes, or tariffs, and sometimes directly through licensing schemes and credit rationing. On the other hand, the private sector usually wields considerable influence with the government, which values the private sector's entrepreneurial role. Effective planning must pay careful attention to this symbiotic relationship.

In addition, neither sector is monolithic. The private sector includes industrialists (both foreign and domestic), small businessmen, farmers, land-lords, artisans, and often important labor unions. There is rarely, if ever, complete mutuality of interests among them. Similarly, governmental power is divided among politicians, bureaucracy, and military in a large number of ministries and organizations which are often quite independent in their objectives and operation. The organizational problems of bringing these divergent elements together and getting them to work together in closer concert to meet long-run national goals are formidable. Typically, a central planning office (CPO) has been created in an attempt to provide the necessary coordination. Since the powers of the CPO vary greatly from country to country, its ability to achieve this coordination has not been uniform. Indeed, a CPO is neither necessary nor sufficient for effective planning. Without a CPO, planning can be organized around particular sectors, whose detailed plans are very loosely coordinated through a ministerial council, the govern-mental budget authority, or representatives of the public and private sectors. (Mexico and Israel are examples of countries which have had satisfactory planning without heavy reliance on a CPO.) On the other hand, if careful sectoral planning, or dialogue with the private sector, or linkages between the CPO and the budgetary authority are ignored, even a plan devised by a technically competent CPO will rarely be well formulated or implemented.

Which organizational framework is most appropriate for any country depends on many factors, including: how economic decisions are made, which sectoral growth strategy is adopted, and what direct and indirect powers are given to planners on the central and sectoral levels. Therefore, we now turn to a brief discussion of various strategies or approaches to planning which a country could choose. For conciseness, a rather abstract view is taken emphasizing the extremes of several approaches while leaving the reader to fill in the continuum.

First, planners can take either an active or passive role in decision making. The "active" planner has some direct control of economic policy. In the limit, the CPO and sectoral planners would have the powers necessary to implement all key aspects of the plan directly. In this case, the distinction between planners and decision makers all but disappears. In such a system, in

3

which the plan is mandatory, other economic agents are subject to the authority of the planners.[2]

At the other end of the spectrum, "passive" planners have little direct control of economic policy. The major role of these planners is to provide critical information about future development alternatives and forecasts to all agents in the economy so that important decisions will be more consistent with common goals than they would be otherwise. The plan itself is indicative,[3] rather than mandatory, with planners acting as advocates and transmitters of information rather than decision makers. Their chief role here is in coordination and monitoring.[4]

Planning can also be characterized by its chain of command. Here we refer only to the "active" aspects of planning. Once again there are two hypothetical extremes. In the one, all decisions are made by a central authority, such as a CPO, which transmits a complete set of instructions to the economy. These can relate to both quantities (taking the form of production targets, import quotas, credit or investment allocations) and prices (wages, taxes, tariffs, or price control guidelines). In contrast to this centralized planning, there are decentralized techniques in which the CPO and sectoral planners send instructions about *how* decisions are to be made. Also, the central planners will usually transmit instructions and guidelines to the sectoral planners. The planner here usually emphasizes price (rather than quantity) policies.[5]

Developing countries fall well within these extremes. The typical ministry of planning is neither GOSPLAN nor the publisher of a prestigious economic newsletter. The Third World is characterized by mixed economies. Planners have little direct control over either the public or private sectors. In dealing with the private sector, the government as a whole, as well as the planning organization, cannot always ignore powerful special interests. Moreover, central planners (e.g., the CPO) rarely have direct control over the government controlled sectors, which are usually managed by a number of separate ministries, often with little coordination. Additional control problems arise if the governmental budget is regulated by a finance ministry which has little interest or involvement in the development of long-run plans.

Nevertheless, almost every CPO controls some economic decisions directly,

---

2. To a certain degree, Soviet-type planning is designed to work in this way. In practice, economic planners have not had such complete powers; see, for example, Bergson [1964] or Nove [1964].

3. "Indicative" planning is common in many developed countries such as Japan, the Netherlands, and France. Excellent discussions of planning in these countries are found in Watanabe [1965, 1970], Netherlands Central Planning Bureau [1965], and Bauchet [1964].

4. For a more complete discussion, see Chapter IV.

5. Several of the chapters in Leeman [1963] discuss the differences between centralized and decentralized planning. For a discussion of recent Eastern European experimentation with decentralized planning, see Kornai [1967, 1974].

such as planning the government's capital budget, approval of direct foreign investment, trade licensing, veto power over certain investment projects, and administration of development assistance programs. While planners usually have more direct influence over the government sector, considerable leverage (through controls and persuasion) can also be applied to the private sector. In addition, while economic decisions are usually made in a decentralized fashion even within the public sector, many of the most important are made centrally —in particular, capital budget allocations and basic fiscal policy.

Thus, the development planner, in both centralized and decentralized systems, has both a passive and active role to play; he helps make and monitor important decisions and designs schemes for improved decentralized planning. While no two planning frameworks are identical in their approach, responsibilities, or mode of operation, it might be useful to attempt to characterize briefly a typical central planner's relationships with other economic agents. Usually, the CPO is responsible for the development of medium- and long-term plans for the economy as a whole, often in the form of Five Year Plans. In building these plans, the planner is engaged in a dialogue with technical specialists and planners in other ministries and the private sector of the economy. The process is complex, time consuming, and filled with compromise. The planner's function is to try to see the whole picture while others pursue more narrow interests. Perhaps even more important is the planner's role in public budgeting. Even when he does not have final authority, he plays an important role vis-à-vis other ministries and the Ministry of Finance in setting investment allocations. Once again, the planner attempts to present the bigger picture over the long run, often in conflict with the realities of the short run.[6]

The planner also engages in a dialogue of give and take with the private sector. For medium-term planning this may take the form of sectoral planning committees which include representatives of various special interest groups. Planners deal with the private sector on a more microeconomic basis regarding individual large scale or foreign investment projects, export and import licensing, as well as price, tax, and tariff policies.

A final point to be emphasized is that the development of a framework and strategy for planning is evolutionary. In many instances, the first planners in a country are a small group of academics, local or foreign, largely carrying out an educational function and, hopefully, training their replacements. As a country gains experience with planning, the organizational set-up may change in response to perceived problems in coordination and implementation. With mixed economies, this will typically imply a diffusion of planning responsibility throughout the economy and increased attention to the sectors and income groups most crucial for attainment of national objectives.

---

6. Tinbergen [1964] is an excellent reference on these problems of the short versus the long run.

## 3. Types of Planning Models

In the previous section, we were concerned with the relationship of planners to other agents of the economy, methods of plan implementation, and various constraints which must be recognized in developing plans and policies. Nothing was said of the methodology of formulating plans and investigating trade-offs or consistency. Formal modelling, qualitative as well as quantitative, is a systematic tool which is available to a planner for these purposes. Model results can provide some of the information necessary for formulating plans and making economic decisions in both the private and public sectors. By using models, the planner is able to study systematically certain economic interrelationships which otherwise might not be easily understood. This process carries over directly into an investigation of possible trade-offs and their magnitude, as well as the internal consistency of a set of plans. In this sense, models are instrumental in character, attempting to relate policies to economic reactions.[7]

It is important to emphasize that while any model should be a reflection of reality, no model is a perfect reflection. This is so for several reasons. A model is an abstraction which can only incorporate certain aspects of the real world. Many economic relationships cannot yet (if ever) be formalized either in quantitative or qualitative terms. Also, all models leave out relationships and details which could, in principle, be included. Not only are very large and comprehensive models expensive to build and to solve computationally, but they are usually more difficult to understand than smaller, simpler formulations. Clearly there are important trade-offs here between a desire to paint the broadest picture possible of an economy and a need for simplicity so that nontechnical planners and policy makers can understand the model's rationale and results.

In order to demonstrate more clearly these trade-offs in model formulation, various characteristics of planning models are reviewed briefly. In this discussion, the work of Tinbergen [1964] is followed closely.

The first important characteristic, or criterion, of a model is its *scope*, which can range from subproject to the entire economy.[8] The appropriate scope is determined by the problems to be analyzed. Thus, national issues such as savings generation, intersectoral investment allocations, or the impact of additional foreign loans are usually central to economy-wide models. On the other hand, choice of technique, location, and size of plant are topics found

---

7. In practice, most economy-wide multisectoral models have included relatively few endogenous policy variables, concentrating instead on formulating consistent projections without explicit linkages with instruments to achieve them. Further discussion on this topic is found in Chapters II and V.

8. The whole world can be included, as is being attempted to a certain degree by Project LINK. See Ball [1973].

in sectoral or project models which pay great attention to detail while treating the rest of the economy as fixed.

*Time* is another very important dimension. Models can be either static or dynamic. Static models generally compare one future date with the present, e.g., now versus five years hence. Dynamic models incorporate endogenous variables from a number (usually between three and five) of time periods, thus providing information to the planner on *how* to get from now to some target year, e.g., yearly investment levels for a five year plan or cumulated investments over the three year subperiods of a twenty year plan.[9]

Another aspect of the model's treatment of time is how far into the future it is designed to project. Model design here is intimately related to the problems to be studied. A short-term model (typically defined as forecasting for at most three years into the future) will often emphasize the role of financial variables in controlling aggregate demand, and may be estimated by econometric techniques on the basis of time series data. Although interesting, and important for formulation of short-term policy, such models are *not* treated extensively in this volume, aside from some general discussion in Chapters III and IV.[10] Rather, the focus here is on models appropriate for medium-term (three- to seven-year horizons) and long-term or "perspective" planning.

The next characteristic is the *focus* of the model, which is often closely related to its degree of aggregation (for a given scope and time horizon). In this sense, essentially three types of medium- and long-term economy-wide models have been applied extensively in developing countries. The first, macroeconomic models, treat the whole economy as one producing sector and are oriented toward forecasts of the major national accounts aggregates. As discussed in Chapter III, the most common representative of this type is the well-known Harrod–Domar model (often extended into a two-gap model by explicit consideration of the foreign trade sector). In contrast with macroeconomic models, there are multisector interindustry planning models which divide the economy into a number of explicit producing sectors. These models form the main subject matter of this volume.[11] A third type of economy-wide model is focused on "dualism," and usually is set up to highlight the dichotomies between two sectors—a large, mostly agricultural "traditional" sector

---

9. A review of the relative costs and merits of static and dynamic models appears in Chapter III.

10. Adequate treatment of the use of these models in developing countries would probably require another volume (and another set of authors), even though use of models in these countries is not nearly so widespread as it is in developed countries. For some reasons as to why this is so, see the chapter cited above.

11. There are wide variations in the number of sectors actually included in these models— the range is from 3–5 to 30–40 or more. Appropriate aggregation levels for different types of problems are discussed in Chapters III, IV, and VI.

and a smaller, dynamic "modern" sector. Although this type of model provides insight into development phases, it has been little used for planning purposes.[12]

A final key characteristic involves the extent of *endogenous choice*—that is, the extent to which projections are made within the model itself. For example, sometimes export levels are projected exogenously and fed into the model and sometimes the model itself computes the appropriate levels. In the latter case, the projections are said to be endogenous. A model is fully determined (or "closed") if all variables or unknowns can be calculated once certain policy variables are fixed and exogenous projections made. Such models are frequently called simulation (or forecasting) models. In other models, there are many alternative growth patterns which are consistent with the set of exogenous variables. Some sort of optimization technique based on the objectives of the plan[13] is then used to close the model. As discussed extensively in following chapters, linear programming is often the technique selected—hence we refer to programming models.

Both in practice and in theory, different types of models are suitable for analyzing different policy problems. As was suggested at the beginning of this discussion, the "useful" model should be focused on a subset of problems. This implies a need for a set of models which together cover the key issues facing the planner. In particular, while economy-wide models are emphasized here, sectoral models can be extremely useful for analyzing many important problems and should not be ignored when selecting the set. A proper division of labor between models helps improve the instrumental nature of models by relating explicitly particular variables (such as trade balances or aggregate growth rates) to each other.

It is also important to note that, for consistency, various planning models should be interrelated; results from one model can and should be input into the others. For example, the savings rate in the Harrod–Domar model is usually exogenous, while it is frequently an endogenous variable in a financial or budgetary model. The assumed rate for one model should be consistent with the rate forecast by the other. Otherwise, when the rates differ, the rationale or meaning of the divergent behavior must be interpreted or explained. These characteristics of models and their relationships both to specific problems and one another are discussed in much greater detail and in a more technical manner throughout the rest of this volume.

---

12. Such models are critical for evaluating the broad lines of a country's development strategy since many dualisms are created by the structural rigidities of imperfect factor markets in less developed countries. Long-term policy simulations are increasingly using 2, 3, or 4 sector models. (See for example, Blitzer and Manne [1974], Chenery and associates [1974], and Kelley, Williamson, and Cheetham [1972].

13. Discussion of objective functions and the treatment of conflicting goals are found in Chapters III and IX. Chapter V discusses relative merits of simulation and optimization models.

## 4. DEVELOPMENT STRATEGY, ECONOMIC PROBLEMS, AND MODEL CHOICE

Planning models should be designed to fit the development strategy of a country as well as its principal economic concerns. Strategy in this context refers to a chosen development path, for example, an export promotion or import substitution orientation. The strategy varies greatly among countries according to size, relations with the world-wide economy, natural resources, level of development, social objectives, and outlook.

The basic approach in multisector planning models is the computation of rather detailed supply-demand balances for a number of aggregate commodities. While final demands (i.e., consumption, investment, and exports) can be computed in a variety of ways,[14] intermediate demands are computed mostly on the basis of input-output coefficients. Therefore, the usefulness of this modelling approach depends, to a great degree, on how important are the interindustry linkages of the economy. And in turn, their importance appears to be mostly a function of the country's size and degree of industrialization.[15]

Not surprisingly, then, these models are, *ceteris paribus*, more useful in larger than in smaller countries. Because of their larger markets, the larger countries tend to have a more diversified industrial base, and, in terms of development strategy, rarely (with the exception of petroleum producers such as Iran or Indonesia) specialize in the export of primary products.[16] During the growth process, a large number of sectors (especially industrial) develop, making multisector consistency an important planning consideration in the investment allocation decision. In fact, input-output tables have now been built for all of the more populous Third World countries except for several of the very poorest.

Economy-wide planning models, based on multisector input-output analysis, are also useful for small countries pursuing an industrialization strategy. These countries (Israel and Taiwan are relevant examples) are seeking to specialize in certain manufactured exports, selected on the basis of comparative advantage, in order to finance otherwise heavy import requirements. Multisector models are useful tools for investigating comparative advantage. As such, smaller countries often use them more for "domestic resource cost" calculations[17] than for intersectoral consistency testing.

Turning from grand questions of development strategy to specific areas of policy concern, we now review the problems discussed in the various chapters in this volume. Needless to say, when several authors are involved, each one's

---

14. For a review of alternative techniques for deriving final demands, see Chapter III.

15. The relationships between development patterns and these characteristics are investigated in Chenery and Taylor [1968].

16. For recent evidence, see Chenery and Syrquin [1974].

17. For a full discussion of these uses, see Chapters VI and VIII.

9

judgment about any specific issue may (and does) differ from that of the others. Hence, when several chapters discuss the same topic, the reader should look at all of them to get a full range of opinions.

Rapid economic growth is a major objective in all developing countries, and perhaps the most frequent use of economy-wide models has been in tracing plausible alternative growth paths over the medium and long run. Indeed, these models, whether macroeconomic or multisector, are uniquely suited to investigating the implications for macroeconomic parameters (such as savings requirements, trade balances, or incremental capital-output ratios) of alternative aggregate growth projections. These uses are reviewed in Chapters III (theoretical discussion) and V.

Intersectoral consistency, another important issue which is very frequently studied using economy-wide models, is the cornerstone of multisector modelling. An input-output matrix is used for relating macroeconomic projections to sectoral production requirements, and vice versa. Chapter V describes how the multisectoral demand and supply balances can be related to the relevant policy instruments and factor uses in order to maintain consistency between objectives and policy solutions. However, since multisector models are numerically constructed with considerable aggregation (for example only one agriculture sector), more narrowly focused models, say for the entire energy sector, are required if the planner is concerned with deriving specific requirements at the detailed sector or process level. In Chapters XI and XII, these problems are discussed.

While economy-wide models are often used to derive sectoral output and investment forecasts for a five year plan, the linkages between these rather aggregate projections and detailed project appraisal work are quite tenuous. Attempts have been made to establish such linkages through using the implied, or shadow, price system implicit in any optimizing model. While these attempts have not yet been entirely successful, several important relationships have been developed and are discussed in Chapter VIII.

Obviously, certain foreign trade issues cannot be separated from either macroeconomic policy or sectoral investment decisions. Almost all economy-wide models have some sort of foreign trade sector. In practice, a wide variety of assumptions can be made concerning the competitiveness of imports and exports (at a given point of time and over the long run), the costs and constraints associated with foreign borrowing, future tariff policies, etc. In Chapter VI, various foreign trade formulations and their policy implications are critically discussed. The important issues include such things as comparative advantage calculations, impact multipliers for foreign assistance, and effective protection rates. Once again we emphasize that, just as with investment decisions, aggregation level puts effective limits on the uses of economy-wide models.

10

Although problems relating unemployment and underemployment to labor skill creation have become increasingly important in recent years, they have not been analyzed systematically in economy-wide models. It is not yet clear how much the models can teach us about these problems, but existing techniques are reviewed in Chapter VII. Among the issues discussed are sectoral employment projections, education planning, surplus labor, and bottlenecks in skilled labor markets.

Similar comments apply to problems of income distribution, which have received even less attention than employment on the part of designers of economy-wide models; however, Chapter V summarizes what has been attempted, along with some suggestions for future research. In a similar vein, Chapter X presents a discussion of possible techniques for analyzing the disparities in regional development which are so important in several countries.

In contrast to these specific problem areas, there are several important general issues in planning which are only now being introduced into models. The first deals with the pursuit of multiple social and economic objectives. Various objective functions, based on economic theory, are discussed and criticized in Chapter III. Chapter IX deals with alternative, nontheoretical techniques which have been developed largely by systems engineers. Largely untested in economy-wide models, these show considerable promise as future tools for investigating a wide range of policy trade-offs.

Economies of scale cut across many economic problems, ranging from project appraisal to foreign trade specialization. Various treatments of this phenomenon are reviewed in Chapter XI. Since scale economies are difficult to measure at an aggregate level and hard to introduce into multisector models, the discussion centers around sector and single project models.

Finally, substitution possibilities exist in all parts of the economy. Substitution in demand is important in drawing implications for both price and income redistribution policies. Similarly, in choosing appropriate technologies, both for aggregate and disaggregate production, substitution in production is of utmost importance. Appropriate methodologies for handling various types of substitution in planning models are the subject of Chapter XII.

In closing this section, it may be useful to reemphasize that some important issues are excluded from discussion in the rest of this volume. First, short-run problems and instruments are largely ignored. As is emphasized in Chapters II and IV, these issues are often important in real world planning; however, the financial and monetary aspects of development policy lie beyond the scope of this book, which focuses on the modelling of the planned structural change of real resource allocations in the medium or long run. Thus, discussion of the short-term influence of changes in relative prices and their effect on technical choice, savings, and consumption is to a large degree omitted, except for

brief treatment in Chapters III and XII. Finally, most of the models discussed are concerned with the expenditure side of national income accounting, leaving out most income creation linkages. If real progress is to be made by augmenting economy-wide models for simulation of planned income redistribution, future research effort will have to be devoted to this topic.

Chapter II

# MODELS AND POLICY: THE DIALOGUE BETWEEN MODEL BUILDER AND PLANNER

JANOS KORNAI

## 1. A SUBJECTIVE INTRODUCTION

I am not a "development planner." I am commenting, more or less as an outsider, on the problems of trying to use mathematical models in the planning of developing countries.

It is true that I am only in part an outsider. For several years I participated intensively in the design and application of mathematical planning models in my country, Hungary. Hungary falls perhaps halfway between a typical developing and developed country. A significant portion of our problems are similar to those of the developing countries: Which should be the leading sectors? What new industries should be established? What should be the rate of industrialization? How can we fit into the international division of labor? How should we distribute the burden of growth between present and future generations? And so on. There is also a similarity between the modelling techniques of our group in Hungary and those discussed in this volume—for example, input-output analysis and static and dynamic linear programming models.

Despite these similarities, I am still an outsider. After all, planning in Budapest is quite different from that in New Delhi or Mexico City. For one thing, the Hungarian economy is based on European economic and cultural traditions. But more importantly, Hungary is a socialist country where the bulk of production is supplied by state or cooperative enterprises, where control of the economy is to a large degree centralized, and where there was considerable experience with nonmathematical planning and a large functioning economic organization at the time that mathematical planning began.

My opinion of mathematical planning or formal economy-wide models was shaped by personal experience in Hungary. It is true that I have participated as a consultant in several research projects which built models for developing countries. I have been present at meetings where competent development planners propounded their opinions. Before that, I tried to review the literature of the problem. Nevertheless, I derived from all this only an indirect impression, without the quality of personal experience. Now, while preparing this study, I reread some earlier material and perused some more recent work as well. I tried to choose "representative" items. I reviewed

primarily the most famous, most quoted works, including the more important ones of the other contributors to this volume. The fact that I did not read these works over a long time period, but almost in one sitting, one after another, probably helped sharpen my general impressions. Here, my objective is not to comment on individual works but rather to give a picture of this general impression. While my remarks do not precisely fit any one specific model, perhaps they give an accurate feeling of the image created by the "average" economy-wide planning model to an outsider.

To this, I must add a few qualifications. First, I concentrated primarily on the evaluation of the mathematical programming models. These closely resemble (from a technical point of view) the models I have worked with myself and feel most qualified to comment on. Second, my remarks are based almost exclusively on journal articles and books. It is possible that the published descriptions are not complete; perhaps much of what the authors have had to say has appeared in unpublished reports or has been said at meetings on the spot. Nevertheless, I believe that the choice the researcher makes in deciding what is most worth publishing, and what he reserves to himself or transmits only to a small circle, reflects his final priorities.

Here I emphasize the items that I believe are missing from these studies. Yet I would like to avoid even the appearance of judging superciliously from the height of some glorious successes. Let me confess that I not only esteem but even envy the high intellectual level and the theoretical standards characterizing these works almost without exception. We Hungarian planners are all self-taught, with skills obtained through hard work, whereas many mathematical development planners have come out of the best schools with a high degree of technical knowledge. I felt, as I read all of these works, that the authors are well acquainted with all the tricks of the art, with those we in Hungary apply, and with many more. I wish that five or ten of the top workers of this group would work in our planning centers in Budapest; the professional quality of the work there would surely improve by leaps and bounds. In addition, I envy the wonderful computing facilities at their disposal; no matter how much our facilities improve, we are always one or two steps behind in computer speed, efficiency of the algorithms, and richness of the program library.

The coin has another side: Any criticism of mine can also be seen as self-criticism. It is always easier to find distortion in the other fellow than by looking in the mirror. Much of the criticism I level at the planning models of developing countries also fits some of my own research and that of other Hungarian model builders.

There are two major topics in this chapter. In section 2, the relations between economic policy makers and model builders, and the dialogue between these two distinct groups, are discussed. Sections 3 and 4 deal with various political implications of development planning models. In other words, section 2 focuses on relations between different groups of *people*, while

sections 3 and 4 emphasize relations between different economic and political *issues*. My remarks are addressed primarily, but not exclusively, to model builders from a model builder. However, much of the material, especially in section 2, is also aimed at policy makers and other participants in the planning process.

## 2. THE MACHINERY OF PLANNING AND MATHEMATICAL MODEL BUILDERS

> The good Boy Scout performs a good deed every day.
> "Boy, was today's good deed difficult!"
> "Why, what did you do?"
> "I led a blind man across the road."
> "And why was that so difficult?"
> "Because he did not want to go!"
>
> (Joke frequently told in Budapest.)

The first mathematical planning models appeared in Hungary in 1957–58. Economy-wide and sector planning, both for the medium and long term, had already been going on in Hungary for about a decade, but exclusively relying on traditional, nonmathematical methods. The scale of planning could be described by two values: (1) The number of people working in the machinery of planning. Hungary is a small country of ten million people. Before the appearance of mathematical planning, the central planning office had a payroll of 500 to 800. In addition, every ministry, the directorate of every industrial branch, every producing company, and every local administrative authority had a planning office. Altogether, tens of thousands of people were busy planning. (2) The number of parameters used in the documentation of the five year plan. There is no accurate count, but a crude estimate of the order of magnitude would be several million.

At the first trials of mathematical planning we had to decide what our relationship to nonmathematical planning should be.[1] Confident of our technical superiority, should we try to assert our independence from the machinery of planning? Should we come forward as competitors, proposing the replacement of traditional planning by mathematical planning? Finally, the following "battle plan" emerged: The task was not the "revolutionary overthrow" of traditional planning but rather its gradual transformation or "reeducation." Having the fanciest models was not the most important thing. It was not even so terribly important, especially at the beginning, that the numerical results of our research be accepted as the basis for the official plan. What was really important was the "infiltration" of formal or mathematical methods into the actual machinery of planning. Everything—the design of the structure of models, the choice of colleagues, the working

---

1. This is dealt with in detail in Kornai [1974].

15

procedures, the presentation and dressing up of results—should be sub-ordinated to this aim. Mathematical planning should not be forced on practical economical leadership but should be built into the actual economic management and become a part of it. Progress should be achieved gradually, step-by-step, so that the planning apparatus would consider mathematical modelling as its own work. The official bureaucracy should accept the pro-fessional mathematical planner as a collaborator. Moreover, even those in the planning process who would not become modellers should at least understand the working of the models; they should help the model builders and also rely upon their help.

In Hungary, this implied that those who started their career as researchers, professors, and academic scholars, were faced with a decision. Some of them gave up their academic positions and took it upon themselves to work as mathematical planners within the planning apparatus of the economic administration. On the other hand, those who were unwilling to do this gradually handed over the day-to-day work to those permanently attached to the planning apparatus. The principal task of researchers and other academic people is the further development of improved methods, and some consulting, while the systematic application of mathematical planning is a governmental job rather than an academic one.

I do not want to idealize the Hungarian situation. We are, frequently, rightfully impatient because of the slow, uneven progress of this penetration, transformation, and reeducation. There is too much conservatism and inertia. The transformation is slowed down by intellectual laziness and by an aversion to getting acquainted with the new methods. Nevertheless, we have made great progress.

Nowadays, there are special groups and departments in the Hungarian National Planning Office with many workers specializing exclusively in mathematical planning. The Planning Office has its own large computer center. Many models have been built—some of them of very large scale, having more than a thousand variables—with the active participation of one or another leading official of the Planning Office. The planning process has several phases which would be unimaginable now without the use of mathe-matical models. There is a repeated dialogue going on between the practical planner and the model builder and, with the mediation of the model builder, ultimately the model. We will return to this later.

My impression is that a very different approach has been taken by the first generation of the mathematical planners in most developing countries. Typically, the initiators of the model, the directors of research, felt that it was most important to generate a good plan, instead of improving planning *per se*, or if it never existed before, creating it. They considered their work as mainly economic research, starting with the design of a model and ending up with the evaluation and publication of the research result. Yet, a more important

impact would have been made if organization and reeducation—in other words, the establishment of modern methods of planning the national economy—had been at the center of their work.

The following is a typical story. An outstanding Western professor, or maybe a talented graduate student, shows up in a developing country. His work is financed by some institution of his native country, a foundation or university, or perhaps by some international organization. He is filled with desire to help and has intellectual interest in research. He completes the work; his report is discussed on location; even a few remarks by local economists may be muttered with proper reverence. There is no great battle over the statements of the model. The professor or graduate student leaves soon after—and life continues just as it was before he came.

This is just like a concert given in a little hick town once a decade by a world-famous violinist. He is listened to with proper reverence but without a real enjoyment of the music: "Bartok, Schönberg—this is too modern, too highbrow for us. . . ." The effect of such an unusual concert would be different if there were better music instruction in the local schools or if there were a town conservatory, quartet, choir, and orchestra to make music available, even on weekdays. If all this is missing, then when the world-famous virtuoso leaves, the little town is left without any music at all.

Returning from music to development planning, even short references to the following questions can hardly be found in the literature. How is the planning process working in the country under discussion? What was the state of planning and its underlying quantitative foundations before the appearance of mathematical planning, and what became of it afterwards? To what degree were efforts to have the model adopted by local groups successful? Was the model sound? What were the most typical objections? A discussion of whether the plan was accepted and "applied" is not what is missing. Everyone agrees that the results of a mathematical model can never be accepted literally, number by number; rather, what is missing is a discussion of how the research, the modelling, affected "planning," i.e., the planning and decision making process as a permanent government activity. Did mathematical planning, at least in this sense, have a lasting effect?

The connections between policymaker and "domestic" model builders are probably closer than the ties with "imported," short-term visitors. Moreover, even in the case of foreign consultants, the real-world experience is somewhat better than one would conclude from publication, or more precisely, from the lack of pertinent published information. In any case, the literature reflects the subjective priorities of the researchers and other model builders; they are not writing about these problems, or hardly at all. Neither positive nor negative feedback is mentioned. How, then, should a model building project be organized in order to make an effective contribution to "planning?" I offer the following set of recommendations based on my own experience, both its

17

successes and setbacks. We emphasize requirements for projects led by academics in countries where there has been little experience with model building. Most of the lessons also hold in more "sophisticated" settings.

(i) *The entire task, each individual phase of it—from data compilation, to design of the model, to appraisal of results—should be performed as a team project.* There should be local people, who are present or future planners, as members of the team. In their selection, their immediate contributions to the current project should not be the only considerations. An equally important or even more important consideration should be: Will they be able and willing to take over the relay stick from us some day, to continue the construction and computation of models similar to those we worked on together? This is typically an area where real pedagogical results can be obtained only by the principle of "learning-by-doing." My impression is that in the few countries where such teams were developed, e.g., in South Korea and perhaps in India, an enduring effect can indeed be found.

(ii) Occasional discussions between the model builders and the local practical economic leaders, economic politicians, and official planners are not enough; rather, a *constant, lively, working relationship* is needed. Here I am thinking of the people who are not participating directly in the team but who have actual planning and economic leadership responsibility. It is no less important to establish lively contacts with local academic economists, who may exert strong influence on public opinion, and who perhaps act as advisers to the local government or planning agencies. If these people observe the activities of the modellers with suspicion or, even worse, with envy and aversion, there can be little hope for acceptance; they will be permanent opponents and critics. The friendlier the contacts with local academic circles, the smoother will be the progress of new methods.

(iii) *The structure of the model should be simple*, especially in the initial phases of introducing mathematical methods and formal models. The degree of complexity should not be set to satisfy the high standards of the university colleagues or the professor in charge of the project; rather it should be adjusted to the intellectual "absorptive capacity" of the local practical planners. The primary consideration should be that the local planners understand and accept the simpler model, consider it their own, and begin to apply it independently. If this "revolutionary" change takes place in the planning process, all the rest can be left to gradual development; in this case, the local planners will be able, by themselves, to change over from simpler to more complex models.

This is a difficult requirement and requires selflessness. It may not add to the academic reputation of the professor directing the research. Sometimes there may be a legitimate need for compromise between these two research objectives. In any case, this criterion is a most important gauge of the *real* goal

of the researcher, the improvement of planning in the country involved, or his own scientific achievement.

(iv) Local decision makers and planners face numerous economic policy problems. *A model,* or rather the series of computations performed with a model, *should be designed to be able to furnish valuable information about the real-world problems of the planners and practical decision makers.* I used the broad wording, "to furnish information," intentionally. We cannot expect our model to give final, decisive answers; it can be considered an accomplishment if it only inspires interesting thoughts, if it furnishes additional points of view for a decision. Neither will I take a stand about the mathematical form that the information should take. Suppose that the problem under consideration is the balance of payments. The balance of payments may be an endogenous variable of the model; it may be a maximand or objective function; or it may be an exogenous constraint subject to parametric variation. In each of the three forms, we may gather information about the mutual relationship between the balance of payments on the one hand and about other economic events and activities on the other.

We also have to take into account an internal dilemma for the researcher, similar to the one already mentioned in connection with the simplicity of the model. Every researcher has one or more pet themes. One is interested in import substitution, another in increasing returns to scale, a third in the length of the time horizon, a fourth in the stability of shadow prices. It is quite understandable, and scientifically very useful, if the researcher views his work in a developing country as an opportunity to experiment with the real numbers of a real economy in connection with investigating his pet interests. It can only be to the advantage of his own research if he discusses such questions with the local practical planners. But he should also be aware of the real weight and importance of his pet theme in the totality of *all* of the problems and development dilemmas of the country in question. His problem may be only one of methodology; even if the issue concerns economic policy directly, it is only one of many such problems. The impossible, to completely ignore one's personal scientific interests, should not be asked. But self-discipline and sober compromise are possible and needed in deciding the weight to give to the problems of economic policy as they are perceived by local policy makers as opposed to those of the research scholar.

(v) With these points in mind, it is highly desirable that *both the structure of the model and the series of computations to be performed with it are fully designed at an early stage.* But even the best thought-through design cannot substitute for an active dialogue between the model builder and the decision makers who will be asked to use it. It is important to emphasize this recommendation, for it is a most important element of the general requirement for a lively working relationship.

The planner and the model builder should try to delineate together the

issues to be analyzed. In any intellectual problem-solving activity, developing a clear formulation of the problem is often more difficult than finding the actual solution. The dialogue between planners and model builders should usually start with the planner thinking aloud about the range of problems which concern him, and the modeller explaining what his tools can accomplish in analyzing them. Ideally, the model builder would later take the results of his computations to a responsible economic politician, to a planner in a high position, and evaluate the results jointly. The economic politician then may ask, "And what would be the result if we did this instead of that?" The mathematical planner then returns to the computer, translates the question into the language of the model, runs one or more new computations, and returns to the planner with the result. Of course the questioning can take the opposite direction as well. The model builder may ask, on the basis of the lessons learned from computed results, whether this or that assumption of the policy maker is realistic.

If I had to judge on the basis of a single phenomenon whether the work of mathematical planners has "matured" in a given country, I would try to observe whether such a question-and-answer process had been developed or not.

(vi) *The estimates, forecasts, and plans of the nonmathematical planners should be utilized to a considerable degree.* We should not strive to generate all of our computations exclusively by a "parthenogenesis," drawing directly from objective statistical sources. This is only one way to approach problems. At least some experiments should be constructed on the basis of numbers obtained from practical, nonmathematical planners. For example, with programming models we frequently use the procedure of describing as constraints certain aggregate targets, which are forecast by nonmathematical methods, leaving the model free in the choice of details. In other words, the model tests whether the aggregate forecast of the planners could be accomplished more efficiently. The interest of the nonmathematical planners is usually increased if they see "familiar" numbers, if they can relate the results obtained by modelling to something they know. The following approach creates confidence: "We are not aiming at something completely different from your ideas. At least as an approximation, we want to investigate how your plans can be realized, only a little bit more efficiently."

I am not proposing that, in the computation phase, we should not deviate courageously from the original ideas of the planners. But gradual change of thought can be assured by calculating variants close to the original ideas as well.

This is complemented by another related proposal: The calculations obtained with the model should be compared carefully with independent nonmathematical plans. One also has to take into account the sensitivity, and possibly even the resistance, of those who developed the original plans; these

20

people would not like their ideas to be shown as stupid by the mathematical planners. I am not proposing a lack of principle but rather special attention to fitting together different arguments and approaches. The superiority of a plan computed using a model should be demonstrated convincingly. No one is convinced by the mere fact that the plan projections were computed by a mathematical model using an electronic computer, not even if we call them "better" or even "optimal," according to an indicator (objective function) designed arbitrarily by us.

The mathematical planner must not believe that, when he debates with practical planners, he is always right, and that the only problem is to convince the other side about his truth. We should be very modest and quite critical of our own work. In many cases the practical planner, relying on long experience, will be right. His naive and subjective estimates will sometimes be more reliable than ours, generated by mathematical models, which are also based on very strong simplifying assumptions. The modeller should approach the men of practice with the double aim of *teaching* and *learning*.

(vii) *The model's results should be summarized in a report clearly understandable to practical people.* This task closely resembles that of a translator. The mathematical planners have developed a peculiar slang, full of such terrifying expressions as "complementary slackness," "two-gap model," "gradualist path," and "turnpike." We have to acknowledge that even academic economists, working in other specialties, do not necessarily understand this slang, to say nothing of the economic politicians. It is sometimes a real headache to determine how to present the end results of computations, involving several hundred thousand numbers and obtained from a large system of equations, in only a few words, tables, and simple diagrams, so that they are really understandable, yet without unnecessary oversimplification.

(viii) Another necessary (but not sufficient) condition for successful completion of the project is that the *practical planners and economic leaders should consider the results meaningful and interpretable.* Unconditional acceptance of our recommendations cannot be expected, and there is nothing wrong with objections voiced to the results obtained by a formal model. But as a minimum requirement, the results should not be considered absurd or naive. In my view it is very important that the computations should not be smiled at behind the back of the model builder. We should not begrudge some expenditure of energy in finding out how the people who are responsible for economic decisions in the country really feel about the results. We should try to provoke a frank discussion and should not relax until we are convinced that the computations are taken seriously.

(ix) Finally, work is not finished with the preparation of a particular set of computations for a given plan. *The proponents of mathematical planning should try to instill a familiarity with their methods and assure their inclusion into the systematic institutional planning framework.* If the work was led by a foreign

21

consultant, it should not be irrelevant to him what happens after he leaves, who is going to continue his work, and under what conditions. Future systematic improvement of the statistical data base (along the lines advocated in Chapter IV), further development of the computational basis of mathematical planning, and training of mathematical planners should be advocated. In the foundation of enduring results, the researcher should be not only a scientist and adviser, but also an organizer and "agitator," a popularizer of modern planning methods.

(x) *Summary.* If the time spent by the leaders of a research project on the construction of a model, securing that data, carrying out the computations, and evaluating and publishing results is considered as taking up 100 percent of their time (that is, if they are unconcerned about whether the methodology itself is being adapted and whether the model's results will have any practical effect in the distant future) then, according to my experience, this "basic working time" may be doubled if the nine above recommendations are carried out. The education and convincing, in words and writing, of both the research team and other practical planners are extremely time consuming.

I have not read anywhere an account of how the working time of the development planning model builder has been divided. But I am probably correct in believing that it is closer to the above described "research" 100 percent than to the "organizing-educating" 200 percent. But as long as this is the case, real penetration of mathematical methods into the planning processes of the developing countries is going to remain very, very slow.

I believe my proposals have much general validity; however, their practical implementation depends on the degree of maturity of nonmathematical planning. It is only clear what aims are worth striving for if there is already organized, institutional, nonmathematical planning. The development of the "battle plan" is more problematic if, at the first appearance of the mathematical planners, there is no or hardly any other kind of planning available. Should we then start exclusively with modelling? Not in my opinion. No matter how much I believe in these methods, I feel that they cannot really stand alone. Life is much more complicated than our greatly simplified and condensed models. We need double-checking tools, including the estimates and "naive" calculations of the practical planners and high-level economic administrators, at least as a complementary control. In a single model, only a few hundred relationships and constraints can be considered. But people working in the central planning agencies and lower-level institutions and enterprises "sense" hundreds of thousands of further constraints and relations, and they can give expression to these in their own estimates. Mathematical planning will develop successfully only when it develops as one element of well-prepared and well-oriented institutional planning, connected by many threads with real economic life in developing countries.

22

## 3. THE SCARCITY OF THE PROBLEMS EXAMINED WITH MODELS

In the previous section there was a detailed discussion of how to establish a closer relationship between model builders, on the one hand, and official government planners and high-level economic administrators, on the other. While agreeing with these proposals, I wish to call additional attention to one particular danger: It is not at all certain that the official planning bureaucracy senses correctly the actual development problems of the country or, more precisely, the relative weights of different problems. Planners can be inhibited by many different factors, ranging from erroneous theoretical economic views to social and political bias. It would be a serious mistake for the model builder to exclude from his investigation those burning questions which the politicians in power would like to forget.

I do not wish to discuss here what kind of recommendations the mathematical planner should propose but rather *what alternatives he should examine*. In my view, the models, and the experiments performed with them, should be constructed in such a way that it would be possible to analyze the conditions and consequences of various social-political trends and various development strategies. For example, in a country in which there is argument about whether there should be agrarian reform, and whether the reform should be moderate or radical, the long-term, economy-wide planning model should be capable of testing the implications of at least a few policy variants.

Of course, in this regard the model builders should not restrict their intellectual contacts exclusively to the circle of government planners. They should also pay attention to what other groups and movements have to say or what they write.

Let us take a look, more concretely, at the key questions of economic policy that have been usefully studied using economy-wide planning models:

(i) The growth patterns between various sectors;

(ii) The structure of foreign trade, import substitution, the trade balance, and the balance of payments;

(iii) Foreign credit and aid;

(iv) Technical development, especially in the allocation of capital and labor;

(v) The scale and proportion of saving and investment. Along with this the time paths of accumulation and consumption, and, ultimately, the division of the benefit and cost between present and future generations.

This list is, of course, not complete. Several other problems, discussed in one study or another, may be added. But I feel that it contains the intersection of the principal problem sets studied in practically every significant research project described in the development planning literature.

The listed problems are extremely important. The criticisms below are not

aimed at diminishing their significance. The themes I will emphasize next are not meant to take their place but to stand next to them at the center of attention. They are important issues which have been largely ignored in previous research in developing countries.

## 3.1 Targets versus Instruments

Economy-wide planning models concentrate their attention primarily on "real" flows such as physical inputs and outputs of the economy, the structure of production, foreign trade, and consumption. The objective of the analysis is to determine numerical, quantitative development targets in these areas. At the same time, these models rarely specify *how* these goals and targets are to be realized. The models are not particularly instrumental in character. This is one of the most important criticisms made by potential users who feel there is nothing they can do with the results of planning models.

In my view, economy-wide modellers who leave careful analysis of instruments to other models (such as short-run econometric models) or to the practical planner working independently are mistaken. One of the most important elements for further research in methodology is how to build instrumental variables and relations into development planning models. Admittedly, this is a difficult task, requiring careful analysis and raising a number of perplexing problems.

One major problem is disaggregation. A model becomes, at least in part, "instrumental" as soon as individual investment projects are included in addition to several rather aggregate sectors. Indeed, the model itself could then decide about whether or not the projects should be accepted. There are several techniques for attempting this. For example, one method is to treat several especially important projects as indivisible integer variables and then link them with the rest of the economy.[2] Another way is to "blow up" one or two key sectors for detailed examination.[3] Finally, there exists a still more comprehensive technique: The development of a multilevel planning system such that aggregate sectors are placed in the higher levels, while in the lower levels disaggregated individual projects are included.[4]

Another important issue is the building of financial variables and relations into the model. While literally all economy-wide models deal with the international balance of payments, there are other financial considerations of equal importance:[5]

(i) The national budget and system of taxation. If there are significant

---

2. For an example of this approach for Korea, see Westphal [1969].
3. Clark [1970] uses this method in the case of Nigeria.
4. This has been attempted for Mexico and reported in Goreux and Manne [1973].
5. The large-scale linear programming model of the Hungarian five year plan for 1971–75 contains a large set of fiscal and financial variables and equations. See Morva and Bager [1972].

regional problems in the country, then the regional budgets are also important;

(ii) The financial requirements and sources of financing investment which usually must be specified in a disaggregated form according to different forms of ownership (for example, state, private capitalistic, small farmer), and possibly according to different sectors;

(iii) Economy-wide balance of private purchasing power and the supply of consumer goods and services, which is very significant from the point of view of possible inflationary tendencies; and

(iv) Credit balances.

Some mathematical programmers object to including financial considerations because a whole series of new constraints would show up in the model, making more difficult any conceptual interpretation of the system of underlying shadow prices. I feel that this objection is irrelevant. It is not necessary and, indeed, is probably impossible for the shadow price system of a long-run, economy-wide programming model for a developing country to have a strong resemblance to a real market price system. I am not going to expound the arguments and counterarguments which are well discussed in Chapters III, V, VII, and especially in VIII.

I should remark here that, in principle, the shadow price system itself is instrumental in nature, usable in the cost-benefit analysis of investment projects; however, use can be made only with great circumspection, care, and much reservation. In cost-benefit analysis and project evaluation, several other sources of information also have to be taken into account. As a result, I cannot agree with the quite widespread point of view that the shadow price system should be the main or even the only instrumental result of such models. Much more important and effective would be the inclusion of the instruments mentioned above; however, their introduction would require some restructuring and reformulating of existing modelling techniques.

## 3.2 *"Physical" versus "Human" Aspects*

Two adjectives originating with Hegel and Marx, "Versachlichung" and "alienation," apply very well to most planning models for developing countries. Although these models describe the flow of objects, things, physical inputs and outputs (and perhaps of money), somehow, living people are missing from them. Let us use an example: The model states that as a result of industrialization, certain changes will occur in the technological structure of production, the capital-output ratio, the balance of payments, and so on. Yet at the same time a deep-seated social change is taking place as a consequence of industrialization. Millions of people become factory workers, giving up their traditional rural living patterns. As cities swell, masses of people stream to the slums. Urbanization, together with the both beneficial and malevolent effects of overturning the whole fabric of society, is as important a consequence of economic development as the deficit in the balance of payments. Despite the

fact that this is well known to every economist and model builder who deals with the developing countries, somehow the convention that it does not belong in the model has become established.

I will try to summarize, at least in key words, which social processes, in my opinion, should be included:[6]

(i) The transformation of the occupational structure;
(ii) The transformation of the structure of learning, training, and culture;
(iii) The transformation of the residential structure (the proportions living in hamlets, towns, cities, and giant metropolises);
(iv) The transformation of property and class relations (small farmer, plantation owner, domestic servant, factory worker, small businessman, big businessman, and so on).

These processes are not simply to be reclassified into sociology, "urban economics," or some other related science; they belong most intimately in the process of economic development; they are accompanying phenomena, causes and effects, goals and methods, all at the same time. Neither should we argue that they cannot be "mathematized," as they are all observable, measurable, and quantitatively describable phenomena.

### 3.3   Allocation versus Distribution—Employment

Although very closely connected with the previous point, distribution questions are so important that they deserve special consideration. Most planning exercises are models of rational allocation of resources. The distribution of the social product among various individuals, groups, and classes is, for the most part, ignored.

The truth is that, in the majority of developing countries, the most acute economic and political problems are mass poverty, unemployment, and underemployment. These are extremely painful problems which, considering the entire Third World, affect hundreds of millions of people. There is no need for lengthy statistical arguments, as the phenomenon is well known and described in hundreds of different documents, official data, statements of politicians, studies of economists and sociologists, and newspaper reports.

The entire economic profession is more or less in agreement that an enduring solution can be effected only by economic growth over a very long time period. Nevertheless, a pertinent question is: What about until then? Should we wait until the economic development of 10, 20, or 50 years somehow overtakes the period of mass misery? And, although with an aching heart, should we leave hundreds of millions of people in destitution until then? Or should something

---

6. Some of these processes are reflected in the Ivory Coast model of Goreux [1973] and Condos and Davis [1973a].

be done urgently? How much of a compensation is a better life in the twenty-first century to people hungering today?[7]

And misery is only one side of the picture. Most economists agree that the typically observed process of development actually *increases* the income inequality in most poor countries (at least in the short run). Should we acquiesce to this as an unavoidable fact of life, or is it possible to do something about it? I really do not have the answer; I only raise questions. But, do not forget that these questions are raised daily in developing countries, not only by the opposition to the establishment, not only by revolutionaries. They are also posed by important supporters of governments, and even by those in power, because an explosion of mass dissatisfaction might threaten their power and position.

Quite intentionally, I do not want to go too far along these lines; I do not wish to discuss changes that are accompanied by a radical transformation of the existing power structure, either political or economic. Instead, as an illustrative example, consider the eventual application of those Keynesian prescriptions that are now adopted without hesitation even by many conservative politicians in developed, capitalist countries. Mass misery in many underdeveloped countries would be quickly reduced if the unemployed were given work opportunities through public works such as building roads, canals, public buildings, schools, and hospitals. This would have little direct foreign exchange cost and would require very few skilled workers. Yet, such projects could absorb a considerable portion of the unemployed and the under-employed. In addition, well-planned public works would be a productive use of labor, for they would enrich the national wealth by creating useful social facilities.

This is an important measure, suggested and urged by the Committee for Development Planning of the United Nations.[8] No one thinks that such a policy, by itself, is sufficient to solve the problem; however, it seems clear that implications of these kinds of policies can and should be tested using economy-wide models. Variables could be introduced into the model to represent the labor-absorbing public works projects, together with equations which assure the consistency of these activities with the rest of the economy.

I have not seen any economy-wide model which deals seriously either with the idea of urgent labor-absorbing public works or with any other economic policy directly aimed at attacking mass poverty and unemployment. Seeing this deficiency, I regard as sterile and grotesque the endless discussions about appropriate time horizons in "welfare maximizing" models. It is a bit ridiculous to debate whether welfare should be maximized over twenty years, thirty years, or over an infinite horizon, when millions of people who are

---

7. Many of the issues raised here are summarized and discussed in Chenery and associates [1974].

8. See United Nations, Committee for Development Planning [1972, 1973].

hungry and unemployed right now are demanding immediate help. The well-known Keynesian saying "In the long run, we are all dead . . ." is true here in the medium run, too; many may starve if economic policy does not provide help soon. I am not against long-run planning; I do not want to push one-sided, short-run considerations. But we must study very carefully the inter-actions between urgent short-run measures focused against mass poverty and unemployment, and the long-run growth of the economy.

The main reason for this neglect is almost certainly the political circumstances in the developing countries. If the local policy makers were really concerned with the organization of public works, they would force the planners to insert such activities into their models. Nevertheless, model builders need not wait for the initiatives of the politicians; they have their own responsibility. Therefore, as an additional explanation, we must look also at the theoretical background of the model builders. I think that, at least in the case of economy-wide models, mathematical planners are strongly influenced by the neoclassical tradition. The typical mode of thought, with perhaps slight exaggeration, is described below.

The country modelled has surplus unskilled labor or open unemployment. *Ergo*, we do not need to regard labor allocation as a constraint for the model. In other words, the purpose of the plan is to solve the conventional neo-classical problem of resource allocation, with scarce resources to be allocated. It does not matter whether this is done in the framework of a firm, or a competitive market economy, or a developing country. All cases are alike since the crucial problem is always the same: The efficient allocation of scarce resources.

I, for one, think that the scope of economics, and within economics the scope of scientific planning, is much wider. Resource allocation is only a narrow subset in the larger set of economic problems.[9] You do not have to be a Marxist, or a Keynesian, or an adherent to the new Cambridge school, but only to be a sound pragmatic economic policy maker to admit that the serious exploration of employment problems simply cannot be left out of any development planning model. The importance of employment is greater, the farther we are from achieving it. It is a somersault in logic to say that since there is surplus labor, we may disregard labor in the model.

Why do the designers of planning models usually think in terms of scarcities, and consider only upper bounds on scarce resources? Why not apply lower bounds on the minimum level of employment, at least for some experiments?

Let me add some qualifications to these critical remarks. What I am criticizing is not planning as such, but formal, mathematical planning. There are countries where some nonformalized planning exercises try to deal with the questions mentioned above. My comments are mainly concerned with

9. The author summarized his critical comments on neoclassical economics in his book *Anti-Equilibrium* [1971].

improving the medium- and long-run economy-wide studies which are discussed in this volume. We can notice signs of improvement. Some of the practical models discussed in Chapters V and VII try to focus on income distribution and employment.[10] It would be very helpful to give wide publicity to these experiments, and to develop further the methodology of formal planning of income distribution and employment.

## 3.4 Disharmonic versus Harmonic Growth

It is easy to understand why developing countries wish to grow as rapidly as possible. Unfortunately, this rush may lead to one-sided, distorted growth and to disharmonies of the following kinds:[11]

(i) Usually physical capital growth is given prominence, and human capital development lags behind;

(ii) Usually the quantitative expansion of output is emphasized, with improvements in the quality of goods and services lagging behind;

(iii) Usually the construction of new housing, schools, hospitals, and roads comes into prominence, and careful and continuous maintenance of old buildings lags behind;

(iv) Usually increases of reproducible national income and wealth are emphasized, and the conservation of the nonreproducible environment lags behind.

The first half of each phenomenon listed above refers to processes which are well defined in conventional statistical accounting, particularly in aggregate indicators of production, physical capital, and consumption. Accordingly, they are easy to include in economy-wide planning models. At the same time, statistical accounting is very deficient regarding the processes in the second half of each of the phenomena. These processes are usually barely treated or completely ignored in compiling national income accounts. Accordingly, they are also neglected in planning models. In economics we have many respectful names: "externalities," "imponderabilia," "public good." The tradition of our profession is to mention them occasionally to demonstrate that we are aware of their importance and then continue the discussion of any problem as if they did not exist. Small wonder that development planning models continue the tradition!

The set of problems just described partly overlaps another set, often called "quality of life." Our policy recommendations for a developing country are based partly on our judgments about the factors influencing the quality of life. I shall discuss only one example, that of consumption.

---

10. Goreux [1973] and Condos and Davis [1973b] on Ivory Coast, and Blitzer and Manne's [1974] model of dualistic economics represent two promising new approaches.

11. For further elaboration of these ideas see the author's book, *Rush Versus Harmonic Growth* [1972].

Almost without exception all models use either demand functions or fixed consumption patterns. The Engel curves which are often used[12] are usually based on the assumption that the consumption pattern of a developing country will simply follow that of the developed countries. Is this really necessarily so? Consider the case of transportation. Leaving aside cost levels, is it beneficial to permit the widespread use of personal passenger cars, which leads sooner or later to pollution, noise, fatal traffic accidents, and complete financial failures of public transport systems? Perhaps it is already too late to reconsider the question in the United States or Western Europe. The automobile is there, and life would stop without cars. But it is not too late to think about this, and about similar aspects of the quality of life, in Nigeria or Burma. Nevertheless, economy-wide planning models, and even sectoral models, rarely treat such problems; in most cases they regard the composition of future consumption as already decided through known demand functions. They tacitly assume that if we raise the illusion of consumer sovereignty, the problem is already settled. Unfortunately, that is not the case. The decision on consumption patterns is extremely complex and full of dynamic externalities. To continue the previous illustrative example: The automobile customer of today decides on his own expenditures for transportation. Buying a car in a developing country, he will enjoy the fact that there are only a few cars on the road. But, in making this decision, together with many other consumers, he does not take into account the future externalities of preferring individual transportation to public transport. All the harmful consequences will fall on future generations, including future car owners and commuters using public transport facilities. Of course, this is only an illustration, showing that the design of future consumption patterns should not be left exclusively in the hands of isolated individuals. The decisions must be supplemented, and if necessary corrected, by planning and active governmental intervention.

## 4. Two Possible Counterarguments

I just described what I see as the missing factors in most development planning models. There are two usual counterarguments brought up in debates. One argument refers to technical difficulties. It states that until now, planning models have been designed mainly for modelling the real sphere, i.e., production, trade, investment, and similar physical activities. I do not find the argument convincing. There are no technical obstacles to adding variables and equations which describe income determination, employment, education, urbanization, and various social characteristics. Mathematical programming is a very flexible device and can be expanded to include a very large set of problems; even when optimizing techniques are not feasible, simulation models can be utilized to investigate many important questions.

---

12. For a discussion of the use of Engel curves in planning models, see Chapter III.

The other counterargument refers to the academic freedom of the research scholar. All criticism is answered by saying that there is no book or article that could not be attacked for leaving this or that problem out of the discussion. I think those using this reasoning are confusing two very different matters: The role of the academic scholar versus that of the responsible planner. I agree with the principle of freedom and sovereignty in the choice of subject matter for academic research, perhaps because I, too, am an academic. The probability of success is, of course, higher when the scholar is researching topics in which his interest is strong.

The situation for the development planner is quite different. He must deal with all socially important questions. The choice of problems cannot depend completely on his personal taste and intellectual interest. He simply does not have the right to neglect any important question, because to do so may harm the country. Perhaps he will not be able to handle all important problems, because of lack of skill or experience, or because of theoretical or technical difficulties, or limited information. These are acceptable excuses. But the intentional exclusion of some problems simply because as an economist he does not find them interesting is never justified.

The dilemma stems from the fact that most designers and builders of planning models are both scholars and planners at the same time. I think they should apply a double moral criterion. When writing a book or an article, or when lecturing at the university, they could follow the principles of academic freedom. But, when developing a model for serious discussion by responsible decision makers, they should adopt the moral criteria of a planner. In that case, they must try to consider all the important questions when building their models. And, furthermore, they must weigh the relative importance of various policy issues on the scales of their social importance rather than their academic challenge.

From these ideas we can draw a general conclusion. We must step out from the narrow circle in which we are moving. The model builder does not make a final political decision; usually, he only explores problems; however, the exploration should be much broader than in the past. We cannot be satisfied with bureaucratic or technocratic "allocation" exercises. A development planning model should demonstrate the consequences of different alternative economic policies on the whole life of the society in question.

Chapter III

# THEORETICAL FOUNDATIONS AND TECHNICAL IMPLICATIONS

Lance Taylor

## 1. Introduction

The purpose of this chapter is to discuss systematically the theoretical bases of economy-wide planning models. Much of the richness of mathematical planning technique comes from its close relationship with economic systems theory. On the other hand, insofar as currently accepted economic theory is an inaccurate description of what really goes on in developing economies, formal planning is likely to be irrelevant. Technical specialists and nonmathematical planners must understand both sides of the models—where they are elegant and where shabby, where realistic and where surrealistic—before they can make a rational decision about whether to use them or not. Some prior thought about the theoretical questions discussed here is required before one can really say "Yes" or "No" to mathematical planning.

Assuming the affirmative answer, one finds that additional choice problems (which really impinge on the first decision) immediately arise. A key point emphasized throughout this volume is that there is no single best model for use by all planning offices. Rather, there is a wide range of possible specifications —an appropriate one in a given country depending on factors ranging from data availability, to the institutional framework for planning, to the specific policy problems under discussion. Many types of models are discussed in this chapter, in an attempt to illustrate what sorts of formulations are likely to be applicable in a variety of practical situations.

The chapter also attempts to provide the potential model builder with a fairly complete summary of best-practice, *applicable* planning techniques (which means that a great deal of the so-called theory of planning is ignored).[1] The vehicle for this effort is a literature survey. Obviously, such a survey cannot develop each point in great detail. The hope is that sufficient motivation and information appear here to allow the reader easy entry into the source literature.[2]

---

1. For a recent review of planning theory, see Heal [1973].

2. Before launching into the discussion, it is probably worthwhile to provide some guidance about the survey's coverage and organization. The literature reviewed is mostly English-language, with a few forays into Spanish. Thorough coverage of European experience (both Eastern and Western) is not attempted, although particular models are picked up when they appear applicable to developing country problems. Due to lack of familiarity on

## 1.1  Readers' Guide

The chapter is organized in sections numbered with single digits (e.g., 2) and subsections numbered with two digits (e.g., 2.2). Within subsections, separate topics are sometimes indicated by small roman numbers (e.g., (ii)). Equations are numbered sequentially within the major sections (e.g., equation (2.2)). In a general way, the topics of the chapter are organized in a definite progression, going from rather simple models to much more complex formulations. By necessity, the presentation also becomes more complex or difficult for the neophyte. Not surprisingly, the frequency distribution of actual applications of the models follows pretty closely the same order.

Substantive discussion begins in the following subsection with a review of aggregate planning models, designed to make medium-term (three to five years) and long-term growth projections. These are the most basic tools of the mathematical planner's trade and have been used, at least implicitly, in plan formulation in at least fifty developing countries.

Several characteristics of the aggregate models are worth noting at the outset, since they carry over to the multisectoral models of later sections. First, they are almost always expressed in real terms. This means both that relative price changes are largely ignored and that interactions of inflation, finance, and flows of funds are omitted from the formulation. These omissions are characteristic of planning exercises and are likely to be remedied only slowly over the next few years.

Second, the specification at best includes a limited set of policy instruments. The models are used to sketch out future growth paths for the economy which seem feasible in terms of estimates of future savings levels, availability of

---

the part of the author, the entire French-language literature on development planning is ignored. Subject to these limitations, the coverage of the survey extends (at least sporadically) through late 1973. I have not cited all the papers I know about in the field, but only those which could be woven into the narrative in what seemed to be an illuminating way. Apologies are offered to all those authors whose work, through misunderstanding or ignorance on my part, is not discussed.

Also, note that since it *is* a survey, the chapter takes a rather academic tone. It is to be hoped that the practicing planner will not be deterred by this—after all, planning models are complicated and lend themselves to professorial exposition. Similarly, the practitioner should not be put off by mathematical derivations he cannot understand—the survey attempts to get to the frontiers of applicable modelling, and the mathematics out there is sometimes fairly difficult. Fortunately, mathematical advice should not be too hard to find, since in principle no derivations here should be out of the technical range of someone who has had a year or two of recent economics graduate study at a good university, and who knows some calculus and linear algebra. This means that most planning offices will have one or more persons capable of following the entire exposition; they can provide the technical backing for a more experienced planner's economic intuition (which is *always* scarcer than simple mastery of technique, in any case). The other chapters in this volume should help in the same way, and the review of the survey's contents should point out the sections most relevant to particular institutional contexts.

foreign exchange, and so on. Shifts in interest rates, forced development of financial markets, trade subsidies and all the other policies to mobilize these resources do not appear in the formulation. Again, the relevant variables may show up in models sooner or later, but to date they largely have not done so.

Third, all aspects of uncertainty—ranging from the price of the major export to the standard error of estimate of the capital-output ratio—are usually left out of the formal model, being dealt with (if at all) by sensitivity analysis. Some preliminary attempts to treat risk and uncertainty more thoroughly appear in the literature and are reviewed below, but they are sporadic and have scarcely penetrated into run-of-the-mill modelling practice.

Finally, institutional limitations on policy appear only in rudimentary form. Political limitations on government action, the role of different government entities in plan design and execution, dependence of the country on the whims of foreign governments and nonresident international business firms and institutions—these and many other forces which deeply affect plan formulation are left out. All one can do is try to select models which fit the appropriate institutional framework. Suggestions on how to do this appear throughout the paper. Note again that all of these comments hold for multi-sector as well as aggregate models.

Section 2 is devoted to a review of static input-output models, which multiply the one or two sectors of the aggregate models to tens or twenties and thereby provide the basis for fruitful communication between macro-planners and sector specialists. The use of input-output models is much less widespread than the aggregate models but is still quite common—the Leontief system has been used at least semiofficially in about thirty developing countries.

Like their smaller aggregate cousins, input-output models are expressed in real terms and are thus more appealing in a planning context in which a "real-minded" entity such as a Ministry of Industry dominates.[3] Even if planning focuses on financial aggregates, input-output still has a role, for it is the best available method to make demand-oriented forecasts of industrial output levels (taking into account price sensitivities of demand, if desired), reconcile them with supply forecasts, consider labor-absorbing implications of alternative technologies, and verify that planned output targets will satisfy overall limitations on available capital, skilled labor, and foreign exchange.

Through all these calculations (and also the numerous consistency checks on economic data which it permits), the input-output system serves as a

---

3. If planning is dominated by the "money-minded" Ministry of Finance, the focus is likely to be on tax receipts, monetary emissions, and such like, which are not easily handled by input-output techniques.

powerful teaching device. When its results are presented in a form accessible to policy makers,[4] the model can be the basis for wide-ranging discussion of trade-offs and policy options. The payoff to mathematical planning comes when it permits the planner to lay out the implications of alternative policies with enough clarity to permit the policy maker to select from the menu before him and point to directions in which it should be extended. Input-output is well set up to achieve this end.

Usual input-output models are static in the sense that they make forecasts for one period, considering only the demand-creating effects of investment. In some contexts, it is also useful to accumulate sectoral investment into capital stocks and take into account the capacity limits these place on production. This can be done formally through the use of the dynamic Leontief model, reviewed in section 3. The dynamic model is most interesting when there is a significant capital goods industry in the country, which is *not* the case in most of the developing world. Planners from small, capital goods importing countries will be best advised not to take the models of section 3 too seriously, since they are somewhat irrelevant to their local problems.[5]

Section 4 is a long discussion of static linear programming planning models. Linear programming (LP) is much more an academician's plaything than the models of sections 2 and 3, but it has been used semiofficially or officially in perhaps a dozen developing countries, including many of the larger and more industrialized ones. The great advantage of LP is that it provides a means for efficient, systematic exploration of the economy's choice set, as delimited by input-output and other constraints. Besides providing a useful computational means to consider trade-offs implicit in the input-output system, LP in principle may be used for decentralized planning since solution of the model provides a set of dual or shadow prices with a Walrasian interpretation. It will be shown that this interpretation cannot be maintained in a strict sense, but that shadow prices from a model may still have a useful "wide-sense" economic meaning. (On this, see also Chapter VIII of this volume.) However, they cannot be used directly to model the impact of such price-distorting government policy instruments as tariffs and indirect taxes. A great deal of section 4 is devoted to establishing these points about shadow prices.

Since linear programming *can* do everything that input-output can, and quite a bit more, practitioners from most institutional contexts should find something of interest in section 4. A variety of model specifications are dis-

---

4. Simplifying results from a complex, disaggregated model is an art form we cannot explore here. It is touched upon in Chapters II, IV, and IX of this volume. See also Kornai [1967, 1974] and Rimler, Daniel, and Kornai [1972].

5. One exception to this blanket statement is point (iii) of subsection 3.3, which discusses a method of computing imports which can also be used in static models (but which fits better analytically in section 3).

cussed, all focused on the problem of making a forecast of where the economy is likely to find itself (in real terms) at the end of a four or five year planning period. A fairly good working knowledge of standard LP theory is assumed, and it is likely that someone completely lacking this will find the discussion difficult.

Finally, section 4 deals with certain economic relations, such as savings behavior, which could in principle be applied in a static nonoptimizing model. Therefore, it is strongly recommended that this section be studied carefully by those attempting to use the projection models discussed in section 2.

Section 5 deals with extensions of the static LP framework into several time periods in order to deal with dynamic investment planning. The problems are similar to those considered in section 3, and the models are best used for longer term (more than five years) perspective planning. In addition, analyzing dynamic models provides useful insights into the behavior of static models, so that people who will actually work with linear programming should find the discussion useful.

Finally, section 6 deals with a variety of other multisectoral models which have been proposed. With the exception of some "simulation" exercises (an attempt is made to define this ambiguous term at the beginning of subsection 6.3), these may not be of immediate interest to practical planners but may become so in the future. At the moment, interested academics can base relevant, policy-oriented research on some of the models discussed, especially if they are interested in forecasting the effects of tariff or tax changes on resource allocation or studying other price-sensitive aspects of economies with fairly well developed market systems.

The reader should also note that five of the major sections close with "Evaluation" subsections, in which additional assessment of the applicability of various model specifications is attempted.

## 1.2 *Aggregate Consistency Models*

At a minimum, all forecasting models try to say something about the growth of GNP over the next half decade or so; some do no more than this. The simplest GNP forecasts are based on the well-known Harrod–Domar model, and we begin with a discussion of its specification. More complicated models for making aggregate growth projections are then discussed, followed by a brief review of models which take into account surplus labor, non-shiftable capital, and balance of payments problems.

(i) The Harrod–Domar model incorporates the simplest of all hypotheses about technology, that the ratio of output to reproducible capital is constant:

$$K(t) = kY(t), \tag{1.1}$$

where $K(t)$ is capital stock at time $t$, $Y(t)$ is output (GNP or a similar concept),

and $k$ is the capital-output ratio.[6] If it is also true that a constant share $s$ of output is saved, then

$$\text{Gross Investment} = I(t) = sY(t) = K(t+1) - K(t) + \delta K(t) \quad (1.2)$$

where $\delta$ is the fraction of capital stock depreciated each period.

Now if $g$ is the rate of growth of output,

$$g = [Y(t+1) - Y(t)]/Y(t) = \Delta Y(t)/Y(t)$$

(where $\Delta$ is the forward difference operator), then capital must also be growing at the same rate, for

$$\Delta K/K = k\Delta Y/K = \frac{k\Delta Y/Y}{K/Y} = \Delta Y/Y.$$

Using (1.2), we therefore have that

$$g = \frac{sY - \delta K}{K} = \frac{s}{k} - \delta, \quad (1.3)$$

which is the basic Harrod–Domar growth equation.

In planning applications, this is usually written in slightly different form as

$$n + p = \frac{s}{k} - \delta,$$

where $n$ is the expected rate of growth of the labor force and $p$ is the rate of growth of productivity. A common question to ask is whether or not the economy is likely to be able to absorb expected employment growth, given historical data on savings and depreciation rates, and the capital-output ratio. Unfortunately, the answer is often "No." The policy problems begin there.[7]

(ii) The Harrod–Domar model emphasizes savings behavior, even though this may not be very stable in a developing country. However, if the data allow it, one can extend the analysis by disaggregating sources of saving. For example, suppose there are different savings propensities out of wage income $W$ and profit income $\Pi$.[8] Then the following two equations must hold,

---

6. See Kuznets [1971] for a thoughtful review of the evidence regarding levels and stability of aggregate capital-output ratios.

7. Of course, many other policy questions can be asked as well, as shown in Chapters II and IV. Also, the Harrod–Domar model can be used for other more technical purposes. For example, equation (1.3) can be rewritten as $g = [I(t)/K(t)] - \delta$. If the economy has grown steadily for some years in the past, then $g$ and $\delta$ will be roughly constant for that period. An "average" value for $I(t)$ over the steady growth period can be used in this equation to infer a benchmark value of $K(t)$, which in turn can be used as a basis for calculating a capital stock time series according to the recursion

$$K(t+1) = K(t) + I(t) - \delta K(t).$$

8. The story which is about to be told applies equally well to any two-way partition of factor payments—agricultural and nonagricultural incomes, for example.

$$W + \Pi = Y,$$

and

$$s_\pi \Pi + s_w W = I,$$

where $s_\pi$ and $s_w$ are savings propensities from $\Pi$ and $W$, respectively. Manipulation of (1.3) and these equations gives a modified growth equation,

$$k(g + \delta) = (s_\pi - s_w)(\Pi/Y) + s_w, \tag{1.4}$$

which can be used to check on savings behavior. For example, if a 4 percent growth rate is desired, while the following parameter values hold: $\delta = 0.03$, $k = 3.0$, $(\Pi/Y) = 0.5$, then (1.4) reduces to $0.42 = s_\pi + s_w$. If the savings rate out of capital incomes is 30 percent, then labor income recipients must save at a 12 percent rate to maintain the postulated rate of growth. This would be a considerable savings rate for low-income people.

(iii) Models based on aggregate production functions can also be used for planning applications, provided that one is willing to assume that the economy behaves "as if" it is competitive, in some generalized way. The standard production function specification is $Y = F(K, L)$, where $Y$ is *net* national product, $K$ and $L$ are capital and labor inputs, and the function $F(K, L)$ is supposed to be homogeneous of degree one (constant returns to scale) and to satisfy various regularity conditions. Over time, the representation of the production function in terms of rates of growth is

$$\frac{\Delta Y}{Y} = \frac{\partial F}{\partial L} \frac{L}{Y} \frac{\Delta L}{L} + \frac{\partial F}{\partial K} \frac{K}{Y} \frac{\Delta K}{K} + R = \alpha_L \frac{\Delta L}{L} + \alpha_K \frac{\Delta K}{K} + R \tag{1.5}$$

where the maintained hypothesis of perfect competition permits the identification of the labor share $\alpha_L$ with the elasticity of output with respect to labor $\partial F/\partial L\, L/Y$ (and similarly for capital), and the symbol $R$ denotes the famous residual. Coupled with a net capital accumulation function of the form

$$\frac{\Delta K}{K} = \frac{s}{k} - \delta,$$

(1.5) provides a basis for growth forecasts based on historical data about factor shares, savings and capital parameters, *and* the residual. It also underlies a series of checks which can be made on the reliability of the national accounts.[9] The growth equation can be extended to consider different types of

---

9. For example, the capital share in GNP is $\alpha_K = (\partial F/\partial K + \delta)K/Y$, an equation relating capital share, marginal product of capital, depreciation rate, and capital-output ratio. One often has information on some of these magnitudes from independent sources (marginal product from balance sheet data, depreciation from engineering replacement requirements, etc.) which can be used to check the estimates in the national accounts through the equation.

labor (Selowsky [1969]), noncompetitive labor market behavior (Bruno [1968]), etc.

(iv) One variant of the multisectoral, neoclassical growth model specification that merits special attention is the dual economy analysis. In one form, this just reduces to a two-sector growth model in which labor moves between the agricultural and industrial sectors in such a way as to equalize wage rates.[10] In another, surplus labor assumptions replace this competitive behavior in the labor market with an institutionally fixed wage in the urban sector and an unemployed reserve army in the countryside or urban slums. These two models are reviewed succinctly by Dixit [1970a]. They have been used extensively in the calculation of shadow prices for project analysis but not for medium-term forecasting.[11]

(v) Another common approach to planning focuses on the bottleneck which may be created by a shortage of capital *goods* (not savings, as in the Harrod–Domar model). As long as one ignores the possibility of importing investment goods (as may be realistic in a large country), this leads naturally to a disaggregation of production into capital goods and consumption goods branches. If it is also assumed that capital cannot be shifted from a sector once installed there (a hypothesis which will come up repeatedly in our discussion), the main choice is where to assign newly produced capital—to the capital goods sector itself or to consumption goods. This decision is the crucial one in the so-called Feldman–Mahalanobis–Domar (FMD) models, once partially applied in Indian planning.[12] The models actually used in India assumed that some fixed proportion of new capital would go to the capital goods industry, and ground out the intertemporal growth consequences of alternative proportions. More flexible schemes are also possible, but this whole family of models suffers from the fact that at reasonable levels of disaggregation there are no pure sectors. Particularly when the ubiquitous input-output connections among sectors are taken into account, it is extremely difficult to segregate published industrial statistics into the FMD capital and consumption classes. For example, products of the "transport equipment" industry (a common classification) can be used as capital goods (trucks), consumer durables (cars), and as intermediate inputs when spare parts are classified as such.

(vi) Finally, we consider the two-gap models, probably the most widely used for forecasting in developing countries. These can be viewed as a practicable generalization of the Harrod–Domar specification to take into account foreign trade bottlenecks, absorptive capacity limits and other disequilibrating phenomena which are rife in the developing world. Foreign

---

10. Long-term simulations from such a model are discussed extensively by Kelley, Williamson, and Cheetham [1972].

11. The surplus labor specification is further analyzed in subsection 4.2, and also in Chapter VII.

12. See Bhagwati and Chakravarty [1969] for a description.

trade is brought into the model via the identity that capital inflows (i.e., the difference between imports and exports) add to investable resources, so that the savings-investment restriction becomes

$$I \leq F + sY \tag{1.6}$$

where $F$ is the amount of capital inflows. Equation (1.6) is called the savings constraint, or "gap."

If investment has a marginal import share of $\Theta$ (typically 30 to 50 percent in small developing countries) and production of a unit of GNP requires imports in the amount $\mu$ (perhaps 10 percent of output value), then the trade constraint or gap faced by the economy can be written

$$\Theta I + \mu Y - E \leq F \tag{1.7}$$

where $E$ is the exogenous level of exports.

The term $F$ enters both of these inequality constraints and is the key to the analysis. Along with output and exports it can be assigned an exogenous current value. Typically, when this is done, only one of (1.6) and (1.7) will be binding, i.e., investment (and therefore the growth rate) will be restricted to a lower level by one inequality constraint than by the other. This dichotomy provides a basis for classification of countries and is also a crude means for assigning foreign aid, since the impact of increased capital inflow on investment is greater when the trade gap (1.7) rather than the savings gap (1.6) is binding.

As with other models of the Harrod–Domar type, note the mechanistic nature of the forecasts. Imports are strictly linked with output and investment levels, as are savings, while exports and net capital inflows are exogenous. Trying to alter many of these "fixed" parameters is at the heart of planning in a developing economy experiencing structural change. However, for forecasting, this is a less serious objection, and the two-gap specification is widely used. Although extremely simple, two-gap models generalize Harrod–Domar in a relevant way and are consistent with the categories in which national accounts data are usually arranged. Macroeconomic planners can do worse than apply two-gap models in a flexible, intelligent analysis à la Chenery and Bruno [1962].

## 1.3 Evaluation

The Harrod–Domar model is robust and is applied "everywhere" in planning exercises, if only as a check on more ad hoc projections. The main question to be asked in any applied context, then, is which variants of Harrod–Domar should be considered? No inviolate rules can be laid down, but the following observations about model selection may prove useful:

(i) When foreign trade problems are important—and they almost always are in developing countries—Harrod–Domar should be generalized to the two-gap specification for applications. If there is some interest in investigating

the effects of tariff or exchange rate changes, the neoclassical two-gap variant of Nelson [1970] may be utilized.

(ii) If planners want to investigate the effects of education reform and skill upgrading, they can do so by generalizing the growth equation (1.5) to take into account more labor skill groups. This sort of study is likely to be most relevant when a country has emerged from an extreme surplus labor growth phase.

(iii) When analysis of financial flows and sources of savings is relevant, the specification of point (ii) of subsection 1.2 may be applied, or generalized. This is applicable especially when there exists evidence of different savings patterns among social classes or income groups, and some redistribution (perhaps to the government through increased taxation) is planned.

(iv) If labor migration and population growth appear to be pressing problems, surplus labor or dual economy models (perhaps with explicit migration and fertility functions) may be applied. Forecasting population movements is treacherous but essential for perspective planning in many countries.

The list could be extended, but the above points may give a flavor of what is possible with existing techniques. An additional caution is that while aggregate models are not costly in terms of either data or calculation, their successful application does require a great deal of economic sophistication and a good "feel" for what is happening in the economy. A purely mechanical application of one of the models described above (or below) is worse than not using a model at all.

## 2. STATIC INPUT-OUTPUT ANALYSIS

The models discussed so far have been aggregative, consistent with national accounts data, and designed to make macroeconomic projections about the evolution of GNP, total employment, the balance of payments, and so on. However, for many planning purposes—particularly as a basis for discussion between sector specialists and those concerned with macroanalysis—more disaggregated growth forecasts are desirable. These are almost always built around an interindustry flow table. This is still an essentially macroeconomic construct, since even the most detailed input-output tables rarely reach down to the plant (let alone the farm!) in their classification. However, the tables do provide a halfway house between macro and micro and are useful for precisely this reason.

### 2.1 The Interindustry Flow Specification

The basic demand-supply balance in the input-output accounting framework is as follows (for sector $i$):

$$X_i + M_i^c = \sum_j X_{ij} + C_i + G_i + J_i + E_i + S_i \quad i = 1, 2, \ldots, n \quad (2.1)$$
$$= \sum_j X_{ij} + F_i$$

where $X_i$ = the volume of gross output from sector $i$;

$M_i^c$ = competitive imports into sector $i$;

$X_{ij}$ = intermediate sales from sector $i$ to sector $j$;

$C_i$ = consumer demand for products of sector $i$;

$G_i$ = government expenditures for products from sector $i$;

$J_i$ = capital formation and replacement demand for sector $i$ products ("investment by sector of origin");

$E_i$ = exports from sector $i$;

$S_i$ = changes in stocks of sector $i$ products;

$F_i$ = total final demands from sector $i$.

Three initial points should be made about equation (2.1):

(i) An assumption implicit in the specification is that each sector produces a single good which can be used interchangeably for consumption, investment, as an export, or whatever. This is a drastic simplification which can create great barriers to communication between macroplanners and sector specialists—for example, saying that demand for all types of "food" output will grow by 10 percent over the next three years does not mean much to the man who specializes in green vegetables for final consumption. About the only palliative for this problem is to try to choose an aggregation scheme which fits the important issues in economic policy. For instance, leading sectors (however defined) should not be lumped together with all the rest, and agriculture ought to be split up into as many sectors as possible. On the other hand, a detailed breakdown of manufacturing sectors is often rather uninteresting, particularly if the overall sector accounts for only 10 or 15 percent of GNP and a smaller share of employment.

(ii) Because each input-output sector does produce many goods, price and quantity indices at the sectoral level have to be constructed for use in (2.1). Ideally, the volume indices should be in terms of producers' prices net of commodity taxes ("basic" prices in the terminology of the United Nations [1968]). In developing countries, the interindustry flow matrix has often been constructed in terms of purchasers' (users') prices, with at best a rough translation to producers' prices on the basis of inadequate information about commercialization margins and a series of proportionality assumptions.[13] For examples of what can go wrong in projections when these rather arbitrary

---

13. Typically, information may be available on total commercialization by row of an input-output table, derived by subtracting the total supply of intermediate goods from a sector (producers' prices) from total intermediate demands (users' prices). In addition, specific information may be available on wholesale and retail margins for consumer goods. In many "producers' price" input-output tables, these margins have just been subtracted from buyers' price flows along the rows, proportionally to total sales in each cell. If commercialization markups differ from cell to cell (as they undoubtedly do) this procedure leads to bias in output projections.

practices are followed, see the United Nations [1968] national account guidelines.

(iii) Finally, the classification of competitive imports $M_i^c$ into sector $i$ is difficult. In principle, only imports of types of "food" or "machinery" which could be produced within the country in the short run and at comparable costs should be considered as competitive. This sort of information can only be obtained from careful interview studies with manufacturers, engineers, economists, and other experts. In practice, the competitive/noncompetitive distinction is often drawn on the basis of foreign trade statistics and industrial census data, supplemented by a priori guesses as to where comparative advantage and/or near-term import substitution possibilities may lie. Even when they are split out, valuation of the competitive imports is difficult, since their world prices plus tariffs (or observable scarcity premium) are often not the same as the prices of comparable nationally produced goods, as the theory to be developed below requires. Clearly, numerous errors can arise in splitting imports into the two categories, but on the other hand treating all imports as being of one type or the other can lead to severe biases in input-output forecasts (again discussed in United Nations [1968]). The best solution is probably to classify imports in the most precise way possible and live with the resulting errors in data.

## 2.2  The Fixed Coefficients Hypothesis

In applied economics, problems like the foregoing are often duly noted at the outset, and then completely ignored in all calculations. Applied input-output analysis is usually no exception; in fact it invokes one additional assumption: $X_{ij} = a_{ij}X_j$, where $a_{ij}$ is a constant.[14] On the basis of this, (2.1) can be rewritten in matrix notation (by dropping subscripts) as

$$(I - A)X + M^c = F, \tag{2.2}$$

which is the basis for almost all the standard calculations.

At the outset, it is worth pointing out that constancy of $a_{ij}$ is really quite a strong assumption: the ratio $X_{ij}/X_j$ does change over time and, in principle, this should be taken into account in applications. There are three ways in which this can be done.

(i) The first is widely utilized in practice. It amounts to making the $a_{ij}$ explicit functions of time, with changes forecast on the basis of more or less formal analysis of how the input structure and product mix of particular sectors have changed in the past and are likely to evolve in the future. Anne Carter's book [1970] on the United States is a good, recent example,[15] and less

---

14. That is, $a_{ij}$ is "estimated" by the ratio $X_{ij}/X_j$ in base year prices, and is assumed not to change in response to changes in other variables endogenous to the planning exercise. Exogenous changes in input-output coefficients are of course permitted.

15. Also see several of the articles in Carter and Brody [1970b].

elaborate studies have been done in developing countries. A more mechanical procedure for updating and forecasting changes in an interindustry flow table has been proposed by Richard Stone.[16] Called the RAS method, it amounts, essentially, to an iterated series of multiplications which bring flows from an old matrix into line with more recent totals for the rows (total sales from a sector for intermediate uses) and columns (total intermediate purchases of a sector), which can sometimes be gleaned from national accounts data. In practice, certain coefficients are usually modified exogenously on the basis of Carter-like sector information and exempted from the RAS procedure.

(ii) A second way of looking at changes in the $a_{ij}$ is in terms of econometric production functions. Long ago, Klein [1953] proposed that the $a_{ij}$ be interpreted as resulting from a Cobb–Douglas production function, with the implication that they should stay constant in *value*, not volume, terms. This was given measured support by Watanabe [1961]; since then a few other studies have indicated at least that the null hypothesis—that elasticities of substitution among intermediate inputs themselves, and between them and primary factors, are equal to zero—should be rejected.[17] Besides Klein, however, no one has proposed a convenient functional representation of intermediate input substitutability for use in applied work. Aside from one or two studies which have adopted the Cobb–Douglas specification (discussed in section 6 below), price-responsive input-output coefficients have not been used in applied models. In view of the econometric results, this carries with it an implicit assumption that goods and factor prices do not change over the forecast period.

(iii) Rather than directly forecasting the input-output ratios, it is possible to state the model in incremental form by replacing the hypothesis of fixed *average* input-output coefficients with

$$X_{ij}(t) = X_{ij}(0) + a_{ij}[X_j(t) - X_j(0)]. \tag{2.3}$$

In this formulation, changes in the input-output ratios are related to increased output levels through the use of *marginal* technical coefficients. Thus, $a_{ij}$ in (2.3) could be estimated, in principle at least, from future project plans. This would encourage a disaggregation scheme emphasizing specific leading sectors. On the other hand, $X_{ij}(0)$ is usually based on an interindustry transactions matrix, stressing historically important sectors. The two classifications may not coincide perfectly.[18]

---

16. For more discussion of RAS and related procedures, see Bacharach [1970].

17. See Tilanus [1966], Griliches and Ringstad [1971].

18. One can also express input-output models in elasticity form—examples are Tims [1968] and van Rijckeghem [1969]—with information requirements similar to those of the incremental models. For more discussion of the two approaches as applied to employment projections see Chapter VII. Subsection 6.2 of this chapter describes how elasticity models can be extended to fully general equilibrium growth simulations.

## 2.3 Planning Applications of Input-Output

Application is based on inverting the $(I - A)$ matrix to find gross output requirements contingent on a forecast of final demands and competitive imports,

$$X = (I - A)^{-1}(F - M^c) \tag{2.4}$$

If one makes the additional assumptions that capital, labor, and noncompetitive intermediate imports are tied to outputs by proportionality relationships, then (2.4) also provides a basis for finding out what quantities of these inputs are "required" by some vector of final demands. For the record, the appropriate formulas are:

$$L = \hat{\lambda}X = \hat{\lambda}(I - A)^{-1}(F - M^c) = \hat{\lambda}^*(F - M^c) \tag{2.5}$$

$$K = \hat{k}X = \hat{k}^*(F - M^c), \tag{2.6}$$

and

$$M^{nc} = \hat{a}_0 X = \hat{a}_0^*(F - M^c) \tag{2.7}$$

where $L$, $K$ and $M^{nc}$ are *vectors* of labor use, capital, and noncompetitive imports required by the net final demand vector $(F - M^c)$, and $\lambda$, $k$ and $a_0$ are vectors of sectoral labor-output, capital-output, and intermediate import-output ratios (also assumed constant for purposes of the forecasting exercise). The "hat" ( ^ ) over these coefficient vectors indicates that they are written along the main diagonal of a matrix otherwise made up of zeroes, and the asterisk denotes "direct-and-indirect" coefficients.

These equations for predicting factor uses are widely used and provide partial answers for a number of questions which often arise during the planning process. Examples are:

(i) Evaluation of specific investment projects: Expenditures on road construction, say, could be plugged in as components of the vector $F$ in (2.5). The sum of the vector $L$ would then be an estimate of total employment resulting directly and indirectly from road construction. Similar calculations could, of course, be made for capital, foreign exchange, and value-added multiplier impacts of the road program. These serve as an important complement to more traditional project evaluation methods, particularly when the expenditure package or investment project is "large" or concentrated in a sector with many interindustry linkages with the rest of the economy.[19]

(ii) When $F$ and $M^c$ in equations like (2.5) to (2.7) are aggregate forecasts of final demands, then $K$, $L$, etc., are predictions of total resources required to meet the final demand forecasts. These can be used to complement purely aggregate studies of whether or not there will be sufficient foreign exchange,

---

19. For more elaboration on this and subsequent points, see Chapter V.

capital, and so forth, over the plan period. If not, then final demand forecasts may be unrealistic and trial and error revision will be necessary. As discussed throughout this volume, this type of error-correcting process underlies any serious planning effort.

(iii) At the same time, the output forecasts from (2.4) provide a basis for dialogue with sector specialists. As mentioned above, this may be hindered by aggregation problems, but it is usually possible. For example, 4 percent aggregate consumption growth may give rise to 3 percent growth in demand for agricultural products, after the input-output calculation. If agricultural supply is only likely to grow at 2 percent, there is obvious need for plan revision. On the other hand, the *consistent* input-output forecast of growth in demand for chemicals (which go largely to intermediate uses) may be 6 percent. If the chemical sector expert is plumping for 10 percent growth without significant import substitution, input-output serves as a valuablereality check on his enthusiasm.

(iv) Although it is largely oriented toward real planning, the input-output system has an implicit price theory, which will be utilized extensively in the sections discussing programming models. If we let $P_i$ be the price of good $i$, $w$ the wage and $r$ the user cost of capital, then competitive behavior in sector $i$ implies that

$$P_i = \sum_j a_{ji}P_j + w\lambda_i + rk_i \tag{2.8}$$

where $\lambda_i$ and $k_i$ are the sector's labor-output and capital-output ratios. Clearly, (2.8) can be rewritten in matrix form (as in equation (4.6) below) and the matrix inverted to express goods prices in terms of factor prices. Given exogenous forecasts of the latter, it has been shown that the resulting forecasts of goods prices often track observed prices fairly well.[20] This type of cost-push price forecast clearly can be used as an element in the formation of monetary policy—as indeed it was, with considerable success, in Chile during the 1960s (Cauas [1972]). In principle, the price forecasts could also be used in conjunction with quantity projections to say something about government revenues, tax receipts, and so on, although this has been done only sporadically in practice.

(v) Finally, note that there are several ways in which competitive imports can be included in the specification. Heretofore, the assumption has been that exogenous quantity forecasts of these imports are available. However, import volumes can also be related to sectoral output or final demand levels by fixed coefficients[21] (which may decline over time to reflect planned import substitution). Alternatively, imports may be calculated by iterative procedures to satisfy exogenously imposed limitations on sectoral capacities. This can be

---

20. See Watanabe and Shishido [1970].
21. Restating the model in algebraic form under these assumptions is left as an exercise to the reader.

done informally through discussions with sector specialists, or formally with the methods discussed in point (iii) of subsection 3.3 below.

## 2.4 Estimation of Final Demand

All these sectoral output and factor use forecasts are conditional on the expected growth patterns of the different components of final demand. We turn now to forecasting techniques for these. Since consumption usually makes up three-quarters or more of final demand in most sectors, considerable effort should be made to predict the $C_i$. The most commonly used formula is

$$\frac{C_i(t)}{N(t)} = \Phi_i \left[ \frac{C_T(t)}{N(t)} \right]^{\varepsilon_i}, \quad i = 1, 2, \ldots, n \qquad (2.9)$$

where $N(t)$ = population at time $t$,

$\quad C_T(t)$ = total expenditure on consumption goods at time $t$,

$\quad\quad \varepsilon_i$ = Engel elasticity (at time $t$),

$\quad\quad \Phi_i$ = constant.

This equation states that sectoral consumption levels depend on expected population and total consumption, via the Engel elasticities. Population projections are usually made by experts, and aggregate (or per capita) consumption growth targets are often set up as goals of the plan.[22] Of course, a major use of models of the type discussed here is to check on just how realistic these goals are, in terms of their probable requirements for primary factors.

In practice, the equation in (2.9) will usually give sectoral consumption forecasts which do not quite add up to $C_T(t)$. The error may be 5 percent or more, and if one wants to avoid it, (2.9) must be linearized around sectoral base year or forecasted reference point consumption levels. If we linearize around the year zero levels (which may provide a less accurate forecast than the future reference point), the appropriate formula is

$$C_i(t) = \varepsilon_i \frac{C_i(0)}{C_T(0)} C_T(t) + \frac{N(t)}{N(0)} C_i(0)(1 - \varepsilon_i), \quad i = 1, 2, \ldots, n. \quad (2.10)$$

---

22. Occasionally, consumption is made endogenous to a "closed" input-output system by additional equations tying $C_T(t)$ to some measure of "income"—commonly the sum of sector value-added levels or the sum of wage payments from the value-added breakdown of the input-output system. The former specification recalls the Keynesian consumption function in that the marginal propensity to consume from total value added must be less than one to assure stability. The latter specification underlies the surplus labor programming models of subsection 4.2, and the turnpike-based terminal conditions mentioned in the appendix to this chapter. Again, the algebraic statement of these revised models is left to the reader. He may find it useful to state the closed model in terms of an $(n + 1) \times (n + 1)$ input-output matrix—the additional row giving factor payments from sectoral production, and the additional column giving the consumption breakdown from the sum of these payments. The very southeast element of this augmented matrix will be zero, unless workers buy services (e.g., domestic ones) from themselves. Chapter V, section 4, reviews such a closed model for Iran.

To guarantee adding-up here, the Engel elasticities must satisfy the condition

$$\sum_i \varepsilon_i [C_i(0)/C_T(0)] = 1, \tag{2.11}$$

which is well known from consumer demand theory.

Engel elasticities for this type of projection are often taken from budget studies and modified informally to satisfy (2.11).[23] There are some well-known problems in transferring this type of cross-section estimate to time series forecasts, but usually nothing is done about them. An alternative source of Engel elasticities is estimation from time series. The national accounts occasionally provide data on consumption levels classified by categories such as "food" and "rent." These are *not* the same as input-output classification categories, so that the time series elasticities can provide only indirect evidence about the $\varepsilon_i$ of (2.9). In addition, the data are often unreliable, since consumption levels may be estimated as residuals by subtraction of other final demand components from sectoral outputs. A final possibility is to borrow Engel elasticities (and also the breakdown of consumption expenditures by sector) from other countries or international cross-section regressions. Some of the pros and cons of doing this are discussed in Chapter IV.

Other components of final demand are usually predicted by more informal means. A planning office may have people specialized in foreign trade and fiscal matters who can provide export and government expenditure forecasts[24] and, in the medium-term, stock changes may be ignored in the accounting or related to output levels, imports, and/or intermediate demands by factors of proportionality. Competitive imports, as a first approximation, are usually related by fixed coefficients either to output levels by sector or else to different components of final demand. The appropriate assumption is a matter of judgment and has to be elected on the scene.

Methods of predicting the vector $J$ of investment demands by origin are discussed exhaustively in section 3. In practice, these procedures may be unnecessary because the main domestic supplier of capital goods in many developing countries is the construction sector, with other capital goods (mainly machinery and equipment) being imported. When this is the case, a careful projection of demands for construction largely suffices for the vector $J$. Not putting an excessive amount of work into forecasting investment leaves resources free for consumption forecasts (which dominate final demand) and consultation with sector specialists on the credibility of the input-output

---

23. If *linear* consumption functions are used in a budget study or time series analysis, then adding-up is automatic. However, constant elasticity demand functions are more common and must usually be corrected.

24. There are usually problems in translating government expenditures from the budget to input-output classifications; the same is often true for exports (and imports), in going from the usual foreign trade classification schemes.

projections. If the interest lies in a plausible plan, this may represent the more rational use of scarce technicians.

## 2.5   Evaluation

Many different types of planning problems arise, and planning models must be designed to fit the questions being asked. If the interest lies in forecasts of the macroeconomic variables for the next five years, one of the aggregate models discussed in subsections 1.2 and 1.3 would probably be used, but its results could still be checked against the sums of sectoral value added, foreign exchange use, and so on, from an input-output forecast. In fact, the summation of sectoral outputs from the disaggregated model may provide a better prediction of GNP than straightforward application of something like the Harrod–Domar equation, particularly if it is anticipated that the output mix will change substantially over the plan period.

Of course, the disaggregated forecasts have many uses themselves, as summarized in subsection 2.3. The disaggregation is especially relevant when the interindustry structure of the economy is well developed (say in a small country when the per capita income is $200 or more, and in any large country); and it is important for planners and policy makers at the center and people in charge of sectors to have effective communication. This may be required under a variety of institutional arrangements, ranging from cases in which the government controls most of investment and needs to apportion available funds among sectors, to cases in which indicative planning with dialogue between public and private sectors is the style. Even in completely free markets, it is useful for planners to know the multiplier impacts of expenditure packages or other policy alternatives they may be considering. For example, if farmers were to adopt new technology in response to governmental encouragement, a large investment outlay in the aggregate would be involved, and the old "agriculture" column in the input-output matrix would have to be replaced by a new one over time. Given the importance of the agricultural sector in any developing country, both the investment and new techniques would have repercussions throughout the economy which even the most laissez-faire government would want to know about. Input-output is the tool that members of such a government would use in determining the economy-wide impacts of their new farming sector.

## 3. DYNAMIC INPUT-OUTPUT ANALYSIS

The multisectoral models discussed in the last section would all be called "static" in the input-output jargon. This means that they have no explicit theory of investment, so that the vector $J$ of final demands for capital goods is on the same footing as all other final demand components.

This situation is radically altered in the so-called "dynamic" input-output model, the subject of this section. This widely used model incorporates an

accelerator-type investment theory in which current demands for investment goods depend on future expected growth of output. As mentioned in the Readers' Guide, there are often good practical reasons *against* making this extension of the static input-output framework—investment demands are hard to forecast and may make a relatively minor claim on total productive resources in the country. Nonetheless, when there is a significant national production capacity for capital goods and high investment rates are anticipated, a case can be made that planners should treat investment as endogenous. Here we review the various methods for doing so.

## 3.1 Basic Assumptions

There are three basic assumptions (often combined) underlying the Leontief dynamic model. The first is that investment demands by origin $(J)$ are related to demands by destination by the following relationship:

$$J = B(D + R) \tag{3.1}$$

where $B$ = a distribution matrix for investment demands;
$\quad\quad D$ = a vector of demands for investment for new capital formation by destination;
$\quad\quad R$ = a vector of replacement demands by destination.

The $i$th column of $B$ in (3.1) represents a breakdown of the basket of goods demanded for investment by sector $i$ from producing sectors. In principle, all columns of $B$ sum to one, when investment flows are expressed (as is usual) in terms of base year unit values.[25] However, if the matrix is interpreted as referring only to nationally produced or competitively imported goods, this will not be the case in many countries because of their dependence on noncompetitive imports for supply of many types of machinery and equipment. Also, many rows of $B$ will be equal to zero, since most sectors produce only for consumption or intermediate demands. Finally, in applications, the coefficients in the columns of $B$ are usually assumed not to change in response to changing capital goods prices. This flies in the face of strong econometric evidence that elasticities of substitution among different types of capital are well above one.[26] Once again, to apply classical input-output, we are obliged to accept strong assumptions about nonchanging relative prices.

The second key assumption is that investment demands by destination are determined by a simple accelerator relationship,

$$D(t) = \hat{k}[X(t + 1) - X(t)], \tag{3.2}$$

---

25. It is conceivable, but not likely, that flows of capital goods might be measured in physical terms, in which case the columns of the $B$ matrix need not sum to one. Again, it is the aggregation problem which almost always rules out this specification in practice. Even for a product as apparently homogeneous as "cement," it makes more sense to talk about dollar-value of output rather than tons produced, for, in fact, there are several kinds of cement which are highly differentiated with respect to both cost and final use.

26. This is well known. See, for example, Sato [1967].

where $\hat{k}$ is a vector of incremental capital-output ratios written along the main diagonal of an otherwise null matrix. The accelerator is assumed to hold as a *technical* relationship. In practice, it may be spread over several years to reflect gestation lags in investment projects. This specification carries with it a number of interesting, though unresolved, problems. They include the following:

(i) Models without a realistic two- or three-year structure of gestation lags cannot provide detail about growth prospects when they are limited by stocks of goods-in-process. Such limitations are practically important, since planners usually are most interested in prospects over the near future. Even if the initial conditions of capital goods formation in the process of gestation can be realistically specified, the adjustment to a set of balanced sectoral growth paths may dominate the economy for three to five years, depending on the investment lags assumed in the model. This is the reason why authors such as Eckaus and Parikh [1968] and Chakravarty and Lefeber [1965] go to great lengths to include gestation lags in their models.

(ii) A counterargument is that solid knowledge about the structure of lags and actual amounts of goods-in-process is extremely difficult to obtain, so that building what is guessed about these things into the model amounts to giving it false precision. This argument is only strengthened by the observation that the length of lags is in part a matter of choice at the plant level. If the model were sufficiently disaggregated it could take this into account, perhaps along the lines of the absorptive capacity restrictions discussed in subsection 5.2.

(iii) Including a complicated lag structure makes the dynamic system harder to understand. It may also lead to instabilities and debugging problems in optimizing dynamic models of the type discussed in section 5.

(iv) On the other hand, aggregation errors are clearly created if a long, complicated set of gestation lags is boiled down to one period. To date there has been no analysis of how severe this problem is likely to be or how it interacts with different sectoral aggregation schemes.

Leaving the applications-oriented reader to sort out this mass of conflicting observations on his own, we turn to a final problem, that of calculating the vector $R(t)$ of replacement investments for use in (3.1). One way of doing this is simply to forecast replacement requirements over the plan period exogenously, assuming that investments made within the plan will not depreciate until well in the future. This type of specification is particularly appealing when one has good knowledge of the sectoral distribution *and* age structure of the existing capital stock.

Another method is to relate replacement requirements to the existing capital stock by some proportionality factors:

$$R(t) = \delta K(t) \qquad (3.3)$$

The vector of "depreciation" coefficients $\delta$ can be obtained on the basis of

actual replacement requirements (if known), industry studies, or various reference books.[27] Replacement requirements can also be related to sectoral output levels, if capital-output ratios are known and it is assumed that the percentage of capacity utilization will remain fairly steady over the plan. This final specification has the advantage of allowing the replacement demands to be subsumed in the input-output matrix (as the reader can easily verify).

## 3.2 The Difference Equation for the Dynamic Model

These formulations permit explicit inclusion of capital accumulation in the forecasting exercise, although it should be recognized that the matrix $B$ and vectors $k$ and $\delta$ are often of dubious quality.[28] The forecast equation, derived from (3.1) to (3.3), is

$$X(t) = AX(t) + H[X(t+1) - X(t)] + F(t), \quad t = 0, 1, 2, \ldots,$$
$$X(0) \text{ given} \tag{3.4}$$

where $H$ is the product matrix $B\hat{k}$, the depreciation vector $\delta$ has been incorporated into the $A$ matrix (along with coefficients for competitive imports, stock changes, and so on), and $F$ is to be interpreted as a vector of final demand totals by origin, excluding investment.

This equation would define a forward recurrence relationship for $X(t)$ if the

27. See, for example, Marston et al. [1953] and Kurtz [1930]. Jorgenson [1971] gives a useful review of "depreciation" theory.

28. If we rule out lifting the $B$ matrix from some other country—favorite sources have been Grosse [1953] and the National Planning Association's compendium [1966]—there remain two common methods to construct $B$ and $k$. The first is based on the use of building permits and investment survey data to estimate construction by destination. This accounts for roughly half of investment. The other major component, machinery and equipment imports, may be estimated from customs data. This may pose problems, since published trade statistics usually only give imports by origin. To find destinations one must have access to detailed customs declarations. This has proven feasible in a few countries. The breakdown of construction and import expenditures (and other minor items such as furniture) gives the columns of the $B$ matrix. Subtracting estimates of replacement investment from the total investments by destination leaves the vector $D$ as a residual. Each component of this vector can be related to the corresponding sector's output change to derive the "marginal" capital-output ratios which make up the vector $k$. Normally, if this process is undertaken for several years, the estimated ratios vary substantially over time. Some sort of regression analysis can then be used to derive an "average" set of $B$ and $k$ coefficients. (The traditional type of average capital-output ratio usually cannot be calculated in developing countries on the sectoral level, for lack of long-term compilations of capital stocks.)

The other method (discussed in detail in Adelman, Cole, Norton, and Jung [1969]) is to base estimates of $B$ and $k$ on the patterns of capital use in recent investment projects. This approach usually suffers from small samples and the fact that new investments large enough to justify writing up a project report may not be representative of the "typical" technology involved in new investments in the country as a whole.

Whether to use one or the other (or both) of these methods is a decision which has to be made on the basis of data available in the country. It is clear, however, that both are subject to considerable potential error, and that the precision of the estimated capital coefficients is not likely to be great.

matrix $H$ could be inverted. Because $H$ has many zero rows corresponding to non-capital goods producing sectors, this inversion cannot be done in (3.4) as it is written, and one must work with a reduced system of equations in which only "state" (stock) variables corresponding to outputs of the capital goods sectors evolve over time. Following tradition, we do not discuss this reduction here[29] and assume that $H$ is already of full rank. This means that (3.4) can be written in the following difference equation form:

$$X(t + 1) = [I + H^{-1}(I - A)]X(t) - H^{-1}F(t), t = 0, 1, 2, \ldots,$$
$$X(0) \text{ given.} \tag{3.5}$$

The general solution to (3.5) for any given time period $t$ takes the form

$$X(t) = [I + H^{-1}(I - A)]^t X(0) + X^*(t), \quad t = 1, 2, 3, \ldots, \tag{3.6}$$

where the first term on the right is the complete solution of the "homogeneous" equation for a Leontief system in which all output surplus over input requirements is reinvested (i.e., in (3.5) the exogenous final demand term $F(t)$ is set identically equal to zero) and $X^*(t)$ is a particular solution of (3.5), based on final demands.

There is a considerable literature on the solution to this homogeneous equation, the behavior of which hinges on the magnitudes of the characteristic values of the matrix $[I + H^{-1}(I - A)]$. One of these will correspond to a balanced growth path for the system, along which elements of vector $X(t)$ stay in fixed proportion to each other and grow at equal, constant rates. Whether or not output levels will converge to balanced growth from arbitrary initial conditions depends on the other characteristic values; if any correspond to growth rates exceeding that of the balanced growth characteristic value, the system will diverge and finally generate negative output levels in some sectors. On theoretical grounds, it is impossible to state when this will occur. With "realistic" matrices, it appears that the unbalanced growth characteristic values predominate, and even when they don't the rate of balanced growth will often be improbably high.[30] Because such growth would dominate the solution (3.6) of the nonhomogeneous equation even when a "reasonable" growth of exogenous final demand is built into the particular solution $X^*(t)$, forecasting output increases from *arbitrary* initial conditions on the basis of (3.5) is not possible.[31]

---

29. In any case, Kendrick [1972b] and Bergendorff, Blitzer, and Kim [1973] describe reduction procedures in detail.

30. Essentially, this is because the model of (3.5) without final demands $F(t)$ resembles a Harrod–Domar model in which the savings rate equals one. Footnote 33 elaborates this point.

31. Many formal discussions of the instability of the Leontief dynamic model are available in the literature, so we do not pursue the matter further here. An excellent applications-oriented analysis is given by Chakravarty and Eckaus [1964]. See also Burmeister and Dobell [1970], Chakravarty [1969], and Jorgenson [1961].

## 3.3   Applications of the Dynamic Model

These problems of forecasting future growth paths largely result from the simple accelerator relationship in dynamic Leontief models—it should not be too surprising that such a rigid mechanism leads to serious inconsistencies if extrapolated too far into the future. Nevertheless, the dynamic Leontief model is one of the few practical methods for making investment and output forecasts, and therefore is widely used. Moreover, there are several ways to get around its instability problem, as follow:

(i) The divergence of the dynamic model solution from balanced growth occurs when the model is run forward in time, i.e., a simulation starting at time zero may give "reasonable" output levels at times one and two but soon thereafter outputs become improbably large or negative. Conversely, a simulation run backward in time from these unsatisfactory output levels would return to the initial conditions. In fact, the stronger result often holds that if (3.5) is simulated back in time from arbitrary terminal conditions, then the solution ultimately converges to balanced growth output proportions.[32] Leontief [1970] capitalized on this stability property with his "dynamic inverse," essentially a recursive procedure for solving (3.4) backward from given terminal conditions. This type of solution has its uses—for example, in providing information on adjustments in the production structure which would have to precede and accompany expenditures on an investment project coming on stream in the terminal year. However, the dynamic inverse is not very useful as a forecasting tool, since it gives no way (other than blind iteration) of modifying guesses at terminal conditions to make the solution approach given initial output levels, if indeed this is possible.

(ii) An approach with more direct emphasis on forecasting is based on the particular solution $X^*(t)$ to the Leontief dynamic system. We develop a simple example here, based on the assumption that each component of the vector of final demands $F(t)$ grows at the same proportionate rate $g: F(t) = F_0(1 + g)^t$, where $F_0$ is the vector of initial final demand levels. We maintain this unrealistic hypothesis only for simplicity—as Hildebrand [1968] shows, most of the following results generalize to the case where the elements of $F(t)$ grow at different geometric rates, are described by polynomials in time, etc.

Given the geometric growth of final demands, it is easy to show that the sequence

$$X^*(t) = (I - A - gH)^{-1}F(t), \quad t = 0, 1, 2, \ldots \tag{3.7}$$

32. The precise statement of conditions is closely related to the "dual stability" theorem for the dynamic Leontief model, conjectured by Solow [1959], and proved by Jorgenson [1960]. Strictly speaking, the theorem refers to the instability of quantities in the Leontief dynamic system and stability of the corresponding dual price system. It is relevant to the analysis of dynamic planning models, and we return to it in subsection 5.4.

satisfies equation (3.4) as long as $g$ is not greater than the balanced growth rate of the closed system, so that all elements of $(I - A - gH)^{-1}$ remain positive. By construction, this solution will demonstrate "reasonable" growth over time[33] and can be expected to track the evolution of final demand quite closely (as long as demand forecasts can be adequately expressed in terms of the simple functions of time listed above, which seems likely). Its major drawback is that $X^*(0)$ from (3.7) will in general not be the same as the "true" initial output vector, assuming that it is known (which is not always the case—planners often have to forecast their plan's base year output levels on the basis of very poor information such as one or two year delayed national accounts). Presumably the particular solution's initial values will be "close" to the true ones, especially if the economy has been growing steadily for a time.

In principle, output forecasts based on the particular solution can be made by forward simulation of (3.7). However, the practice has not been quite so straightforward, largely because exogenous technical change is usually built into the $A$ and $H$ matrices. When coefficients change over time in a linear difference equation such as (3.5), it is impossible to derive particular solutions of the type we have been discussing. If the coefficients do not change "too much," successive approximations procedures can be used to solve (3.5), and the constant coefficients solution can be used as a guide in setting up these procedures.[34]

---

33. In fact, for the special case of equal geometric growth of all components of final demand, Johansen [1972] shows that the Harrod–Domar growth equation (1.3) applies in the dynamic system, where $s$ and $k$ are weighted averages of sectoral nonconsumed output shares and capital-output ratios, the weights depending on efficiency prices of the type discussed in the next section. Also, the growth rate $g$ is equal to $sg^*$, where $g^*$ is the balanced growth rate of the closed Leontief system. In this way, savings can offset the "improbably high" value of $g^*$ referred to near the end of subsection 3.2, which reflects the reinvestment of all surplus in further growth.

34. For example, when $A$ and H are constant, the particular solution shown in (3.7) will result from the following successive approximations (where superscripts on $X(t)$ denote the step in the approximation process and superscripts on $\Delta$ now denote repeated applications of this difference operator to all elements of a vector):

$$X^{(0)}(t) = (I - A)^{-1}F(t),$$
$$X^{(1)}(t) = (I - A)^{-1}\{F(t) + H(I - A)^{-1}\Delta F(t)\}$$
$$= \{I + (I - A)^{-1}Hg\}(I - A)^{-1}F(t) \tag{3.8}$$

$$X^{(2)}(t) = (I - A)^{-1}\{F(t) + H(I - A)^{-1}\Delta F(t) + [H(I - A)^{-1}]^2\Delta^{(2)}F(t)\}$$
$$= \{I + (I - A)^{-1}Hg + [(I - A)^{-1}Hg]^2\}(I - A)^{-1}F(t), \text{ etc.}$$

From the matrix power series in the second lines of (3.8) there is convergence to the (3.7) solution since

$$\{I + (I - A)^{-1}Hg + [(I - A)^{-1}Hg]^2 + \cdots\}(I - A)^{-1}$$
$$= \{I - (I - A)^{-1}Hg\}^{-1}(I - A)^{-1}$$
$$= (I - A - Hg)^{-1},$$

and the last term is the coefficient matrix of $F(t)$ in $X^*(t)$.

Finally, note that several linear programming models have used particular solutions of the Leontief dynamic system to set postplan terminal conditions. This is discussed in the appendix on terminal conditions at the end of this chapter.

(iii) Other investigators have relaxed Leontief's key assumption that no excess capacity is permitted in the economy. Their procedure has been to specify exogenously the growth of capital stock or capacity by destination and then use (3.1) and (3.2) to determine $J(t)$, the vector of investment demands by origin at time $t$. In each period, then, the economy must satisfy inequality relationships of the form

$$X(t) + W(t) = AX(t) + J(t) + F(t),$$
$$\hat{k}X(t) \leq K(t),$$
$$W'(t)[K(t) - \hat{k}X(t)] = 0, \tag{3.9}$$

where the first line is a modification of the basic demand-supply balance equation (3.2), the second line constrains each sector's output $X_i(t)$ to be less than or equal to its exogenously specified "capacity" $K_i(t)/k_i$, and the third line defines a "balancing" vector $W(t)$. The $i$th element of $W(t)$ is equal to zero or the amount by which sector $i$ capacity falls short of total demand for the sector's product (calculated on the right side of the first equation in (3.9)). When positive, this quantity can be interpreted (for a traded goods sector) as an endogenously generated volume of competitive imports which allows sector supply to meet demand. For a nontraded goods sector, a positive $W_i(t)$ becomes an explicit capacity shortfall, to be met by some sort of demand restriction. In sectors where there is excess capacity, such imports or shortfalls do not exist, and the corresponding entries in $W(t)$ are zero.

A number of variants on this "almost consistent" model exist. In his later United States work, Almon [1970] specified investment by destination semi-exogenously. The pioneering application in developing countries was by Bergsman and Manne [1966]. They calculated investment by destination, assuming a geometric growth of output between the base year and a consistently projected final year. However, they apparently used projected capacity levels in place of $X(t)$ to calculate intermediate demands on the right side of the first line of (3.9), leading to *overestimates* of these demands from

---

In his earlier forecasting exercises for the United States, Almon [1963] used the successive difference expansion shown in the first lines of each step in (3.8). Since he worked with time-varying technology matrices, he could not analytically prove convergence to a particular solution but, in fact, observed it after three to five steps. In another application, a planning team in South Korea (Adelman, Cole, Norton, and Jung [1969]) generated forecasts by using the rule

$$X^{(i+1)}(t) = (I - A)^{-1}\{F(t) + H[X^{(i)}(t + 1) - X^{(i)}(t)]\}$$

which underlies the matrix multiplier chain appearing in the second lines of (3.8). They also reported rapid convergence.

sectors with excess capacity. These in turn produced overestimates of short-falls $W_i(t)$ for sectors with deficient capacity. Clark and Taylor [1971] devised a simple iterative procedure to solve (3.9) in a Bergsman–Manne model for Chile, thus approaching consistency as closely as this framework allows. Interestingly enough, a more complicated variant of the Clark–Taylor algorithm was used twenty years ago by Chenery, Clark, and Cao–Pinna [1953] for a static input-output analysis of Italian trade prospects. This was not followed up in the literature, although Arrow [1954] gave a proof of their algorithm's convergence when all the $W_i(t)$ can actually be traded.

(iv) Finally, forecasts of capital stock growth can be made endogenous to the model, while still permitting excess capacity (but ruling out capacity shortfalls in nontraded sectors, so that the model becomes fully consistent). The natural way to choose the paths of capital stock growth is via some optimization procedure, specifically by multiperiod linear programming planning models. We return to these in section 5, after describing in the next section their one-period cousins.

## 3.4 Evaluation

All the algebra in this section should not obscure the fact that the dynamic Leontief model is not, after all, based on a very convincing set of assumptions. The very fact that the accelerator—the simplest of investment theories—gives rise to the problems just recorded indicates that a satisfactory treatment of investment in dynamic planning models may be a long time coming.

However, dynamic models at least incorporate capital accumulation in a consistent manner. The practitioner has to ask whether the benefits of using the model to treat investment as both a final demand item and a source of new capital goods outweigh the costs. The costs clearly depend on the quality of data on investment flows (which may range from nonexistent to fairly credible) and the availability of computational facilities.[35] The benefits are likely to be greatest when planners operate in an environment in which it is important to know about the growth of the domestic capital goods industry. This will almost always be the case in a large country, where capital goods imports tend to be replaced by domestic production fairly early in the growth process. If a small country is, by choice or necessity, engaged in this type of import substitution, or if it appears that savings or balance of payments constraints may be particularly irksome over the plan period, then working through a fully dynamic plan exercise may help point out possible alternative timing patterns for investment projects which will widen bottlenecks. As always, the emphasis should be on using the model as a tool of exploration, to see what options in its pattern of growth the economy has, and how these can

---

35. At least a medium sized computer (and attendant staff and auxiliary equipment) is required to deal with a disaggregated dynamic input-output model. Storing and manipulating the required data is a substantial task in itself.

be exploited to best advantage. All large models, wisely used, are effective devices for learning about the range of real policy choices which planners have. Dynamic input-output is no exception.

## 4. STATIC LINEAR PROGRAMMING (LP) MODELS[36]

A natural complement to the input-output production specification is optimization of some welfare function to select the "best" pattern of final demand and resource allocation from the many which are possible. Since input-output technological assumptions are all of a constant coefficients (linear) type, linear programming is the appropriate computational means for doing this. Many multisectoral LP planning models have been developed and are reviewed in this section.

There are two ways of looking at LP optimization in planning. The first is based on the idea that parametric programming methods provide a fairly cheap means of exploring the frontiers of the economy's choice set, so long as it can be described in terms of linear inequalities. As we will see in detail, three types of restrictions seem to enter the specification of applied planning models. The first reflects real limitations on economic growth that are easily and realistically modelled. Examples are input-output balances, bounds on total factor uses, and the balance of payments constraint. The second type of constraint represents an attempt to capture important but not well understood limitations on growth. Examples are absorptive capacity restrictions on the amount of investment which can be undertaken in a given industry at a given time, upper bounds on saving which reflect the limited freedom of action of the government in fiscal and monetary matters, and "political" constraints such as requirements for certain regions to grow at specified rate, lower bounds on the level of employment the economy must generate, and upper bounds on imports which would threaten already established but inefficient industries. Finally, some constraints are included in the model on an ad hoc basis for purely technical reasons, to avoid overspecialization in trade, "flip-flop" consumption patterns, and other forms of extreme behavior to which linear systems are prone. All these constraints together may make up a fairly realistic approximation to the set of feasible alternatives faced by the real side of the economy. The linear programming simplex algorithm is an effective means to get out to the boundaries of this set (which input-output models normally cannot do), and parametric programming transforms the exploration of the boundaries from a heavy burden to a fairly cheap and straightforward educational exercise.

---

36. This and the next section presuppose knowledge of elementary linear programming theory, particularly its duality and complementary slackness aspects. Background material on the economic interpretation of LP is available in Dorfman, Samuelson, and Solow [1958], Gale [1960], Dantzig [1963] and many other sources. Kendrick [1970, 1972c] and Manne [1974a] give detailed reviews of LP planning models which complement the present one.

The second view emphasizes the ability of an LP model to simulate a general equilibrium or competitive resource allocation, complete with the prices from the dual solution. This is an appealing construct, and explains much of the interest of academics in these models. Nonetheless, the similarity of the model solution to a Walrasian equilibrium is often very faint, particularly on the price side. Anticipating the detailed discussion later in this section, we can note two main problems:

(i) In a sense, the shadow price system will often be too close to that of a competitive system. That is, in each sector the price of output will be set to marginal cost, marginal consumption utilities will be set to prices, and so on, *but in addition* the only wedges between shadow prices for the same good in different uses will come from other shadow prices on primal constraints of the second and (especially) the third types. This means that the models do not permit easy analysis of the effects of changing *preexisting* price wedges, such as the tariffs and indirect taxes which proliferate in developing countries. Such analysis lies at the heart of much of the project analysis literature (e.g., Harberger [1968]), and it would be desirable to incorporate it into planning exercises. Optimization does not permit this to be done easily, although some other techniques now in the developmental stage (discussed in section 6) may allow this extension.

(ii) The other problem is similar: The ad hoc restrictions necessary for primal stability pick up their own shadow prices, which can usually be interpreted as taxes and subsidies. A finance ministry with extremely effective tax and transfer divisions would be indispensable if one were to attempt to implement the model's shadow prices in a serious way, for example in invest- ment project selection. Given the way finance ministries operate in developing countries, applying all the shadow taxes and subsidies, and therefore shadow prices, is a forlorn hope.

In short, present-day models do not approach a Walrasian competitive resource allocation, with its attendant dual prices. Shadow prices often have a useful "broad sense" interpretation—e.g., a high shadow price on an employ- ment lower bound will show that this policy goal may be difficult to achieve— but their interpretation as reflecting an economy in full general equilibrium easily breaks down.[37] They are also very useful in the model debugging process and help guide the imposition of ad hoc restrictions. But in the final analysis, a well-tuned primal will probably predict more accurately the evolution of

---

37. One might add the observation that all techniques for calculating efficiency prices require unpalatable assumptions and consequences thereof. Programming approaches are not obviously worse than assuming economy-wide perfect competition *now*, as in Harberger [1968], or using wholesale approximations to the solution of a nonlinear dynamic optimizing model, as in Little and Mirrlees [1969]. See Chapter VIII for a review of possible uses of the LP dual solution in project evaluation.

quantities in the economy than its dual will predict the evolution of prices.[38]

### 4.1 Investment Theory and the Golden Rule

We proceed by way of examples, since there are far too many LP planning models in the literature for easy summarization. To finesse this numbers problem, the argument is developed in terms of representative models, with different authors' contributions discussed as they are relevant to the issue at hand. The first topic considered is formulation of forward-looking theories of investment, necessary even in a static model because there is no natural way to determine investment demand in a given year without considering the future growth of the economy.[39]

The simplest way to generate investment endogenously is to fix a priori the rates of growth of capital stock in the plan year. Table 1 shows in "detached coefficients" form a simple set of type one model constraints built around this specification. We peruse the table in detail to illustrate the detached coefficients representation, which will be used repeatedly.

**Table 1: Detached Coefficients Tableau of an LP Model for Year "$t$" in which Post-Terminal Capital Growth Rates are Exogenous**

|  | (1) $X(t)$ | (2) $C_T(t)$ | (3) $J(t)$ | |
|---|---|---|---|---|
| (1) $P'(t)$ | $-(I-A)$ | $\xi$ | $\begin{bmatrix} I \\ 0 \end{bmatrix}$ | $\leq -\bar{C}(t)$ |
| (2) $R'(t)$ | $\hat{g}H$ | | $-I$ | $\leq 0$ |
| (3) $w(t)$ | $\lambda'$ | | | $\leq \bar{L}(t)$ |
| MAX | 1 | | | |

The area inside the central rectangle in Table 1 corresponds to the matrix $A$ of the following primal and dual linear programming problems:

| *Primal* | *Dual* |
|---|---|
| MAX $c'x$ | MIN $p'b$ |
| subject to $Ax \leq b$ | subject to $p'A \geq c'$ |
| $x \geq 0$ | $p' \geq 0'$. |

The activities of the primal problem here (elements of the vector $x$) are written along the top of the table. The resource constraints (corresponding to $b$) are

---

38. See Nugent [1970] for a slightly dissenting opinion and a clever use of the dual to explore distortions in the Greek economy.

39. That is, a theory is necessary if investment is to be included as an endogenous variable. An alternative is simply to make the vector of investments by origin exogenous, and use linear programming to explore resource allocations, and consumption and trade patterns which maximize the objective function, contingent on the given investment demands. In many contexts, it is not obvious that much would be lost by doing this.

written in the right margin. The dual variables (elements of $p$ in the dual problem) are written in the left margin, and the transposed primal maximand weighting vector (or dual constraint vector), $c'$, is written along the bottom of the problem matrix.

Each row of the central matrix in Table 1 represents a set of inequality constraints. The first row can be written in elaborated form as follows:

$$\begin{bmatrix} \xi_1 \\ \cdot \\ \cdot \\ \cdot \\ \xi_n \end{bmatrix} C_T(t) + \begin{bmatrix} 1 & \cdot & \cdot & \cdot & \cdot & 0 \\ 0 & \cdot & \cdot & \cdot & \cdot & 1 \\ 0 & \cdot & \cdot & \cdot & \cdot & 0 \\ 0 & \cdot & \cdot & \cdot & \cdot & 0 \end{bmatrix} \begin{bmatrix} J_1(t) \\ \cdot \\ \cdot \\ \cdot \\ J_m(t) \end{bmatrix}$$

$$\leq (I - A)X(t) - \begin{bmatrix} \bar{C}_1(t) \\ \cdot \\ \cdot \\ \cdot \\ \bar{C}_n(t) \end{bmatrix}. \quad (4.1)$$

This is essentially a consolidation of input-output equations (2.2) and (2.10), written as inequalities. The $\xi_i$ (lumped together in the vector $\xi$ in Table 1) are the coefficients of $C_T(t)$ in the expenditure function (2.10): $\xi_i = \varepsilon_i C_i(0)/C_T(0)$. The $\bar{C}_i(t)$ are shorthand for the constant terms in the same equation.[40] The $J_i(t)$ are investment levels by origin, the only other final demand items in this model. We assume that only sectors 1 through $m$ produce investment goods. This explains the subscripts in the vector $J(t)$ in (4.1), as well as the zero entries in the matrix multiplying this vector. When (4.1) is rewritten in compact notation, it becomes

$$\xi C_T(t) + \begin{bmatrix} I \\ 0 \end{bmatrix} J(t) \leq (I - A)X(t) - \bar{C}(t), \quad (4.2)$$

which is simple translation of the first row of Table 1.

Assume that capital stocks will be fully utilized in the plan year (supposed to be sometime in the future). This means that $K(t) = B\hat{k}X(t) = HX(t)$, where the matrices $B$, $\hat{k}$, and $H$ are as defined in section 3 (with the new convention that $H$ has dimension $m$ x $n$, with column $i$ expressing sector $i$'s requirements for each of the $m$ capital goods).[41] Using the assumed fixed

---

40. As discussed in a recent paper by Ginsburgh and Waelbroeck [1974], it is not difficult to extend the methods of Chapter XII to several variables and determine the make-up of the consumption basket *via* approximations to a complete system of demand equations. This alleviates some of the problems with the price system discussed in subsection 4.3, but for simplicity we do not discuss this refinement in detail here.

41. Note that the $K$ vector here represents average as well as incremental capital-output ratios. The analysis is little changed if $\Delta K(t) = H\Delta X(t)$ is used instead.

growth rates for each capital stock, gross (=net) investment in the $i$th capital good is

$$J_i(t) = K_i(t + 1) - K_i(t) = g_i K_i(t),$$

where $g_i$ is the exogenously specified growth rate of $K_i(t)$, coming perhaps from investors' expectations of future growth in the economy, or planners' perceptions of them.[42] The vector representation of these equations is:

$$
\begin{bmatrix} J_1(t) \\ \cdot \\ \cdot \\ \cdot \\ J_m(t) \end{bmatrix}
=
\begin{bmatrix} g_1 & \cdot & \cdot & \cdot & \cdot & \cdot & \cdot & 0 \\ \cdot & & & & & & & \cdot \\ \cdot & & & & & & & \cdot \\ \cdot & & & & & & & \cdot \\ 0 & \cdot & \cdot & \cdot & \cdot & \cdot & \cdot & g_m \end{bmatrix} HX(t) \qquad (4.3)
$$

In compact inequality form, (4.3) appears in the second row of Table 1.

Labor requirements appear in the final row of the table. Total labor use (which equals $\sum_i \lambda_i X_i(t)$, where the $\lambda_i$ are labor-output ratios) should not exceed the fixed labor supply $\bar{L}(t)$:

$$\lambda' X(t) \le \bar{L}(t). \qquad (4.4)$$

Note that in this model, the labor constraint is the only one which really limits the optimal value of the maximand. There are no bounds on output imposed by the existing stock of capital at the start of the plan since constraints on capital stock (4.3) merely induce positive investment levels in the plan year of the optimal solution. In this sense, labor is the model's only "primary factor."

Since $C_T(t)$ is being maximized,[43] it will be positive in any sensible problem. This means that, in terms of the shadow prices written along the left margin of Table 1, the consumption activity must just "cost out," so that

$$P'(t)\xi = 1. \qquad (4.5)$$

This equation is represented by the second column of Table 1. We will see shortly that each $P_i(t)$ is the cost per unit of producing good $i$. Since $\xi_i$ is the marginal consumption share of that same good, (4.5) says that the marginal

---

42. One can also specify growth rates for sectoral output levels. This alternative leads to an interpretation of the dual solution different from that when capital stock growth rates are specified, which is discussed below.

43. Other maximands besides aggregate consumption or its value in utility terms are used in applied programming models, but consumption is the most common and easily interpretable (particularly in terms of varying consumption weights to trace out the transformation surface), so we stick with it here. Chapter IX provides a survey of alternative methods of setting objective functions and the interaction of objectives and constraints in an optimizing exercise. This latter issue is also perceptively analyzed by Marglin [1967], while Adelman and Sparrow [1966] discuss the effects of specifying alternative objective functions on the solution of a particular applied programming model.

cost of the consumption activity is just equal to one, its marginal "utility" in the LP maximand.[44]

When $C_T(t)$ is positive, all production activities will also operate at positive levels, since all sectors must contribute at least indirectly to final demands in any one sector, under reasonable assumptions on the input-output matrix.[45] One of the basic theorems in linear (mathematical) programming states that whenever the marginal benefits are less than the marginal costs for a given activity, that activity will not be positive. Similarly, whenever an activity is in the optimal solution for a linear program, that activity exactly costs out in the above sense. This property is referred to as "complementary slackness." In terms of the dual problem outlined above, this condition implies that for an optimal solution, $(p'A - c')x = 0$. By complementary slackness, the first column of Table 1 represents a matrix *equation*:

$$-P'(t)(I - A) + R'(t)\hat{g}H + w(t)\lambda' = 0 \tag{4.6}$$

Also, all the investment activities will run at positive levels as long as the growth rate vector $g$ is strictly positive and the system remains feasible. The third column of Table 1 thus gives another set of equations:

$$P_i(t) = R_i(t), \quad i = 1, 2, \ldots, m. \tag{4.7}$$

The combination of (4.6) and (4.7) is the price-equals-cost relationship for all sectors in the economy,

$$P_i(t) = \sum_{j=1}^{n} P_j(t)a_{ji} + w(t)\lambda_i + \sum_{j=1}^{m} g_j P_j(t)h_{ji'} \quad i = 1, 2, \ldots, n, \tag{4.8}$$

where the $h_{ji}$ are elements of the matrix $H$. Observe that the rental price or cost to the user of the $j$th type of capital in the equation (4.8) is given by $g_j P_j(t)$, so that the rates of growth $g_j$ double as own-rates of return to capital in this model.

Specifications of this type are often used to forecast investments by sector. The method is simple and practicable, and this probably explains its popularity. As noted, it has interesting duality aspects in that growth rates and rates of return of the several capital goods are equalized in the consumption-maximizing solution,[46] but these are mentioned only sporadically in the

---

44. We note again the simple nature of the linear objective function, which assumes constant marginal utility for each consumption good at all income levels. This weakness makes any parametric testing of welfare trade-offs in income distribution most difficult. See Chapters IX and XII for discussions of techniques for handling more realistic and helpful objective functions.

45. Of course, this presupposes that domestic production is the only possible source of supply, an assumption that is relaxed when imports are permitted. Chakravarty [1969] gives precise conditions for all elements of the inverse matrix $(I - A)^{-1}$ to be positive, which is equivalent to the assertion in the text.

46. There is a strong family resemblance between this result and the so-called Golden Rule of accumulation (von Neumann [1945], Phelps [1961]), which states that the growth and profit rates of capital stocks should *all* have the same value along the steady growth path with the highest sustainable level of consumption per head.

applied programming literature.[47] However, three variant specifications which focus on the real side do exist:

(i) The first was just described—investment in the plan year is determined by growth rates for the several capital stocks. In practice a single growth rate for all types of capital is usually chosen.

(ii) The second approach looks back in time instead of forward to find a rule for defining the profit rate. The crucial assumption is that there is no lag between investment expenditures and new output (instead of the positive lag assumed in section 3). If it is also true that all sectors grow at a constant rate $g$ between now (year zero) and the plan year $t$, the following relationships will hold:

$$\frac{J_i(t)}{\sum_{\tau=0}^{t} J_i(\tau)} = \frac{\sum_j h_{ij} X_j(0)(1 + g)^t}{\sum_j h_{ij} X_j(0)[(1 + g)^{t+1} - 1]/g} = \frac{g(1 + g)^t}{(1 + g)^{t+1} - 1} = S(g;t), \quad (4.9)$$

where $S(g;t)$ is defined by the last ratio. Also, the sum of investment between now and year $t$ should just equal the increment in capacity,

$$\sum_{\tau=0}^{t} J_i(\tau) = \sum_j h_{ij}[X_j(t) - X_j(0)]$$

so that

$$J_i(t) = S(g;t) \sum_j h_{ij}[X_j(t) - X_j(0)].$$

In matrix form this becomes

$$J(t) = S(g;t)H[X(t) - X(0)].$$

The similarity with the second row of Table 1 is striking—except that the (now unique) growth rate $g$ has been replaced by the quantity $S(g;t)$ and a constant vector $S(g;t)HX(0)$ is subtracted. The net result is a slightly modified investment theory and a different profit rate. (The value of $S(g;t)$ will be just a few percentage points bigger than $(t + 1)^{-1}$—the inverse of the number of years contained in the planning period—as long as $g$ is "small.")

Coefficients such as $S(g;t)$ which summarize the entire investment profile of a plan in one number are called "stock-flow conversion factors" in the literature. Chenery and Bruno [1962] and Manne [1963] were perhaps the first to use them in the form just described. The stock-flow method has the advantage of giving a forecast of investment in the plan year based on an assumed value of the overall growth rate *during* the plan, not after it. Of

---

47. An exception is Weisskopf [1967], who selects values for his $g_i$ (set equal for all types of capital) from profitability (not growth) considerations. The theory of the dual interpretation of the $g_i$ is developed further by Bruno [1967a]. The reader may verify that the Golden Rule actually applies in our simple model by showing that, aside from a constant term, labor payments (in shadow prices) equal total consumption—the other clause of the Rule.

course, when the model is actually solved it will usually turn out that the postulated within-plan growth of GNP is not exact. Iteration on $g$ to achieve consistency is feasible, since the value of $S(g;t)$ is not sensitive to $g$ itself, as Manne has demonstrated.

(iii) This desirable consistency property may no longer hold when one takes the obvious step and works with a separate within-plan growth rate and stock-flow conversion factor for each sector—iterating to make a few dozen $g_j$'s come close to each other in the investment specification and model solution can be very time consuming, even if each $S(g_j;t)$ is not a sensitive function. This problem does not arise when different post-plan growth rates for sectoral outputs are postulated.[48] Formally, the investment equation in this case would be

$$J(t) = H[X(t+1) - X(t)] = H\hat{g}X(t). \tag{4.10}$$

This specification of growth rates "by destination" naturally gives rise to a new version of the price-equals-cost equation:

$$P_i(t) = \sum_{j=1}^{n} P_j(t)a_{ji} + w(t)\lambda_i + \sum_{j=1}^{m} P_j(t)h_{ji}g_i, \quad i = 1, 2, \ldots, n. \tag{4.11}$$

Careful comparison with (4.8) shows that *each sector* now has its own rate of profit $g_i$, as opposed to the previous hypothesis that *each type of capital* has its distinct own-rate of return. This may be a better description of the real economy since it can be rationalized in terms of sectoral capital stocks which cannot be shifted once installed. The previous hypothesis that each type of capital has the same own-rate in all uses is consistent only with perfect competition when all capital goods are freely movable among sectors. This distinction will come up again, and the reader ultimately has to decide which specification he prefers.

## 4.2 More Investment Theory and Surplus Labor

When there are two general types of goods—"consumption" and "investment"—in an LP model, an obvious way to choose the amount of each one to produce is to put them both in a welfare function and maximize it, subject to the relevant technological constraints. This sort of specification is sometimes used in applied planning models, and we consider its implications here. To ease comparison of results with the dynamic models of section 5, it is best to work not with investment itself but with its result—capital stock in the year after the plan. This means that the vector $K(t+1)$ of post-plan capital stocks should be included in a linear welfare function of the form:

$$\text{Welfare} = C_T(t) + \bar{P}'(t)K(t+1).$$

---

48. These growth rates could be calculated from a particular solution of the Leontief dynamic model, based on a mixture of hypothesized growth rates of final demand components. Eckaus and Parikh [1968] follow a somewhat similar procedure in their dynamic LP model for India. See the appendix on terminal conditions at the end of this chapter.

The only difference between this specification for the maximand and that of the last subsection is the inclusion of the term $\bar{P}'(t)K(t+1)$ which gives welfare weight to post-plan capital stock.[49] This and other aspects of a full model specification are summarized in Table 2.

The first row of this table represents sectoral demand-supply balances— exactly the same as in equation (4.1) or (4.2). Row (2) says that $K(t+1)$, the capital stock vector in the post-plan year, cannot exceed the sum of investment and the plan year's capital. Row (3) is the labor constraint, and row (4) restricts capital use in the plan year to be less than, or equal to, its supply. The fifth row puts a priori upper limits on the amounts of each capital stock which can be accumulated in the economy up to the plan year. Thus, unlike the model shown in Table 1, labor is not the only primary factor.[50] And, as just discussed, the maximand of the primal problem contains both consumption in the plan year and post-plan levels of capital stock.

Suppose once again that the consumption activity $C_T(t)$ runs at a positive level. All goods will be produced and some use made of all types of capital; hence, columns (1), (2), and (4) describe vector-matrix equalities. Since depreciation is not considered, the vector $K(t+1)$ is also positive, and column (5) represents an equality.

**Table 2: Detached Coefficients Tableau of an LP Model for Year "$t$" with Post-Terminal Valuation of Capital Stock in Year "$t+1$"**

|  | (1) $X(t)$ | (2) $C_T(t)$ | (3) $J(t)$ | (4) $K(t)$ | (5) $K(t+1)$ |  |
|---|---|---|---|---|---|---|
| (1) $P'(t)$ | $-(I-A)$ | $\xi$ | $\begin{bmatrix} I \\ 0 \end{bmatrix}$ |  |  | $\leq -\bar{C}(t)$ |
| (2) $R'(t)$ |  |  | $-I$ | $-I$ | $I$ | $\leq 0$ |
| (3) $w(t)$ | $\lambda'$ |  |  |  |  | $\leq \bar{L}(t)$ |
| (4) $S'(t)$ | $H$ |  |  | $-I$ |  | $\leq 0$ |
| (5) $P'(t-1)$ |  |  |  | $I$ |  | $\leq \bar{K}(t)$ |
| MAX |  | 1 |  | $\bar{P}'(t)$ |  |  |

The relationships among shadow prices from all these equalities are easy to write down. Column (5) indicates that,

$$\bar{P}_i(t) = R_i(t), \quad i = 1, 2, \ldots, m. \tag{4.12}$$

49. The problem of choosing the vector of weights $\bar{P}(t)$ for the post-plan capital stocks is not a trivial one—in fact it has not been resolved to general satisfaction. A discussion of some of the proposed solutions is deferred to the appendix on terminal conditions at the end of the chapter.

50. For expositional purposes, we have here constrained capital stocks in the plan year. For numerical applications, initial stocks are the constraining factors. These are usually estimated by taking gross output levels as given and assuming no surplus capacity. For a good example of how this is done, see Manne [1966].

This together with the fourth column equation means that,

$$S_i(t) = P_i(t-1) - \bar{P}_i(t), \quad i = 1, 2, \ldots, m. \tag{4.13}$$

Substitution into the first column equality gives the usual price-equals-marginal-cost condition that;

$$P_i(t) = \sum_{j=1}^{n} P_j(t)a_{ji} + w(t)\lambda_i + \sum_{j=1}^{m} [P_j(t-1) - \bar{P}_j(t)]h_{ji}. \tag{4.14}$$

If each capital stock's own-rate of interest is *defined* as

$$r_j(t) = [P_j(t-1) - \bar{P}_j(t)]/\bar{P}_j(t),$$

then the capital cost term at the right-hand end of (4.14) can be rewritten as

$$\text{Capital cost} = \sum_{j=1}^{m} r_j(t)\bar{P}_j(t)h_{ji}.$$

Since the $S_i(t)$ in (4.13) cannot be negative, the own-rates $r_j(t)$ will be non-negative, too—as long as some nonzero valuation is assigned to post-terminal capital. With this proviso, the price-equals-cost equation (4.14) is the same as in the model of Table 1, i.e., equation (4.8) still holds, except that its $g_j$ terms should now be replaced by $r_j(t)$.

Choice in the model of Table 2 is expressed by the inequality relationships of column (3):

$$P_i(t) \geq \bar{P}_i(t), \quad i = 1, 2, \ldots, m. \tag{4.15}$$

Equality here means that the cost of the $i$th good, $P_i(t)$, does not exceed its exogenously specified use-value, $\bar{P}_i(t)$ in investment—in this case, $J_i(t)$ will normally be positive. Of course, $J_i(t)$ will be zero when the cost of the $i$th good exceeds its value as an investment. If this condition holds and $\bar{P}_i(t)$ is increased, (4.15) will ultimately be satisfied with equality—in this sense a sufficiently high valuation on the $i$th capital stock in the post-terminal year will assure that some investment in this type of capital takes place in the plan.

In light of the last subsection's results, it is of interest to examine the relationship between wage payments and consumption (and growth rates and interest rates) in this model. This can be done by writing down the condition that the primal maximand equals the dual minimand at the optimal solution,

$$w(t)\bar{L}(t) - [C_T(t) + P'(t)\bar{C}(t)] = \bar{P}'(t)K(t+1) - P'(t-1)\bar{K}(t)$$

$$= \sum_{j=1}^{m} \bar{P}_j(t)\bar{K}_j(t)[g_j(t) - r_j(t)] \tag{4.16}$$

where $g_j(t)$ in the last line is the rate of growth of the $j$th capital stock: $g_j(t) = [K_j(t+1) - \bar{K}_j(t)]/\bar{K}_j(t)$. The last line itself is derived by simple manipulation of the preceding line.

Equation (4.16) says that the difference between total shadow wage pay-

ments and total consumption (on the left of the first equality) is equal to a weighted average of the *differences* between the rates of growth and rates of return of the several types of capital—the weights being the shadow price valuations of the capital stocks themselves. If growth rates equal own-rates of interest, a modified Golden Rule applies; the wage bill is equal to consumption in this case. However, the Golden Rule does not *have* to hold in this model, i.e., the growth rate of a certain type of capital need not be equal to its own-rate of return, as was always the case with the model of Table 1. This has a number of interesting implications when labor is not scarce and there are no other binding constraints on primary factors (such as skilled labor or land). In this case, the row (3) constraint of Table 2 is not binding and $w(t)$, its shadow price, is equal to zero. From (4.16), this means that the consumption activity $C_T(t)$ will run at a positive level only when own-rates of return $r_j(t)$ significantly exceed capital growth rates $g_j(t)$. Consideration of "plausible" values for these variables indicates that this may be unlikely.[51]

Equation (4.16) is thus a warning that low consumption levels may be expected in models without binding labor (or other primary factor) constraints. This is a serious problem in practice, especially in dynamic LP models, as we will see in section 5. At this point, it is useful to discuss a method for maintaining "reasonable" consumption levels when the model does not have binding labor constraints. This can be done by following the investment project analysts (Marglin [1974], Little and Mirrlees [1969]) in putting a lower bound on consumption by assuming that each *employed* worker receives an institutionally fixed wage, which he spends only on consumption goods. In terms of the classification of constraints made in the introduction to this section, this could be viewed as a type-two constraint of a political nature.

Formally, this surplus labor specification amounts to the replacement of the nonbinding labor constraint (row (3) of Table 2) with a restriction of the form:

$$\bar{v}\lambda' X(t) - C_T(t) \leq \sum_{i=1}^{n} \bar{C}_i(t) \tag{4.17}$$

where $\bar{v}$ is the fixed wage.[52] Since the "price weights" in the sum of the consumption function constant terms on the right side of (4.17) are all equal

---

51. Note that the $r_j(t)$ have to be quite a bit bigger than the $g_j(t)$ to permit a positive consumption activity $C_T(t)$ because of the negative consumption "floor" term involving $\bar{C}(t)$ on the left side of (4.16). Taking this into account along with an average value of the sectoral capital-output ratios of about three would imply that *total* consumption (valued in shadow prices) in the plan year ought to be about 30 percent of the shadow price value of the capital stock. On the average, this would require the terms $[g_j(t) - r_j(t)]$ on the right of (4.16) to have a value of about $-0.3$ when the shadow wage $w(t)$ equals zero. This in turn means that the $r_j(t)$ would have an average value of about 0.35 when capital stock growth is taken into account. Higher values of consumption would imply higher rates of return, but even 0.35 begins to strain the bounds of credibility.

52. To save notation, the symbol $w(t)$ is retained for the shadow price on constraint (4.17) —the interpretation of $w(t)$ obviously changes.

to unity, the constraint says that the worker's consumption level is guaranteed *in terms of base year prices.*

When binding, (4.17) is equivalent to the key assumptions of all simple labor surplus models that only workers consume and that investment is financed from what is left of profits after consumption is paid for. Shadow profits cannot be spent wholly on investment because consumption is subsidized in shadow price terms. The existence of the subsidy can be verified by noting that when the shadow price $w(t)$ on constraint (4.17) is positive, the cost-equals-utility condition (4.5) for consumption must be replaced by

$$P'(t)\xi - w(t) = 1. \qquad (4.18)$$

That is, the shadow cost of a marginal increase in consumption exceeds unity (its marginal welfare valuation) by the amount of the shadow wage subsidy $w(t)$. Well-known corollaries are that investment is implicitly taxed, that the shadow price valuation of a new worker's marginal product is less than the shadow cost of his consumption, and that the welfare gain from hiring the new worker is just equal to the shadow price value of the loss of investable surplus his employment entails.[53]

Although appealing, this specification has not been widely used in practice. Lefeber [1968] gives a good intuitive description of the labor surplus model and presents illustrative results from a small static model with a constraint resembling (4.17). Manne [1974b] uses linear programming to investigate dynamic shadow price behavior in a similar context, and a number of optimal growth versions exist as well (e.g., Newbery [1972]).

## 4.3 Second-Best Problems and Foreign Trade[54]

There were very few substitution possibilities in the models just discussed. Each good or service was produced using one and only one technique, with no imports allowed as a substitute. These models were purposely over-simplified to focus attention on their investment theories. It is now time to

---

53. The last statements are standard allocation rules for labor surplus economies. They follow from rearrangement of (4.18), followed by multiplication by the fixed wage $\bar{v}$: $\bar{v} = P'(t)\xi\bar{v} - w(t)\bar{v}$ or $v = P'(t)\xi v - [P'(t)(I - A) - S'(t)H]\lambda^{-1}v$ where $\lambda^{-1}$ is the *vector* of sector output-labor ratios $\lambda_i^{-1}$, and the second equation follows from manipulation of the price-equals-cost equations for the labor surplus model (which are the same as (4.14) except that each term $w(t)\lambda_i$ is multiplied by $v$). The second equation says that welfare from consumption of a new worker (just equal to the amount $v$ he consumes) is equal to the shadow price valuation of the loss in investment this new consumption entails. This follows, since the right side is just the loss of investable surplus caused by hiring the new worker—i.e., the shadow price valuation of his completely consumed wage payment minus his imputed marginal productivity averaged across sectors by the $\lambda^{-1}$ vector. Since employment and therefore workers' consumption is subsidized, the wage exceeds the marginal product and their difference is positive.

54. See Chapter VI for additional views on many of the topics discussed in this and the next subsection.

shift focus toward basic resource allocation problems by widening the choice set of the model to resemble more nearly practical LP applications. The most common extension of the basic models discussed above, and the topic of this subsection, is the inclusion of choice through foreign trade. In particular, we will discuss a model where imports are noncompetitive and linked with fixed coefficients to consumption, investment, and gross output, but exports can be selected in an efficient way to meet balance of payments requirements.

Table 3 gives a representative specification. The first three rows are as in Table 1, respectively stating balances for goods, investment flows (assumed to be determined by exogenous capital stock growth rates, as in subsection 4.1), and labor. Two more final demand categories are included in the first row—exports $E(t)$ and government expenditures $G(t)$—but its interpretation remains unchanged. Row (4) states that noncompetitive imports for intermediate uses, $M^X(t)$, are determined by

$$M^X(t) = \sum_j a_{0j} X_j(t),$$

where the $a_{0j}$ are input-output coefficients. Similarly, row (5) determines imports of noncompetitive capital goods through the fixed growth rate mechanism, while row (6) relates noncompetitive imports for consumption, $M^C(t)$, to total consumption activity $C_T(t)$.

As was emphasized in section 2, all of these balances, in principle, refer to flows of physically distinct goods and services. Of course, in practice, sectoral outputs are index numbers but the physical interpretation remains—nothing has been said so far about prices. Row (7), which refers to the current account balance of payments, is an exception—imports and exports have to trade off in this constraint at some price ratios. As long as the country is "small" (which in most cases is a reasonable assumption), these trading prices—$\pi^X$, $\pi^C$, $\pi^J$, $\pi^E$—can be assumed to be fixed outside the model. An important question remains, however: What values should be assigned to them?

Two possibilities naturally present themselves, and both are explored in some detail here because they illustrate a set of important issues implicit in the interpretation of results from an LP planning model in terms of a Walrasian general equilibrium system.

The first possibility is to set the $\pi$'s equal to the world prices of the traded goods. In practice this may be difficult to do, because observed prices of tradables within the country will include the effects of tariffs, quotas, and other trade restrictions. However, if we set domestic prices by convention equal to one and assume for simplicity that tariffs and subsidies are the only commercial policy instruments used, then under competition the following relationship must hold:

$$1 = (1 + t_i)\tilde{\pi}_i, \quad i \text{ indexes traded goods} \tag{4.19}$$

where $t_i$ is an ad valorem tariff-cum-subsidy rate and $\tilde{\pi}_i$ is a "frontier price" index for traded sector $i$ (c.i.f. for imports, f.o.b. for exports), converted to

**Table 3: Detached Coefficients Tableau for a Planning Model with Endogenous Exports and a Savings Constraint**

| | (1) $X(t)$ | (2) $M^x(t)$ | (3) $C_T(t)$ | (4) $M^C(t)$ | (5) $J(t)$ | (6) $M^J(t)$ | (7) $E(t)$ | (8) $J_T(t)$ | (9) $V(t)$ | |
|---|---|---|---|---|---|---|---|---|---|---|
| (1) $P'(t)$ | $-(I-A)$ | | $\xi$ | | $\begin{bmatrix} I \\ 0 \end{bmatrix}$ | | $I$ | | | $\leq -[\bar{C}(t)+G(t)]$ |
| (2) $R'(t)$ | $gH$ | | | | | | | | | $\geq 0$ |
| (3) $w(t)$ | $\lambda$ | | | | | | | | | $\leq L(t)$ |
| (4) $P^x(t)$ | $a'_0$ | $-1$ | | | | | | | | $\geq 0$ |
| (5) $P^J(t)$ | $g_0 h'_0$ | | | | $-I$ | | | | | $\geq 0$ |
| (6) $P^C(t)$ | | | | $-1$ | | $-1$ | | | | $\geq 0$ |
| (7) $Q_I(t)$ | | $\pi^x$ | $\xi_0$ | $\pi^C$ | | $\pi^J$ | $-(\pi^E)$ | | | $\geq F(t)$ |
| (8) $Q_S(t)$ | | | $-1$ | | | | | | $(1-s)$ | $\geq G_T(t)-G_T(0)-C_T(0)+(1-s)V(0)$ |
| (9) $Q_J(t)$ | | | $1$ | | $e'$ | $1$ | | $-1$ | | $\leq 0$ |
| (10) $Q_V(t)$ | | $-1$ | $1$ | $-1$ | | $-1$ | $e'$ | $1$ | $-1$ | $\leq -C_T(t)$ |
| MAX | | | $1$ | | | | | | | |

Note $e'$ is the vector $[1, 1, \ldots, 1]$. Other symbols are defined in the text.

the national currency by a nominal exchange rate. Writing the balance of payments in world prices amounts to using the $\tilde{\pi}_i$ of (4.19) in row (7) of Table 3, assuming that it is possible to calculate them.[55]

The procedure has much to recommend it, not least a theorem by Diamond and Mirrlees [1971] to the effect that in many second-best situations it is optimal for production to be efficient. In the context of international trade, this means that domestic rates of transformation ought to be the same as world rates, or that domestic prices of all imported intermediate and capital goods ought to be equal to their world prices (times the exchange rate). Since in input-output almost all goods are intermediates, the theorem would seem to imply that in planning models the balance of payments should be written in terms of world prices, so that production efficiency will prevail.[56]

This is all well and good as far as it goes, but it leaves at least two questions unanswered:

(i) The first, more practical question has to do with the fact that trade restrictions already exist in abundance in developing countries. It is natural to inquire how the economy is likely to respond if the government modifies these wedges it has driven between producer and consumer prices, import and domestic user prices, and so on.

One way of looking at the effects of tariffs begins by setting all the $\pi$'s in the foreign exchange constraint equal to one, so that domestic rather than world relative prices rule. From (4.19), this means that traded goods prices will then be tariff-ridden—one may suppose that the government *chooses* to impose tariffs as in (4.19) and at the same time gives the private sector a real resource transfer in the amount $F(t)$, the term on the right side of constraint row (7) in Table 3. If the private sector acted "as if" it were maximizing total consumption subject to its technological constraints, the assigned prices of traded goods, and the transfer given it by the government, a competitive resource allocation would result from solving the linear program.[57] Assuming that each tradable good is traded and that the model consists only of rows (1) to (7)

---

55. A reliable data source for frontier prices may not be readily available. The customs data on dollar trade volumes may or may not be reliable in a developing country; in any case, there are considerable problems in constructing volume indices of exports and imports on a basis consistent with the industrial census data which usually underlies the input-output table. If tariff data are appropriately compiled—say for an effective-protection study—one could "estimate" $\tilde{\pi}_i$ by the quantity $(1 + t_i)^{-1}$, but this is clearly a crude procedure. (For more on such data problems, see the appendix to Chapter VI.)

56. We note in passing that the Diamond–Mirrlees theorem is the essential justification for the well-known Little–Mirrlees [1969] recommendation that investment projects should be valued in terms of world prices. For more on this, see Chapters VI and VIII.

57. An implicit additional assumption is that the economy really acts as if it were maximizing a single utility function, so that the initial wealth distribution and income effects are irrelevant in determining demand levels.

of Table 3, column (7) indicates that the usual relationship between the (shadow) prices of tradables, world prices and tariffs

$$P_i(t) \geq Q_f(t)(1 + t_i)\bar{\pi}_i \qquad (4.20)$$

would hold, for each traded good $i$. In this expression, $Q_f(t)$ is the shadow price on the tariff-included foreign exchange constraint, the "shadow exchange rate."

One could then change the $t_i$ and investigate how sectoral production levels would rise and fall, total employment would change, and so on. Side calculations would show how the official, or world price, balance of payments, government budget, and other interesting aggregates would respond to these experimental tariff variations. Naturally, the same technique could be applied to shifts in indirect taxes and quantity restrictions. A number of studies describe calculations of this type (e.g., Lage [1970]). The results are interesting, and the method should probably be pursued.

(ii) In a more academic vein, one might even consider generalizing this approach into a problem in which the government would choose tariffs (or taxes, or quantitative restrictions) to optimize the already suboptimized private sector consumption, subject to the balance of payments in world prices and constraints of its own on such things as foreign debt repayment or purchase of a certain bill of goods.

Analysis of this kind of double optimization problem gave rise to the cited Diamond–Mirrlees theorem, as well as to many other theoretical papers proposing second-best rules for taxation and efficiency prices for public enterprises (e.g., Dixit [1970b], Atkinson and Stiglitz [1972]). We cannot review this literature here, but only note that it may prove suggestive for applied models in the future. For computational reasons, these will almost certainly have to take the form of the nonlinear Walrasian models reviewed in section 6. In the LP trade model we have been discussing, it is easy to show that the government's optimization of tariffs subject to certain linear constraints *and* the optimal solution to the program of the first seven rows and columns of Table 3 gives rise to a highly nonlinear problem.[58]

In summary, writing the balance of payments in terms of tariff-ridden domestic relative prices can best be interpreted as an artifice or trick, possibly misleading but potentially useful nonetheless. Its only justification is that price relationships such as (4.20) hold in the dual solution to the private sector optimization problem; i.e., *within* the shadow price system of the optimizing problem there are *exogenous* tariff wedges between world and

---

58. However, finding solutions may not be completely out of the question, since the problem fits a simplified version of the variable coefficients LP algorithm discussed by Dantzig [1963]. The resulting shadow price system has a number of interesting characteristics, as discussed by Cardwell [1973].

domestic prices. Varying these tariffs to see what happens to real quantities is a tempting experiment.[59]

## 4.4 Specialization Problems and Foreign Trade

Turning to another trade-related aspect of the shadow price system, assume again that there is positive consumption, all goods are produced, and all types of capital used. By complementary slackness, equalities will then hold down columns (1) through (6) of Table 3. Appropriate substitutions give the following two sets of equations among the shadow prices:

$$P_i(t) = \sum_{j=1}^{n} P_j(t)a_{ji} + w(t)\lambda_i + \sum_{j=1}^{m} g_j P_j(t)h_{ji} + Q_f(t)[\pi^X a_{0i} + g_0 \pi^J h_{0i}],$$

$$i = 1, 2, \ldots, n, \quad (4.21)$$

and

$$\sum_i P_i(t)\xi_i + Q_f(t)\pi^C \xi_0 = 1. \quad (4.22)$$

The first set contains the price-equals-marginal cost relationships for all sectors, analogous to (4.8). Equation (4.22) is a slightly elaborated version of (4.5) and has the same interpretation.

These equations clearly put many restrictions on the price system. There are only $n + 2$ variables in the $n$ equations (4.21), and (4.22) adds one equation more. Thus the exogenous specification of one absolute price determines the whole system! If one sets a value for the foreign exchange shadow price $Q_f(t)$, for example, then the wage $w(t)$ and all other prices follow from it.

Now consider column (7). Since we are still ignoring rows (8) to (10), it takes the form,

$$P_i(t) \geq Q_f(t)\pi_i^E, \quad i \text{ indexes exportable goods.} \quad (4.23)$$

Complementary slackness here means that equality holds for the $i$th price when the $i$th good is actually exported. Hence, export of any single good adds one equation to (4.21) and (4.22) and completely determines the price system. Another export would add an inconsistent (usually) equation in the prices. Therefore, *only one good will be exported*. Table 3 describes a constant returns model with very many goods and very few factors of production. It is not surprising that there should be strong tendencies toward specialization and

---

59. Perhaps it is worth reiterating that equation (4.20) is a behavioral relationship which one would expect to hold under competition when a good is traded subject to tariffs. Simple addition of government revenue constraints, the balance of payments in world prices, and so on, to the first-stage optimization problem we have been discussing would destroy the simplicity of (4.20) by bringing other shadow prices into the equation. It is perhaps feasible to interpret the augmented equation in terms of tariffs and subsidies—see Evans [1972]—but the additional shadow prices become confusing very rapidly. We will get a taste of this in the subsection 4.5 discussion of the savings constraint, another example of a realistic type two restriction which gives rise to hard-to-understand shadow prices.

abrupt, "knife-edge" responses to traded goods price changes in such a system.[60]

Practitioners have reacted to this overdeterminism in varying ways (and with varying degrees of awareness of what was really going on). Once again we selectively catalog their solutions, with an eye to those most appropriate for future model building efforts.

(i) Clearly, more factors help alleviate the price congestion, by bringing more factor prices into sectoral cost functions on the right-hand side of (4.21). For example, the model of Table 2 would help out in this context, since its rates of return to capital are endogenous, because there are explicit bounds on the capital stock. Similarly, each additional type of *fully employed* labor has a positive shadow wage. With fixed coefficients, there is, of course, no assurance that each labor type will be fully employed, but labor-labor or labor-capital substitution activities make it more likely.[61]

(ii) Bringing in more shiftable factors attacks overdetermination at its roots, in the cost functions, but cannot eliminate the problem completely. Inventiveness and data begin to run out when three or four types each of labor and shiftable capital have been accounted for—numbers far short of the number of sectors. An obvious additional step is to impose (type-two or -three) "capacity" limitations on sector outputs. Each constraint adds a specific shadow price to its sector's cost function, permitting complete freedom of variation for goods prices. Unfortunately, interpretation of such constraints is difficult. There is no clear relationship between their shadow prices and those on the capital stock demand-supply balances. Nor is it obvious whether the capacity prices are long run or short run. Probably the cleanest way to side-step these problems is to drop the overall capital balance constraints and assume that capital is not shiftable among sectors once installed. Shadow prices in any given year are then based on *sectoral* rates of profit and are quite

---

60. Samuelson [1953] gives the classic analysis of why constant returns models with more goods than factors have strong tendencies toward specialization in trade. Of course, most of the forces which work against specialization—fluctuating prices for single export products, limited storage facilities, selling costs—are left out of the analysis. They shouldn't be, but it is not clear how to bring them into applied models. Also, note that the result stated about exports (along with others in this survey) implicitly assumes nondegeneracy in the LP planning model specification.

61. Partly because of computational costs and partly because of limited data, factor substitution beyond a few two-variable trade-offs has not been widely used by linear programmers. Of course, there is much econometric evidence for capital-labor substitution, and recent econometric studies (e.g., Dougherty [1972b]) suggest that elasticities of substitution among different types of labor are well over unity. In a recent model of Mexico, Manne [1973a] makes tentative but welcome steps in the direction of building in substitution among labor types. Other models have implicitly allowed substitution by making the education system endogenous and responsive over time to derived demands (usually based on a fixed coefficients technology) for different types of labor. See, for example, Adelman [1966], or Blitzer [1972]. All these models are described in more detail in Chapter VII.

free to vary. They are also "short run." To get "long run" prices, one would have to solve a full dynamic linear programming model. As we will see in discussing the model of Table 4 in the next section, this might be prohibitively expensive.

(iii) Partial palliatives for overdetermination are also available on the demand side. The most obvious is relaxation of the rigid Engel curve specification of the consumption function. This can easily be achieved by adding type-three constraints which permit sectoral consumption levels to vary between bounds constructed at some levels "above" and "below" the Engel line (Bruno [1966]). Each binding constraint carries with it a shadow price, which can be interpreted as a tax or subsidy on consumption of the corresponding good. Whether these sumptuary measures are feasible in the real world is debatable, but they do allow elimination of equation (4.22), one restriction less on the basic shadow price system. If one works not with ad hoc consumption restrictions but with an approximation to a complete system of demand equations, as in Ginsburgh and Waelbroeck [1974], these same results can be achieved with less violence to the dual by allowing quantities consumed to vary in response to changes in consumers' prices instead of vice versa. If this approach proves computationally practicable, it should be followed.

(iv) Upper and lower bounds on volumes traded rule out specialization in export markets at the cost of introducing shadow prices which must be interpreted as export taxes and subsidies. A more sophisticated variant specification is based on piece-wise linear approximations (see Chapters VI and XII) to falling export marginal revenue curves (or rising import marginal cost curves).[62] Shadow prices then carry the interpretation of "optimal taxes on exports" (or tariffs on imports), in the traditional trade theory sense.[63] In either case, if the model is constrained by a nonfrontier price foreign exchange constraint, these shadow prices in effect are tariffs on tariffs. Their connection with the economy's actual price system is tenuous.

(v) Finally, if competitive imports are introduced into the system (by adding

---

62. Several authors (e.g., Chenery and Raduchel [1971], Manne [1973a]) justify a negative relationship between export volumes and prices (or an increasing relationship between import volumes and prices) on the basis of "rising national supply prices." This is incorrect in a constant returns system, in which supply prices are given only by cost functions such as (4.21), and other explicit price-quantity curves can only come from the world market. (In fairness, it should also be added that the cited authors' models are executed correctly, despite their faulty interpretation.) Other models with decreasing export revenues include those of Bruno [1967a] and Foxley, Clark, and Jul [1973], which, respectively, deal with foreign sales of Israeli oranges and Chilean copper.

63. These approximations require inclusion of additional terms in the objective function to operate. Ginsburgh and Waelbroeck [1974] point out that these represent the welfare of the rest of the world, so that the whole objective function can be interpreted as a weighted sum of the country's welfare, and that of its trading partners. Varying the weights is one way of assuring balance of payments equilibrium.

activities similar to $E(t)$ in Table 3, but with signs of coefficients reversed everywhere), they can, in principle, satisfy all domestic demands and permit certain industries to shut down. In this specification, equations (4.21) are relaxed into price less-than-or-equal-to cost inequalities; the inequalities like (4.23) (with direction reversed) are added to permit comparison of foreign and domestic costs of potential imports. The model naturally chooses the cheaper of these two alternative sources of supply.[64] Clark [1970] and Weisskopf [1967] constructed make-or-buy models of this type to examine import substitution strategies in Nigeria and India, respectively, and Clark, Foxley, and Jul [1973] conducted investment project analyses in Chile with the same methods.

### 4.5 The Savings Constraint

Although expressed in shadow price terms, the level of savings is determined endogenously by the interaction of consumption maximization and the investment demand specification in the models discussed so far. This is made possible by the real, technological nature of the primal constraints (including the balance of payments which is basically "technological"). Optimization provides a price system and allocation of goods to different uses. Savings is part of this allocation.

In practice, the rate of savings from such models is usually "too high," both in terms of historical observations and plausible projections of the volume of savings the government will be able to mobilize through its fiscal and monetary policies. Putting an upper bound on savings becomes essential, therefore, to reduce the model's savings rate from its approximate Golden Rule level.

Consumption is bounded most elegantly through a postulate that it gives declining marginal welfare as it increases. In terms of Table 1, this involves replacing the "1" in the maximand row by a concave function $\omega[C_T(t)]$, which in turn would require modification of (4.5) to the form

$$P'(t)\xi = \partial\omega/\partial C_T(t). \tag{4.24}$$

The function $\omega$ represents planners' preferences for savings. That is, in the Table 1 model, consumer demand behavior is described by the vector $\xi$ and investors' animal spirits guesses about future capital stock growth appear in the matrix $\hat{g}$. Planners essentially ask through $\omega(C_T)$ how output composition and levels must vary until these two sets of preferences are met. When this

---

64. This criterion is "domestic resource cost," sketched by Chenery [1961], interpreted in linear programming terms by Bruno [1967b], and discussed further in Chapters VI and VIII. Naturally, the foreign versus domestic cost comparisons are only valid at full general equilibrium; away from equilibrium, they may in fact point the wrong way. Also, if the model is set up to describe private sector behavior subject to a tariff-ridden foreign exchange constraint, the make-or-buy decision rule remains domestic resource cost but expressed in terms of tariff-ridden shadow prices. The private sector does maximize total consumption but subject to the wrong opportunity costs for traded goods.

happens, savings is determined endogenously, in shadow price terms, to fit consumers', investors' and planners' tastes. There is no great computational barrier to adding this single nonlinearity to an otherwise linear problem, but curiously the specification has been little used.[65] (But see Chapter XII for some examples.)

Lacking a declining utility function, the next best thing is to impose a type-two upper bound inequality constraint on savings. Particularly in multi-sectoral models, this turns out to be difficult because savings is naturally a residual—*current* price output minus *current* price consumption (in a closed economy). Yet in the world of the model, current prices are shadow prices. In our discussion of the balance of payments, we have already seen the problems which arise when we attempt to constrain the shadow price system. These get even worse when savings is constrained.

The practice has been to impose a savings constraint in base year prices. Sometimes one can do this without creating great interpretation problems in the shadow price system, e.g., in the surplus labor model discussed in subsection 4.2 (equation 4.17) there is a savings constraint. In general, however, the accounting relationships necessary to make sure that savings in base year prices equals investment in base year prices are quite complicated. Their shadow prices are at least equally complicated and can only be interpreted as a set of investment taxes and consumption subsidies. Coupled with the taxes and subsidies discussed in the last subsection, these would surely overload any finance ministry which tried to impose them.

These problems can be seen in the quite typical savings constraint specification appearing in rows (8) to (10) and columns (8) and (9) of Table 3. The new activities defined by the columns are total investment in base year prices, $J_T(t)$, and gross national product, $V(t)$. Row (8) gives the "marginal" savings constraint per se, which can be written as:

$$[V(t) - V(0)] - [G_T(t) - G_T(0)] - [C_T(t) - C_T(0)] \leq s[V(t) - V(0)]$$
$$= S(t) - S(0).$$

This says that the potential savings increase is the product of the marginal savings rate $s$ and the increment in GNP over the base year, $V(t) - V(0)$. The left side of the inequality is the increment in GNP less increments in total consumption and government expenditures, a quantity closely related to the increment in total investment. With consolidation of constant terms, this constraint can be written in more compact form as

$$V(t) - G_T(t) - C_T(t) \leq sV(t) + s_0, \qquad (4.25)$$

where $s_0$ is a constant.

65. Declining utility functions for total consumption have actually been used more in dynamic than static planning models. We return to this topic in subsection 5.2. There we will also discuss upper bound absorptive capacity constraints on investment, which effectively limit savings.

Row (9) defines total investment in base year prices as the sum of investments in each sector, and row (10) adds up the components of GNP. Substitution of (4.25) and rows (7) and (9) into row (10) gives the following restriction on investment:

$$J_T(t) \le sV(t) + s_0 + F(t) + \sum_i (1 - \pi^i)M^i(t) - \sum_i (1 - \pi_i^E)E_i(t). \quad (4.26)$$

Total investment cannot exceed national savings plus foreign savings plus the sum of tariffs on imports less subsidies on exports.[66] The presence of the capital inflows term $F(t)$ in both (4.26) and the balance of payments constraint clearly places the Table 3 model in the two-gap family. As discussed in subsection 1.2, often only one of the gap constraints will turn out to be binding.[67]

Shadow prices of the new constraints are also closely related. The complementary slackness principle applied to column (8) shows that $Q_J(t) = Q_V(t)$, while column (9) gives $(1 - s)Q_s(t) = Q_V(t)$. Substitution into other columns shows that:

(i) $Q_V(t)$ should be subtracted (via a subsidy) from the traded prices of all imports and exports (i.e., $Q_f(t)$ times the appropriate $\pi_i$ in the balance of payments), except the price of capital goods imports.

(ii) When a domestically produced good is used for investment purposes, its price $R_i(t)$ should be $P_i(t)$ plus $Q_V(t)$.

(iii) The quantity $[s/(1 - s)]Q_V(t)$ should be subtracted from the left side of the complementary slackness equality (4.22) which holds when the total consumption activity $C_T(t)$ enters the solution. Since by (2.11) the $\xi$'s multiplying the prices in (4.22) sum to one, this is equivalent to a subsidy on each consumption price.

Putting all this together, we conclude from (i) and (ii) that traded goods should be priced at the level $Q_f(t)\pi_i$ for investment uses; from (i) and (iii), the price for consumption uses should be $[Q_f(t)\pi_i - (1 - s)^{-1}Q_V(t)]$, which can be a substantial subsidy. Since even more complex rules (given in (ii) and (iii)) apply for nontraded goods, imposing a savings constraint adds substantially to the already burdensome tasks of the finance ministry hidden behind the LP solution if it is to be used directly to induce market responses.

---

66. The statement is fully true if the balance of payments is in terms of world prices; otherwise, the last two terms of (4.26) are hard to interpret.

67. The easiest way to think of gap models is in LP terms; certainly Chenery and Bruno [1962] so cast their original formulation, and the input-output-based model of Tims [1968] can be interpreted in the same way. A dynamic, optimizing two-gap LP model was developed by Chenery and MacEwan [1966]. Taylor [1971] used control theory to show that the sequence of binding gaps is usually predictable over time in this kind of model: first absorptive capacity constraints (discussed in the next section) tend to bind, then savings, then balance of payments. Of course, an atemporal model like that of Table 3 may find itself at any point along this sequence.

The specification of savings restrictions in Table 3 is representative,[68] and as long as total consumption is being maximized such constraints usually turn out to be binding. The modified Golden Rule savings behavior implicit in the unconstrained model is evidently not a good description of how savings is generated in developing countries, and the purpose of the additional constraints is to bring the model solution closer to the statistics. More elegant ways to get the desired result (such as using welfare functions with declining marginal increments or "soft" absorptive capacity constraints) have not been used widely to date.

### 4.6   Other Topics

Despite its formidable length, this section does not cover all the problems which can be analyzed with multisectoral LP models. Here follows a brief list of other topics which model builders might consider.

(i) Aside from the models which concentrate on the make-or-buy decision with respect to imports, relatively little work has been done at the aggregate level of choice on technique. In part, this simply reflects the lack of readily available data on alternative columns for the same sector in the input-output matrix; however, for selected sectors, there is no doubt that these could be estimated. There is obvious policy interest in studying possible employment-creating effects of alternative techniques in labor-intensive sectors such as construction and some types of agriculture. LP models are an ideal tool for evaluating the macroimpacts of new technologies, and model builders should expand their efforts in this direction. Chapters VII and XI contain further suggestions along these lines.

(ii) Externalities are another topic which can be studied fruitfully in a programming model (particularly if one is willing to put credence in its Walrasian characteristics). At the sectoral and regional level, models have been used to unravel some of the complexities of industrial complexes and scale economies, as discussed in Chapters X and XI. There is also some literature in developed countries on environmental problems, focused on externalities. No doubt this will be extended sooner or later to the developing world.

(iii) The whole range of problems created by uncertainty has not been touched. Although applied multisectoral model builders have to date almost uniformly avoided consideration of uncertainty, there is no reason for them to continue to do so in the future—at least on key problems. These might include consideration of probable fluctuations of prices in key exports,

---

68. Variant specifications relate savings in base year prices to some measure of disposable income and/or payments assigned to specific factors of production according to the breakdown of value added in the input-output table. (For an example of the latter, see Tendulkar [1971].) The ultimate effect of these other specifications on the solution to the planning model is similar to that of the constraints discussed here.

imprecision in estimates of important parameters,[69] and so on. There has been analysis of such problems at the sectoral level (e.g., Kornai [1967, 1974]), and techniques for solving at least some sorts of stochastic LP problems are fairly well developed (Sengupta [1972]). This is another area where slow but steady advance may be expected over the next few years.

### 4.7 Evaluation

All of the algebra we have just struggled through may have diverted attention from the ultimate question one must ask about any formal planning model: Just how useful is it? This question about LP models is best phrased in terms of the two interpretations discussed at the beginning of this section.

Regarding the second one—that LP models provide a replica of a competitive resource allocation with shadow prices that could readily be used for decentralized decision making—the judgment must be that existing models fall short of what might be desired. Although it is clear that shadow prices reflect in some general way the real resource trade-offs in the economy, they obviously fail to do so in detail. There are simply too many implicit taxes and subsidies in the shadow price system for the model to be completely credible. And on the other side of the coin, it is extremely difficult to build preexisting taxes into the model, to ask how the solution will respond to changes in these policy instruments.

Nonetheless, experience has shown that the prices *are* useful in measuring the trade-offs implicit in any particular LP model, and that these trade-offs are of interest to policy makers. This has to do with the first interpretation of LP given above—that it is a useful means of exploring the frontiers of the opportunity set facing the economy. These frontiers may not be well known to model builders (which explains in part the need to impose ad hoc restrictions), but any idea at all as to their location and how the constraints fit together can be of use.

To drive this point home, it is useful to contrast LP results with those of the nonoptimizing models discussed in section 2 and 3. If well managed, the latter will provide a consistent forecast of future growth prospects for the economy, and some sensitivity analysis. An optimizing model will provide a forecast of the frontier of the choice set, perhaps 2 or 3 percent "better" in terms of its own welfare function than that resulting from a consistency model.[70] More importantly, parametric variation of the solution will provide detail on the

---

69. Standard errors really have no meaning for many of the parameters which are used in economy-wide models, since they are based on point estimates; but some parameters such as Engel's and export demand curves' elasticities are estimated econometrically, and one might consider taking their associated probability distributions into consideration in model formulation.

70. Efficiency gains by optimization over projection models have not been explored much in the literature. The cited figures are a consensus of other authors of this volume, and are verified in the experiments of Bergendorff, Clark, and Taylor [1973].

slope and curvature of the choice frontier. Despite the ad hoc constraints, this information is at least somewhat accurate, and useful. For example, good projections of how much growth can be expected from additional foreign aid, or how much investment is likely to decline if the urban wage goes up, can be extremely important for policy makers. In a similar vein, shadow prices may have clear policy implications, even if they do not have a strict market interpretation. If the shadow cost of rapid development of a lagging region or meeting a minimum employment objective is high, such a goal will probably be difficult to achieve in the real economy as well as in the world of the model.

Of course, getting useful information from the model is not a trivial under-taking. As discussed in Chapters II and V, scores of variant solutions may be necessary to trace out enough trade-off curves for a useful discussion between model builder and policy maker, and still more iterations will be necessary to deal with problems uncovered in a successful discussion. Furthermore, the structure of the models makes them more useful for answering some questions than others—they will give a more accurate forecast of the real impacts of an increase in the savings rates than of a revision in tariff policy.

These and other benefits of modelling can be quite real. So can the costs. It may take a five-man team of good quality a year to get enough data to-gether for a good LP model, to have the data inserted into the computer program package for solution, and verified there. During this process and in deriving solutions thereafter, much computer time may be required. All of this takes monetary and (more important in a developing country) human resources. Obviously, each planning director has to make his own decision about whether to undertake such a model, after considering data requirements (as outlined in Chapter IV) and some of the detailed results which may be possible (Chapters V–VIII). By planning office standards, the cost-benefit ratio may seem fairly high, but in comparison to many other expenditures made in developing countries (jet planes for the prestige of the local airlines, steel mills which produce at three times world prices), it is probably in the acceptable range.

## 5. DYNAMIC OPTIMIZING MODELS

Like their static cousins, dynamic planning models can be viewed from several angles. For example, they are earthly representations (with feet of clay obtruding) of the ideal models for which turnpike theorems are proved. For obvious computational reasons, they have finite horizons as well as all the ad hoc characteristics of the static models discussed in the last section. Still, dynamic planning models reflect a part of the turnpike's purity, and the diligent planner should at least sample some of the philosophy of that ideal.[71]

71. Turnpike literature is vast and difficult. The reader should begin his reconnaissance with surveys (good ones are by Chakravarty [1969], Turnovsky in Burmeister and Dobell [1970], and Koopmans [1964]) and proceed wherever his tastes lead him. Other interesting

He should also learn a bit about Ramsey-type optimal savings models,[72] although these will be discussed to a certain extent below.

In more pedestrian fashion, dynamic models can be seen as static programming models which repeat themselves over time. Successive periods are linked together through capital accumulation equations. In linear models, these usually take the accelerator form discussed in section 3; in nonlinear optimal growth models, the accelerator is somewhat relaxed by the possibility of within-period capital-labor substitution, but next period's capital stock is still the sum of this period's stock and net investment. These simple hypotheses impose a distinctive time structure on both the primal and dual solutions of dynamic optimizing models. This often proves useful in designing solution algorithms, as discussed in subsection 5.3.

To date, such "dynamic decomposition" algorithms have been applied only to nonlinear models, although there is no obvious reason why they could not be extended to the linear case as well. On the other hand, most models actually developed have been linear, solved by brute force application of standard LP computer routines. Since the dynamic model linear programming tableau (for example, Table 4) is built by "piling up" tableaux from static models, strict limits have been imposed on the number of sectors and periods to keep the problem manageable.[73] Typical exercises involve a dozen or so sectors and at most, five or six periods (artificially elongated to encompass several years each). This degree of aggregation can be bothersome in practical planning for reasons already discussed: highly aggregated sectoral forecasts do not provide a good basis for communication between macroplanners and industrial specialists, and putting two or three years in one time period means that the model can say little about very short term changes in the economy. This may not be serious when perspective planning is being emphasized. In other contexts the size limitations of dynamic LP models limit their usefulness. To repeat, there is no single type of model that can give insight into all planning problems.

## 5.1 Within-Period and Between-Period Optimality Conditions

The computational problems with dynamic planning models are a direct result of size—the time to solve a linear programming problem usually

---

articles (partially discussed in the appendix on terminal conditions) are by Murukami, Tokoyama, and Tsukui [1970] and Tsukui [1968], who apply turnpike theory to a planning model in which consumption is tied directly to sectoral value added. Maximization of consumption is replaced by maximization of the value of terminal capital stock, and rapid convergence to a turnpike growth path is demonstrated.

72. These models are also the subject of a huge literature. Clear introductions are given by Arrow and Kurz [1970] and Dorfman [1969]. To my knowledge, no surveys exist as yet.

73. This is true even when all possible substitutions are made to reduce the number of constraints in the model. Bruno, Dougherty, and Fraenkel [1970], Manne and Weisskopf [1970], and Bergendorff, Blitzer, and Kim [1973] describe such size-reduction procedures.

increases roughly with the cube of the number of constraints, and many of these, such as the input-output balances and the balance of payments constraints, simply must be repeated from period to period to give a sensible problem. The capital stock equations are about the only part of the specification where the model builder has some freedom of choice. Here, the most constraint-saving assumption is that each type of capital is shiftable and may be moved among sectors at will. A dynamic model with shiftable stocks requires accumulation equations only for the few types of capital typically produced in the country; adding-up restrictions within each period's constraint set guarantees that capital demands will not exceed the totals available. The model of Table 2 can easily be expanded into a dynamic linear program of this type. The reader is encouraged to do this and to interpret the primal and dual inequality relationships along the lines that follow.

The problem with shiftable capital stocks (stressed last section) is that they easily give rise to overspecialization which may be unacceptable in a highly aggregated description of the economy.[74] For this reason, detailed analysis of a model with nonshiftable capital stocks is of some practical interest, although it may increase the costs of computation. Table 4 gives a three-period example.

The optimality conditions in both primal and dual solutions of Table 4 decompose neatly into within- and between-period classes. We begin with the former, using "P" and "D" in equation numbers to distinguish primal and dual relationships.

Assume that, for the optimal solution, $C(t)$, $X(t)$, and $J(t)$ are all positive. In the dual, then, price-equals-cost equations are given by columns (1), (5), and (10),

$$P'(t)(I - A) = R'(t)\hat{k} + w(t)\lambda'. \tag{5.1D}$$

Of course $R(t)$ and $w(t)$ are factor shadow prices in this equation. They are the dual variables related respectively to the capital and labor supply restrictions in the primal:

$$\hat{k}X(t) \leq K(t)$$
$$\lambda'X(t) \leq \bar{L}(t). \tag{5.1P}$$

Again in the dual solution, comparison of the costs of producing sectoral outputs from (5.1D) with the benefits of using them in consumption and

---

74. If one works with a dozen traded goods and a half-dozen factors in a dynamic model, then only six of the traded goods will usually be produced domestically in a given period. Although it may make a lot of sense to shut down overprotected industries in developing countries, a planner cannot recommend this on a wholesale basis. For this reason, it may behoove him to work with a model less inclined to propose highly specialized patterns of resource allocation.

**Table 4: Detached Coefficients Tableau for a Dynamic Planning Model with Nonshiftable Capital Stocks by Sector**

| | (1) X(1) | (2) C(1) | (3) J(1) | (4) D(1) | (5) X(2) | (6) C(2) | (7) J(2) | (8) D(2) | (9) K(2) | (10) X(3) | (11) C(3) | (12) J(3) | (13) D(3) | (14) K(3) | (15) K(4) | |
|---|---|---|---|---|---|---|---|---|---|---|---|---|---|---|---|---|
| (1) R'(1) | $k$ | | | | | | | | | | | | | | | $\le \bar{K}(1)$ |
| (2) P'(1) | $-(I-A)$ | $\xi_1$ | $\begin{bmatrix} I \\ 0 \end{bmatrix}$ | | | | | | | | | | | | | $\le -\bar{C}(1)$ |
| (3) S'(1) | | | $-I$ | $B$ | | | | | | | | | | | | $\le 0$ |
| (4) Q'(1) | | | | $-I$ | | | | | $I$ | | | | | | | $\le \bar{K}(1)$ |
| (5) w(1) | $\chi$ | | | | | | | | | | | | | | | $\le \bar{L}(1)$ |
| (6) R'(2) | | | | | $k$ | | | | $-I$ | | | | | | | $\le 0$ |
| (7) P'(2) | | | | | $-(I-A)$ | $\xi_2$ | $\begin{bmatrix} I \\ 0 \end{bmatrix}$ | | | | | | | | | $\le -\bar{C}(2)$ |
| (8) S'(2) | | | | | | | $-I$ | $B$ | | | | | | | | $\le 0$ |
| (9) Q'(2) | | | | | | | | $-I$ | | | | | | $I$ | | $\le 0$ |
| (10) w(2) | | | | | $\chi$ | | | | | | | | | | | $\le \bar{L}(2)$ |
| (11) R'(3) | | | | | | | | | | $k$ | | | | $-I$ | | $\le 0$ |
| (12) P'(3) | | | | | | | | | | $-(I-A)$ | $\xi_3$ | $\begin{bmatrix} I \\ 0 \end{bmatrix}$ | | | | $\le -\bar{C}(3)$ |
| (13) S'(3) | | | | | | | | | | | | $-I$ | $B$ | | | $\le 0$ |
| (14) Q'(3) | | | | | | | | | | | | | $-I$ | | $I$ | $\le 0$ |
| (15) w(3) | | | | | | | | | | $\chi$ | | | | | | $\le \bar{L}(3)$ |
| MAX | | $\omega_1$ | | | | $\omega_2$ | | | | | $\omega_3$ | | | | $\bar{Q}'(3)$ | |

investment activities determines whether the latter will run at positive levels. The relevant inequalities are:

$$P'(t)\xi \geq \omega_t,$$

$$P'(t)\begin{bmatrix} B \\ 0 \end{bmatrix} \geq Q'(t). \tag{5.2D}$$

Finally, demands for consumption and investment cannot exceed total sectoral supplies:

$$\xi_t C_T(t) + \begin{bmatrix} B \\ 0 \end{bmatrix} D(t) \leq (I - A)X(t). \tag{5.2P}$$

$D(t)$ in this balance equation is the vector of investment levels by destination at time $t$, and the other notation is as in the last section.

All of these relationships[75] hold *within* any period of the dynamic model solution. They look very similar to the static model conditions derived in the last section; in fact they would follow from the maximization of the functional $\omega_t C_T(t) + Q'(t)D(t)$ (which is essentially GNP in terms of shadow prices) subject to technical restrictions (5.1P) and (5.2P). Clearly, all that has been said about static LP planning models with nonshiftable capital stocks applies to "each period's" model here.[76]

How are capital stocks $K(t)$ and investment valuations $Q'(t)$ generated for each year's static problem? The former clearly come from the accumulation relationships in rows (4), (9), and (14) of Table 4:[77]

$$K(t) + D(t) \geq K(t + 1)$$
$$K(1) = \bar{K}(1). \tag{5.3P}$$

The dynamic conditions on capital goods prices are given by the complementary slackness conditions on columns (9), (14), and (15),

$$Q'(t - 1) = Q'(t) + R'(t),$$
$$Q'(t_f) = \bar{Q}'(t_f), \tag{5.3D}$$

where equality follows from the fact that all capital stock levels will be

---

75. In their derivation, some consolidations have been made from Table 4. The second line of (5.2D) consolidates complementary slackness conditions in columns (3)–(4), (7)–(8) and (12)–(13). The inequality (5.2P) consolidates rows (2)–(3), (7)–(8), and (12)–(13).

76. In particular, there is a distinct possibility that when the labor constraint is not binding there will be low levels of consumption, as discussed in subsection 4.2. This is a recurrent problem in dynamic models, and we return to it in the next subsection.

77. Note that this formulation assumes that all capital stocks, by sector of usage, are known for the initial period. This, together with the strict accelerator relationship for investment, severely restricts sectoral growth possibilities in the near term. To avoid these problems of rigidity, Manne and his associates (e.g., Blitzer, Cetin, and Manne [1970] or Manne and Weisskopf [1970]) have recommended fixing only aggregate base year investment, while allowing the model to choose its own investment breakdown. While this introduces some errors of national accounting, these authors feel that the extra flexibility is worth this cost. In any case, base year investment by sector of destination is rarely known accurately.

positive (if they begin positive) and $t_f$ is the last period in the model.

Condition (5.3P) is readily interpreted as summing investment by destination $D(t)$ and the existing level of capital stock $K(t)$ to get the next period's capital. The price equation (5.3D) can be thrown into a form similar to those discussed in section 4,

$$r_i(t) = \frac{Q_i(t-1) - Q_i(t)}{Q_i(t)} = \frac{R_i(t)}{Q_i(t)}, \quad i = 1, 2, \ldots, n \qquad (5.4)$$

which defines sectoral own rates of return to capital $r_i(t)$ by changes in the capital prices $Q_i(t)$ over time. Within each period, however, $R_i(t)$ (and therefore $r_i(t)$) is determined by the constrained maximization of $\omega_i C_T(t) + Q'(t)D(t)$ described above. By equation (5.3D), $Q'(t)$ and $R'(t)$ then determine the *preceding* period's capital goods prices $Q'(t-1)$. In other words, the capital price equations (5.3D) run naturally backward in time from given terminal values $\bar{Q}'(t_f)$,[78] while the accumulation equations (5.3P) run forward from $\bar{K}(1)$. Information to guide each forward or backward time step comes from the within-period static maximization involving both $K(t)$ and $Q'(t)$. In mathematical programming terminology, the entire model can be described as a "two-point" boundary value problem (the two vector space points being initial conditions on capital stock levels and terminal conditions on their values) of the type traditionally considered in the calculus of variations or optimal control theory.

## 5.2 Specialization Problems and Proposed Remedies

The inequality relationships in (5.2D) provide much latitude for specialization of final demands into either consumption or investment activities. This same problem exists in static models like the one shown in Table 2, which also place valuations on both consumption and investment in the maximand, but solutions come easily in a static world, since adjustment of the objective function weights to get "reasonable" values for all final demand components is straightforward. Such tuning is more difficult in dynamic models, where it must be done indirectly via the dynamic price equations (5.3P).

Attempts to avoid final demand specialization in dynamic LP models are common in the literature. The main goal of such attempts has been to avoid "flip-flop" behavior in consumption, i.e., zero consumption in all but one

---

78. Dynamic models have their own endogenous mechanisms for generating investment demands up to the final period. There, however, something has to be done to insure that "enough" capital is passed on to post-terminal years to make the future economically viable. In practice, the devices already discussed in subsections 4.1 and 4.2 are used in the last period of dynamic LP models to assure positive investment. The most common approach is to put some valuation on post-terminal capital stock, as in Table 2. Ways of determining numerical values for the parameters of the valuation function are discussed in the appendix to this chapter.

period, often the last.[79] There has also been interest in avoiding extreme specialization in investment expenditures by sector of destination, which occurs frequently in nonshiftable capital models of the type being considered.[80] Details on some of the proposed remedies follow:

(i) Unpleasantly low levels of total consumption can be avoided by placing type-three lower bounds (usually increasing with $t$) on $C_T(t)$. This is done explicitly by Chakravarty and Lefeber [1965] and Eckaus and Parikh [1968] (collectively known as *CELP*), and more subtly by Manne [1970]. The latter works with what he calls a "gradualist" objective function, in which initial consumption and its asymptotic growth rate are parameters. This formulation leads neatly to a long-run steady growth solution of the planning model, based on the idea that only initial consumption increments which can be sustained forever are permitted. Unfortunately, this growth path turns out to be inefficient, in the sense that transitory, nonsustainable consumption increments at specific points in time (which could increase total discounted welfare from consumption) are ruled out. This rather abstruse sounding criticism has some bite: gradualist models have a difficult time turning short-term resource increases (such as temporary reductions in capital outflows due to foreseen downward fluctuations in the schedule of debt repayment) into welfare-increasing "blips" upward in consumption or investment. Shadow prices on the temporarily available resources may fall dramatically as a result. Stability in the primal is (as is often the case) purchased at the cost of instability in the dual. Moreover, the interpretation of the dual is made difficult by the fact that the gradualist constraints themselves pick up shadow prices. Like the shadow prices on the lower bounds on consumption in the *CELP* specification, these can only be interpreted as subsidies for consumption. The gradualist formulation may be illuminating in policy discussions, since its results are easily summarized in terms of one exogenous parameter (the asymptotic consumption growth rate), but ultimately both it and the *CELP* model put only lower bounds on consumption growth—a somewhat inelegant technique at best.

(ii) Upper bounds on components of GNP besides consumption clearly act as lower bounds on the latter. Savings constraints are often imposed to this end. Also, a binding labor (or other primary factor) constraint helps maintain positive consumption, for the Golden Rule type of reasons discussed in subsection 4.2. Dynamic models with full employment show fewer

---

79. This will automatically occur in strictly linear models without a labor (or other primary factor) constraint when consumption is valued by geometrically declining weights in the objective function. Chakravarty [1969] and Westphal [1971] present illuminating examples.

80. Investment specialization is common even in aggregated optimal growth models of the type considered in the theoretical literature. For examples based on the Feldman–Mahalanobis–Domar models of subsection 1.2 (which feature nonshiftable capital), see Ryder [1969] and Weitzman [1971].

tendencies toward flip-flop than the *CELP* model, in which labor is ignored.[81]

(iii) Suppose that the welfare weight $\omega_t$ in the first inequality of (5.2D) depends on the level of consumption $C_T(t)$. This is the specification discussed at the beginning of subsection 4.5, and equation (4.24) can be rewritten with a time subscript as a price-equals-marginal-utility relationship,

$$P'(t)\xi \geq \partial\omega_t/\partial C_T(t).$$

If the derivative of $\omega_t$ goes to infinity as $C_T(t)$ approaches zero, the above condition guarantees a positive consumption level. Dynamic programmers have been more willing than their static counterparts to use approximation techniques and incorporate the isolated nonlinearity of this specification into their models. The results reported by Carter [1967], Barr and Manne [1967], Westphal [1971], and Goreux [1973] show that consumption fluctuations are duly moderated by decreasing marginal utility.[82]

(iv) One could also consider replacing the second set of inequalities of (5.2D) by some sort of marginality conditions, to insure positive levels of investment to all destinations and also to limit total investment from above (and total consumption from below). The latter consideration in part motivates the "absorptive capacity" constraints built into many dynamic linear programming models. In simplest form, these are upper bounds on sectoral investment levels in a period (or the rates of growth of investment between periods). Although often imposed only in the hope of generating "nice" solutions to LP models, such restrictions do fit into type two of our classification because they reflect "decreasing returns" to investment resulting from a host of real but not well-understood phenomena tied up variously in "learning-by-doing," engineering injunctions that it takes time to "break in" a new plant, and so on. Many such grumbles are reviewed by Eckaus [1973]. In the same article, he proposes that the amount of capacity which actually comes on stream within a period is a certain declining function of appropriately lagged investment and uses the function to develop smooth consumption growth in the *CELP* model. A welcome characteristic of his specification is that each unit of investment ultimately is translated into capacity on a one-for-one basis, so that absorptive capacity limitations are only short run. Somewhat earlier, Dorfman [1969] proposed an alternative formulation in which the amount of new capacity is a declining function of the ratio of invest-

---

81. For example, Bruno, Dougherty, and Fraenkel [1970] work with skilled labor constraints in their dynamic LP model and have no problems with consumption flip-flop. Making consumption endogenous via surplus labor restrictions, as in subsection 4.2, should also work, although this has not been done in developing country practice. (But again see Murukami, Tokoyama, and Tsukui [1970] for an exception.)

82. There are some problems with credibility of utility functions which are curved enough and/or discount rates which are high enough to generate "reasonable" savings rates. This is discussed in subsection 5.3. See also Goreux [1973] for a serious (and largely successful) effort to put *all* the restrictions of consumption theory into an LP planning model.

ment to existing capacity, even in the long run. Dorfman and Thoreson [1969] used this function in a set of interesting variations on the Chenery and MacEwan [1966] dynamic two-gap model. Finally, much the same considerations have crept into the optimal growth literature under the name of the "Penrose effect" (see Uzawa [1969]) and also into various cost-of-adjustment econometric theories of investment demand. Given the number of eminent hunters pursuing the absorptive capacity hare, there is reason to hope that a definitive functional relationship (complete with parameters) will be bagged sooner or later. For the moment, the interested practitioner had best follow cautiously the suggestions of Eckaus or Dorfman.

## 5.3 Optimal Control Models

The foregoing discussion implies fairly strongly that "nonlinearizing" various parts of the dynamic LP specification is one way of guaranteeing that the model's solution will be stable. If one imposes all the nonlinearities simultaneously, then the linear program becomes a model of optimal growth, in the usual sense of that term in the literature. There has been some experimentation with numerical solution of these models. A brief discussion of an example with nonshiftable capital stocks (similar to the model solved by Kendrick and Taylor [1970]) may serve to illustrate some of the advantages and drawbacks of this approach. To simplify notation, the model is set up in terms of continuous time, but the reader can make the obvious translation to discrete time for comparison with the model of Table 4.

The objective, as usual, is to maximize some welfare function based on consumption. In this case however, a discounted criterion function $U[C_1(t),\ldots,C_n(t)]$[83] with declining marginal within-period "utility" from each consumption good is assumed, so that consumption proportions are not fixed by the Engel coefficient vector $\xi$ of the linear programs:

$$\text{MAX } \bar{Q}'(t_f)K(t_f) + \int_0^{t_f} e^{-\rho t}U[C_1(t),\ldots,C_n(t)]\,dt. \tag{5.5}$$

---

83. Almost all practitioners use some specialization of the general form,
$$U[C_1,\ldots,C_n] = \sum_i a_i[C_i - \bar{C}_i]^{b_i}$$
as their utility function. For one-sector models, the variant $U(C) = (1-\eta)^{-1}C^{1-\eta}$ is often used, where $\eta$ is the elasticity of marginal utility with respect to consumption. From evidence reviewed by Chakravarty [1969] and Kendrick and Taylor [1971], it appears that if the discount rate $\rho$ is set to a "reasonable" value then $\eta$ may have to be as large as two or three to enforce "reasonable" savings patterns in these models. This has to be interpreted as a planners' preference, since it is unlikely that an individual's "utility" from consumption would drop off so rapidly—when $\eta$ is equal to three, the marginal utility from a consumption increment is only equal to the *inverse of the cube* of the consumption level already attained! In a planning model, this is a utility gain low enough to induce low savings rates at the beginning of the program and, therefore, slow but steady rates of capital accumulation and income growth over time.

Besides the welfare integral, the terminal value of capital stock is assumed to enter the maximand.

Material balances are similar to those of the linear program

$$0 = (I - A)X(t) - \begin{bmatrix} B \\ 0 \end{bmatrix} D(t) - C(t) \qquad (5.6)$$

where notation is as before, except that $C(t)$ is now a vector of sectoral consumption levels. For simplicity, intermediate inputs and the proportional makeup of each sector's capital stock basket are assumed to be determined by the usual fixed coefficient matrices $A$ and $B$, although this could be relaxed.

Production functions depend on capital, labor, and time (for technical progress):

$$X_i(t) = X_i[L_i(t), K_i(t), t], \quad i = 1, 2, \ldots, n \qquad (5.7)$$

and full employment reigns,

$$\sum_i L_i(t) = \bar{L}(t). \qquad (5.8)$$

Finally, capital accumulation is not set equal to investment but rather a declining function of it, to capture the absorptive capacity phenomenon:

$$\dot{K}_i(t) = dK_i(t)/dt = f_i[D_i(t)], \quad i = 1, 2, \ldots, n. \qquad (5.9)$$

Total discounted "surplus" in this economy is:

$$H(t) = e^{-\rho t} U[C_1(t), \ldots, C_n(t)] + Q'(t)\dot{K}(t)$$

where $Q'(t)$ is a vector of valuations assigned to the increases in capital stocks, $\dot{K}(t)$. When applied to this economy, the Maximum Principle of Pontryagin et al. [1962] states that necessary conditions for (5.5) to be maximized subject to the foregoing constraints are:

(i) The surplus $H(t)$—usually called a Hamiltonian—should be maximized at each time point with respect to the technological restrictions (5.6) to (5.9). This determines all flow variables, including investment, analogously to the within-period optimization discussed in subsection 5.1.

(ii) Capital stocks are determined by equation (5.9), running forward in time from initial conditions $K_i(0) = \bar{K}_i(0)$.

(iii) The investment valuations $Q_i(t)$ are determined by the differential equation

$$\dot{Q}_i = -[P_i(t) - \sum_j a_{ji} P_j(t)] \frac{\partial X_i(t)}{\partial K_i(t)} \qquad (5.10)$$

where the $P_i(t)$ are shadow prices of the commodities in the economy, dual to equations (5.6). Equations (5.10) run naturally backward in time from terminal conditions $Q_i(t_f) = \bar{Q}_i(t_f)$.

The similarities with the dynamic LP models just discussed are striking, with differences only in detail. In the LP model, GNP in shadow prices is maximized in each time period as opposed to the surplus $H(t)$ (which takes into account utility generated by intramarginal consumption units), and the control model substitutes nonlinear equalities for the programming model's linear inequality constraints. As the reader can verify, necessary conditions for maximization of $H(t)$ in each period are strictly analogous to (5.1D) and (5.2D). Equation (5.10) for investment valuations is very similar to (5.3D), when one observes that the right side of (5.10) is a measure of the value of the marginal product of the capital stock in sector $i$, equivalent to the $i$th component of $R'(t)$ in (5.3D).

Comments on the LP model carry over practically verbatim to the control formulation. In particular, specialization in production and trade would be ruled out in an open economy version of this model by nonshiftable capital stocks; flip-flop consumption behavior doesn't occur because of the declining marginal utilities in the utility function; and specialization in investments by destination is not a problem as long as the $f_i$-functions in (5.9) are sufficiently curved.

If one is willing to work in the optimization mode, models like the present one are worth considering. Efficient solution algorithms can be designed to fit the structure of the problem,[84] and many of the troublesome rigidities of dynamic LP models are smoothed out. It is a moot point whether future optimizing dynamic planning exercises should be carried out in the linear programming or optimal control frame.[85]

---

84. Dependable algorithms involve the following steps: (i) specification of a nominal "history" of capital stock growth; (ii) integration of (5.10) backward in time from terminal conditions and simultaneous maximization of the Hamiltonian subject to technical constraints (all this takes place with the nominal capital stock levels in the relevant functions); (iii) integration of (5.9) forward, calculating new capital stocks from the investment levels from the maximization in (ii); and (iv) continuing with this form of integration "in circles" until convergence is reached. Although other solution methods have been proposed (Radner and Friedmann [1965], and Mirrlees [1967]), this one seems fairly robust. In particular, it avoids numerical problems which can stem from the dual instability of (5.10) and (a linearized version) of (5.9) discussed below. The main difficulty is the maximization of the Hamiltonian in step (ii), but this can probably be done with the algorithms discussed in subsection 6.1. A somewhat secondary problem is that this solution technique generally requires knowledge of the derivatives of all the functions in the model. These can usually be evaluated numerically, but derivation of the relevant formulas may be very time consuming. Computer programs are now being developed which may ease the task of symbol manipulation.

85. To date, most optimal control models—and most dynamic LP models as well—have been developed by academics. Demonstration multisectoral models were solved by Radner and Friedmann [1965], Friedmann [1968], and Kendrick and Taylor [1970] in the late 1960's. Bergendorff, Blitzer, and Kim [1973] and Martens and Pindyck [1973] suggest differing approaches to solving models hybrid in specification between the dynamic LP's and the highly nonlinear optimal control models cited here.

### 5.4 Evaluation

Either dynamic LP or optimal growth models can be used to generate quantity forecasts similar to those resulting from the dynamic Leontief model of section 3. They are thus likely to be useful to planners in institutional circumstances which favor dynamic input-output, i.e., when the economy has significant capital goods capacity or faces sharp limitations on savings and investment.

In addition, the dynamic optimizing models can, in principle, shed light on a number of other problems:

(i) They can be used to set discount rates for investment project analysis. One popular approach to finding shadow prices is to assume that the economy will behave optimally in the future, so that the dual solution to this optimizing problem will provide shadow prices appropriate for project selection. If the planning model is sufficiently aggregative and nonlinear, the shadow prices may not even be subject to many of the objections raised in sections 4 and 5.

There is a huge theoretical literature in this area which cannot be summarized here. Newbery [1972] and Taylor [1973] have attempted numerical calculations of shadow prices at the aggregative level. In the disaggregated dynamic LP models, the author who has paid most attention to optimal discount rates is Manne [1973a] in his DINAMICO model for Mexico. He finds that the own-rates of interest—the $r_i(t)$ of equation (5.4)—have similar and quite plausible values across sectors. Whether this carries over into other model specifications is a topic worth exploring.

(ii) "Comparative dynamics" in a broad sense also falls within the purview of these models. They can clearly deal with such things as the effects of different patterns of import substitution over time and the economy-wide impacts of different time-phased investment packages[86] which are beyond the reach of static formulations. There are also a number of dynamic externalities that are relevant to development planning, a good example being the learning-to-export functions analyzed by Bruno [1970] and Manne [1973a]. Dynamic models can play an extremely useful educational role by opening the eyes of planners to the importance of economic processes which require a number of years to work themselves out.

(iii) There is much to be said for "perspective" planning which attempts to outline future development possibilities over a 10- to 20-year horizon. Dynamic optimizing models are the only readily available means for tracing out these long-term trade-offs in a consistent manner. Despite the sketchy nature of such results, they can be useful in building up the exogenous pro-

---

86. An interesting example would be a study on economic *and* ecological grounds of the automobile/highway/oil refinery transportation investment complex versus some of its alternatives.

94

jections needed for more detailed short- and medium-term planning as outlined in sections 2 and 4.

On the other hand, dynamic optimization is not without its problems. We have already seen that it is costly in terms of both manpower and computation.[87] Moreover, the main purpose of dynamic optimization is to provide an investment theory. In the optimal growth variant, for example, investment is determined by the interactions of equations (5.9) and (5.10). There are two problems with this. The first, and more abstract, objection is that it can be shown that the two sets of equations share the same coefficient matrix (with (5.9) linearized about the optimal growth path), except that signs are reversed and the matrix is transposed. Thus the dual stability properties of the price and quantity solutions to the dynamic Leontief system which were alluded to in section 3 also characterize the optimizing models. This casts some doubt on the economic relevance of the problem, since there is much theoretical debate (summarized by Burmeister and Dobell [1970], pages 405–6) about whether or not a decentralized economy can conform to the capital stock pricing rules of (5.10), in part because of their instability.[88]

The other objection, probably more relevant in practice, is that optimization may not provide a very accurate investment forecast. It may well be that for quantity-side comparative dynamics and forecasting, behavioral investment equations in a simulation model (such as those discussed in the next section) are more appropriate than those resulting from optimization of a planner's preference function.

In summary, the dynamic models are most likely to be useful when dynamic externalities are suspected to be important, when capital goods or savings capacity in the economy is tight, or when there is interest in analyzing shadow prices (of factors of production, at least) for project analysis. To this must be added the observation that it is always useful to have a *completely* consistent multisectoral projection of how the economy is going to look over the long term, and that dynamic optimizing models are one of the few available methods for generating such perspective plans and long term trade-off frontiers.

## 6. NONOPTIMIZING ECONOMY-WIDE MODELS

So far, we have interpreted optimization as a device for either exploring the choice set of the economy or for generating something approaching a Walrasian general equilibrium resource allocation. Still another interpretation

---

87. Realistically speaking, a dynamic LP exercise might tie up several Ph.D. economists and appropriate assistants for a year or two, and $5,000 or $10,000 of support costs before it is completed. These estimates assume that considerable work will be required in gathering and "laundering" data, but this is essential in most developing countries doing any type of model for the first time.

88. Dual stability/instability of the quantity and price equations could also give rise to numerical problems in solving dynamic models by dynamic decomposition, although this is not likely to be the case if the algorithm in footnote 84 is used.

is that optimization is a means of using up the excess degrees of freedom in a realistic quantity-side model specification. As soon as the rather rigid assumptions of either static or dynamic input-output are relaxed, excess degrees of freedom arise in the model from many sources: excess capacities, the possibility of substituting capital for labor along production functions, substitution of different goods in consumption functions, and so on. In this section, we discuss ways besides optimization of coming up with enough additional conditions to make the quantity solution of the planning model determinate. In particular, the first two subsections are devoted to truly Walrasian models (as opposed to the optimizing approximation) which can be solved numerically, while the third subsection examines a variety of more ad hoc methods for closing model specifications. It is important to remember, in at least the developing countries, that these types of models are still quite untried and experimental.

## 6.1 Constant Returns Models

The simplest characterization of an economy in which factor substitution and demand responsiveness to prices reign is based on constant returns to scale and consumption by a single "household." A small example is an $n$-sector, two-factor model with Cobb–Douglas production functions:

$$X_i = L_i^{\alpha_i} K_i^{(1-\alpha_i)}, \quad i = 1, 2, \ldots, n \tag{6.1}$$

in which $L_i$ and $K_i$ are the labor and (shiftable) capital employed in sector $i$. Demands for these factors are determined by the cost minimization equations:

$$L_i = \alpha_i P_i X_i / w,$$
$$K_i = (1 - \alpha_i) P_i X_i / r, \quad i = 1, 2, \ldots, n \tag{6.2}$$

where the $P_i$ are sector price levels, $w$ is the wage, and $r$ is the user cost of capital. Equations (6.1) and (6.2) together imply the price-equals-cost relationships

$$P_i = \Theta_i w^{\alpha_i} r^{(1-\alpha_i)} \quad i = 1, 2, \ldots, n \tag{6.3}$$

where $\Theta_i = [\alpha_i^{\alpha_i}(1 - \alpha_i)^{(1-\alpha_i)}]^{-1}$.

If $\bar{K}$ and $\bar{L}$ are the total factor endowments of the economy, then income is given by

$$Y = w\bar{L} + r\bar{K}, \tag{6.4}$$

and sectoral consumption demands are

$$D_i = D_i(P_1, P_2, \ldots, P_n, Y), \quad i = 1, 2, \ldots, n. \tag{6.5}$$

If these demand functions are derived from a utility function, then total expenditures $\sum_i P_i D_i$ will automatically equal $Y$.

Now suppose that, subject to some normalization rule (such as $w + r = 1$), arbitrary values of the two factor prices are chosen. Via the cost functions

(6.3), $w$ and $r$ will determine goods prices; they similarly determine income $Y$ from (6.4). Goods prices and income together give total demands $D_i$ from (6.5).

On the supply side, factor and goods prices give labor and capital input proportions $a_{Li} = L_i/X_i$ and $a_{Ki} = K_i/X_i$ from (6.2). By using the calculated demand levels $D_i$, excess demand for the factors can be calculated from the equations

$$E_L(w, r) = \sum_i a_{Li} D_i - \bar{L} \qquad (6.6)$$

and

$$E_K(w, r) = \sum_i a_{Ki} D_i - \bar{K}. \qquad (6.7)$$

In equilibrium (which can be shown to exist and be unique as long as there is only one household),[89] these excess demands must be zero. Computationally, equilibrium can be attained in at least two different ways. One is simply to apply an algorithm to drive the excess demands to zero, i.e., to find the minimum of a quantity such as $(E_L)^2$. (By Walras' Law, if one of two excess demands is driven to zero, then the other one must also be at zero.) Such algorithms are readily available and were applied by Chenery and Raduchel [1971] and Raduchel [1972] in solving multisectoral, multifactor models.

The other approach is to follow Scarf [1969] and use an algorithm similar to the simplex method of linear programming fame to find general equilibrium solution points in the price space. This can be done by searching for a point at which excess demands for goods *and* factors are zero, or else searching only in the factor price space after going through a reduction of the type just described. In either case, computational experience shows that a problem with a score of excess demand functions can be solved in a half-hour or so on a fast, third generation computer. A successful application of the Scarf algorithm (to a small problem) is described by Shoven and Whalley [1972].

In general these exercises demonstrate that factor substitution may be an extremely powerful means of attaining full employment of resources in a developing economy. Given the importance of this and other results, further work with these models is clearly warranted. They should permit a series of interesting comparative static exercises in certain areas, which we can delimit fairly precisely on the basis of previous results and common sense:

(i) As long as make-or-buy specialization problems are evaded by the

---

89. Arrow and Hahn [1971] give a recent, definitive treatment of general equilibrium theory. See their Chapters 2 and 9 for proof of the assertions in the text. Unfortunately, uniqueness and stability of equilibrium need *not* obtain when more than one household exists, e.g., when there are separate consumption functions of the form of (6.5) for recipients of labor and capital incomes. Such a specification would be of much greater use in analyzing income distribution than the present one.

models, including decreasing prices of exports, increasing costs of imports, exogenous specification of volumes traded, and so on, then the reduction procedure just sketched can handle specifications far more complex than the simple Cobb–Douglas case considered here. One general characteristic of constant returns technology is that cost functions, such as (4.8) and (6.3), are independent of scale of production. The computational procedure makes use of this fact and can be easily extended to deal with quite general production functions involving primary and intermediate inputs, as long as nonincreasing returns apply [90] (decreasing returns can always be accommodated by the inclusion of sector-specific dummy factors, e.g., "entrepreneurship").

(ii) Data requirements are extremely severe for this type of model. Production function parameters have to be estimated (or guessed), and a complete set of demand functions must be specified. If only local comparative static exercises are contemplated, both production and demand functions can be approximated by various elasticity schemes (essentially all Hicks–Allen elasticities of substitution on the production side, and a complete set of price and Engel elasticities—computed, for example, by the Frisch [1959] scheme—on the demand side), but analysis of "large" changes clearly requires full parametric representation of production and utility functions. In a developing country, even complete sets of production and demand elasticities may lie well beyond the range of the econometrically possible.

(iii) One clear advantage of the Walrasian models is that they permit easy incorporation of existing price distortions in the economy, such as tariffs and subsidies, institutionally fixed "subsistence" wage rates, exogenous wedges between wage levels for the "same" type of labor in different sectors, and so on. Simulation of effects of changes in the magnitude of distortions should prove illuminating.[91] Optimization of taxes and tariffs subject to the government's budget constraint is another possibility.[92] New problems may appear

---

90. Fixed coefficient intermediate inputs can be handled by replacing the $P_i$ in (6.2) and (6.3) by net prices or values added $P_i^* = P_i - \sum_j P_j a_{ji}$ and by premultiplying the final demand vector $D$ by the Leontief inverse $(I - A)^{-1}$ in (6.6) and (6.7). The more interesting case of intermediate input substitutability can be handled through the derived demand equations for inputs. With Cobb–Douglas production functions, for example, the equations are $X_{ji} = \gamma_{ji} P_i X_i / P_j$ ($\gamma_{ji}$ is the exponent of $X_{ji}$ in the production function for $X_i$). These allow one to show that sectoral costs (and therefore goods prices) finally depend only on factor prices and also permit the replacement of all $X_{ji}$ terms by price terms in sectoral goods balances. After these manipulations, the general equilibrium solution for the economy reduces to finding factor prices which equate factor excess demands to zero, as before. Taylor and Black [1974] elaborate on the detail involved in Cobb–Douglas assumptions.

91. All this assumes that hard data can be found about the nature and extent of price distortions—not necessarily the easiest task in the world.

92. That is, one would use a general equilibrium solution model as part of a larger optimizing system, along the lines discussed in subsection 4.3. If some gradient method is used to find optimal policies subject to the general equilibrium solution, then one would want a rapid means for finding out how the latter varies with respect to "small" changes of

when this is seriously attempted, however, for complete description of the government's action requires consideration of its financial role and how it impinges on private asset choices (Raduchel [1972]). Opening real planning models to financial influences is a research task which will not soon be completed.

(iv) The Chenery–Raduchel models which were actually solved had only a few factors of production and, as mentioned above, experience with Scarf algorithms shows that they become quite costly when more than about twenty excess demand functions (for goods and/or factors) are included. This means that neither approach may be able to handle the make-or-buy problems discussed in subsection 4.3 if there are many sectors.[93] Note that choice of technique alone does not rule out specialization in a constant returns economy. This is true even when there are many factors, if factor proportions do not differ greatly among sectors.[94]

(v) The simple Cobb–Douglas example given here does not contain savings and investment functions. These can be added at will (and in current prices!), but, as usual, may lead to an overdetermined system in which differing *ex ante* plans have to be brought into mutual conformity *ex post*, perhaps through adjustment of some equilibrating variable. As discussed in a similar context in Chapter V, one usually cannot impose investment levels (or exogenous investment demand functions) *and* behavioral functions for savings by source without at the same time introducing an equilibrating variable such as the total government tax receipts or the balance of payments gap which moves to insure that the savings-investment equality holds *ex post*. Appropriate behavioral assumptions may vary from country to country, as may the institutional considerations which ultimately should dictate the selection of equilibrating variables. However, explicit consideration of savings and investment linkages is necessary in any planning exercise, particularly when the model is made dynamic by addition of capital accumulation equations to the ones considered here. Once again, research on appropriate treatment of this problem is likely to continue for a long time, especially since the Cambridge Criticism has shown

---

policy instruments. Chenery–Raduchel algorithms (themselves based on gradient methods) may do this more efficiently than Scarf algorithms, once an initial general equilibrium solution is found. This subject merits exploration.

93. Apparently, no one has attempted to solve a make-or-buy problem for a nonlinear economy. One would probably have to work with excess demands for both goods and factors to do so, since specialization comes into play in the excess demand functions for goods. Intuitively, it appears that Scarf algorithms may be more suitable than gradient methods of the Chenery–Raduchel type for this problem, since small changes in prices can lead to discontinuous jumps in sector output levels to and from zero. This conjecture, however, has not been verified by example.

94. This is important in aggregate models, which may have nearly linear transformation surfaces and corresponding tendencies toward specialization even when there are more factors than goods. For examples, see Johnson [1966] and Taylor [1973].

that different specifications of equilibrating variables in the savings-investment equality are intimately tied in with income distribution analyses of a type now fashionable in developing countries. (See again Chapter V.)

(vi) Finally, any model based on current economic theory has to assume perfect competition, or something very close to it (i.e., simple forms of non-competitive behavior such as monopoly or discriminating monopoly can also be included). This means that we sweep two serious problems under the rug. The first is another facet of the Cambridge Criticism—even when the economy is approximately competitive, we know we cannot with good conscience work with capital and labor aggregates such as enter equation (6.2). The aggregates don't exist and too much distribution theory is already built into the model by the assumption that "capital's marginal product" equals the rate of profit. Second, developing economies obviously have enough elements of oligopoly, unresponsive pricing rules, and so on, to render the competitive description of price formation very suspect. If we had a better theory of prices and economic power than the Walrasian one, model builders would clearly use it. At the moment, however, all that can be said is that an LP model is likely to be a poor facsimile of a Walrasian economy, while a nonlinear constant returns model will be a better one. On these grounds, the models of this subsection are clearly to be preferred. If competition is basically the only game in town, you might as well play it with elegance.

## 6.2 Johansen Models

Leif Johansen ([1960] and [1968]) has developed a method closely related to the models just discussed for making price-endogenous, multisectoral forecasts of economic growth. Basically, he proceeds by logarithmically differentiating the equations characterizing a Walrasian competitive equilibrium with respect to time in order to get a simultaneous system of equations which are linear in all growth rates. A set of growth rates is specified exogenously and a matrix inversion then suffices to calculate the other growth rates in the system.[95] This complete set of growth rates can then be applied to base year values of prices and quantities to get a prediction of the state of the economy two or three years in the future (which appears to be about the range of validity of the basic log-linear approximation). The forecasting process can stop there, or else a complete new general equilibrium solution can be derived (this may be done fairly easily since the log-linear projections should be close enough

---

95. The reader can use our Cobb–Douglas model to test his understanding of this procedure by logarithmically differentiating equations (6.1), (6.2), (6.5), and the additional conditions $X_i = D_i$, $\Sigma L_i = L$, and $\Sigma K_i = \bar{K}$. This will give a set of $5n + 2$ independent linear equations in $5n + 5$ growth rates. If the growth rates of total employment $\bar{L}$ and the wage $w$ are set exogenously (the latter is essentially a normalization for the price system), then the growth rate of capital stock $\bar{K}$ can be used to determine the growth rate of total expenditure on consumption $Y$, or vice versa. For reasons discussed in the text, Johansen chooses the former alternative.

to the new general equilibrium values to allow solution of the equilibrium equations by simple gradient methods) to provide a basis for another forecast step.

Most of the comments of the last subsection apply directly to Johansen's models and need not be repeated. In his forecasting exercises for the Norwegian economy, he finessed the problems raised in points (iii) to (v) by, respectively, not including a government expenditure balance (so that direct tax rates and government deficits are both endogenous and implicit), fixing exogenously values for exports and competitive imports and specifying total net investment exogenously (but allowing competitive mechanisms within the model to allocate total investment among sectors). These are practical assumptions in the context of a forecasting model and probably should be followed in similar cases in the future.

A specific problem of the Johansen approach is that a completely consistent base year specification of the economy (both in price and quantity terms) must be developed to provide initial conditions for the forecast differential equations. In practice, this may require fairly rough and ready assumptions and modifications of the basic data (which usually must be garnered from a variety of inconsistent sources in any case). A specific strength is that only a matrix inversion is required for the first-stage forecasts and not the application of relatively complicated nonlinear equation solving techniques. This can be a great advantage in the developing countries, where computer wizards who can make the last subsections's methods work are scarce. In addition, the basic methodology is easily adapted to a variety of comparative static exercises—for example, the analysis of the effects of tariff changes.[96] In view of its robustness and the range of problems with which it can deal, it is surprising that the Johansen technique has not been applied more widely.

## 6.3 Simulation Models

"Simulation" is not a precise word. Sometimes it is used to describe the process of making a number of solutions of a model in order to find out how it responds to variations in parameters and other changes in specification. Since one must go through this type of analysis to make sense out of any model, it is probably better to reserve the term "exploration" or "numerical experimentation" for this process.[97]

Another use of the word is to describe the numerical solution of dynamic models made up of differential (or difference) equations which are too complex for analytical solutions or simple qualitative analysis. In this sense, Johansen's models are simulations, as are exercises with the dynamic input-output model.

---

96. That is, one can analyze tariff changes in the fixed capital stock short run. See Taylor and Black [1974] for an example.

97. The latter term is used by Varsavsky and Calcagno [1971] for a series of planning exercises in Latin America.

In this subsection, we consider models with specifications richer than in the dynamic Leontief model. This implies that additional relationships must be specified to close the model and make the solution determinate. Evidently, one does not have to follow Johansen and close the model in a Walrasian way; many more possibilities exist. This lack of uniqueness also contributed to the imprecision of the word "simulation;" it almost seems that as many ways of closing models have been used as there are model builders. The following catalog is incomplete and only attempts to indicate the range of existing options.

(i) From a scientific point of view, the most interesting simulations are undoubtedly historical. A long span of time series data permits fairly complete "calibration" of the model[98] and invites counterfactual experiments of various kinds. An early, fruitful example is the input-output analysis of the differential impacts of supply and demand influences on Japanese growth by Chenery, Shishido, and Watanabe [1962]. Like many simulation exercises, these are based on the open Leontief model, with no real production restrictions.[99] A complete general equilibrium model was applied recently to Japanese historical statistics by Kelley, Williamson, and Cheetham [1972]. They use a two-sector growth model, which permits a number of comparative dynamic counterfactual experiments. Both of these groups of studies use some economic theory and give reasonably structured results. Although their lessons for policy makers are not direct, these exercises clearly add to the general understanding of an economy's long-run behavior patterns.[1]

(ii) In developed countries, econometric macromodels are intensively simulated as a means of forecasting. Such models will undoubtedly be used more and more in the developing countries, but they are now at a stage at best comparable to that in the United States when the Klein–Goldberger model was constructed in 1953. The reasons for this lag are manifold. Most developing countries do not have quarterly time series for the national

---

98. Simulation is in part an estimation technique, and "calibration" really means modifying parameters and functional specifications until the model "tracks" some set of time series to an intuitively pleasing degree of precision. Since most models typically have many more parameters than there are observations to track, and rely little on economic theory for a priori specification, they are underidentified—calibrations tend to be non-unique in inverse proportion to theoretical richness of the models.

99. That is, demand determines production through the input-output system. Production forecasts in turn lead to employment forecasts, through either fixed employment-output ratios or production functions in which capital stock has been determined by cumulation of investment. The well-known Cambridge forecast models (Stone [1964]) have the latter specification.

1. As discussed in Chapter V, simulations of changes in the income distribution have recently been undertaken in many developing countries. These have mostly been based on the Leontief closed model, but general equilibrium models of the type discussed in subsection 6.1 are on the way. See Adelman and Robinson [1973] and Adelman and Tyson [1973].

accounts so that all econometric models suffer from lack of degrees of freedom. Moreover, in many countries the reputation for accuracy of even the existing accounts is not exactly compelling. Using econometric methods to extract maximum information from minimally acceptable data is not necessarily the best use of scarce resources in a planning office. Perhaps more basic is the problem that there is very little theoretical guidance on how to construct econometric models in developing countries. Advanced country models are all basically Keynesian and deal with the effect on employment of changes in aggregate demand. This point of view reveals little about policy alternatives in countries facing extreme surplus labor, balance of payments rigidities, or both. Some interesting beginnings (e.g., Behrman [1972]) have been made in attacking these problems, but real success may await a new theoretical synthesis. In most places, it certainly awaits more data.

(iii) A third group of models (Holland and Gillespie [1963]; Kresge [1971]; and Luft [1968]) is something of a cross between typical econometric models used in developed countries and the theory-based models of the two preceding subsections. As in the econometric models, functional specification in these simulations is tailored (at least in part) to the institutional detail of the economy; however, they also resemble the general equilibrium models in that supply and demand effects both enter fully into the specification. The builders of these models might well argue that they represent the best of both worlds. A critic might reply that they really give the worst. The institutional detail may add little in the absence of statistical parameter estimation—even "t"-tests of coefficients add a degree of rigor to econometric estimation which is completely lacking in ad hoc calibrations. And, in comparison to the parsimonious specification of production functions and complete systems of demand equations in the neoclassical models, the simulation models' price-quantity demand curves and industry cost curves add parameters but detract from understanding general equilibrium effects. The debate between proponents of these different modelling techniques is partly theological and will not be resolved here, but it is probably fair to say that simulation models (as construed in this paragraph) have been neither so widely nor so fruitfully applied in developing countries as have general equilibrium models or their optimizing counterparts.

(iv) Finally, all the variants on the Leontief dynamic model discussed in section 3 really can be classed as simulations. As was stressed previously, these models are robust and readily applicable. Despite their somewhat limited frame of reference, they are undoubtedly the most directly useful form of "simulation" for planners in developing countries.

## 7. CONCLUSIONS

Summarizing the foregoing is obviously out of the question, so these conclusions will be kept as short as possible. The main thing to be stressed is that

multisectoral planning models, despite their evident drawbacks, actually are useful tools in practice. How far any particular planning office wants to push beyond applying the static, open input-output model is the relevant question, and it is probably one that should be asked in most places. After sufficient quantities of time, money, and high-powered talent have been invested in them, dynamic or optimizing models (or models of the type discussed in the last section) undoubtedly shed light on the problems of the real economy. Unfortunately, they do not answer the critical question: Do they provide enough illumination to justify their own construction? Only the shorthanded director of planning—perhaps aided by some of the observations in this volume—is in a position to make that investment decision.

## Appendix on Terminal Conditions

Much of the planning model literature is devoted to the formulation of terminal conditions, probably with inadequate justification. The fact is that rollover planning is the rule in all countries, with new medium-term plans being drawn up every three to five years. Indeed, people who formulate plans are *really* concerned only with the next two or three years, since projects and policies which for one reason or another are not interesting to the government but have to be included anyway can be conveniently stashed away in the last years of the plan and then ignored. In such circumstances, a practical man's enthusiasm for debate on how to specify post-terminal capital stocks thirty years hence is likely to be nil. If fairly arbitrary specification of terminal conditions has little effect on the next three years, that is all one really needs to know. The following points about how to set terminal conditions should be interpreted with this in mind.

In practice, setting terminal conditions amounts to specifying an investment theory for the last year of the plan in a dynamic model, since within-plan investments are taken care of by the model's optimization process. This has been done either by relating capital stocks to the flow variables in the last year[2] or by putting a valuation on post-terminal capital stocks (as in subsection 4.2). Both methods are discussed in the points that follow. The presentation is somewhat disjointed, listing many suggestions by many authors (including some untried proposals from the present writer). This reflects the state of the art. There is little agreement among model builders about how terminal conditions really ought to be set.

(i) The simplest possible approach is to tie capital in the last year of the plan to the levels of the flow variables of that year. Even in multisectoral models, this is often done only for *aggregates* such as total capital and consumption, so that in effect the economy is treated as having only one sector. There is a considerable literature on setting terminal conditions in finite horizon, one-sector optimizing models, and multisectoral programmers have relied extensively on this. One specification that is often used is based on the suggestion of Sen [1967] that terminal capital be tied to terminal consumption by a relationship such as[3]

$$C_T(t) = (1 - s)X(t) = (1 - s)K(t)/k \qquad (A.1)$$

where $s$ is an assumed saving rate and $k$ is the capital-output ratio. This

---

2. This is not the same as the specification discussed in subsection 4.1, where *investment* was related to other flow variables.

3. For simplicity, year $t$ throughout this appendix refers to the last year of the plan, so that year $t + 1$ is the first post-plan year.

method is simple, but, at least in *continuous* time models with malleable capital, it is not a satisfactory solution. The problem arises because when there are no terminal conditions in these models, capital stock will be run down to zero in the last instants of the plan to give maximal consumption. Condition (A.1) will not prevent this, since it is essentially only a constraint relating the *derivative* of the capital stock to its level and can be satisfied for an arbitrarily small stock level at the very end of the plan (Sydsaeter [1970]). This problem does not arise directly in models with lower bounds (usually zero) on net accumulation and discrete time, but the force of Sydsaeter's argument still makes complete acceptance of the method somewhat difficult.

(ii) Formulas such as (A.1) can be derived on other assumptions. For example, if it is assumed that consumption will grow at a rate $g$ beginning in the last year of the plan, then $C_T(t + \tau) = C_T(t)(1 + g)^\tau$ where ($\tau = 0, 1, 2, \ldots$) indicates time counting from year $t$. Substituting this expression into the accumulation equation for capital stock gives the difference equation:

$$K(t + \tau + 1) - K(t + \tau) = [K(t + \tau)/k] - C_T(t)(1 + g)^\tau$$

which has the solution:

$$K(t + \tau) = \frac{C_T(t)}{(1/k) - g}(1 + g)^\tau, \quad \tau = 0, 1, 2, \ldots \qquad (A.2)$$

For $\tau = 0$, this reduces to $K(t) = C_T(t)/[(1/k) - g]$, a relationship which could be used in place of (A.1). This specification is perhaps more interesting than (A.1), for the foregoing derivation is exactly the same as the one underlying the particular solution (3.7) to the Leontief dynamic model. The multisectoral generalization of (A.2) is

$$K(t + \tau) = H(I - A - gH)^{-1}\xi C_T(t)(1 + g)^\tau = \Phi C_T(t)(1 + g)^\tau,$$
$$\tau = 0, 1, 2, \ldots, \quad (A.3)$$

where the vector $\Phi$ is defined by the second equality and the other notation is as in sections 3, 4, and 5.[4]

(iii) Manne ([1970] and [1973a]) and members of the *CELP* team (Eckaus and Parikh [1968]) use a formulation similar to (A.3) with $\tau = 0$ as a constraint on capital stocks in the terminal year, except that separate post-terminal growth rates for different components of final demand are permitted. In detail, this approach is implemented by writing commodity balances (ignoring trade) in the first post-plan year in the form

$$(I - A)X(t + 1) = \xi C_T(t + 1) + BD(t + 1).$$

If we continue to assume that $C_T(t + \tau) = C_T(t)(1 + g)^\tau$, and also postulate

---

4. Throughout this appendix we assume, for simplicity, that the matrix $H$ is of full rank.

that investment by destination grows at a constant rate $n$, $D(t + \tau) = D(t)(1 + n)^{\tau}$, then we have, after appropriate substitution,

$$(I - A)X(t + 1) = \xi C_T(t)(1 + g) + BD(t)(1 + n).$$

If $X(t + 1) = X(t) + \hat{k}^{-1}D(t)$, we finally derive

$$[(I - A)\hat{k}^{-1} - B(1 + n)]D(t) = \xi C_T(t)(1 + g) - (I - A)X(t), \quad \text{(A.4)}$$

which can be solved for $D(t)$. Note that even though (A.4) is a material balance equation set for year $t + 1$, all of its variables refer to year $t$ so that it acts as an effective constraint on investment in the final plan year.

(iv) We now turn to the method of setting terminal conditions in which some valuation of post-terminal capital stocks is included in the objective function, as summarized in Tables 2 and 4. The simplest possible specification along these lines is actually based on a modification of Table 2: drop $\bar{P}'(t)K(t + 1)$ from the objective function and add lower bound constraints of the form $K(t + 1) \geq \bar{K}(t + 1)$. These constraints will generate shadow prices (which we can call $\bar{P}'(t)$), and the story goes as before. The trick is to guess appropriate post-terminal levels of the capital stocks. One approach has been to assume growth rates of capital stocks between years zero and $t + 1$, and use these to figure out the $\bar{K}(t + 1)$. Another method might be to specify exogenously some "desired" level of *post*-terminal consumption $C_T(t + 1)$. Then application of (A.3) will give a vector of desired post-terminal capital stocks.

(v) One way of implementing the actual Table 2 specification can be illustrated if we revert for a moment to the one-sector specification, in which equations such as (A.1) and (A.2) permit valuation of the scalar post-terminal capital stock via valuation of post-terminal consumption $C_T(t + 1)$. A welfare weight $\omega$ is assigned to $C_T(t + 1)$ in the objective function, and, by (A.2), this is equivalent to putting a valuation of $\omega k/(1 - kg)$ on post-terminal capital stock. One way to calculate $\omega$ is as the discounted value of consumption in the immediately post-terminal year, $\omega = (1 + \rho)^{-1}$, where $\rho$ is a social rate of discount.[5] Another approach is to include the discounted value of the entire stream of post-terminal consumption (still growing at a constant rate $g$) in the objective function:

$$\omega = (1 + \rho)^{-1} \sum_{i=0}^{\infty} [(1 + g)/(1 + \rho)]^i.$$

This method (perhaps first used by Chenery and MacEwan [1966]) evidently gives a much greater weight to $K(t + 1)$ than simple discounting of $C_T(t + 1)$.

---

5. Choice of $\rho$ leads into a huge literature in investment project analysis which cannot be summarized here. Many linear programmers seem to elect values ranging between 5 and 10 percent but provide little justification for their choice.

For a model with many time periods this may be of little import, since the objective function weight for post-terminal consumption would itself be heavily discounted. Sensitivity analysis in Westphal [1971], Chapter 6, roughly supports this conjecture.

(vi) The need to specify some relationship between the capital stock *vector* and the scalar $C_T(t + 1)$ prohibits easy generalization of this one-sector method to multisectoral models, because the multiplier $k/(1 - kg)$ does not have an immediate analog when there are many capital goods.[6] One possible approach is to note that from (A.3), $K_i(t + 1) = \Phi_i C_T(t + 1)$, $i = 1, 2, \ldots, n$. Each component of the capital stock vector is proportional to post-terminal consumption, and the proportionality factors can be interpreted as "ratios" of a capital-output matrix and a matrix of "consumption propensities" permitted by post-terminal balanced growth. On the basis of this analogy to the one-sector case we may set the capital stock valuations $\bar{P}_i(t) = \omega \Phi_i$. Another approach could be based on the formula for goods prices in the first year of post-terminal balanced growth,

$$P'(t + 1) = [\lambda'(I - A - gH)^{-1}\xi]^{-1}\lambda'(I - A - gH)^{-1}, \qquad (A.5)$$

i.e., the direct and indirect labor costs per unit of output of each good in balanced growth, divided by direct and indirect labor costs of the consumption demand basket.[7] Multiplying these prices by one plus the growth rate (= interest rate), $g$ would provide a set of period $t$ prices which could be used for the $\bar{P}'(t)$. Both these methods have some appeal, although as far as I know they have not been tried in practice.

(vii) Finally, one can use optimal growth theory to find terminal capital stock targets. The method is to compute the balanced growth state that would be optimal if one were on it—a generalization of the Golden Rule. One would then maximize utility over a finite horizon, subject to the condition that the economy reach the optimal balanced growth path at the end of the planning period. This is reviewed thoroughly in the one-sector context by Mirrlees and Stern [1972]. In a multisectoral planning model with consumption dependent on value added, Murukami, Tokoyama, and Tsukui [1970]

---

6. Bruno, Dougherty, and Fraenkel [1970] note the problem, and end up setting each $\bar{F}_i(t)$ equal to $(1 + \rho)^{-1}$, i.e., they discount capital stock levels, not consumption.

7. This relationship can be derived by noting that the price system corresponding to the balanced growth (at rate $g$) particular solution of the dynamic Leontief model must be

$$P(t + 1 + \tau) = w(t + 1)(1 + g)^{t+1-\tau}\lambda'(I - A - gH)^{-1}, \quad \tau = 0, 1, 2, 3, \ldots.$$

Moreover, from the Golden Rule applied to year $t + 1$, we derive

$$w(t + 1)\bar{L}(t + 1) = w(t + 1)\lambda' X(t + 1) = w(t + 1)\lambda'(I - A - gH)^{-1}\xi C_T(t + 1)$$
$$= P'(t + 1)\xi C_T(t + 1) = C_T(t + 1).$$

This chain of equalities implies that $w(t + 1) = [\lambda'(I - A - gH)^{-1}\xi]^{-1}$ and substitution into the difference equation for the prices (with $\tau = 0$) gives (A.5).

use turnpike theory to find the final-year balanced vector of outputs and then maximize total output to these proportions. Convergence to the turnpike during the plan is reported to be rapid. Ginsburgh and Waelbroeck [1974] discuss finite programming approximations to post-terminal conditions of this type.

Chapter IV

# QUANTITATIVE FOUNDATIONS AND IMPLICATIONS OF PLANNING PROCESSES

TSUNEHIKO WATANABE

## 1. INTRODUCTION

In this chapter we are concerned with the quantitative or numerical foundations of planning; that is, the adequacy and accuracy of the social and economic data base. It is important to review systematically the relationships between the planning process and quantitative methods for several reasons. First of all, there have been considerable lags between the theoretical development of planning models and their operational implementation in the economies of developing countries. In attempting to explain this, the lack of appropriate data for, and credible results from, planning techniques is one of the crucial features to be examined. Planners can scarcely expect wide support from either the private sector or governmental agencies unless they can provide a quantitatively well-founded empirical picture of the national economy. This, in turn, requires the organization of a good data system.

Secondly, all economy-wide plans have to contain quantitatively consistent planning indices, as well as some analysis of trade-offs, possibly through optimization. If these are lacking, the plan may be easily sidetracked by alliances between different government agencies and pressure groups—as will be shown through examples below. A good data system is one of the prerequisites for formulating consistent plan indices (along with theoretical and technical considerations, as discussed in other chapters); a fundamental difficulty faced by developing country planners has been a lack of reliable data and the ability to process them adequately.

Lastly, improved quantitative foundations may facilitate better applications of planning and programming techniques than otherwise might be achieved. For example, some of the econometric techniques that have been utilized in the national planning in several developed countries could not be recommended if only poorly compiled data were available; with poor data, the straightforward use of these techniques might often produce misleading results.[1]

---

1. An example may be found in the use of the Cobb–Douglas production function. Even with a statistically good correlation coefficient, which can very often be obtained from poor quality data (especially for capital stock), it is very risky to draw specific quantitative conclusions about potential output of the national economy using the function's estimated parameters when the data underlying the estimation do not inspire much confidence.

Although major parts of this chapter are devoted to rather technical appraisals of the data system and its processing, e.g., data reliability, data, revision, the pros and cons of using borrowed data, and so on, it is useful to begin with a discussion of the quantitative foundations of different planning techniques, particularly in regard to the working of the planning process and the use of models to assure internal consistency of both plan productions and their data base.[2] Sections 2 to 4 deal with how quantitative methods are used by the planner, while sections 5 to 10 discuss data requirements of different modelling techniques and appropriate statistical sources.

## 2. THE COORDINATING ROLE OF THE PLANNER

As was emphasized in Chapters I and II, the planning process is an accumulation or repetition of a government's coordinating efforts among a large number of different economic and social units, working together to produce a desirable pattern of national management of the society concerned. For this attempt to be successful, a common understanding of the process of planning is necessary. A dialogue between government planners, policy makers, and other technicians and representatives of important economic and social units participating in the process of plan building is often mentioned as one of the most important prerequisites of the plan and its implementing policies on a real-world economy.

The coordinating effort is necessarily a time consuming and frustrating job for the planning office, even though it is absolutely essential. This problem may become more acute in the following situations: (i) where the planning office is newly organized in relation to other governmental agencies (producing conflict between newer and older organizations over power configurations); (ii) where actual implementation of the plan is in the hands of other government agencies, *not* the planning office (as is likely to be the case in most countries); (iii) where financial aggregates such as the money supply and the level of government spending are determined by agencies differing from the planning office in terms of both institutional prerogatives and accepted tenets for policy formation (e.g., the rule of balanced budgets in annual terms might be strongly supported *and* applied by a powerful finance ministry not inclined to consider the long-term developmental implications of its policies); and, (iv) where reliable and accurate information on individual production processes, especially in private sectors, is not available to the planning office (in practice, the available information may reduce to some kind of weighted average figures for industry as a whole, or for a group of enterprises, unless considerable funds have been spent for collecting the necessary information).[3]

---

2. Discussions of the planning process also appear in Chapters I and II.

3. Subsection 4.4 of Chapter XI shows clearly why such information can be completely misleading at the national level.

Effective remedies for these problems may be achieved to some extent through institutional reorganization. For example, the creation of a coordination division in the planning office, with most of its staff transferred from other existing governmental agencies, might be an important reform. Another important requirement for the planning office is to improve its ability to influence or persuade other organizations and their personnel regarding plan indices. This ability can be increased in several ways, although the typical long-run procedure would be through educational efforts.[4] Well-prepared quantitative foundations of the plan are a great help in this effort. They reinforce the planner's arguments in the process of plan building, especially if they maintain nationally consistent characteristics. In addition, well-prepared quantitative foundations can help significantly to reduce the time required in the planning process, which itself is a kind of trial and error attempt to reach desired and mutually acceptable targets.

## 3. QUANTITATIVE FOUNDATIONS FOR PLANNING

A well-prepared quantitative foundation can be characterized as follows. First, it has to be derived from a good data system,[5] since poor data may easily produce confusing implications which could distort the planning process. Forecasting and the monitoring of short-term adjustments depend upon a precise and rapid data collection and processing system. Decisions based upon poor forecasts might produce much worse effects than those based on a purely qualitative foundation. For example, poor performance of national economic projections, if they are repeated for a considerable period, would eventually destroy the credibility of a plan.

Second, a well-prepared quantitative foundation of the planning process should use appropriate model formulations with proper linkages to operational policy instruments. For example, the Ministry of Finance and the Central Bank are concerned generally with money variables, such as the surplus of deficit in the government budget and the balance of payments; they may not consider a planning model constructed only with constant prices and other real variables to be well-prepared. Also, an agency which is engaged primarily in short-term policy adjustment may not be sufficiently

---

4. Here educational efforts may imply the following two elements: (i) the first corresponds to the learning-by-operation, where during the course of dialogue, participants may come to have better knowledge about planning techniques, the nature of interdependence in the economy, the usefulness of conditional forecasting, and so forth; (ii) the second corresponds to a more formal type of education, such as maintenance of an advanced training institution on planning. See, for example, the French experience in Cohen [1969].

5. Several international organizations have sustained efforts to impose their methods of statistical collection and inference in developing countries, often providing technical assistance to improve the collection of demographic, industrial, and agricultural census, employment statistics, price and wage data, trade statistics, and so on, which all contribute to a unified national income accounting system. See, for example, United Nations [1968].

persuaded by a long-term plan that ignores intermediate considerations. For this reason, planners often apply a variety of models requiring data valid for different periods of time, reflecting the nature of the planning framework (real-term based, money-term based, or a mixture), the degree of openness of the economy (foreign trade and capital flows), and the dominant problems to be evaluated by the quantitative plan (such as growth, sectoral investment, unemployment, income distribution).

Finally, a well-prepared quantitative foundation has to have considerable flexibility in order to shed light on possible trade-offs under different combinations of targets and constraints. This is mainly due to the fact that coordination in the planning process, at least from the viewpoint of its quantitative foundations, can usually be achieved by performing a sizable number of quantitative experiments with different sets of targets, instruments, and constraints, such as higher growth with more foreign aid or lower growth with considerable absorption of unemployment. In order to perform these experiments effectively, numerical and computational modifications of the planning models and alternative specifications of structural relationships must be attempted, in response to suggestions made by other governmental agencies and responsible private participants. In general, this kind of flexibility can be maintained only by the preparation of different types of models and data, which must be mutually consistent. This implies that the planning office may have to study many aspects of a national economy simultaneously, which complicates the data manipulation and consistency requirements.

## 4. FORECASTING, CONSISTENCY, AND OPTIMIZATION MODELS

Two important aspects of the quantitative foundation of the planning process are economy-wide planning models and their corresponding data requirements. The theoretical nature and limitations of economy-wide planning models have been reviewed in Chapter III; their quantitative applicability and limitations are discussed here.

Applied planning models have to be able to deal with a wide variety of questions about the economy. Broadly speaking, these can be classified under two headings—how to manage demand and how to manage supply.[6] Demand management relates mostly to short-term problems, while supply management is mostly related to long-term planning. In addition to this difference in the planning period, the administrative responsibility of demand management is usually undertaken by the Ministry of Finance and the Central Bank, since most of the relevant policy instruments are money-based variables such as changes in the discount rate, the supply of money, government expenditures, and government revenues. On the other hand, supply management is more

---

6. A general discussion of this dichotomy is found in Tinbergen [1964] and Lewis [1966]. For a country example, see Japan, Economic Planning Agency [1965a].

concerned with technology-oriented or physical variables. One of the most important requirements of national planning is to maintain consistency between demand and supply management, despite the fact that in particular models emphasis is usually placed on one or the other (e.g., a short-run demand model may presume some predetermined rate of potential output growth, determined from long-term considerations). For this reason, the planning office probably should prepare at least two kinds of economy-wide planning models, one demand oriented (short term) and the other supply oriented (long term).

The role of these two models in the planning process will be to supply a quantitative basis for the dialogue between planners and the other participants. In order to be useful for this purpose, these models may have to fulfill at least the following three functions: forecasting, consistency, and optimization. Economic (and possibly social) forecasts are frequently required in economy-wide planning in order to estimate feasible medium- or long-term development patterns. In addition, short-term economic forecasts may also be needed in order to make short-term economic policies, such as stabilization measures, effective. In the planning process, several alternative forecasts, based on different sets of exogenous and policy variables, are usually desirable. These alternatives then serve as a good point of departure for further detailed dialogue. In some cases, the policy alternative tests will be directly requested by a special group, such as the Ministry of Finance.

Consistency in economy-wide planning and programming is usually understood in terms of economically or technologically feasible relationships between disaggregated or sectoral breakdowns and national aggregates, but it can also be interpreted in a broader sense. For example, lack of "technological consistency" may originate from structural characteristics of developing economies. During the last several decades there has been a common belief that active use of foreign (advanced) technologies would be a great help in promoting rapid economic development. Following this conjecture, the capital-labor mix of the best-practice techniques developed in advanced countries might be introduced into sectoral or national planning. In most cases, however, the use of these techniques is inconsistent with prevailing structural characteristics. That is, the skilled labor needed in using best-practice techniques effectively is generally quite scarce in developing nations; at the same time, these techniques frequently require relatively small inputs of unskilled labor and would lead to further problems of unemployment and underemployment. Since it is rarely desirable to pursue a single policy objective, such as rapid industrialization in this case, the above stated possible side effects should not be overlooked by the planning office.

Lastly, planning based on both demand-oriented and supply-oriented models may be enriched by putting the analysis in an optimizing framework. One of the largest payoffs from optimization in planning models comes in the

115

form of assessments of possible trade-offs and of changes in efficient frontiers derived from the models.[7] This information may be especially important for developing economies, where prevailing relative price differentials from inadequately functioning markets might not provide useful guidelines for decentralized decision making.

We now present an illustrative example of the use of quantitative planning models in the planning process. Needless to say, the present example is only one way of using quantitative models.[8] The process described is heavily dependent upon appropriate and reliable data to be discussed in the next section.

The first task of the planning office will be to prepare some estimates of the rate of expansion in national productive capacity. Estimates derived from a Harrod–Domar model are typical at this stage. As has been indicated in Chapter III, the Harrod–Domar estimate of growth is sensitive to the values assumed for the expected rate of growth of the labor force, the rate of growth of productivity, the rate of capital stock depreciation, the rate of saving, and the incremental capital-output ratio. The planning office, therefore, should indicate the feasibility of these several alternative estimates of the rate of growth; for example, it should investigate whether the assumed range of variation in the capital-output ratio is reasonable both historically and internationally.

This process will likely stimulate discussion among the various agents involved in the planning process. For example, the Ministry of Finance may criticize the Harrod–Domar growth estimates because their assumed saving behavior seems too optimistic, especially from the viewpoint of the government budget. The Ministry of Industry may also say that the assumed incremental capital-output ratios appear too low from the viewpoint of possible future technological change. From these reactions and those of other governmental agencies and professional people, the planning office may start another round of experimentation, based on a recalculation of the Harrod–Domar estimates but using a different set of values for such things as the incremental capital-output ratios and the saving rate, or by experimenting with another model such as a neoclassical growth model, or a two-gap model. The revised estimates would be discussed by the interested parties and the process repeated until a "tentative" agreement on the rate of potential growth is eventually reached.

Having established, for working purposes, a "tentative" agreement on the rate of potential aggregate growth, the planning office should next take into consideration other important aspects of growth such as short-term demand adjustments and changes in sectoral production. The assumed rate of potential

---

7. For fuller discussions of optimizations, see Chapters III, VIII, and IX.

8. The example closely resembles the experience of Japan and several of the more developed countries.

growth will have to be introduced into final demand projections which feed into input-output studies to derive intermediate demand. Total demand is then compared with domestic supply (especially imports). Sectoral or industry experts may start their active participation at this stage by providing alternative estimates of sectoral demand and supply either using formal models or their own expert knowledge. The aggregate of these sectoral estimates will deviate, in general, from the level of national intermediate demand and supply as computed from the economy-wide model.[9] The planning office will then attempt to provide consistent forecasts incorporating these independent estimates, perhaps by revising the input-output model. The point is that quantitative experimentation at this stage might become very complicated and time consuming if the underlying statistical information is of poor quality. Sometimes it may be impossible at this point to produce a unique solution involving agreement among all the sectoral input's productions. Even so, the planning office should proceed since the subsequent stages of the planning process are designed to produce revisions which result in consistent plans.

Assuming general consistency has been achieved between a proposed national rate of growth and the corresponding national demand and sectoral growth rates, the planning office will begin to reassess these rates of growth in terms of various policy questions. These include: (i) what will happen to these rates of growth if other important policy considerations such as a high level of employment, price stability, balance of payments equilibrium, or desirable income distribution are emphasized; (ii) what will be the government expenditures required, especially public sector investment during the planning period, and is this amount compatible with the financial constraints of the economy concerned; (iii) what will be an appropriate relationship between medium- or long-term supply management and necessary short-term demand adjustments; and, (iv) what will be the relationships between the positive considerations discussed above and normative plans which may be derived from an optimization model?

In general, these reassessments will cause the planning office to extend the planning dialogue and may eventually require the repetition of the entire quantitative preparations of the plan. Although repetition of quantitative preparation and experimentation may not be pursued operationally exactly as outlined above, due to the lack of proper statistical information, computer

---

9. This can happen for several reasons. The planning office sectoral estimates may be based on averages of data from several firms and thus not be representative of actual technology. (The planners may not have enough power to pry detailed technological data out of the private sector, even if they want to.) Or the sectoral forecasts may be based on engineering or physical information, perhaps of foreign origin for new technologies at least, which are inconsistent with money-based sectoral aggregates. Finally, production sectors often represent significant concentrations of economic power, and they may be able to force *their* growth forecasts on the planners, even if the latter know they are inconsistent in some way.

facilities, or skilled man-power in most less developed economies, it is important for a planning office to recognize that the planning process itself will generate new sources of information which will be validated as they are included in a consistent quantitative framework.

## 5. THE DATA SYSTEM: SOURCES AND FORECASTING MODELS

In economic studies, there are three different kinds of data available—time series, cross-section, and cross-country. Time series data, in principle, are generated from long-run historical observations, while the latter two data are obtained from variations among different economic units within very short time periods. The economic and statistical implications of various data, however, do not depend solely upon differences in observation periods. For example, cross-section data on consumption, based on family budget surveys for different income groups, may bring out more significant structural changes than data based on a 15-year time series. This is because differences in present consumption expenditures observed from a family budget survey reflect much larger income variations than are likely to occur in a 15-year period.

In other words, the long-run implications of structural change may be better revealed by cross-section than time series data. This might also hold for cross-country data, although there are additional problems with respect to data comparability.[10] Also, the degree of statistical variation in the observed samples, one of the most important prerequisites for effectively applying present econometric techniques, is generally smaller in time series than that in the other two kinds of data.

On the other hand, the availability of cross-section data (such as a family budget survey or an industrial census by size of firm), is usually limited because cross-sectional information on some important economic variables is quite difficult to collect.[11] For example, appropriate price data for cross-section estimates of consumption functions are very hard to derive. Systematically compiled cross-country data have become more readily available recently through the continuous efforts maintained by international organizations (such as the UN, FAO, ILO, IMF, and IBRD). The coverage and availability of cross-country data, however, are generally more limited than those of the other two kinds of data. This is especially true if we pay due attention to the problem of appropriate international conversion rates.[12]

Let us now discuss the nature and limitations of available data from the viewpoint of forecasting. The common statistical techniques applied for economic forecasting (short-, medium-, and long-term) are usually based on

10. The best examples can be found in Houthakker [1957], and Lluch and Powell [1973].

11. Sometimes cross-section data reduce to single-point estimates. This is often the case with input-output matrices or capital-output ratios.

12. For discussions of international conversion rates, see Gilbert and Kravis [1954], David [1972, 1973], and Balassa [1973].

time series data, especially in developed economies. Economic forecasts based upon cross-section and cross-country data have not been used extensively in developed countries.[13] In the case of developing economies, the reliability of time series data is generally quite poor, as is well known, although most developing countries have already started to compile national income accounts following broadly the UN [1968] standards.

With a relatively short period of time series observations in national income accounts and relatively poor quality statistical information, it would be useful to construct a simple aggregate economic model and to use it for *ex post* forecasting in order to improve data reliability, especially of national income accounts. A simple aggregate economic model may include a consumption function, an investment function, an import function, and related identity equations. The consumption function may be specified as a function of income variables (e.g., disposable income, national income or GDP) and other variables such as the size of population. If the model is viewed as demand oriented, the investment function may be described as the function of changes in output variables (e.g., GDP or some form of capacity utilization), exogenous government investment (including foreign investment), and other related variables; where estimates of the existing capital stock are available, they should also be added. The import function could be specified as a function of output variables (e.g., GDP or some form of capacity) and other related variables such as relative prices or changes in foreign trade indicators.[14]

*Ex post* forecasts derived from a simple aggregate model may then be used fruitfully for improvements in data reliability. For example, the cross-section estimates of income elasticity with respect to consumption expenditures, which might be derived from family budget studies, may be used to test the estimated consumption function. The international comparative studies on consumption expenditures (Houthakker [1957], Weisskoff [1971], Lluch and Powell [1973], and Lluch and Williams [1973]) may also provide useful checks. Values of impact multipliers which can be calculated from *ex post* forecasts may also provide a reasonable basis for judgment of data reliability. For example, whether or not the addition of an extra unit of government investment would generate a reasonable amount of direct and indirect increase in total output (e.g., GDP) may be used in systematically assessing the data.

Simple aggregate economic model building might not be useful for short-term *ex ante* forecasting, since the dualistic nature of developing countries is a significant barrier to drawing meaningful forecasts from this kind of model. For example a mixture of fundamentally different technologies, traditional

---

13. For example, Chenery's studies on the patterns of economic growth [1960], which use cross-country data to a considerable extent, have been utilized mostly in the context of development studies, even though they may provide an appropriate methodology for projecting possible structural changes in the production system in some of developed countries.

14. For an example of this approach to Korea, see Adelman [1969].

(labor-using) and modern (labor-saving), may generate biased forecasts for levels of output, employment, or imports. These considerations would lead to the use of another type of analysis, such as the Leontief input-output model, for forecasting purposes.

In principle, input-output statistics should not be viewed as time series data. Even though the compilation of an input-output table may be expensive and time consuming, its usefulness for assessing economy-wide data reliability might be greater than that from applying simple macroeconomic models, because the input-output statistics will reveal useful information about sectoral structure. For example, the direct and indirect requirements of sectoral production for a given bill of final demand may be compared with the existing capacity of domestic production in the key sectors. This would be useful in examining the consistency of disaggregated data.[15]

Although both simple macroeconomic models and input-output models may be more useful in assessing data reliability through *ex post* forecasting than through *ex ante* forecasting, future economic projections are an important application of economy-wide planning models. Therefore it may be worthwhile to discuss a feasible method for applying national income and input-output statistics in making these projections. As has been pointed out above, predictability itself sometimes may be poorer using these formal models than when using more naive types of forecasts such as a simple blowup of GNP components or sectoral output levels.[16] However, one of the more important gains from attempting to use models to make forecasts lies in the ability to draw implications from the model's solution regarding structural interdependence in the economy. Furthermore, the appropriate sensitivity analyses which are required in order to test the feasibility of economic planning can only be made within a modelling framework.

## 6. The Data System: Consistency Models

The second aspect of the data system concerns consistency. Although the consistency problem may have to be examined first with regard to qualitative or theoretical assessments of national planning and programming, quantitative procedures which could satisfy this criterion are desirable and should be prepared, especially with respect to the necessary data system. Important basic properties for a consistent data system would include the following:

(i) A system of national income accounts, built around an interindustry flow table, is the most desirable format for data compilation. However, maintenance of a fully articulated national accounting system at a very detailed level may not be necessary. For example, detailed accounts of "Household and Private Nonprofit Institutions" including taxes, transfers,

---

15. For a fuller discussion, see Chenery and Clark [1959] or Chapter V.
16. See, for example, Arrow and Hoffenberg [1959], and Hatanaka [1960].

and income from property could be replaced with a simple account such as private consumption expenditure and savings versus compensation of employees and other personal income. Similarly, consistency requirements may be satisfied by accounts for net national income at factor cost by industry (preferably with the same sectoral classification as the input-output table) instead of a very detailed set of income accounts.

(ii) The accounting system should be based on as many independent sources of data as possible, to assure its internal consistency. For example, personal consumption in developing countries is often estimated as a residual, gross product less the sum of investment, government expenditure, and the trade surplus. Since, for analytical purposes, a residual estimate of consumption is useless, it should be supplemented by independent data on consumer expenditures—from household surveys, for example.

(iii) Stratification of data often helps immensely in gaining insights into the economy. For example, an industrial census classified by firm size, the nature of technology and organization (modern versus traditional), labor requirements (skilled versus unskilled) and the vintage and origin (national versus foreign) of the capital stock should be compiled, even if only every five years. Also, annual family budget surveys should be classified according to such things as region, income class, and type of work to give highly useful demographic and income distribution information.

(iv) Data on foreign trade, especially commodity statistics, should be prepared using the same sectoral classification as the domestic input-output breakdowns. In general, industrial census and other production data are collected on the basis of the ISIC (International Standard of Industrial Classification) or its variants, while trade statistics are based on the SITC (Standard International Trade Classification). These two schemes differ to a considerable extent, which may in turn lead to some inconsistency in estimates of sectoral demands and supplies.[17]

(v) One of the most difficult obstacles in maintaining quantitative consistency between the sectoral levels and national aggregates may come from the nonexistence or poor quality of price indices. There are several types of prices used in the valuation of economic activities. For example, producer's price and purchaser's price, c.i.f. and f.o.b. prices, market price and factor cost, with or without excise taxes, and tariffs are all suitable in different cases. The system of price indices and their mutual relationships, therefore, cannot be easily synthesized. Furthermore, price indices in developing nations may frequently be disturbed by regional autonomies and differences which are aggregated into national indices. The planning office may have to devote considerable effort to collecting appropriate price data, and in this respect,

---

17. It may not be necessary to discard one of these two classifications, since both classifications may be useful, especially for the purpose of checking the data reliability. See also the relevant discussion in Chapter VI.

the use of well-designed sampling surveys or of foreign data might be strongly recommended.[18]

(vi) The last consistency problem involves the inclusion of socio-economic information based upon regional and demographic breakdowns. Statistics on education, income distribution, regional rates of unemployment, and vital statistics are often needed. These data may reveal differences in structural characteristics of the society which can be used to reduce the gap between technically advanced plan formulation and the administrative procedures necessary for its implementation.

## 7. THE DATA SYSTEM: OPTIMIZATION MODELS

The appropriate data system for optimization models can be studied from the following two viewpoints: (i) the data required in the stage of model building, and (ii) that needed for assessing the model's results. The former can be divided into information about (a) the objective function and (b) data for structural parameters and constraints. Estimates for (b) are in most cases supplied through data based on physical or technological information. These include input-output coefficients, sectoral capital-output ratios, sectoral labor-coefficients, the levels of required production, and the available amount of capital and labor stocks. Here, it is not crucial to determine each coefficient uniquely because optimization models have considerable degrees of freedom in varying supply and demand patterns. For example, both existing input-output coefficients and advanced (new alternatives) technical coefficients can be included simultaneously in a programming model. Here, the use of data generated in advanced economies is to a considerable extent justified. The technological feasibility of using borrowed production techniques for planning has to be carefully examined ahead of time; otherwise inconsistencies with actual structural characteristics may emerge. Nevertheless, the collection of detailed technological data, both from domestic and foreign sources, is quite desirable.

The information needed to formulate objective functions will usually be a mixture of objectively observed data with subjective or policy-determined data. For example, if the objective function to be maximized over a specified planning period is the discounted sum of utility of consumption per capita, estimates of population size would correspond to the objectively observed data, while the determination of the time discount rate and elasticities of marginal utility would reflect the subjective judgments revealed during the planning process.

Although economy-wide optimization models should not be assessed solely

---

18. A problem that arises in inflationary economies is that the finance ministry may wish to misconstrue or even alter price data for political purposes and/or to hold down wage demands by government employees. A planning office or statistical office may lack sufficient power to put an end to this sort of interference with its data source.

through examination of their computed shadow prices, it is often important to attempt such an evaluation.[19] For example, an optimizing model may indicate, through its dual solution, that the two key scarce resources over the next 10 years will be foreign exchange and skilled labor. From the viewpoint of quantitative judgments of trade-offs, differences between various runs of the model using alternative sets of constraints, objective functions, and structural parameters may be very important.

## 8. DATA UPDATING

An appropriate data system for economy-wide planning would have to contain a mechanism for updating or revising existing data—or in other words, the use of statistical techniques to supplement and check the estimates made by national income accounts. There are three alternative approaches to this task.

(i) First, a properly designed sampling survey, probably small in size, could be used in investigating significant changes of existing information. For example, changes in inventory stocks of important raw materials, including agricultural products, could be estimated annually or quarterly using a stratified sampling procedure. More specifically, the sampling ratio for important economic units such as large firms or special regions or districts could be unity, while smaller sampling ratios might be applied for other units in a systematic sampling procedure. Even though information based on sampling procedures might be fragmental, its systematic usage might be sufficient for making many of the needed data revisions.

(ii) Second, various statistical techniques, particularly simple regression estimates, can be applied to updating. In this case, the important criteria are purely statistical, including coefficients of determination adjusted by the degrees of freedom and acceptable $t$-values for the estimated coefficients, rather than theoretical. For example, private consumption expenditures in the national income accounts may be updated by the use of a simple regression such as:

$$P \cdot C = \alpha_0 + \alpha_1 X,$$

where, $P \cdot C$ = private consumption expenditures in the national income accounts (valued at current prices) and, $X$ = the total amount of current consumption reported in the family budget survey, plus governmental consumption expenditures from the budget (also valued at current prices). Theoretically speaking, this regression equation may not be very satisfactory, since no relative price terms are included; however, if the statistical fit is good, it may yield quite satisfactory approximations. The fundamental idea in this updating procedure is the use of purely statistical techniques without paying too close attention to theoretical properties.

---

19. For a more complete discussion of this process, see Chapter VIII.

Updating may also have to be extended to matrix-type data, such as the input-output table. Since most input-output matrices usually are at least of $10 \times 10$ size, and frequently much larger, the updating procedure may have to handle at least 50 or more individual coefficients. If the updating procedure were applied coefficient by coefficient, it would be almost impossible to complete without consuming huge amounts of time and human resources. Even though it is advisable to use specific updating devices for important key coefficients, it is also desirable to have an updating device for the input-output matrix as a whole. The RAS row and column correction technique, developed by Stone and others, seems best for this purpose.[20]

(iii) Lastly, updating devices with closer links to economic theory, such as econometric model building, can be utilized. During the last decade advanced countries have made considerable progress with econometric model building, especially in connection with national economic planning and policy analysis.[21] Although it may be too early to say that econometric model building, which is typically based on a Keynesian theory of national income determination, is widely applicable for structural analysis in developing countries, it might be a useful technique for updating data. The results based on econometric models could be more useful than those derived from purely statistical techniques because econometric models can handle economic interdependence and simultaneous relationships explicitly. (It is not necessary to construct econometric models using Keynesian orthodoxy, but alternatives are rare.)

## 9. BORROWED DATA

As a procedure for estimating necessary statistics that are not domestically available, borrowed data do play a useful role. Their use in planning has often been understood as analogous to the use of borrowed technology in the process of industrialization. The borrowed data are usually quantitative information relating to technologically or economically well-established relationships in some other (usually advanced) nation's experience. For example, some engineering data on production processes are impossible to obtain in developing countries simply because these technologies themselves have not been utilized so far (even though the planning authority may be considering their adoption within the near future). Thus, one category of borrowed data may be a set of quantitative (and qualitative) information which is not available but whose need may be quite pressing. Most data in this category relate to engineering processes in narrowly defined production activities.

A second category of borrowed data is information that is not only technology-oriented but also contains some important economic relations. A representative example in this category would be capital-output ratios in various manufacturing sectors. Capital-output ratios, in a statistical sense, are weighted

20. For descriptions of the RAS method, see Bacharach [1970].
21. See, for example, the work on Project LINK (Ball [1973]).

averages of the capital-output coefficients of individual production activities, where the weights are derived from each unit's share of domestic supply. Therefore, in borrowing data of this kind, there would be two problems relating to the appropriateness of the engineering information as well as the economic weighting scheme. As noted earlier, borrowing engineering information may be justified since much of this information is missing in a developing country; but, borrowing the economic weights will have to be examined quite carefully, since the structural characteristics in the two economies may be entirely different. Table 1 illustrates the problem. American capital-output ratios of various manufacturing sectors in 1947 and two sets of Japanese capital-output ratios using corresponding classifications for 1955 are compared.[22] The two

**Table 1: Capital-Output Ratios**

|  | (1)<br>United States<br>(1947) | (2)<br>Japan (1955)<br>(economy-wide) | (3)<br>Japan (1955)<br>(large scale<br>firms only) |
|---|---|---|---|
| Manufacturing Totals | .191 | .213 | (not available) |
| Processed Foods | .228 | .140 | .146 |
| Textiles | .308 | .174 | .400 |
| Lumber & Wood Products | .438 | .282 | .382 |
| Paper and its products | .458 | .195 | .483 |
| Printings | .394 | .179 | .399 |
| Chemicals | .428 | .284 | .584 |
| Petroleum and Coal Products | 1.256 | .287 | 1.252 |
| Rubber Products | .334 | .162 | .302 |
| Leather Products | .110 | .093 | .219 |
| Nonmetallic Mineral Products | .870 | .406 | .581 |
| Metal Products | .432 | .202 | .750 |
| Machinery | .475 | .340 | .453 |
| Transport Equipment | .467 | .324 | .475 |

columns for Japan represent ratios for the nation as a whole (column 2) and large-scale firms only (column 3). As may be seen from the table, the national averages between two countries differ considerably, while the degree of similarity between columns 1 and 3 is very high. This may imply that the use of the borrowed data for economy-wide coefficients (in this case, the use of the American averages as the Japanese national capital-output ratios) would lead to biased estimates of capital requirements, even though the use of such data when investigating large firms may provide reasonable estimates. These ideas

---

22. The American figures are derived from the Harvard Economic Research Project [1953] and represent mostly incremental capital-output ratios. The Japanese data come from Japan, Council of Industry Planning [1958].

extend beyond capital-output ratios and include the usage of borrowed input-output coefficients, labor coefficients, and so forth.

A third category of borrowed data is both more ambitious and riskier to use than the preceding two. This category includes the structural parameters of behavioral equations estimated for other countries. The marginal propensity to consume in consumption functions, the elasticity of substitution in production functions, and the relative price elasticity in foreign trade equations, are relevant examples. The assumption is that borrowed parameter estimates for some carefully selected equations might be more reliable than estimates derived from direct domestic observation. The usefulness of borrowed data of this sort depends heavily on the theoretical specifications used in the borrowed studies and their appropriateness to the economy being planned. An extensive discussion in this respect can be seen in Weisskoff's study of consumption functions [1971] as well as in Houthakker's pioneering study on the Engel elasticities [1957]. Needless to say, since there are always several theoretical variations or alternatives in the specification of structural equations, extensive sensitivity analysis is essential.

## 10. MONITORING PLAN PERFORMANCE

So far, our discussion has centered around the preparation and application of quantitative planning and necessary data requirements. These may be seen as necessary conditions in an efficient planning process, but they are certainly not sufficient. Here, we briefly discuss a remaining necessary condition—the monitoring of plan implementation or performance. It is important for the planning process to have a good monitoring mechanism to provide regular and intensive assessments of how plans are being carried out. Important questions include why planned aggregate or sectoral production targets have not been achieved, or why unexpected price increases have occurred, or trade balance estimates have deviated from *ex ante* projections.

Although some of this performance monitoring will have to be done qualitatively, quantitative monitoring is also desirable. Quantitative checks may prove more useful in the planning office's attempts to persuade other agents to adhere more closely to the plan. In addition, such monitoring is important in learning about how to improve the planning process itself. There are a number of requirements which have to be met by the planning office in the development of an effective mechanism for these purposes. (i) Continuous efforts must be made in collecting and updating economic data. Changes in the most strategically significant input-output coefficients have to be made constantly. (ii) The new and updated data should be used to test, at regular intervals, the structural specification of the various planning models which are being used. If an input-output model is being used, the components of the final demand vector, especially consumption and capital formation, should be checked annually. (iii) The models themselves may have to be rerun with

revised estimates of certain exogenous variables, such as the level of net foreign aid, the exchange rate, or the marginal savings propensity. These steps should provide considerable help in reducing the gap between the planned and actual situations.[23]

---

23. In this regard, see Tinbergen [1964] for an excellent discussion of these planning methods during the implementation process.

Chapter V

# INTERSECTORAL CONSISTENCY AND MACROECONOMIC PLANNING

PETER B. CLARK

## 1. INTRODUCTION

This chapter discusses the ways multisectoral models can be used to test the consistency of alternative resource allocation programs and to estimate trade-offs among key economic variables used for macroeconomic planning.[1] The focus is on assessments of the compatibility of critical aspects of a plan with all other aspects and with given social objectives. This is often done by increasing interdependency in a Leontief system by further "closing" it, i.e., by bringing more demand elements into the matrix inversion which calculates supply requirements as functions of exogenous demand.[2] Adding relationships (either technical or behavioral) to the demand-supply balances at the core of the model allows more endogenous variables to be incorporated into feedback loops so that they become mutually consistent. Inclusion of behavioral relationships which involve critical policy instruments, as opposed to mere definitions, is an important part of this "model-closing" process. However, the alternative ways in which an open Leontief model can be closed must be tempered by the planner's judgment about whether they represent some behavioral or institutional reality.

Most applications of input-output techniques follow the lines just laid out —the initial specification includes only final demands from which consistent output levels with their dependent resource requirements are calculated. However, practical examples show that it is often necessary to extend this type of consistency calculation in one or more directions. The augmentation of the basic model depends upon the planner's perception of a country's key problems and their effective policy resolution; for example:

(a) In Sri Lanka, the employment mission from the ILO [1971] found that the balance of payments problem so dominated the economy that it

---

1. Each of the macromodels described in Chapter III, section 1.2 (from Harrod–Domar growth models to two-gap models) test macroeconomic consistency. This chapter deals exclusively with multisectoral models and the macroconsistency which can be derived from the multisectoral framework.

2. Usually a "closed Leontief model" means that the consumption vector is solved for endogenously, along with output. We shall extend the use of this term to include the conversion of any exogenous variable in the usual Leontief model to one estimated endogenously.

would be a useless exercise to focus directly on increased investment for employment creation. Balance of payments variables such as exports, imports, and foreign aid were put at the heart of a consistent planning system used to analyze employment policies, *given* the required amount of trade improvement;

(b) On the other hand, the Colombia ILO mission [1970] was much freer to model possible employment creation policies because of the country's viable international trade sector. Hence, the mission's analysis was essentially (but not formally) based on direct and indirect employment patterns derived from an open Leontief model.[3]

(c) In Korea, sector investment planning and project choice dominated the policy picture, so that the Leontief system was closed in a way which focused on investments required to sustain growth.[4]

(d) Similarly, in India a series of models were constructed which put emphasis first on import substitution and later on capital goods production and investment timing, because these variables seemed to be the key to growth in a large, mostly autarchic economy.[5]

Another important distinction drawn throughout this chapter is that *consistency* calculations are not a test of what we define as economic *feasibility*. A model may have numerous solutions which are internally consistent but completely infeasible from the macroeconomic viewpoint. A model produces feasible plans only if it includes supply considerations in one of the following ways:

(a) By putting primary resource restrictions on foreign exchange, initial capital stock, savings, labor supply, and so on, within an optimizing model of the type discussed in sections 4 and 5 of Chapter III. Solutions from such a model illustrate the economy's capacity to allocate resources consistently to satisfy demand targets, but subject to its overall primary resource limits;

(b) By being elaborated into a general equilibrium model in which both demand and supply adjustments are made in order to reach an equilibrium. Normally, endogenous price determination is the equilibrating adjustment process;

(c) By simulation studies (using input-output models) coupled with close

---

3. No model was published in the ILO report, but the modelling of employment problems has dominated the Colombian economic literature for several years. Studies include Nelson, Schultz, and Slighton [1971]; Thorbecke and Sengupta [1972]; and Perry [1972].

4. See the model described in Adelman, Cole, Norton, and Jung [1969].

5. Prominent in the sequence of models were those of Manne and Rudra [1965], Srinivasan, Saluja, and Sabherwal [1965], Bergsman and Manne [1966], Chakravarty and Lefeber [1965], and Eckaus and Parikh [1968].

communication between model builders and the people in the economy who decide on and implement policy. In this case feasibility is in part a matter of judgment (Lefeber [1966]), based on information transmitted outside the model. Both the exogenous information[6] and the feasibility of the model's results should increase during the planning process itself through observation by planners of how entrepreneurs and government officials react to plan proposals.

If this last type of test were the only concern of the planner, then static or dynamic tests of feasibility would be the only requirement of planning models. However, input-output models can be used as dynamic simulators of alternative development programs. Tracing the structural changes required to move from one set of targets to another set defines policy trade-offs. These can be mapped by parametric variation of a static model for a given target year or traced over time in a dynamic framework. Used in this way, simulation models are equivalent to the recursive solution of a series of time interdependent static models and provide a flexible alternative to dynamic linear programming models as a means for testing dynamic feasibility.[7] Here the feasibility of the resulting plan can be judged by calculations made outside the model itself. Although their solution may not be on the efficiency frontier, multisectoral simulation models compensate for this by being able to sketch out a great many consistent alternative plans at low cost.

After a preliminary formal discussion of consistency in the next section, we will concentrate on economy-wide multisectoral models which can be used to analyze two critical development planning problems—consistent multisectoral investment planning (sections 3, 5, and 6) and a balanced program of income (or consumption) redistribution (section 4). While a large number of consistency models could be reviewed, we only give detailed attention in each section to one empirically tested model (two examples from Indian experience and one from Iran) which could readily be adapted for use in most developing countries. The reader is encouraged to imagine how to make these simple models more complex by incorporating specifications from the next three chapters which consider the special problems of a consistent international trade strategy (Chapter VI), employment planning and human capital formation (Chapter VII), and the use of shadow prices for project evaluation (Chapter VIII). The concluding section of this chapter discusses the use of consistency models for development planning.

---

6. See sections 6 and 8 of Chapter IV for a discussion of how to update and make data more consistent during the planning process.

7. A basic premise of this chapter is that in at least some countries, LP is likely to be too complicated and costly for routine use by planning offices. We do refer, however, to certain LP models as guidance on how a simulation model should behave as it increases its social efficiency.

## 2. ELEMENTS OF AN INPUT-OUTPUT CONSISTENCY MODEL

The basic relationship of all consistency models is the distribution equation, or commodity balance, which equates[8] total supply with all categories of demand:

$$X_i + M_i^c = \sum_j a_{ij}X_j + C_i + G_i + N_i + R_i + S_i + E_i \qquad (2.1)$$

This relationship calculates the domestic output plus competitively imported supplies of the $i$th good which are sufficient to meet all demands for intermediates, household consumption $C_i$, government expenditure $G_i$, net and replacement investment $N_i$ and $R_i$, inventory accumulation $S_i$, and exports $E_i$.[9]

Equation (2.1) illustrates the type of consistency tested by almost all input-output models—that sector supplies are required to satisfy all demands, including endogenously generated intermediate demands. Some planning uses of this type of consistency calculation are outlined in section 2.3 of Chapter III. The simplest consistency test is where all final demand elements as well as competitive imports are specified exogenously and added into a vector $\bar{F}$.[10] Then a single matrix inversion permits us to estimate sectoral production levels. The inverse of the technology matrix is used to trace the direct and indirect intermediate demand produced by a given final demand vector. Using matrix notation, the output vector $X$ may be solved for using the following relationship:

$$X = [I - A]^{-1}(\bar{F} - \bar{M}^c) \qquad (2.2)$$

where final demands $\bar{F}$ and competitive imports $\bar{M}^c$ are set exogenously. These output requirements will be consistent with the targeted final demand. Competitive imports also can be linked to domestic production or total supply and may be interpreted as sectoral import substitution targets, as discussed in Chapters III and VI.

In addition to the consistent pattern of each element of demand and supply

---

8. In the medium term and in some sectors, it may be efficient to allow for excess capacity and/or to permit excess stocks to accumulate. In this case the strict equality in (2.1) might be replaced by an inequality, as it is in programming models. Capacity shortfalls could indicate the need to reduce consumption expenditures to make a feasible plan, for example.

9. Most input-output studies combine all investment ($N_i$, $R_i$, and $S_i$) into gross investment demand $J_i$. Furthermore, because $G_i$ and $E_i$ are often taken as exogenous, the practitioner selects either the consumption or gross investment vectors as the given targets. By varying these targets while holding the trade gap fixed, a consumption-savings trade-off can be traced. This reduces the consistency model to the familiar two-gap model where the trade gap is assumed to dominate. Note that feasibility is not directly tested since savings are not determined endogenously.

10. Noncompetitive imports can be treated as a separate row in the technology matrix and as exogenous elements of final demand; these definitions are required to maintain the appropriate account of the demand for foreign exchange.

which the multisectoral analysis yields, model solutions also can be utilized to give consistent estimates of factor input requirements both at the sectoral and aggregate level. If one makes the heroic (but often necessary) assumption that factor use is proportional to sectoral production, then it is a simple matter to derive factor employment patterns which are consistent with the vector of exogenous final demand targets. The appropriate specification for a static Leontief system is:

$$L = VX \tag{2.3}$$

where $L$ is a vector of factor input requirements and $V$ is a matrix of factor productivity ratios $[v_{ij}]$ representing the input of factor $i$ per unit of gross output in sector $j$.[11]

This simple input-output model serves to illustrate the previous points about increasing the degree of "closedness" of the system. The two calculations (first solving for outputs, then resource requirements) can be made in one step if the whole equation set is expressed in partitioned matrix form as:

$$\begin{bmatrix} I - A & 0 \\ -V & I \end{bmatrix} \begin{bmatrix} X \\ L \end{bmatrix} = \begin{bmatrix} \bar{F} \\ 0 \end{bmatrix} \tag{2.4}$$

The upper rows in the partitioned matrix on the left-hand side represent the basic input-output system (2.2), while the lower part represents the factor demand equations (2.3). Since a well-known rule about the inversion of partitioned matrices[12] shows that the inverse matrix will also have a northeast corner made up entirely of zeros,

$$\begin{bmatrix} I - A & 0 \\ -V & I \end{bmatrix}^{-1} = \begin{bmatrix} (I - A)^{-1} & 0 \\ V(I - A)^{-1} & I \end{bmatrix} \tag{2.5}$$

the vector $L$ of employment levels has no direct interaction, no feedback, into the commodity balances found in the upper part of the partitioned matrix. Typical interdependencies (sometimes called closed-loop specifications) which might be added to an input-output model to link the southwest and northeast quadrants of the partitioned matrix include the relationships between labor productivities and public education expenditure, capital stock coefficients and investment demand, excise tax rates and government expenditure, or the functional distribution of income and the size distribution among consuming households.

Whenever the northeast elements of one of these feedback linkages are absent (i.e., when this type of demand remains exogenous in the commodity

11. Scarce primary resource factor supplies may include various categories of skilled labor, capital goods, and noncompetitive imports which require foreign exchange or indirect taxes which contribute to government savings.
12. See Intriligator [1971], p. 488.

balance equations), the unknowns $X$ and $L$ can be calculated in sequence. But whenever a Leontief model is "closed" to complete one or more of the feedback links, then a simultaneous solution is required to determine the interdependent output and factor use estimates. This solution cannot be decomposed into recursive steps. Then, and only then, shall we say that the factor resource allocations are *mutually consistent* with the other endogenous variables in the model.

One purpose of consistency modelling is to increase our knowledge and understanding of how an interdependent system operates. Variables from systems which are fully decomposable, which can be solved recursively, should not be thought of as interdependent. The output pattern is not dependent upon the factor availability or productivity; production may not be consistent with factor employment. Policies affecting resource use will have no impact on supply consistency because no feedback loop exists in the specification.

### 3. CLOSING THE LEONTIEF MODEL: INVESTMENT

Investment planning is the single most important policy instrument in the hands of the public sector. Capital accumulation for capacity expansion is fundamentally interrelated with all other resource allocations in the economy, and it is presumed that efficient investment planning can lead to optimal employment of all other resources. Therefore, often the first variable to be closed in a planning model is investment, particularly since many capital expenditures are under direct control of governments in developing countries and can have significant impact on growth patterns in the medium term.

Net investment by sector of origin is often calculated through an accelerator relationship as follows:

$$K(t) - \bar{K}(0) = B[X(t) - \bar{X}(0)] \qquad (3.1)$$

where elements of the vector $\bar{K}(0)$ are initial amounts of each type of capital available in the economy, $\bar{X}(0)$ is a vector of initial output levels, and $B$ is a matrix of coefficients $b_{ij}$ giving the amount of capital type $i$ required for an additional unit of output in sector $j$.[13] While the specification gives an estimate of the capital accumulation required from the base year ($\tau = 0$) to the target year ($\tau = t$), note that a static consistency model omits all intertemporal planning problems (for example, lag structures of capital gestation and learning functions required to reach full capacity) which characterize dynamic models.

At the minimum, we can use this equation to test whether the output levels

---

13. Here the definition of a consistent investment program by sector of destination is adeptly swept under the rug by the specification of the $B$ matrix. See Chapter III, section 3.1 for an evaluation of the pitfalls likely to be encountered when using an accelerator.

derived from (2.2) can be produced with the vector of capital stocks resulting from accumulation of annual gross investments by sector of origin, $J(\tau)$,

$$K(t) - \bar{K}(0) = \sum_{\tau=0}^{t} J(\tau). \tag{3.2}$$

These two determinations of capital growth will usually *not* be consistent because the factors which limit the rate of sectoral capacity expansion (i.e., absorptive capacity and gestation lags) may have a different sectoral distribution than the factors which inhibit the growth of total final and intermediate demand. The amount of tolerable error will depend on how much policy interest lies in precise investment planning and on judgments as to the quality of the data.

A more complex planning problem can be based on projections of sectoral production levels desired in the future, say at the end of the next five-year planning period. Consistent production estimates can be derived for given final demands with the aid of an input-output model. Then, using the accelerator specification, the target year capital stock is estimated. The planner is then free to devise investment theories which relate capital accumulation to the targeted production levels, thereby closing the model so that the final investment demand is consistent with the endogenous program of capacity expansion. There are several ways this can be done; we have chosen an example from Indian experience because it incorporates a realistic set of assumptions about available data for investment planning and the options open for public policy.

In the context of the Indian Fourth Plan, a great deal of importance was attached to investment, as mentioned above. One of the earliest and most interesting tests of the investment targets of that plan was made by Manne and Rudra [1965]. Because of computer limitations and because most intersectoral choices were already obvious to policy makers, they chose to model "consistency requirements" in the static Leontief tradition rather than attempt a linear programming study.

Interindustry demands were dominated by the near block-triangularity of the Indian input-output table. It could be partitioned into three independent groups of industries: (i) agriculture based production and processing for final consumption; (ii) the mining, metals, machinery, and wood products industries, which comprised the investment goods producing sectors at the focus of the Indian import substitution strategy; and (iii) a third group of intermediate product industries, including fuel, power, transport, and chemicals.

The authors concluded that, because of this economic structure, successful implementation of agricultural plans would be essential in order to achieve proposed household consumption targets but would have only second-order importance (via farmers' income changes) on the demand for industrial

135

production. On the other hand, output targets for key industrial sectors would depend upon the government's willingness to maintain high aggregate investment rates regardless of the behavior of agriculture (which depends upon good monsoons and other stochastic phenomena). A shortfall among industrial production targets would directly affect the domestic investment program and the import substitution strategy India had planned for conservation of foreign exchange. Moreover, underachievement of output targets among intermediate products would have diffuse impact throughout the economy. Thus the planning model attempted to derive investment patterns which were consistent with future production targets rather than to focus directly on consumption planning.

The Manne–Rudra consistency model has almost exactly the same relationships as those in equations (2.1) and (3.1). Two further equations were added: One, to relate investment to the desired change in capital stocks $[K(t) - \bar{K}(0)]$, and the other, to calculate the deficit on merchandise account of the balance of payments where noncompetitive imports were linked to output levels. They are:

$$J(t) = d[K(t) - \bar{K}(0)], \tag{3.3}$$

where $d$ is a constant stock-flow conversion factor; and

$$\sum_i \bar{M}_i^c + \sum_i M_i^{nc} = \sum_i \bar{E}_i + W. \tag{3.4}$$

Imports are separated in (3.4) into exogenous and endogenous categories, where the latter, noncompetitive imports $M_i^{nc}$, are tied to sector output levels by fixed coefficients. The former, competitive imports, are treated as target variables to be altered exogenously to maintain a reasonable foreign aid gap $W$. Final demand is here defined as net of endogenous fixed investment and includes household and government consumption, exports, and exogenous fixed investment.

After substitution of (3.1) and (3.3) into (2.1), these equations can be solved to give sectoral output levels in terms of non-investment final demands by inverting the matrix $[I - A - dB]$. This is a way of "endogenizing" investment since demands for the four capital goods $J_i$ in the system can be computed from (3.3) once the sectoral production for the target year is known. The stock-flow conversion factor $d^{14}$ is used to calculate the share of gross fixed capital formation which will occur in the terminal year of the plan period (1970–71) as a share of the 10-year investment requirements called for to achieve the final demand targets set for 1970–71.[15]

14. See the explanation of this factor in Chapter III, section 4.1, where it is defined in equation (4.9).

15. Under the strong assumptions of a 2-year gestation lag (representing an average for all 30 sectors) and a constant rate of investment throughout the whole 10-year period (for each sector), Manne and Rudra settled on a single stock-flow conversion factor for all sectors.

In this model the current account balance of payments gap is not a fixed resource constraint, as it would be in a linear programming model.[16] Manne and Rudra explain that competitive imports and other parameters were adjusted during the course of numerical experimentation so that the trade gap would be in a feasible range of what India might expect to secure from foreign loans and grants. Since these are not policy, but target variables, these adjustments imply confidence that import licensing, tariffs or an active import substitution policy were economically, politically, and institutionally feasible and would induce the desired results.

Since sectoral levels of production and competitive imports do not substitute for each other as functions of the relative scarcity of domestic factors of production as compared with the exogenous supply of foreign exchange (exports and the foreign trade gap), the model is insensitive to relative costs and cannot be used directly to explore India's international comparative advantage.

If more foreign aid were available to India than was predicted by Manne and Rudra's adjustment of $W$, it would not be absorbed in the 1970–71 resource allocations implied by the model's solution. Thus the planner must use the estimate of $W$ judiciously. There is nothing implied by the solution about feasible or efficient levels of foreign capital inflow. The judgments of feasibility come from outside the model. Import licensing arrangements might be set up to attempt to induce the import pattern projected by the model, but even doing this probably would not lead to the sectoral output targets calculated by the model. Thus the consistency model is designed to explore the implications of structural change at the normative rather than operational policy level.

A model of this type can be used to bring alternative growth paths and policy options into consideration in the planning process if it is used as a basis for discussion with agents in the economy who can provide the planner with informed judgments about the plausibility of the model's solution. As a result of this interaction, the feasibility of the plan is increased because the judgment and knowledge of those with whom the planner confers will become implicit in later solutions of the model. In this case, what exactly can one learn from the initial solution of the Manne–Rudra "open" consistency model?[17]

In the Manne–Rudra calculations, two sets of exogenous terminal year targets were fixed: (i) an ambitious development program drawn from the

16. Since the planner selects the most viable import substitution investments from exogenous information, equation (3.4) defines the trade gap $W$ as the balancing residual between the exogenously determined level of exports and competitive imports and the endogenous noncompetitive imports associated with the terminal year domestic production pattern.

17. First, before solving the model, the planner must collect much exogenous information and projections, including: final demand estimates; import substitution targets; the permissible range of the trade gap; and an updating of the technology matrix from its base year values reflecting changes in relative prices and the impact of technological change.

objectives of India's Perspective Planning Division [1964]; and (ii) a more pessimistic view of what would be feasible. These implied different 10-year average growth rates for the aggregates of gross capital formation, government consumption, household consumption, and gross domestic expenditure. Beyond this, variation in the values of other critical parameters permitted the authors to generate a much wider range of solutions for interpretation and discussion with policy makers. Runs differed from one another by: (i) the degree of endogenous investment left to the model; (ii) changes in the agricultural sector's capital-output ratio; (iii) altering the degree of block-triangularity found in the technology matrix; and (iv) evaluating the effects of the machinery import substitution program.

The credibility which a policy maker is willing to give to the results of a static consistency model depends upon his own estimate of the feasibility of the policy changes implied by the planner's simulations. He must compare alternative economic situations at the end of the plan period but in a static model learns nothing of the transition process. Moreover, the policy maker must judge whether the planner has selected key parameters to vary which are proxies for policy options actually at the discretion of the policy maker. Explicit specification of policy instruments in planning models will reduce the degree of judgmental interpolation required of the policy maker.

## 4. CLOSING THE LEONTIEF MODEL: CONSUMPTION AND INCOME DISTRIBUTION

In the previous section we discussed a relatively simple method for exploring the consistency of sectoral investment plans because of investment's importance as an effective policy instrument. We turn now to the problem of testing consistency among targets. Society's welfare is often expressed in the level and distribution of its consumption. In this section we shall extend the usual method of closing a Leontief system which relates consumption directly to sectoral output by developing a closed-loop specification by first relating output to the personal distribution of income from which consumption patterns are easily derived. Thus a planner can focus directly on the impact of various income redistribution schemes upon induced sectoral demand patterns.

National planners and their model builders have tended to overlook distributional problems until open unemployment in major urban centers and underemployment in the service sector and rural areas become political liabilities. There are as yet unresolved problems associated with attempts to graft distribution and employment considerations onto the typical economy-wide multisectoral planning model.[18] One of the most interesting efforts to

---

18. See Chenery and Associates [1974] for a general discussion of these models.

date is described in Working Paper No. 12 of the ILO Employment Mission,[19] which visited Iran from November 1971 to January 1972, because the model is small and embodies most of the relationships we wish to study.

The model we shall describe is not beyond the means of most LDC planning offices or their staff, since it was specified, estimated, solved (with many variations), analyzed and written up in a few months by a team of five people. A similar model has been constructed for Sri Lanka (Pyatt et al. [1974]), because Pyatt believes it is important to introduce Keynesian elements into the Leontief framework in order to analyze effective demand questions normally omitted from planning models.

The Manne–Rudra consistency model closed the static Leontief system by making endogenous the capital capacity expansion, inventory investment, and some imports, but set household consumption as a terminal target. Pyatt's model lets gross fixed investment remain exogenous as target variables but makes endogenous the generation of personal income and the payment of all other factors. The model is built around a set of accounting relationships, most of which are definitions without much behavioral significance. The model does, however, give consistent projections because it balances simultaneously seven sets of accounts: (1) commodities, (2) domestic income, (3) government income, (4) rest of the world, (5) indirect taxes, (6) direct taxes, and (7) a combined capital account of savings by source.

The structure of the accounting relationships can be seen in Table 1 (drawn from Table 11.1 of Pyatt [1973] but with a different notation and somewhat simplified to eliminate detail important only in Iran). Our exposition of the model's structure will follow row by row the framework of accounts shown in Table 1.[20]

As in all static Leontief models, the first relationship is a commodity balance similar to equation (2.1) but omitting competitive imports. Final consumption is distributed among $k$ types of institutions (i.e., $k = r, l, h$, and $g$—rural, low income urban and high income urban households, and government, respectively). Government consumption, exports, and gross investment demand are all exogenous.[21]

Consumption expenditures are a linear function of the total income earned

---

19. We shall refer to this report as Pyatt [1973] because he was the senior author and formulated the model's specification based on his previous experience working with the new United Nations System of National Accounts [1968].

20. This table is presented as an example of the complexity of the accounting relationships this type of model requires.

21. Pyatt distinguishes between exogenous vectors of private ($\bar{I}^p$), public ($\bar{I}^g$) and foreign ($W$) investment in columns 23 to 25 of Table 1 because his accounting system attempts to map sources of savings in rows 23 to 25 directly into their final uses. However, since this classification is entirely exogenous, the savings-investment balance can be tested equally well in aggregate terms.

**Table 1: The Framework of Accounts for Pyatt Model of Iran***

| Expenditures | Live-stock 1 | Other agric. 2 | ... | Con-struc-tion 11 | Owner of dwell-ing 12 | $\sum$1 to 12 13 | Households Rural 14 | Urban low 15 | Urban high 16 | G |
|---|---|---|---|---|---|---|---|---|---|---|
| 1. Livestock | $X_{1.1}$ | $X_{1.2}$ | ... | $X_{1.11}$ | $X_{1.12}$ | $\sum_j X_{1.j}$ | $C_{1.r}$ | $C_{1.l}$ | $C_{1.h}$ | $\bar{C}$ |
| 2. Other agriculture | $X_{2.1}$ | . | | . | $X_{2.12}$ | $\sum_j X_{2.j}$ | $C_{2.r}$ | $C_{2.l}$ | $C_{2.h}$ | $C$ |
| ⋮ | ⋮ | ⋮ | | ⋮ | ⋮ | | ⋮ | ⋮ | ⋮ | |
| 11. Construction | $X_{11.1}$ | | | . | $X_{11.12}$ | $\sum_j X_{11.j}$ | $C_{11.r}$ | $C_{11.l}$ | $C_{11.h}$ | $C$ |
| 12. Owner of dwelling | $X_{12.1}$ | $X_{12.2}$ | ... | $X_{12.11}$ | $X_{12.12}$ | $\sum_j X_{12.j}$ | $C_{12.r}$ | $C_{12.l}$ | $C_{12.h}$ | $C$ |
| 13. $\sum$1 to 12 | $\sum_i X_{i.1}$ | $\sum_i X_{i.2}$ | ... | $\sum_i X_{i.11}$ | $\sum_i X_{i.12}$ | $\sum_i\sum_j X_{ij}$ | $\sum_i C_{ir}$ | $\sum_i C_{il}$ | $\sum_i C_{ih}$ | $\sum$ |
| 14. Rural | $V_{r.1}$ | $V_{r.2}$ | ... | $V_{r.11}$ | $V_{r.12}$ | $\sum_j V_{rj}$ | $V_{rr}$ | — | $V_{rh}$ | $V$ |
| 15. Low urban | $V_{l.1}$ | $V_{l.2}$ | ... | $V_{l.11}$ | $V_{l.12}$ | $\sum_j V_{lj}$ | — | $V_{ll}$ | $V_{lh}$ | $V$ |
| 16. High urban | $V_{h.1}$ | $V_{h.2}$ | ... | $V_{h.11}$ | $V_{h.12}$ | $\sum_j V_{hj}$ | — | — | $V_{hh}$ | $V$ |
| 17. Government | $V_{g.1}$ | $V_{g.2}$ | ... | $V_{g.11}$ | $V_{g.12}$ | $\sum_j V_{gj}$ | — | — | — | |
| 18. $\sum$14 to 17 | $\sum_k V_{k.1}$ | $\sum_k V_{k.2}$ | ... | $\sum_k V_{k.11}$ | $\sum_k V_{k.12}$ | $\sum_j\sum_k V_{kj}$ | $\sum_k V_{kr}$ | $\sum_k V_{kl}$ | $\sum_k V_{kh}$ | $\sum$ |
| 19. Imports | $M_1^a$ | $M_2^a$ | ... | $M_{11}^a$ | $M_{12}^a$ | $\sum_j M_j^a$ | $M_r^c$ | $M_l^c$ | $M_h^c$ | $M$ |
| 20. Indirect taxes | $T_1^i$ | $T_2^i$ | ... | $T_{11}^i$ | $T_{12}^i$ | $\sum_j T_j^i$ | $T_r^i$ | $T_l^i$ | $T_h^i$ | |
| 21. $\sum$13 + 18 + 19 | $X_1$ | $X_2$ | ... | $X_{11}$ | $X_{12}$ | $\sum_j X_j$ | $C_r$ | $C_l$ | $C_h$ | $C$ |
| 22. Direct taxes | — | — | ... | — | — | — | $T_r^d$ | $T_l^d$ | $T_h^d$ | — |
| 23. Private | — | — | ... | — | — | — | $S_r^p$ | $S_l^p$ | $S_h^p$ | $S$ |
| 24. Government | — | — | ... | — | — | — | — | — | — | |
| 25. Foreign | — | — | ... | — | — | — | — | — | — | |
| 26. $\sum$21 to 25 | $X_1$ | $X_2$ | ... | $X_{11}$ | $X_{12}$ | $\sum_j X_j$ | $Y_r$ | $Y_l$ | $Y_h$ | |

GDP at factor cost $= \sum_j\sum_k V_{kj} + \sum_k\sum_k V_{kk} + E_f$.
* Adapted from Table II.1, Pyatt et al. [1973].

by each type of household (rural, low income urban and high income urban) plus government:

$$C_{ik} = \bar{c}_{ik} + y_{ik}Y_k \quad \text{for} \quad k = r, l, h, \text{ and } g, \tag{4.1}$$

where $\bar{c}_{ik}$ is the intercept term, $y_{ik}$ is the marginal propensity to consume the $i$th good by each household of type $k$, and $Y_k$ is personal income aggregated across all households of type $k$ plus government $Y_g$.

Substituting (4.1) into the balance equation (2.1), the two vectors of unknowns are domestic production (columns 1–12 of Table 1)[22] and personal

22. Our references to this table will be given henceforth as elements of the "Pyatt" matrix ($P$). Thus we shall describe the values of sectoral output, which appear as the sum of all rows of columns 1 to 12, as the vector whose elements are $P_{26.01}$ to $P_{26.12}$ which accounts for all inputs to production. Outputs are distributed along rows 1 to 12, summing also to sectoral production as elements $P_{1.26}$ to $P_{12.26}$.

| 14 to 17 | Exports | Indirect taxes | Σ 13 + 18 + 19 + 20 | Direct taxes | Savings | | | Σ 21 to 25 |
|---|---|---|---|---|---|---|---|---|
| | | | | | Private | Government | Foreign | |
| 18 | 19 | 20 | 21 | 22 | 23 | 24 | 25 | 26 |
| $_k C_{1.k}$ | $\bar{E}_1$ | — | $X_1 - I_1$ | — | $\bar{I}_1^p$ | $\bar{I}_1^g$ | — | $X_1$ |
| $_k C_{2.k}$ | $\bar{E}_2$ | — | $X_2 - I_2$ | — | $\bar{I}_2^p$ | $\bar{I}_2^g$ | — | $X_2$ |
| ⋮ | ⋮ | ⋮ | ⋮ | ⋮ | ⋮ | ⋮ | ⋮ | ⋮ |
| $_k C_{11.k}$ | $\bar{E}_{11}$ | — | $X_{11} - I_{11}$ | | $\bar{I}_{11}^p$ | $\bar{I}_{11}^g$ | | $X_{11}$ |
| $_k C_{12.k}$ | $\bar{E}_{12}$ | — | $X_{12} - I_{12}$ | | $\bar{I}_{12}^p$ | $\bar{I}_{12}^g$ | | $X_{12}$ |
| $\sum_k C_{1k}$ | $\sum_t \bar{E}_t$ | — | $\sum_t (X_t - I_t)$ | — | $\sum_t \bar{I}_t^p$ | $\sum_t \bar{I}_t^g$ | — | $\sum_t X_t$ |
| $_k V_{rk}$ | — | — | $Y_r$ | — | — | — | — | $Y_r$ |
| $_k V_{lk}$ | | | $Y_l$ | — | — | — | — | $Y_l$ |
| $_k V_{hk}$ | $-\bar{E}_h$ | $\bar{T}_h^r$ | $Y_h$ | — | — | — | — | $Y_h$ |
| $_k V_{gk}$ | — | $T_g^r$ | $Y_g$ | — | — | — | — | $Y_g$ |
| $\sum_k V_{kk}$ | $-\bar{E}_h$ | $T^i$ | GNP at mkt. p. | — | — | — | — | GNP at mkt. p. |
| $_k M_k^c$ | $\bar{E}_f$ | — | $M^a + M^c$ | — | $\bar{M}_p^b$ | $\bar{M}_g^c$ | — | $M$ |
| $_k T_k^i$ | | | $T^i$ | — | | | — | $T^i$ |
| $'' + \bar{G}$ | $E$ | $T^i$ | | — | $\bar{I}_p$ | $\bar{I}_g$ | — | Total |
| | — | — | — | — | — | — | — | — |
| $_k S_k^p$ | — | — | $\sum_k S_k^p$ | — | — | — | — | $\sum_k S_k^p$ |
| | — | — | $S_g$ | — | $K$ | — | — | $S_g + K$ |
| | $W$ | — | $W$ | — | $T_p^s - K$ | $T_g^s + K$ | — | $T_p^s + T_g^s + W$ |
| at mkt. p. | $M$ | $T^i$ | Total | — | $\bar{I}_p + T_p^s$ | $\bar{I}_g + T_g^s + K$ | $-W$ | — |

income ($P_{26.14}$ to $P_{26.16}$ and also $P_{14.21}$ to $P_{16.21}$) from which household consumption and savings are drawn.[23]

$$X = AX + yY + \bar{F}_x. \qquad (4.2)$$

The trick of paying sectoral value added directly to households was adopted in order to answer the overriding policy issue in Iran, "Where is the market for industrial products going to come from?" Note that the functional distribution of income (given in Table 1 by rows 14 to 17) is not based on the normal separation of sectoral value added into payments to different primary factors. Model builders attempting to work with the size distribution of income encounter great difficulty with the usual national accounts presentation, which separates value added into wages, salaries, employee's

---

23. Double entry accounting in Table 1 is shown by the fact that row and column totals must be equal.

contributions to social security, payments to entrepreneurs and property plus retained earnings, depreciation, and indirect taxes less subsidies. One can readily observe there is some, but not too much, correspondence between these categories and the "basic" factors of production (labor, land, and capital); nor is there any apparent translation into the institutional categories which characterize the personal distribution of income. However, for Iran, perhaps we are fortunate; the accounts given by Pyatt [1973] have in one way or another arrived at this conversion due to the simplicity of the sectoral/factoral/institutional classifications.[24]

$Y_k$, the income received by the 4 consumer groups ($P_{14.26}$ to $P_{17.26}$) is derived by summing across the columns of Table 1 for rows 14 to 17:

$$Y_k = \sum_j v_{kj} X_j + \sum_k c_{kk} Y_k - \bar{E}_k + \bar{T}_k^r, \quad \text{for } k = r, l, h, \text{ and } g, \quad (4.3)$$

where the $v_{kj}$ are fixed proportion value-added coefficients for factor earnings paid by sector $j$ to institution $k$, and the $c_{kk}$ represents income paid by households to domestic servants, income paid to owners of buildings, and wages and salaries paid by government to civil servants and military.[25] The income generation equations (4.3) also includes $\bar{E}_k$, net factor income payments abroad (by income group $k$), and $\bar{T}_k^r$, government transfers paid to $k$th group of recipients (i.e., nonresident oil sector payments received by government as indirect taxes and then transferred to the personal sector).

If we collapse all exogenous final demand into a vector $\bar{F}_x$ relating to equation (4.2) and $\bar{F}_y$ for equation (4.3), we can simultaneously solve for the vectors $X$ and $Y$ by inverting the partitioned matrix of input-output and value-added coefficients:

$$\begin{bmatrix} X \\ \hline Y \end{bmatrix} = \begin{bmatrix} I - A & -C_x \\ \hline -V & I - C_y \end{bmatrix}^{-1} \begin{bmatrix} \bar{F}_x \\ \hline \bar{F}_y \end{bmatrix} \quad (4.4)$$

The model produces output and income vectors which are *mutually consistent* because they are computed simultaneously in a fully determined system. (The other variables included in the model are calculated only *after* the matrix inversion (4.4) has been completed.) The interactive consistency between outputs and income results from the closed-loop system in which production leads to factor earnings, which leads to income determination, which leads to expenditure patterns, which leads to production requirements needed both to supply the goods and to create the income flows. The feedback is created in

24. Pyatt reports that the ILO has financed additional work on these accounting conversions for Sri Lanka where the national accounts have been divided into twelve factors of production which receive value added and pay it out to 21 different types of households (see Pyatt et al. [1974]).

25. We have shown the variables in Table 1 rather than the parameters, so that the flows might be summed to define macroeconomic variables.

this specification by closing the model with an endogenous expenditure system, i.e., the non-zero elements $C_x$ in the northeast partitioned matrix of equation (4.4) which are functionally related to the distribution of income (as defined by the equations in the lower half of the partitioned matrix).[26]

The Pyatt model collapses all imports $M$ into a single vector, row 19 of Table 1.

$$M = \sum_j m_j^a X_j + \sum_k m_k^c Y_k + \overline{M}^b \qquad (4.5)$$

where $m_j^a$ represents a proportional intermediate import coefficient for sector $i$, $m_k^c$ is a coefficient for consumption goods imported by the institution of type $k$, and $\overline{M}^b$ is the exogenous value of capital goods imported by the private sector $\overline{M}_p^b$ and the government $\overline{M}_g^b$.

Rows 19 through 26 of Table 1 give a detailed account of Iran's government sector, the balance of payments, and the savings-investment balance. Because of Walras' Law and equation (4.4), all these relationships can be boiled down directly into the equations:

$$
\begin{aligned}
e[(I - C_y) - C_x]Y &= \text{Private Savings} \\
&= eVX - [e(I - A)X - (e\overline{F}_x + e\overline{F}_y)] \qquad (4.6) \\
&= \text{Total value added} - [\text{Outputs net of} \\
&\qquad \text{intermediate inputs} - \text{Exogenous} \\
&\qquad \text{final demands}]
\end{aligned}
$$

in which $e$ is a "summing vector" $[1, 1, \ldots, 1]$ of appropriate dimension. Of course, many other variables are implicit in this equation relating total payments and uses. As can be seen in the last rows of Table 1, in the Iran model they include the following variables: government income $Y_g$, total indirect taxes $T^i$, total direct taxes $T^d$, total savings $S$, private savings for the $k$th income type $S_k^p$, government savings $S_g$, current account deficit of the balance of payments $W$, net capital transfers from private sector and government to the rest of the world $\overline{T}_p^s + \overline{T}_g^s$, a transfer item $\overline{T}_g^r$ reflecting the difference between export receipts and net factor payments abroad $\overline{E}_f$.

The reader may consult Pyatt [1973] for the behavioral and accounting relationships he imposes to determine *all* these variables, or (better) may attempt to work out plausible equations for himself on the basis of Table 1.[27] The main point to be made here, however, is that the savings-investment balance (4.6) must still be respected. *All* the variables just discussed enter into

---

26. Because of the feedback from factor payments to consumption, the Pyatt model has an element of complexity not appearing in the simple Leontief model (2.4), where the northeast corner is a zero matrix.

27. One of the strong points of Pyatt's work is his meticulous attention to accounting relationships. As should be obvious from the discussion, this is a very complicated business, but it is a necessary one if detailed consideration of the government accounts is of interest (as may or may not be the case in a given planning situation).

equation (4.6) through one accounting relationship or another, as inspection of Table 1 will verify. Therefore, one more equilibrating variable must be created to permit consistency if one wants to specify all of them exogenously. In Pyatt's case, this is the capital transfer variable (among income recipients) denoted by $K$ in the far southeast corner of Table 1. In an Iranian context this may be appropriate; in another context, one might want to maintain the savings-investment identity by specifying some other variable as endogenous. Obvious candidates are total government investment, the value of some sort of government transfer, the trade gap, and so on.[28] But once again, in any extension of the model, one must make sure that equation (4.6) is satisfied.

Pyatt's model is the culmination of several studies which attempt to measure the effects of income redistribution on consumption patterns and resource use. Most of these are based on a simpler specification similar to equation (2.4), in which factor payments do not feed back to consumption. The size distribution of income is simply assumed to be modified, with two principal effects usually observed. First, redistribution from high income recipients will reduce personal savings, but only insofar as marginal propensities to save rise with incomes—the overall rate of savings will not be affected when the consumption function is linear.[29] Since empirically estimated consumption functions are not greatly curved, the savings reduction may not be large. Second, high income recipients may have consumption baskets containing a disproportionate share of capital-intensive goods, or goods with a high import content, and so forth. Hence, redistribution may lead to a *reduction* in the overall capital-output ratio (through a shift of the total consumption basket toward less capital-intensive goods) and an *increase* in the growth rate for a given savings rate.

The usual methodology for studying the effects of the redistribution of income among specified categories of recipients has the following basic features:

(a) a pattern of income redistribution is assumed, based either on targets for the lowest group, on taxation possibilities, or on other social objectives;

(b) the impact of the redistribution on savings and total investment is calculated from aggregate consumption functions for each group plus assumptions as to external capital flows;

(c) the total consumption of each income group is broken down into component parts using Engel curves or other forms of the demand function;

----

28. Here again the reader can test his ingenuity. Try writing a simplified Pyatt model, for example, and show how government investment can be endogenized to satisfy equation (4.6) through appropriate modifications to the northeast partitioned matrix in (4.4).

29. This is a theorem perhaps first stated by Lubell [1947].

(d) the new levels of total consumption for each commodity are used in an input-output system to determine changes in production, imports, and employment, which are then compared to an initial projection without income redistribution; and

(e) second round effects, as in Pyatt, may be calculated by an iterative procedure feeding the effects of changed factor payments in (4) back into the consumption vector and following down through (1) to (4) again. This amounts to a matrix multiplier expansion of the inverse matrix found in equation (4.6).

One important use of this methodology is to estimate the effects of a hypothetical income redistribution on the factors limiting growth: domestic savings, external capital flows, investment requirements, and foreign exchange. Once these are determined, the effect on total output can also be estimated. The welfare effects of income redistribution can then be summarized as:

(a) a growth effect (positive or negative);
(b) a redistribution effect (positive); and
(c) an employment effect (hopefully positive).

The studies made so far are inconclusive as to the general nature of the effects of income redistribution on aggregate growth and employment. In many of the cases studied, the effects measured have been relatively small. For example, moving from a Brazilian to a British income distribution would, in Cline's [1972] estimate, have little effect on total employment in Brazil. The savings rate would fall, and so would the aggregate capital-output ratio, because of the shift in consumption patterns. Reasoning from the Harrod–Domar equation (1.3) of Chapter III, aggregate growth might be slightly increased if negative responses from domestic and foreign investors (and other factors omitted from the model) do not work too strongly in the opposite direction.

In preparing the Fifth Five Year Plan (1974–78), the Indian Planning Commission [1973][30] has made use of a variant of this methodology that provides a useful example of this model's advantages, as well as its limitations. The Indian approach is designed to test the feasibility of bringing the lowest 30 percent of the income recipients up to a specified minimum consumption standard (20 rupees a month in 1960 prices) by 1978.[31] This would involve a 60 percent rise in the average per capita consumption of this group over the 5-year period. It is further assumed that income redistribution would not affect the overall rate of growth of GDP (taken to be 5.5 percent), and that a

---

30. Srinivasan, Saluja, and Sabherwal [1969] made a similar exploration of the implications of alternative income distributions.

31. The same target tested by the Manne–Rudra model [1965].

reduction in the average per capita consumption of the top 30 percent of income recipients of 3 percent (instead of an increase of 16 percent with no redistribution) would therefore be required.

The analytical procedure used by the Planning Commission follows the steps outlined above. The consumption functions of different groups of income recipients were estimated from family budget studies, while exports and public consumption were kept unchanged. The new final demands were then translated into production and import levels by means of a 66-sector input-output model.

One of the most interesting results of these simulation experiments is the effect that redistribution of consumption would have on the production levels of most industrial sectors.[32] In 22 of the 66 sectors consumption redistribution causes a change in the annual growth rate by *more* than 1 percent. Requirements for food grains and textiles are appreciably increased, while consumer durables are significantly lower.

The feasibility of this type of redistribution policy depends in the first instance on the possibilities for limiting upper income consumption through taxation, which in the Indian context would have to be mainly in the form of indirect taxes on luxury consumer goods. In principle, it would be possible to compute the level of excise taxes needed on the basis of the price elasticities for each commodity. If this income transfer is found to be possible, feasibility will then depend on the supply elasticities of food production and the ability of Indian policy makers to change the supply structure of the economy.[33]

While the Indian model shares the weaknesses noted above in not being able to analyze the process of income generation or the instruments for intervening in it, it does represent one of the most significant attempts by a government body to explore the implications of distributional policies for planning. Other governments have been committed to the redistribution goal. In 1971 the Chilean government shifted 9 percent of GDP from the upper income brackets to the worker class. A similar test of static consistency of this strategy was made by Chile's Center for Planning Studies, (Foxley [1973]), which simulated the Allende government's plan for consumption redistribution as outlined in the 1971–76 development program, ODEPLAN [1971]. Static tests of consistency, of course, ignore the dynamics of the redistribution problem. They fail to study the short-term supply imbalances caused when half-completed investment projects or new investments with gestation lags

---

32. These results must be carefully evaluated because they simply indicate the production changes which should accompany an altered consumption pattern. Note the model has not closed consumption as the Pyatt model does, nor does it endogenize the investment requirements needed to transform the output capacity as earlier consistency models of India have.

33. Both conditions require judgment which falls beyond the scope of the consistency model.

would impede the restructuring of the economy to meet a target of redistributed consumption.[34]

## 5. DYNAMICALLY CONSISTENT INVESTMENT PROGRAMS

It has been noted above that one element of feasibility would be a test of the intertemporal consistency of a plan. The same multisectoral demand and supply patterns found in the commodity balances (2.1) may be traced through time in order to test dynamic consistency. This is particularly important whenever investment lags are lengthy or when planners anticipate major structural changes in final demand which cannot be easily met by imports or stock changes.[35] These may include the effects of income redistribution, eliminating excessive foreign debt, implementing land reform, or planning an educational reform.

In sections 5 and 6 we consider in some detail intertemporal consistency models, with special emphasis on planning the time phasing and choice of sectoral investment programs. The static models discussed thus far have made various short-cut assumptions in their treatment of the accumulation of investment into new capital stock. Again in the Indian context, attempts were made to make the simplifying assumptions as innocuous as possible. One of the major outcomes of this was to replace the stock-flow conversion factor found in Manne and Rudra by an accelerator in the next generation of Indian planning models. In this section we discuss the 30-sector target consistency model of Bergsman and Manne [1966]. This model's principal applications were the construction of consistent investment profiles for the period 1965–75, and an analysis of the long-run impacts on the balance of payments of early import substitution.[36]

The model took, as given, the 1970–71 and 1975–76 projections of the

34. The dynamics of the Chilean case were studied by Bergendorff and Clark [1973] using a 13 (annual) period dynamic economy-wide model. The model's simulation of this once-and-for-all income shift illustrates how an abrupt restructuring of demand will cause a severe cyclical disequilibrium among all macroeconomic variables in the medium term. A policy of gradual redistribution would not cause the same degree of structural imbalance. In either case, unless policy instruments are found to maintain the new purchasing power within the working group for a time period (about 7 years in the Chilean case) sufficient for the pattern of domestic supply to permanently adjust to the newly imposed pattern of demand, the goal of consumption redistribution cannot be permanently maintained. For a provocative examination of some of the theoretical reasons for the unequalizing spiral of income concentration, see Bacha and Taylor [1974].

35. See also Chapter III, section 3 for a discussion of the uses of dynamic consistency models.

36. In this section we focus almost entirely on the practical problems of using a model of the Bergsman–Manne type to study medium-term adjustment problems. See Chapter VI, section 3, for an evaluation of the study's policy conclusions for India's development strategy and the time phasing of foreign aid. Further technical details are discussed in Chapter III, section 3.3.

economy from the static consistency models of Manne and Rudra [1965] and Srinivasan, Saluja, and Sabherwal [1965]. Dynamically consistent sectoral supply (output and import) patterns were tested with a simulation technique which we outline briefly. Different runs were made using exogenous data chosen to reflect the planner's hypotheses about potential inconsistencies in the plan's targets or policies. The model's specification of "shock absorbers" indicates the planner's evaluation of what actually could be adjusted to achieve *ex post* consistency, i.e., what variables were subject to policy influence.

The sectoral commodity balances have the same form as equation (2.1), except that all variables now carry time subscripts.[37] Noncompetitive imports are specified as endogenous variables (related to output levels). Competitive imports $M_i^c$ are a residual supply category defined as the difference between excess demand and production and are called "equilibrating" since they represent changes in planned import substitution.

Some parts of the terminal year investment demand are given exogenously by the static consistency models used to set the plan targets; other parts are estimated endogenously as adjustment factors.[38] The endogenous investment specification is derived from the accelerator relationship described in equation (3.1). In the Bergsman–Manne model the terminal year accelerator incorporates exogenous post-terminal growth rates $r_i$ set as target rates of sectoral capacity expansion:

$$J_i(T) = \sum_j b_{ij} r_j X_j(T)(1 + r_j)^{\Theta_j - 1} \qquad (5.1)$$

where $\Theta_j$ is the average gestation lag for investment in sector $j$.

In the first round of calculations competitive imports are set at zero. Then, using matrix notation, one can substitute equation (5.1) into (2.1) and solve for the terminal year production levels:

$$X(T) = [I - A - Br(1 + r)^{\Theta - 1}]^{-1} \bar{F}(T) \qquad (5.2)$$

These are compared with the exogenous target year values (either 1970–71 or 1975–76). The differences in production estimates can be interpreted as the equilibrating competitive imports. The solution strategy involves backward recursion from the consistent terminal year targets to the known initial conditions. The last year of India's Third Five Year Plan, 1965–66, was used as the initial year for the planning exercise. Thus, the process began with

---

37. Actually the variables of the Bergsman–Manne model are all rates of growth, but we will discuss the model as if the variables were absolute levels in order to maintain comparability with other models discussed in this chapter.

38. One could not expect the investment estimates derived with a closed static Leontief model using a stock-flow conversion factor $d$ (looking backward in time) to agree exactly with investment patterns estimated by an accelerator (looking forward to post-terminal output requirements).

consistent demand and supply patterns for three points in the time, between which Bergsman and Manne interpolated to obtain estimates of sectoral values of output, input-output coefficients and all exogenous final demands in the intraplan years. Sectoral investment was made consistent using the following accelerator specifications:

$$J_i(t) = \sum_j b_{ij}[X_j(t + \Theta_j) - X_j(t + \Theta_j - 1)], \quad 0 < t < T \quad (5.3)$$

In this way total demand and domestic supply are compared in the commodity balances (2.1) for the intraplan years leaving $M_i^c(t)$, the equilibrating imports, as the residual. $M_i^c(t)$ may take either a positive or negative value, representing a supply shortfall or excess. However, for nontraded goods, the residual cannot be interpreted as potential imports and therefore requires another adjustment mechanism. Bergsman and Manne suppressed excess demand for nontraded consumption goods by lowering the exogenous sectoral consumption demands included in $\bar{F}(t)$, and in the nontraded service sectors by adjusting $X_i(t)$ sufficiently to make $M_i^c(t) = 0$. The only substantial sectoral inconsistency remaining after these adjustments was in the urban construction sector during early years of the Fourth Plan, which caused the model to be called "almost consistent."

There are many ways to bring about consistency in a dynamic model. Some model builders relax the rigid requirement for a balanced transition from "known" initial conditions. This is especially true when they use a lagged accelerator because it is difficult to estimate the sectoral capital formation-in-process at the initial year.[39] Bergsman and Manne judged that it was most realistic to ignore the model's prediction that the urban construction industry might not expand sufficiently in the short run. Others might have taken this as a binding constraint and shifted investment around throughout the intraplan period in order to compensate for the deficient capacity as quickly as possible.[40] In the meantime, output levels could be held below their interpolated values. Similarly, when plausible, other elements of demand such as

39. A criticism frequently levelled at input-output models is that they have no past. Unlike econometric models, their behavior is seldom verified over an historical period. Hence, initial conditions for dynamic models which incorporate multiple year investment lags are usually simplified in one of two ways: (a) point estimates are made from actual observed figures, and capital-in-process is made a function of given preplan sectoral growth rates (assuming no change in capacity utilization); or (b) the gestation lag is reduced to one period by aggregating time. Celasun [1972] introduces non-uniform gestation lags into a Bergsman–Manne type multisectoral simulation model for Turkey. Bergendorff and Clark [1973] used a 3-year lagged accelerator to estimate initial year capital utilization and partially finished investments by forcing the endogenous variables of the model to track the actual path of all sectoral and aggregate values given for each year of a 5-year preplan period.

40. Taylor, Ide, and Sheshinski [1971] have developed a simulation program which incorporates an incremental investment-shift function to minimize sectoral supply shortfalls while maintaining full intersectoral consistency.

consumption and inventory accumulation might be varied during early years of a plan.[41] A final "shock absorber" evident in the real world is excess capacity, which permits supply to vary at a rate different from changes in demand. This seems to be important in solutions to dynamic optimizing models.[42]

After all supply adjustments have been exhausted, the planner must still check the consistency of the resources required. *Ex post* evaluation of the balance of payments gap and of savings needs varied considerably among solutions of the Bergsman–Manne model, depending upon the import requirements of alternative dynamic investment programs computed by the model. The dynamic input-output model alone gives inadequate tests of economic feasibility of both exogenous targets and endogenous variables. The model is simply a tool used to structure discussions with policy makers which forces assumptions to be made explicit.

## 6. OTHER APPLICATIONS OF CONSISTENCY MODELS

The importance of evaluating the intersectoral consistency of an investment program has been demonstrated by the planning experience of India, Turkey, Chile, Korea, Israel, and Japan. These are all economies where the complexity of the interindustry flow matrix has exceeded a critical level,[43] and where there has been considerable import substitution in the capital goods sectors.

A great number of input-output models have been built for application in developing countries. The following discussion of three country applications is presented to illustrate possible applications and should not be seen as an exhaustive list of "successful" applications.

Perhaps the most effective use of multisectoral consistency models for investment planning is provided by Korea during the preparation of the Second Five Year Plan. This involved extensive use of a 43-sector consistency model. There is good documentation[44] of how alternative investment pro-

---

41. Two schools of thought prevail among development planners concerning the realism of and likely speed of adjustment to an optimal growth path. For example, Manne [1970] describes the computational advantages of a "gradualist path" of consumption, while Eckaus and Parikh [1968] consider it an unrealistic requirement to expect consumption to grow smoothly during a period of transition from unbalanced to balanced growth.

42. See Chapter III, section 3.3 for other applications of dynamic Leontief models.

43. The density of the transactions matrix where this threshold occurs could be computed. The rationale for defining a minimum interdependent structure is recognized by Griffin and Enos [1970] when they point out that "comprehensiveness and consistency in planning will be more important in economies in which interindustry flows are large, institutions are well adapted to modern needs, and foreign trade is relatively unimportant, i.e., in economies where the growth impetus originates in the domestic industrial sector."

44. Adelman [1969], Cole and Lyman [1971], Jo and Park [1972], and Robinson and Byung-Nak Song [1972].

grams were used in an extensive committee system of indicative planning to encourage coordinated and complementary action among the industrialists of the private sector.

Investment planning seems to have been a sufficient input to public policy formation at the time of the Second Plan, so long as the Korean economy was not too complex and used a relatively centralized system of resource allocation. However, a more sophisticated but similar consistency model proved to be less useful during the preparation of the Third Plan. The need for direct investment planning was less since market efficiency had strengthened. Then government planners turned more heavily to econometric projection models of increased detail, including models of price determination, whose solutions provide a comprehensive and consistent perspective for indicative planning.

The State Planning Organization (SPO) of the Turkish government used a modified version of the Tims [1968] consistency model to set the internal balance in its investment program for 37 sectors within a macroeconomic framework for the 1973–74 Plan. The major objective of this model (see Turkey, SPO [1972]) was to derive alternative sectoral investment programs as functions of a number of exogenous parameters. These included: sectoral export levels, private savings propensity, tax rates,[45] a fixed pattern of sectoral import substitution, and the growth rate of GDP. The principal experiments focused on the effects of changing the targeted rate of GDP growth, observing its effect on consumption and the government budget. Unfortunately the model was not used to test the impact on the macroeconomic aggregates of alternative patterns of import substitution. This could be very important in order to get some notion of Turkey's comparative advantage during its transition phase to membership in the European Economic Community.

Clark and Taylor [1971] developed a dynamic consistency framework of the Bergsman–Manne type for Chilean investment planning. The planning model for Chile was designed to make detailed demand projections throughout the planning period which could be tested for consistency with known production expansion: i.e., information about investment plans, projects in preparation, and changes planned in the pattern of imports and exports.

The Chilean dynamic input-output model utilized terminal targets set by a static optimizing model. The flexibility of the software package designed to control the policy simulations accommodates large amounts of exogenous data previously collected by sector coordinators and stored in computer-oriented data banks. This routine permitted low cost and rapid consistency tests of alternative targets, parameter values, policies, and resource limits. In addition, the Chilean Planning Office developed a dynamic linear programming model covering the same period of time. Comparison of the solutions of the dynamic consistency model with the dynamic optimizing system reveals that

---

45. Government savings were the endogenous residual item discussed in connection with equation (4.5) which implies no upper bound on the marginal rate of saving.

there would be an efficiency (and welfare) loss of only a few percentage points of GDP (and aggregate consumption) if the solution to the consistency model rather than the optimizing model was followed by the economy.[46] This stems from the importance of small changes in the time-phasing of sectoral investment.

## 7. Use of Consistency Models

Having reviewed some of the consistency specifications actually used to plan multisectoral investment patterns we must still ask whether their solutions produce new and useful information.[47] How does the planner use the model's output? For example, suppose the solution of a consistency model calls for an expansion of 7.4 percent in textiles, of 3.9 percent in food processing, of 14.2 percent in transportation, and 11.8 percent in electrical equipment manufactures. These sectoral changes are planned for in the fifth year of the plan; all are mutually consistent and occur simultaneously with a 6.3 percent increment of GDP, reduction by 1.2 percent in the unemployment rate, and a growth of the trade gap by 19 percent. If this information were computed in a static model, the figures would represent an average annual change over the period of the model. Otherwise the estimated sectoral growth rates and the aggregate behavior they constitute may show considerable intraplan variance from year to year when taken from the solution of a dynamic consistency model. What use can the planner make of our hypothetical model's results?

First of all, the solution is not a prediction. The significance of the results depends upon the relative stability[48] of the values taken by each variable, relative to all other feasible alternatives. Dialogue with policy makers will determine the degree to which changes by the economic structure are socially and politically desirable. Utilizing this proxy for a social welfare function, if variables are fairly well behaved, the model's results in some sense give an outline for a plan. Just how useful this is depends in part on the country's planning organization. For example, in planning agencies where sector coordinators work with the functional ministries of agriculture, industry, housing, transport, health, education, and so on, the pattern of sectoral investment derived from a solution of the model can be compared with private

---

46. The 10-year value of aggregate consumption discounted at 8 percent given by the solution of the optimizing model exceeded the value of the same variables from the consistency model by 3 percent. See Bergendorff, Clark, and Taylor [1973].

47. On this point the record is not clear. Most authors report the type of model used and some of the results. There are no accounts of the decisions taken and policies revised based on information derived from economy-wide consistency studies.

48. Here parametric variation of key parameters, made singly or as interrelated changes of several parameters, are the normal sensitivity tests. Variation of resource constraints (which trace trade-offs on the efficiency frontier) is not possible as it would be in LP. With simulation models, one is not sure whether or not the patterns of resource use calculated endogenously by the model are the most efficient allocations.

sector projects and capital budgets being evaluated by public ministries. The coordinator's function will be to collect potentially useful projects sufficient to flesh out the skeleton of the plan provided by the multisectoral consistency model. For an agency without coordinators, a more formal approach may be required.

Another important use of an economy-wide multisectoral model has come from linking sectoral models and other studies of partial equilibrium behavior to the aggregate consistency framework. Interrelated models help create consistency among analytical foci of different parts of an economy (micro versus macro, sectoral versus aggregate, regional versus national, linear versus nonlinear behavior, target groups versus social welfare).

Not all variables of different models have to be directly linked or even maintain exactly equivalent values to be useful for consistency checks. For example, a savings rate in one system may be derived from household behavior and government surpluses, while in another model, savings are defined as a national accounts identity (a residual category). The latter may have theoretical and definitional meaning but is in reality collecting all the unexplained behavior in the system. The artful planner will recognize when it is legitimate to use a macrovariable as a control for a partial equilibrium analysis or vice versa. The explanation of and rationalization of different estimates of key macroparameters help make explicit the underlying technical, behavioral, and institutional assumptions often hidden within the macroeconomic analysis embodied in a development plan.[49]

Can projects be selected as part of a strictly nonoptimizing consistency framework? The answer may be a qualified yes, if planners maintain the appropriate consistencies.[50] Bergendorff, Clark, and Taylor [1973] compare the investment patterns derived by a dynamic input-output consistency model (described in Clark and Taylor [1971]) with the investment mix and timing recommended by the solution of an intertemporal optimizing model. Since many of the choice elements in a consistency framework are fixed to grow at exponential rates, or follow other smooth growth paths, the behavior of the variables of the consistency model strikingly contrasts with that of the investment programs derived from an optimizing model. The latter obtains its greater efficiency by "bunching" and "switching" competitive imports, investment, and the sectoral allocation of foot-loose factors over time. The authors say, "to a degree, economic intuition and rules-of-thumb about investment advice, can explain these things. This in turn, suggests that artful

---

49. Multilevel models are an attempt to impose a consistency criterion over decentralized, sectoral, or partial equilibrium behavior. See Kornai [1969] and [1973] and Goreux [1973] for expositions concerning the maintenance of consistency by multilevel planning.

50. See Chapter VIII, sections 3 and 4 for discussion of how the logic of shadow prices can be used within the framework of a consistency planning model as a guide for project selection.

juggling of the time-phasing of investment in a simulation model such as the one considered here might help raise its efficiency rating." The authors go on to discuss principles which govern the interrelationship between sectoral capital-output ratios, tariff rates, and shadow exchange rates. Furthermore, if labor is a redundant resource, labor could be brought directly into the analysis as was done by Weisskopf [1967].[51]

While it is impossible to apply the same selection criterion in a consistency framework as the full optimizing model, a wide range of solutions may be produced with the consistency model. This array of alternatives may be presented to policy makers as a set of policy options representing trade-offs among objectives. Policy makers can then select the strategy they prefer. From careful analysis of the multisectoral results the planner can determine what factors are causing the elements of supply and demand of each sector to behave as they do. With these rules in mind, the same logic may then be imposed upon the subset of elements which comprise each sector, namely, groups of projects.

This approach may overlook some indirect effect lost at the sectoral level due to aggregation bias. Furthermore exogenous information should enter the calculus whenever possible. However, by constant work with a portfolio of projects, a sector planner can effectively replace optimization by a combination of logic and selective complete enumeration techniques. Using the sectoral investment time pattern as a guide, the plan can present project selections which may be more efficient than other macroeconomic choices (made by partial equilibrium criteria) because of their consistency with a balanced set of aggregate goals.

---

51. See the evaluation of Weisskopf's treatment of this problem in Chapter VI, section 3.

Chapter VI

# THE FOREIGN TRADE SECTOR IN PLANNING MODELS

## T. N. SRINIVASAN

## 1. INTRODUCTION

The importance of foreign trade for development is a continuing theme in the economic literature. Both the classical "trade as an engine of growth" doctrine and the modern two-gap planning models reflect this importance. Opening an economy to external trade has two important implications: (i) Given trade, domestic production and use of each commodity can differ, with production exceeding (falling short of) use in the case of exported (imported) commodities. Thus, even if there are no production commodity changes with the introduction of trade, welfare could be improved as long as there are substitution possibilities in consumption or use. (ii) Insofar as technology permits substitution in production, introduction of trade makes it possible to reallocate resources in production along the lines of comparative advantage, thereby making an additional contribution to GNP. Thus, trade contributes to welfare by efficiently reallocating resources in consumption and production. That balanced trade contributes to the welfare of the trading partners was not grasped by mercantilists of yore and still is not, by their modern counterparts.

The extent of improvement in efficiency brought about by trade depends on the extent to which a country relies on trade. Insofar as some developing countries are much more dependent than developed countries on international trade for essential commodities, particularly those incorporating non-traditional technology, the success of their growth strategy will depend on the success with which their domestic production and use structure reflects changing trade possibilities. At initial stages of development, countries do not have industries that produce capital goods or chemicals, even though consideration of comparative advantage may involve setting up such industries in the course of development. In fact, comparative advantage in a dynamic context may involve either substitution of produced inputs (made available through foreign trade and/or domestic production) for exhaustible resources, and/or responses to changing factor endowments and technology. However, in the short and medium run, the cost of domestic production of these goods is literally infinite for such countries. Indeed, there are relatively small countries for which it may never be optimal to set up a domestic capital goods

industry.[1] Hence, less developed countries *must* trade, either in the short run or forever, in order to accumulate capital and to grow, just as small regions in a country have to trade with other regions in the same country.

External resource inflow into a country has important implications for development for two reasons. First, such an inflow augments the country's capacity to import.[2] Second, it enables the country's domestic expenditure to exceed its income or, to put it in familiar terms, it makes it possible for the country to invest more than it saves. Indeed, these two aspects of foreign resource inflow are at the very heart of the two-gap models of development.

We can thus distinguish two aspects of external trade activities, the comparative advantage or efficiency aspect and the resource augmenting aspect. The literature on effective rate of protection (ERP), domestic resource cost (DRC) of foreign exchange, and dynamic comparative advantage can be termed as dealing with production efficiency in the context of trade.[3] The literature on the shadow price of foreign exchange,[4] based on a general equilibrium or programming model, relates to both aspects, while in the literature based on partial equilibrium models, the two aspects tend to get mixed up.

In discussing these two aspects, one could approach them from a descriptive (i.e., positive) point of view or, alternatively, from a policy (i.e., normative) point of view. Later, we shall show that evaluation of import substitution strategies of development adopted by many developing countries through the computation of the spread of ERP's afforded to various production activities, or the DRC's implicit in them, represents the positive point of view. On the other hand, the determination of investment allocation in a static or dynamic optimizing model, as well as the specification of criteria for project selection (given trading possibilities), represents the normative point of view. Insofar as the ERP's or DRC's prevailing at any point of time are used either to predict or direct resource flows, these also have a normative aspect.

In what follows, we shall first discuss the different ways in which foreign

---

1. See Part VI of Robinson [1963].

2. This is always true in the short run whether the capital inflow is in the form of grants, "hard" loans, or direct private investment. However, loans and private investment naturally involve obligations in the future to amortize capital, pay interest, or repatriate profits.

3. The concept of Effective Rate of Protection (ERP) was developed because tariffs are often levied on both inputs and outputs of a process, so that the nominal tariff on output does not reflect fully the protection afforded to domestic resources (value added) used in production. The related concept of Domestic Resource Cost (DRC) measures the cost of domestic resources used in earning or saving a unit of foreign exchange. See Bruno [1972a], Corden [1971], and Krueger [1966, 1972], and sections 3 and 4 in this chapter for further discussion of these concepts.

4. The shadow price of foreign exchange is the increment in social welfare associated with a unit increase in the availability of foreign exchange. This should be distinguished from overvaluation or undervaluation of domestic currency under a fixed exchange rate system.

trade possibilities have been treated in economy-wide planning models. Then we shall comment on the calculation and use of ERP, DRC, and the shadow price of foreign exchange. We shall conclude with a discussion of some of the problems that arise in real-world planning of the foreign trade sector, particularly in a world full of tariff and nontariff barriers to trade, project- and/or commodity-tied aid flows, and bilateral barter trade arrangements.

## 2. MULTISECTOR PLANNING MODELS INCORPORATING FOREIGN TRADE

A model, by definition, is an abstraction of reality. A successful or, more appropriately, a useful model will retain sufficient elements of reality for the purpose in view. However, data and computer capacity limitations may impose severe constraints in this regard, particularly in the treatment of foreign trade.

Let us begin with the typical commodity balance of a planning model:[5]

$$X_i + M_i \geq (Int)_i + C_i + I_i + E_i, \tag{2.1}$$

where:  $X_i$ = gross output of sector $i$,

$M_i$ = "competitive" imports of commodity $i$,

$(Int)_i$ = intermediate demand for commodity $i$,[6]

$C_i$ = consumption demand for commodity $i$,

$I_i$ = investment demand for commodity $i$, and

$E_i$ = export demand for commodity $i$.

If it were possible to include a constraint row for every possible commodity and service that potentially or actually could be demanded or supplied in every relevant period, no problems would arise and all the variables in the above constraint could then be defined in physical units. It is immediately obvious, however, that even in the least developed economy in the contemporary world, the number of distinct commodities in use is so large that assigning a constraint for each such commodity is infeasible. Thus, aggregation into commodity groups becomes inescapable.

To be sure, the degree of aggregation of commodities, as well as time (days, weeks, months, quarters, years, or a number of years), depends upon the use to which the model is to be put, the availability of data, and computer capacity limitations. In aggregating a number of commodities into a single commodity group, valuation weights are needed. A number of conceptual as well as data availability problems arise in choosing among the possible valuation weights, for instance, the choice between domestic producer's or

---

5. For clarity we have suppressed the time subscript $t$ associated with the variables. Thus we should have denoted by $X_{it}$, the gross output of sector $i$, period $t$, etc.

6. It is usual but not always necessary to express $(Int)_i$ as $\sum_j a_{ij}X_j$, the sum of intermediate sales calculated on the basis of input-output coefficients $a_{ij}$. See Chapters III and V.

market prices for domestically produced commodities; or between c.i.f. or tariff-inclusive prices for imports (or market prices in the case of commodities whose imports are subject to tariffs *and* quota restrictions); or between f.o.b. or tax or subsidy-inclusive prices for exports, and so on. Data availability may impose severe limitations in achieving consistency in the aggregation procedure adopted for different components of the demand and supply sides of the commodity balance relating to an aggregate sector. These difficult problems, though not germane to our present discussion, are discussed briefly in the appendix to this chapter.

In optimizing models, aggregation introduces an additional problem with respect to exports and competitive imports, insofar as they are endogenous. For, unless specific constraints are introduced to prevent it, in an optimal solution, either $E_i$ or $M_i$ or both will be zero. However, given that commodity $i$ is an aggregate of a number of commodities, even if, from an optimality point of view, each commodity constituting the aggregate will either be exported in positive amounts or imported in positive amounts (but not simultaneously imported and exported in positive amounts), in the aggregate commodity $i$, both exported and imported goods may be included. Thus, the optimal solution of an aggregated model may be at variance with the truly optimal solution that would have been obtained in a more disaggregated model.

A similar problem arises when aggregation is made with respect to seasons of a year or regions within a country. It may be optimal for a country to import a commodity in one season and to export it in another, if storage costs are high. It may be optimal for one region of a country to export a commodity but for another region of the same country to import it, if internal transport costs are sufficiently high. Thus, aggregation will result in distortions of trade flows. To minimize these aggregation biases, ad hoc constraints are often introduced, placing bounds on the imports and exports of each trading sector. However, it is difficult to avoid arbitrariness in the specification of such bounds.

Even if there are no aggregation difficulties, it may still be desirable to specify upper bounds on exports and imports of each trading sector, because it is usually unrealistic to postulate that foreign demand for exports is infinitely elastic. To take into account the fact that an increasing volume of exports can be made only at decreasing unit prices, and still remain within a linear programming framework,[7] requires approximation of the marginal revenue curve (associated with a given downward sloping demand curve) by a step function, as in Figure 1.

---

7. See Chapter XII for a discussion of this and other approaches to nonlinearities. Of course one could abandon linear programming in favor of nonlinear programming and avoid piece-wise linear approximations. For some early exercises in nonlinear programming see Chenery and Kretschmer [1956] as well as Chenery and Uzawa [1958].

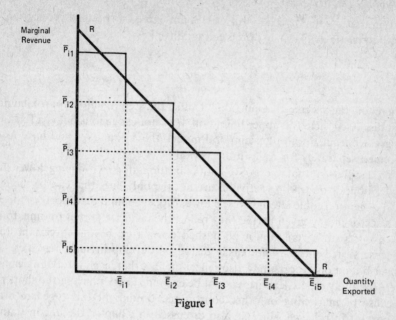

Figure 1

Thus instead of a single export variable $E_i$, we would have a number of variables $E_{i1}$, $E_{i2}$, ..., etc., and a number of constraints such as:

$$0 \le E_{i1} \le \bar{E}_{i2}, \ldots, E_{i,k-1} \le \bar{E}_{ik}, \quad \text{and so on.}$$

Then, by assumption, each unit of exports up to quantity $\bar{E}_{i1}$ can be made at a value of $\bar{P}_{i1}$, while each unit between $\bar{E}_{i1}$ and $\bar{E}_{i2}$ will fetch a lower value $\bar{P}_{i2}$, and so on. Total exports of $i$ will then equal $E_i = \sum_{k=1}^{K} E_{ik}$ and the export earnings will equal $\sum_{k=1}^{K} \bar{P}_{ik} E_{ik}$, an approximation to the area under the marginal revenue curve. Since by construction $\bar{P}_{ik} \ge \bar{P}_{ik+1}$, in an optimal solution $E_{ik} > 0$ implies that $E_{ij} = \bar{E}_{ij}$ for $j < k$; this prevents inconsistencies in which positive exports at marginal unit value $\bar{P}_{ik}$ are being made while exports at a higher marginal value are not being made to the maximum feasible extent. Though this step function approach is straightforward, often $K$ is set at 1 so that only a single upper bound constraint $E_i \le \bar{E}_i$ is imposed. Similarly, if the foreign supply of imports is not infinitely elastic, so that the marginal cost of imports rises with volume, one can also approximate the upward sloping marginal cost curve with a step function. Again the step function may have only one step, resulting in a single upper bound for imports.

There is yet another reason why one may wish to impose an upper bound on imports. Very often, the planning authorities have a specified target for import substitution in a given trading sector. A typical, but by no means the only, way in which this is reflected in a model is to impose a constraint

159

stating that competitive imports should not exceed a specified proportion of total domestic availability of the commodity; i.e.,

$$M_i \leq \alpha(X_i + M_i) \quad \text{or} \quad M_i \leq \frac{\alpha}{1 - \alpha} X_i$$

where $\alpha$ is the specified proportion.[8] Unlike the step function approximation just discussed, here the upper bound on $M_i$ is not exogenous but is a function of gross output. In an intertemporal model, these bounds would have to be specified separately for each future period.[9]

We emphasize that the above rationalizations for introducing lower and upper bounds on trading activities are not the only ones that can be thought of. To mention some alternatives: a lower (upper) bound on exports (imports) of a sector in any given period may reflect the fact that even if optimal to do so, exports (imports) cannot be pushed down (up) beyond a certain limit because vested interests not easily dislodged develop in such activities. An upper bound on exports may also reflect the fact that, even if foreign demand were infinitely elastic, exports cannot be expanded very much in the short run because of marketing or other constraints. Bounds of this type are often important in practice, since as also discussed in Chapter III, unconstrained optimizing models have strong tendencies toward trade specialization in their commodity aggregates.

The imports included in the $M_i$ terms of equation (2.1) are called competitive imports, or imports that substitute, unit for unit, with domestic production. In planning models, a second category of imports, called "noncompetitive" imports, is often introduced to reflect the fact that production in any sector will often involve the use of some inputs for which there is neither current domestic production capacity nor any possibility of establishing capacity in the medium to long term.[10]

As mentioned earlier, in small countries, a significant number of commodities fall into the category of noncompetitive imports. If $z_i$ is the foreign exchange required to procure the noncompetitive imports needed per unit of

---

8. See, for instance, Chakravarty and Lefeber [1965] or Eckaus and Parikh [1968]. The shadow price associated with this constraint (when binding) indicates the cost (in terms of the objective function) of forced import substitution past the point of maximum comparative advantage. Note, however, that because of the aggregation difficulties discussed above, a high shadow price on this constraint is only indicative of inefficiency until confirmed by detailed commodity studies.

9. There are many other approaches in the literature to bounding competitive imports, including parametric variation of the rising import cost curves discussed earlier (Manne [1973a]), quotas on the amount of foreign exchange assigned to certain import classes (Cardwell [1973]), attempts to include tariffs in the model specification (Evans [1972]), and so on. Flexibility and policy implications of these different specifications vary; the interested reader should consult the sources cited.

10. See Chapter III, section 2.1, iii, for a discussion of this dichotomy.

domestic output in sector $i$, the total amount of foreign exchange spent on such imports can be expressed as $\sum_i z_i X_i$. This sum will then be included as part of the total import bill (another part is, of course, total competitive imports, $\sum_i M_i$). This way of introducing noncompetitive imports is equivalent to adding a row to an input-output matrix, analogous to the rows corresponding to factor inputs such as labor or capital.[11]

We now turn to the balance of payments (BOP) constraint. In principle, it is simple to write down:

Foreign exchange spent on imports

    $-$ Foreign exchange earned by exports $\leq$ Foreign capital inflow.   (2.2)

In practice, however, a number of conceptual and data problems arise. For instance, if the competitive imports have been expressed in domestic market prices, then only the foreign exchange actually spent on securing these imports should be included in (2.2). Of course, if the difference between the c.i.f. price of imports and the domestic market price to producers is exactly equal to the tariff, this should be easy to do. Similarly, in the case of exports, if the difference between the producers' price and f.o.b. realization is only an export tax or subsidy, the correction needed to convert $E_i$ defined in domestic market prices to its foreign exchange equivalent would be simple. Such simplicity is rare due to the costs of distribution, commercialization, insurance, storage, and so forth, which separate border prices from market or producer prices.

There is yet another aspect of aggregation that crops up in converting $E_i$ and $M_i$ to their foreign exchange equivalents. In the commodity balance equation (2.1), a unit of $E_i$ is equivalent to a unit of $M_i$. However, the foreign exchange cost of a unit of $M_i$ and foreign exchange earned by a unit of $E_i$ could differ for a number of reasons: (i) the commodity composition of exports and imports of sector $i$ could differ; (ii) even for the same commodity, export and import prices will differ as exports are valued f.o.b. while imports are valued at c.i.f.; and (iii) the average tariff on imports included in $M_i$ may be different from the average subsidy on exports included in $E_i$.

We have so far conducted our discussion under the assumption that our economy trades with a single entity called "rest of the world," allowing unique export and import prices to be defined. However, trading in the real world takes place in blocs, with varying degrees of convertibility between currencies. Hence, in principle, separate trading activities (with corresponding upper and lower bounds) would have to be introduced for trade with each major bloc. Corresponding balance of payments constraints would also have to be introduced. Kornai [1967] has moved a step in this direction by

---

11. Given that the different sectors import different baskets of noncompetitive intermediate inputs, aggregation problems are reduced if one works with several additional rows, one for each major type of noncompetitive imports. The single row mentioned in the text is often an aggregate of a multi-row import matrix.

introducing two separate BOP constraints accounting for Hungary's trade with Eastern and Western blocs.

## 3. Foreign Trade in Planning Models: Applications

Let us now turn to a discussion of the uses to which planning models have been put in analyzing the growth implications of foreign trade possibilities and external resource inflows. Planning models can be of a consistency type in which one derives the gross output and investment levels consistent with exogenously specified final demands, with no elements of choice present. Alternatively, they can be of an optimizing variety, in which there are alternative ways of achieving specified targets and the model chooses one of these so as to maximize some objective function. Consistency models can of course be used to generate information, useful for choosing among policies, by running the model once for each policy combination. But the essential difference between the two lies in the optimizing model's making trade choice endogenous. We confine our discussion here mostly to optimizing models since we focus on foreign trade choices.

The primary analytical tool in these models is sensitivity analysis. Basically, there are three sets of parameters associated with the foreign trade activities in a planning model: (i) parameters that enter the objective function (which might appear if the objective is specified as minimizing the volume of the foreign resource flows required to achieve specified targets for consumption, investment, and so on, or if the objective is the weighted sum of domestic and foreign resource cost of achieving the same targets); (ii) parameters related to the lower and upper bounds on exports and imports of different sectors, as well as those related to noncompetitive imports; and (iii) parameters related to external resource inflow. By solving a model for alternative specifications of the parameters, one can gain valuable insights.

The range of issues analyzed quantitatively by the use of planning models is indeed very wide. For instance, the implications of the import substitution strategy are explored in different ways in different models. Weisskopf [1971] induces increasing import substitution in his target-year linear programming model for India by increasing the relative weight of foreign resources in the objective function, which is a weighted sum of domestic and foreign resource costs. The former are the labor (wage) costs associated with achieving terminal year targets for aggregate consumption, exports, and so on. Foreign resource costs are the foreign exchange costs of financing the competitive and noncompetitive imports required to achieve the given targets. Other constraints include the usual commodity balances, constraints on capacity, and lower bounds on competitive imports as a proportion of domestic availability. Exports are exogenous. Thus there is no explicit BOP constraint since, given exogenous exports, the cost of foreign capital inflow is included in the objective function through foreign exchange costs. Algebraically the objective

function is $\Theta^L L + \Theta^M M$ where $L$ and $M$ represent domestic and foreign resource costs, respectively. The relative weight $\Theta^M/\Theta^L$ could be interpreted as an exchange rate.

The comparative advantage or efficiency implications are seen by ranking the industries according to the exchange rate at which the domestic production activity first becomes profitable. Thus, the higher the ratio has to be set before it is optimal to have domestic production of a commodity, the less desirable it is from the point of view of comparative advantage and, hence, import substitution.

An alternative (similar though not identical) ranking of sectors is obtained by examining the ratio of the shadow price of the commodity balance constraint of a sector (2.1) to the import price of its output. This shadow price is obtained from a run in which domestic costs are assigned a zero weight (i.e., $\Theta^L = 0$) in the objective function. As such it represents the minimal marginal import content of domestic production. This is so because, given $\Theta^L = 0$, foreign resource costs are minimized so that the shadow price of the commodity balance constraint represents the additional foreign exchange cost associated with a unit increase in the output of the sector—in other words, the marginal import content of domestic production. Thus, the ratio of shadow price of domestic production to import price represents the relative foreign exchange content of domestic production as compared to imports. As such, the higher the ratio, the less attractive the sector is from the point of view of import substitution.

In Weisskopf's model, the resource augmenting aspect of foreign capital inflow is depicted in two ways. If the growth targets with respect to consumption, exports, investment, and so on, are unchanged while the relative weight of the foreign resource cost in the objective function is varied, a trade-off between external capital inflow and domestic savings is derived. As is to be expected, as the relative weight of external resource cost is increased, more domestic savings and less foreign capital are used to achieve the given targets, and the substitution of domestic savings for foreign resources becomes increasingly costly. Alternatively, one can view the economy-wide incremental capital-output ratio as a measure of efficiency of investment in the model. As the relative weight of foreign resource cost increases, the capital-output ratio rises, reflecting increasing costs of import substitution or, equivalently, the increasing productivity of foreign resource flow.[12]

Tendulkar [1971] also works with a target year linear programming model for India. His objective function is aggregate consumption in the target year.

---

12. Two other studies concerned with the make-or-buy problem of import substitution in a static LP model are Bruno [1967a], which compares import substitution with export expansion alternatives at a fairly aggregate sector level, and (similar to Weisskopf's study) a static LP study of Nigeria, Clark [1970], which specifies an LP model with project data in order to test alternative import substitution strategies.

Two variants of the model are considered: (i) the open-loop variant, in which it is assumed that domestic savings can be raised to any extent required so that foreign resource availability becomes the binding constraint on investment; and (ii) the closed-loop variant, in which a limit on the ability to raise domestic savings is set through fixed (but different) marginal propensities to save out of wage and non-wage incomes. Other constraints include commodity balance constraints, upper and lower bounds on export activities, capacity constraints, lower bounds on competitive import activities, and a BOP constraint with an exogenously specified external resource flow.

The sensitivity analysis consists in varying the level of the exogenously specified external resource flow. The resource augmenting aspect of external resource flow is measured by its shadow price, the additional consumption generated by an additional unit of this resource. Not surprisingly, the closed-loop variant yields a higher shadow price at each level of this flow, the difference narrowing as the level of the flow increases. This reflects the fact that in the closed-loop variant, additional foreign resources increase import capacity as well as domestic investment capacity, while in the open-loop variant, they break only the import bottleneck.

Tendulkar also presents the incremental capital-output ratios, which, as expected, are higher in the closed-loop model and fall in both as the external resource flow increases. Though Tendulkar does not present such results, one could, in principle, obtain a ranking of sectors according to comparative advantage by ranking them with regard to the level of foreign resource inflow at which competitive imports of each sector first appear in the optimal solution. This ranking would, of course, differ between the two variants of the model, since the savings-generating capacity of production in a sector (via its payments to labor and capital) is given a value in the closed-loop (but not in the open-loop) model.

Manne and Weisskopf [1970] present an intertemporal model in which three alternative patterns of capital inflow are specified, all starting from the same initial year inflow but representing differing rates of decline over time. The marginal propensity to save is limited to a maximum rate of 0.20. The maximand is the *increment* $\Delta$ in aggregate consumption in the first year, given that the initial year's consumption *level* $C_0$, as well as the growth rate $g$ of the *increments* in following years, are exogenously specified. Thus, $\Delta$ is maximized subject to:

$$C_t = C_0 + \Delta\left[\frac{(1 + g)^t - 1}{g}\right], \tag{3.1}$$

and all other constraints. This is the so-called "gradualist" consumption path requirement.[13] Manne and Weisskopf show that the aggregate incremental capital-output ratio, as well as the shadow price of foreign exchange, increases as the rate of decline in aid flow increases.

---

13. See section 5 of Chapter III for more details regarding this objective function.

Bergsman and Manne [1966], in their "almost consistent" model of India's Fourth and Fifth Five Year Plans (as proposed in 1965), compare the time paths of the BOP under alternative strategies of development. The strategies are defined in terms of aggregate growth and import substitution targets. The model postulates consistency (between demand and supply of output of each sector) only for the terminal (target) years of the two plans. An unusual feature of this model as compared to other static models is its use of inter-polation techniques to approximate time paths of crucial variables.[14] Its most striking result is that even though faster import substitution (in the sense of more rapid decline in the ratio of imports to domestic output) in the capital goods sectors requires higher imports to be used in building up domestic capacity and, therefore, larger trade deficits in the early years, these are more than offset by the imports saved in later years. Thus the sum of trade deficits during the 10 years (whether discounted at 0 percent or 10 percent per annum) is less in the case of the faster import substitution strategy. The policy implication is that a larger external resource flow in the early years (to build up capacity in import substituting industries) *decreases* the total aid (over the 10 years) needed to sustain the growth targets.

The Chenery and MacEwan [1966] model for Pakistan does not take external capital inflows as a datum but as a choice variable to be optimized explicitly. Their objective function is the sum of three elements: (i) the sum of discounted consumption over the planning horizon; (ii) the weighted value of terminal year GNP; and (iii) the sum of discounted capital inflow multiplied by a negative number representing the cost of a self-reliance policy independent of need for capital inflows. Production is aggregated into just two sectors: tradables (export or import substituting) and nontraded production. Three alternative forms of aid flow are postulated. In the first, the "cost" of self-reliance is specified while the optimization procedure determines the year by which aid is reduced to zero and the discounted sum of aid flows. In the second, the aid termination date is specified while its shadow price and total amount (discounted) are endogenously determined. In the third, only the discounted sum of foreign aid is specified, while the shadow price of aid and its termination date are determined through optimization.

The most interesting feature of the Chenery–MacEwan dynamic optimization solutions is that they fall into a time pattern—an initial period in which aid is used to push investment to its upper limit of absorptive capacity, with capacity creation for traded goods production and nontraded goods production being evenly divided; a middle period in which investment growth is slowed while its composition is shifted in favor of capacity creation for tradables and during which aid flows are phased out; and a final period in which aid is reduced to zero and balanced growth in both production sectors

---

14. This is discussed in detail in Chapter V.

is achieved. This pattern of aid utilization is very similar to that reported by Bergsman and Manne [1966] and is typical of planning models in which capital inflows early in the planning period can be used without rapidly increasing costs to build up capacity with a long-lasting payoff, as in Bruno [1974]. As noted earlier, Chenery and MacEwan also find that aid in the first part of the planning period is used to build up capacity for import substitution. The shadow price of aid conforms to the predictable pattern, falling with the volume of aid and rising with increases in absorptive capacity and marginal propensity to save.

Some of the most interesting studies in this context are the various planning models for the Israeli economy reported by Bruno, Dougherty, and Fraenkel [1970]. This study is an illuminating one. The objective function is the sum of two components: the sum of discounted consumption plus the discounted value of the terminal capital stock. Three alternative versions of the model are considered. In the first, no savings constraint is imposed and the time pattern of aid inflow is subject to choice, given its fixed total discounted sum. In the second, the aid inflows are flexible but a savings constraint is imposed. In the third, no savings constraint is imposed but aid inflows are specified for each period with no intertemporal transfers permitted. The discount rate used in the objective function (10 percent) is higher than that (8 percent) specified for aid discounting.

In the solutions in which there is flexibility for choosing the time pattern, it is optimal to obtain more aid initially and to repay it in later years by expanding exports and by import substitution. The pattern of comparative advantage is also indicated by the ranking of industries according to overall order or profitability. Though a decrease in foreign aid availability leads to the expansion of exports from different sectors at different points in time, thereby showing that the profitability of different sectors changes over time, nevertheless, within each time period the relative profitability rankings of the sectors remain substantially the same. As in all the models discussed so far, the shadow price of foreign aid flow falls when the level of aid inflow is increased, and rises when domestic savings are increased. This last observation reflects a complementary relationship between foreign and domestic savings which often occurs in these models because additional foreign inflow permits additional production (by easing the "trade gap" restriction on noncompetitive imports), which in turn permits additional savings through the Tendulkar closed-loop mechanism.

### 4. CRITERIA FOR PROJECT SELECTION: GENERAL EQUILIBRIUM APPROACH

Let us now turn to criteria that have been proposed in the literature for the selection of investment projects in general and export promoting or import substituting projects in particular. One approach is to use a full general

equilibrium intertemporal optimizing model to generate a set of shadow prices for resources and outputs. These shadow prices are then used to determine whether a proposed project yields a positive net benefit, with only those projects yielding positive benefits being selected. Logically, if the projects are of sufficient importance and size that the shadow prices will be altered once they are included, the programming model has to be run again to determine a new set of shadow prices. These may in turn lead to the inclusion of other projects and the dropping of some. This procedure has to be repeated until all the excluded projects yield nonpositive net benefits at the shadow prices of the last iteration. Such an iterative computation may be costly. However, if the projects are small enough and the model has enough substitution possibilities built into it, the shadow prices are likely to be insensitive to the inclusion or exclusion of a few projects.

The use of shadow prices derived from a general equilibrium model to evaluate projects has some attractive features. It makes logically equivalent the three apparently different investment criteria based on return to capital, domestic resource cost of earning or saving foreign exchange, and social marginal productivity.[15] We define a "project" by $(n + m)$ coefficients, $a_i(i = 1, 2, \ldots n)$ and $f_j$ $(j = 1, 2, \ldots, m)$ where $a_i$'s represent inputs (if negative) and outputs (if positive) of the project in terms of commodities and $f_j$'s represent primary factor inputs. If we denote by $p_i$ the shadow price of commodity $i$ and $v_j$ the shadow price of a unit of service from factor $j$, the net benefit of the project is:

$$B = \sum_{i=1}^{n} a_i p_i - \sum_{j=1}^{m} f_j v_j. \tag{4.1}$$

If $B > 0$, the project is to be selected.

Now this criterion, $B > 0$ where the social productivity of the project is positive, can be interpreted in different ways. Suppose the $m$th factor is capital whose unit shadow price is $K$. Let the shadow rate of return on capital be $r$. Then, by definition, $v_m = Kr$. Thus $B > 0$ is equivalent to:

$$\sum_{i=1}^{n} a_i p_i - \sum_{j=1}^{m-1} f_j v_j - f_m Kr > 0,$$

or,

$$\frac{\sum_{i=1}^{n} a_i p_i - \sum_{j=1}^{m-1} f_j v_j}{f_m K} > r. \tag{4.2}$$

In this way of looking at the criterion of selection, $f_m K$ is the value of capital invested in the project and $\sum_{i=1}^{n} a_i p_i - \sum_{j=1}^{m} f_j v_j$ is the shadow rent earned by the capital invested. Their ratio is the rate of return earned by capital invested in the project. This criterion thus amounts to saying that the

---

15. To demonstrate this, see Bruno [1967b].

project should be selected if it earns a rate of return on capital at least as high as the shadow rate $r$.

Before we demonstrate the equivalence of this criterion to the domestic resource cost criterion in the case of projects involving tradable goods, let us draw attention to another attractive feature of this general equilibrium approach. It is this: if the shadow prices are correctly computed and are unaffected by the acceptance or rejection of the project, the net benefit of the project can be estimated from factor prices alone by using the coefficients of direct and indirect factor use. To show this, let us denote by $f_{ji}$ the *direct* and *indirect* amount of factor $j$ needed to produce one unit of commodity $i$.[16] Without loss of generality, let us assume that the project produces commodities $1$ to $k$, and uses as input commodities $k + 1$ to $n$. Then by definition $a_1, \ldots, a_k$ are positive and $a_{k+1}, \ldots, a_n$ are nonpositive. Then the value of the project's output is $\sum_{i=1}^{k} a_i p_i$. The direct and indirect amount of factor $j$ used in the project is $\bar{f}_j$ given by:[17]

$$\bar{f}_j = f_j + \sum_{i=k+1}^{n} (-a_i) f_{ji} \qquad (4.3)$$

(the negative sign in $-a_i$ is introduced to account for the fact that $a_i$'s are nonpositive). The benefit of the project evaluated using these total (direct and indirect) factor use coefficients is:

$$B' = \sum_{i=1}^{k} a_i p_i - \sum_{j=1}^{m} \bar{f}_j v_j$$

or,

$$B' = \sum_{i=1}^{k} a_i p_i - \sum_{j=1}^{m} [f_j - \sum_{i=k+1}^{n} a_i f_{ji}] v_j$$

or,

$$B' = \sum_{i=1}^{k} a_i p_i + \sum_{i=k+1}^{n} a_i ( \sum_{j=1}^{m} f_{ji} v_j) - \sum_{j=1}^{m} f_j v_j. \qquad (4.4)$$

Now, if the shadow price $p_i$ of the $i$th commodity has been correctly calculated, then it should equal the cost of direct and indirect factor inputs used in its production. That is $p_i = \sum_{j=1}^{m} f_{ji} v_j$. Hence:

$$B' = \sum_{i=1}^{k} a_i p_i + \sum_{i=k+1}^{n} a_i p_i - \sum_{j=1}^{m} f_j v_j,$$

or,

$$B' = \sum_{i=1}^{n} a_i p_i - \sum_{j=1}^{m} f_j v_j = B, \qquad (4.5)$$

---

16. The coefficients $f_{ji}$ are easy to compute if one assumes that each commodity is produced by one activity using all inputs in fixed proportions. If we allow substitution between inputs, we can still compute $f_{ji}$ as if the fixed-proportions assumption held, as long as the inclusion of the project does not change the shadow prices of commodities or factors.

17. Commodities not involved in the project, either as input or as output (i.e., those with $a_i = 0$) are counted in $k + 1$ to $n$.

where the last line follows from (4.1). This equivalence has the following important implications: even if one does not have the correct shadow prices of commodity inputs, as long as one has data on total factor inputs of a project and the correct shadow prices of factors, the true social benefit of a project can be calculated. This has some relevance for the Little–Mirrlees criterion to be discussed below.

Turning now to a project producing tradable goods, let the first primary factor be foreign exchange. Let $\bar{f}_{1i}, \bar{f}_{ji}$ be the total (direct and indirect) use of foreign exchange and domestic primary factor $j$, respectively, in the production of nontradable commodity $i$. Let the project produce tradable goods $1$ to $k$, with the world price, in foreign exchange, of tradable good $i$ being $p_i^f$.

Then, the foreign exchange *earned* or saved by the project is $\sum_{i=1}^{k} a_i p_i^f$. The foreign exchange *used* directly or indirectly through the tradables content of nontradable goods employed by the project (the negative sign of $a_i$ is to allow for the fact that $a_i \leq 0$ for inputs) is:

$$\sum_{i=k+1}^{n} (-a_i)\bar{f}_{1i} + f_1.$$

The amount of domestic factor $j$ used directly or indirectly through the factor content of nontradables by the project is:

$$\sum_{i=k+1}^{n} (-a_i)\bar{f}_{ji} + f_j.$$

Now, by definition, the benefit of the project is

$$B = \sum_{i=1}^{n} a_i p_i - \sum_{j=1}^{m} f_j v_j.$$

If we denote the shadow price of foreign exchange as $v$ then, if the shadow prices have been calculated correctly:

$$p_i = v p_i^f, \quad i = 1, 2, \ldots, k \tag{4.6}$$

and

$$p_i = v \bar{f}_{1i} + \sum_{j=2}^{m} \bar{f}_{ji} v_j, \quad i = k + 1, \ldots, n. \tag{4.7}$$

Hence:

$$B = v \left[ \sum_{i=1}^{k} a_i p_i^f \right] + \sum_{i=k+1}^{n} a_i \left[ \sum_{j=2}^{m} \bar{f}_{ji} v_j + v \bar{f}_{1i} \right] - v f_1 - \sum_{j=2}^{m} f_j v_j,$$

or,

$$B = v \left[ \sum_{i=1}^{k} a_i p_i^f - f_1 - \sum_{i=k+1}^{n} (-a_i)\bar{f}_{1i} \right] - \left[ \sum_{j=2}^{m} [f_j + \sum_{i=k+1}^{n} (-a_i)\bar{f}_{ji}] v_j \right] \tag{4.8}$$

or,

$B = v$ (Net foreign exchange earned or saved by the project) $-$ (Domestic resource cost of the project).

Thus, if $B > 0$, $v >$ Domestic resource cost of project/Net foreign exchange earned or saved. This ratio represents the domestic resource cost (DRC) of earning or saving a unit of foreign exchange by the project. The project should be selected if the DRC is less than the shadow exchange rate.

## 5. Criteria for Project Selection: Partial Equilibrium Approach

Let us now turn to a set of project selection criteria based on partial equilibrium analysis.[18] We will discuss first the Little–Mirrlees [1969] criterion. This should, perhaps, be more properly described as an approximation to a general equilibrium approach rather than a partial equilibrium one. Be that as it may, the basic assumption behind their criterion is that, for tradable commodities, the shadow price is indeed the marginal border price. If this assumption is accepted,[19] we can draw upon our earlier demonstration of the equivalence between the calculations based on the project's direct factor and commodity input coefficients and calculations based on total factor input coefficients, and modify it somewhat to derive the Little–Mirrlees criterion.

As before, let the first $k$ commodities be tradables. Instead of dividing the inputs (direct and indirect) used in producing a unit of a nontradable commodity into foreign exchange and domestic factors, let us divide them into inputs (again direct and indirect) of tradable commodities ($f_{qi}$ representing the input of tradable commodity $q$ per unit of commodity $i$) and domestic factors ($f_{ji}$ representing the input of domestic factor $j$ per unit of commodity $i$). Then, the net benefit $B$ of the project is given by:

$$B = \sum_{q=1}^{k} \left\{ a_q + \sum_{i=k+1}^{n} f_{qi}a_i \right\} p_q - \sum_{j=1}^{m} \left\{ f_j + \sum_{i=k+1}^{n} f_{ji}a_i \right\} v_j,$$

or

$$B = \sum_{q=1}^{k} \bar{a}_q p_q - \sum_{j=1}^{m} \bar{f}_j v_j, \tag{5.1}$$

where $\bar{a}_q = a_q + \sum_{i=k+1}^{n} f_{qi}a_i$, and $a_q$ is the direct use of output of tradable $q$ in the project, and $\sum_{i=k+1}^{n} f_{qi}a_i$ is the indirect use or saving of tradable $q$ arising out the use or production of nontradable $i$ in amounts $a_i$. Similarly, $\bar{f}_j = f_j + \sum_{i=k+1}^{n} f_{ji}a_i$. The project is chosen if $B > 0$.

The $p_q$'s are known once it is specified whether the extra supply is to come from a reduction in exports (in which case $p_q$ is the marginal f.o.b. price) or from an increase in imports (in which case $p_q$ is the marginal c.i.f. cost). The

---

18. See Bacha and Taylor [1971] for a discussion of some partial and general equilibrium methods of calculating the shadow price of foreign exchange.

19. Implicit in this is the assumption that optimal trade policies are being or will be followed. See Sen [1972] for a discussion of the implications of this assumption and its failure to hold.

determination of the domestic input shadow prices $v_j$ will be taken up later. The attractiveness of the Little–Mirrlees criterion is that the $\bar{a}_i$'s and $\bar{f}_j$'s can be estimated fairly accurately without excessive data gathering and computation, though the calculations of $p_q$ and $v_j$ pose more serious problems.[20]

Another widely discussed partial criterion is based on the so-called effective rate of protection (ERP). The concept of effective protection was originally intended as a descriptive tool to indicate the magnitude of net protection conferred on a production activity once the protection afforded to both its outputs and inputs is taken into account. The ERP of an activity is the proportionate change in value added brought about by the tariff structure as compared to free trade. For instance, let us consider an activity which produces $n$ outputs at levels $a_1, \ldots, a_n$ and uses $m$ inputs at levels $a_{n+1}, \ldots, a_{n+m}$. For simplicity, we suppose all commodities are tradable. Let the world prices of all inputs and outputs be unity (by choice of units), and let the tariff rate (ad valorem) on commodity $i$ be $t_i$. Then assuming the input-output coefficients fixed, we can write:

$$\text{Domestic value added (Under free trade)} = \sum_{j=1}^{n} a_j - \sum_{k=n+1}^{n+m} a_k; \tag{5.2}$$

$$\text{Domestic value added (Under tariffs)} = \sum_{j=1}^{n} a_j(1 + t_j) - \sum_{k=n+1}^{n+m} a_k(1 + t_k); \tag{5.3}$$

$$\text{Change in value added} = \sum_{j=1}^{n} a_j t_j - \sum_{k=n+1}^{n+m} a_k t_k; \tag{5.4}$$

$$\text{Effective rate of protection} = \frac{\text{Change in value added}}{\text{Free trade value added}},$$

or,

$$\text{ERP} = \frac{\sum_{j=1}^{n} a_j t_j - \sum_{k=n+1}^{n+m} a_k t_k}{\sum_{j=1}^{n} a_j - \sum_{k=n+1}^{n+m} a_k}. \tag{5.5}$$

Now, define $\Theta_i = a_i/\sum_{j=1}^{n} a_j$  $i = 1, 2, \ldots, n + m$. Clearly, for $i = 1, \ldots, n$, $\Theta_i$ represents the value of the output of commodity $i$ as a proportion of the total value of output, the values being at free trade prices. For $i > n$, $\Theta_i$ represents the value of input $i$ as a proportion of the value of output. With this notation, we can rewrite (5.5) as:

$$\text{ERP} = \frac{\sum_{j=1}^{n} \Theta_j t_j - \sum_{k=n+1}^{n+m} \Theta_k t_k}{1 - \sum_{k=n+1}^{n+m} \Theta_k}. \tag{5.6}$$

---

20. For more details of data derivation, see the appendix to this chapter.

In the case of a single output (i.e., $n = 1$) the equation (5.6) takes the simple form $t_1 = (1 - \sum_{k=2}^{m+1} \Theta_k)\,\text{ERP} + \sum_{k=2}^{m+1} \Theta_k t_k$. Here the nominal tariff $t_1$ on output is a weighted average of the effective tariff and the tariffs on inputs. If this activity does not involve any imported inputs at all, nominal tariff and ERP coincide. Otherwise, they can differ very much, depending on the range of variation in tariffs.

The suggested use of ERP in policy making was based on the idea that ERP in some sense represented a change in "net" price per unit brought about by the tariff structure. Indeed, this is the case if we assume that the production coefficients are constant and independent of prices. If we further assume, as in the case of Little–Mirrlees, that the free trade prices are the true shadow prices, a wide spread between ERP's would represent a distortion of the relative "net" prices of various activities as compared to free trade. This was further taken to imply that the industries with relatively high ERP's would have gained resources (and expanded) at the expense of those with low ERP's. Thus the spread of ERP's was taken as a measure of inefficiency in resource allocation. As a corollary it was suggested that, in evaluating new investment projects, those that involved the expansion of industries with low ERP's should be preferred.

There is by now a vast literature on the ERP theory, particularly on its resource flow implications. Interested readers can refer to Corden [1971], Grubel and Johnson [1971], and the papers in a symposium on effective protection in the *Journal of International Economics* [August 1973]. For our purposes it is enough to summarize the main conclusions of this debate. First, it is not generally correct to interpret the ERP as a proportionate change in some "net" price or proportion of value added. A sufficient condition for such an interpretation to be valid is that the production structure exhibit what is known as "functional separability" between domestic primary factors and tradable inputs. This means that the production function $F$ relating output $Q$, domestic factors $D_1, D_2, \ldots, D_n$, and tradable inputs $M_1, M_2, \ldots, M_m$, can be written as $Q = F[f(D_1, \ldots, D_n), M_1, \ldots, M_m]$ where $f$ is a function only of $D_1, \ldots, D_n$. Thus each domestic factor affects $Q$ through its effect on $f$. Fixed input-output coefficients is a special case of a functionally separable production structure.

Even if this separability assumption is made, the only assertion that one can make regarding resource flows is that if a change in the tariff structure increases the ERP of one industry relative to another, leaving the ERP of all other industries relative to the latter unaltered, this one industry will attract domestic resources. But nothing can be said about resource flows if a number of relative ERP's are changed. Thus, the resource flow implications of ERP's are limited even from a theoretical point of view. Further, if we abandon the implicit assumption that the observed resource usages, given the tariff structure, represent an equilibrium configuration, widely divergent ERP's at a

point in time could be consistent with dynamic adjustments taking place as the economy moves toward a less inefficient structure of resource use. As such, not too much should be read from the wide divergence observed in ERP's at any point of time.

The fact that ERP rankings are poor predictors of resource pulls in a general equilibrium context has been empirically demonstrated by, among others, Evans [1972] and Taylor and Black [1974]. Evans assumes a Leontief fixed-proportions technology while Taylor and Black experiment with a Leontief as well as a Cobb–Douglas technology for intermediate inputs. In addition to demonstrating that the data gathering and computation costs needed to elaborate such a general equilibrium model are not very much more than that used in computing ERP's, these models show that the relatively insignificant effect of large tariff changes on macro variables such as GNP may conceal substantial sectoral effects, that are often incorrectly predicted by ERP's. Thus a 10 percent cut in all tariffs and subsidies in the Taylor–Black model resulted in an increase of only 0.21 percent in aggregate consumption in the case of a Cobb–Douglas technology for both primary and intermediate inputs. However, the largest sector output increase was 8.81 percent (for nitrates) and the largest output decrease was 10.29 percent (for food).

Before concluding our discussion on tariffs, we should take note of the literature on the theory of the "second best" as applied to foreign trade policies. Dasgupta and Stiglitz [1974], following an earlier paper by Ramaswami and Srinivasan [1968], raise the following issue in particular:

> In an open economy, in which the government is pursuing various trade and tax policies and where some of the policy instruments are optimally chosen but the others are not, and in which, as a consequence, domestic price ratios differ from international price ratios, what is the appropriate relationship between international prices, domestic prices, and shadow prices in benefit-cost analysis?

It will be noted that, under the assumptions made above, the comfortable world of Little–Mirrlees—in which the border prices were the shadow prices—disappears. Dasgupta and Stiglitz summarize their results in the form of a set of rules, or criteria, to be followed in devising public policies. These rules naturally depend on the constraints on policy instruments. In particular, they show that the Little–Mirrlees criteria do not hold if: (i) there is a government budgetary constraint; or (ii) there is a constraint on foreign capital inflow; or (iii) there is an import or export quota on one or more commodities; or (iv) the level of net imports of a particular commodity (e.g., steel) influences (nonoptimally) some policy instrument (e.g., public investment) of the government. They endorse the earlier conclusion of Ramaswami and Srinivasan [1968] that intermediates should not be taxed in a centrally controlled economy and, if only trade taxes can be levied, the output of intermediates should not be changed from what their levels would be at world prices.

173

## 6. Some Practical Problems

We now turn to a few practical problems associated with the planning of the foreign trade sector that are not yet reflected in any planning model. We have already touched upon the fact that aid flows are very often tied to purchases within the donor country (and only of commodities included in some specified list). Aid use may also be restricted to the import requirements of specific projects. At the very least, a realistic planning model should distinguish two categories of foreign exchange: tied versus free exchange. This would further mean that, with respect to exports and imports, the relevant unit prices have to be estimated separately for transactions in each type of exchange. In fact, more than two types of foreign exchange may have to be recognized.[21]

The planning models discussed here concentrate exclusively on the investment needed to create export or import substituting production. The investment in marketing, such as the cost of penetrating a new market or substantially expanding an already existing market, is not recognized adequately, if at all.

Uncertainty, an important feature of the real world, is also neglected. Most models and criteria for project appraisal proceed on the assumption that there is a single known "world" price for each tradable commodity. Not only do world prices fluctuate, but there need not even be a reliable long-term expected price around which these fluctuations take place.

Another important aspect of trade not adequately covered by models is the question of technological change and transfer brought about by planning a window to the rest of the world. Though this factor is recognized as important (see Vernon [1970]), it has not yet been incorporated into a quantitative model. This is not just a question of testing specific hypotheses about the differences between industries or firms in the export sector and those selling exclusively in the domestic market. Rather, it is more a question of "planning" technical change through trade. This is a relatively unexplored area.

In conclusion, it can be said that although valuable insights have been obtained from the planning models regarding the foreign trade sector, we are still a long way from building a model that incorporates most of the significant aspects of this vital sector in relation to development. It is also worth emphasizing that a policy model, however realistic and sophisticated, is no substitute for policy implementation. And therein lies the rub.

---

21. See Bhagwati and Eckaus [1970] on cost of aid tying. Also see Kornai [1967] on the introduction in a planning model of separate balance of payments relating to different trade blocs.

# Appendix on Data Problems

Some of the data problems that arise specifically in the context of the foreign trade sector have been referred to in the text. Here we discuss several more.

One of the problems commonly encountered in aggregating trade data to conform to the sectoral classification of an input-output or programming model is that countries very often follow one commodity classification system in their industrial census and a different one for their trade data. This problem, though irksome, is probably not as serious as those that arise in estimating the amounts and unit prices of each traded commodity.

In countries where, in addition to trade taxes, there are exchange controls, in principle, there is a second source of data on foreign trade, namely the exchange control authorities. But, it will be rare indeed if the two sources agree with each other. Part of the problem is due to normal leads and lags: exports (imports) get recorded by the customs at the time of shipping (arrival), while exchange control authorities record the same transactions only at the time of receipt (payment) of equivalent foreign exchange from (to) the foreign importer (exporter). Accounting practices may create differences. For instance, on imported equipment financed by supplier's credit, the customs authority normally will record the entire value of the machinery as imports. The exchange control authorities record only the downpayment, unless they follow an accounting practice in which the entire value is recorded as payments in current account and the difference between the value and downpayment as an inflow entry in the capital account. A third source of possible difference is the treatment of imports or exports on government account depending on whether such transactions are exempt from some of the exchange control and/or customs regulations.

Countries which have exchange controls typically also have a plethora of export promotion schemes, capital-outflow controls, and so on. Incentives for over-invoicing or under-invoicing transactions abound in such countries. For instance, if there are restrictions on capital outflows, these restrictions can be and are overcome by over-invoicing imports. This device also may be resorted to by multinational corporations, if the less developed country imposes limits on the repatriation of profits. Over-invoicing of imports of equipment from an overseas subsidiary or headquarters achieves two purposes: it illegally repatriates profits and at the same time inflates the capital base to which the repatriated profits are often related. Of course there is a cost to the firm of over-invoicing, namely the extra import duty that has to be paid. Whether on a net basis over-invoicing is worthwhile depends on the risks involved (both of detection and of having to arrange a deal with a foreign supplier which is not a subsidiary) and on the severity of restrictions.

Under-invoicing of imports can take place if import duty saved by doing so exceeds the cost of having to obtain foreign exchange in the black market to pay the supplier the difference between true value and invoiced value. Under-invoicing also can occur if the residents of the importing country have investments in the exporting country and the exporting country has capital outflow restrictions.

Exports may be under-invoiced in order to export capital or to finance illegal imports through smuggling. Exports may be over-invoiced if the marginal domestic cash subsidies or import allowances to exporters are so high that, even after allowing for the cost of buying foreign exchange in the black market, a profit remains.

The foregoing discussion should indicate that it is by no means a simple matter to determine whether recorded data correspond to reality. Given time and resources, one could attempt to check the data reported by one country against the data on the same transactions as reported by its trading partners. However, too much cannot be expected from this since: (i) numerous and complex leads and lags are involved; (ii) different countries may have differing accounting periods; (iii) different countries may report data on different bases (c.i.f. versus f.o.b.); and (iv) some illegal transactions involve falsification of records both at origin and destination!

All this has rather unfortunate implications for modelling the foreign trade sector in general and the application of Little–Mirrlees criterion in particular. However, use of explicit modelling in policy making, even if based on such data, may perhaps lead to better decisions than decision making without modelling, since the latter approach has to be based on the same imperfect data.

In conclusion, let us make one final remark on the data needs of the Little–Mirrlees approach. Even without using the inverse of an elaborate input-output matrix, it is often possible to estimate fairly accurately the direct and indirect use of tradables and primary factors in a project by a few (often 2 or 3) rounds of adding inputs, inputs of inputs, inputs of inputs of inputs, and so on. This may permit consideration of a more detailed (and more up to date) input structure than that included in the level of disaggregation of a typical input-output matrix. However, the difficult issues of deriving the shadow prices of domestic factors and the social rate of discount remain. But these issues are pertinent for almost any approach to project appraisal.

176

Chapter VII

# EMPLOYMENT AND HUMAN CAPITAL FORMATION

CHARLES R. BLITZER

## 1. INTRODUCTION

There is no use asserting that employment and human capital formation have been the primary interests of people who work with formal planning models; instead, until very recently, labor absorption and skill creation variables have entered only tangentially, if at all, into most planning exercises. Things that were considered important—balance of payments, capital requirements, intersectoral resource allocation—of course, have been considered more carefully in model formulation, and model builders can flatter themselves that they have said something about these issues. But they certainly have said little about job creation; of course, the rest of the profession has not said much either.

Naturally, a few exceptions to this generalization have appeared over the years, particularly in recent ones. The type of labor force planning with the longest history probably is the so-called manpower or employment projections approach, which essentially derives labor demands as functions of sectoral output levels through fixed coefficients (perhaps changing over time according to predetermined productivity trends). Once output projections are made, then labor "requirements" predictions follow mechanically. These can be compared to supply projections, and, if it looks as if demand for some type of labor will significantly exceed supply, steps such as scaling down output projections or recommending increases in supply of the relevant skill groups can be taken.[1] (Detailed analysis and criticism of this methodology appears in section 2 and the appendix to this chapter.)

A natural extension of the manpower approach is to embed both the sectoral output and employment projections into some sort of consistent forecasting framework. This is often done in connection with input-output exercises, either of the static or dynamic variety. However, the essential methodology is not altered by basing output projections on the Leontief inverse matrix, and we do not go into great detail on this variant here. We do discuss at somewhat greater length attempts to incorporate employment into a fully consistent

---

1. At its simplest the manpower methodology reduces to projecting output growth with a Harrod–Domar model and then tying demand for a single type of labor to the output projection with a fixed coefficient. Although unsophisticated, this methodology has underlain the employment projections in more than one national planning document.

linear programming framework. The natural way to do this is to retain fixed coefficients, tying demands for different labor types to the output levels of each production activity,[2] and to put upper bound constraints on the supply of each labor category. When binding, these labor constraints obviously limit the solution and pick up positive shadow prices—"shadow wages" in this case. As discussed in section 3, these shadow wages often turn out to be unstable and of unlikely magnitude, suggesting that something is wrong with the basic specification. On neoclassical grounds, this is not so surprising— fixed coefficients imply that derived demands for labor must be very wage-inelastic, i.e., big changes in wages will be required to compensate small changes in employment. The simulated market within the shadow price system is just behaving as theory would predict it should.

Returning to the real market, however, the observation has been that relative wages for different skill and/or education classes of labor have been rather insensitive to changes in supply. As usual, this can be rationalized in various ways. Neoclassical economists read an inflexible wage structure as evidence for rather high elasticities of substitution among different labor types—small wage changes lead to big shifts in employment patterns, or vice versa.[3] Reformed neoclassicals (in the United States, at least) have tended to explain these findings in terms of jobs requiring specific sets of skills which can be provided by people with widely differing descriptive characteristics— education, race, sex, age, and so on.[4] Although potentially relevant to developing countries, this way of looking at the labor market has not yet been incorporated into formal planning models. Two level constant elasticity of substitution production functions may provide a method for accommodating these divergent substitution possibilities. The neoclassical, high elasticity of substitution approach has been used a bit in economy-wide models, which are reviewed in section 3. It also is an implicit assumption underlying many planning models which focus on the production process within the educational system. These models, plus some manpower-oriented variations, are covered in section 4.

Employment and distribution tend to merge as issues when one takes a more classical view of the world. If the supply of labor is quite elastic at some

---

2. In the linear programming formulation, there may be more than one production technique for each sector. The range of labor-output ratios may be quite wide within sectors such as agriculture, construction, or commerce. There is less variation in more capital-intensive sectors such as electricity generation or steel production.

3. On this, see Bowles [1969], Dougherty [1972a, 1972b], and references in the latter papers. Note also that high elasticities of substitution among different labor types imply that fixed coefficients manpower forecasts are essentially useless, since their basic assumption is that it is impossible to replace one type of labor with another. Manpower people have been heavily criticized by neoclassicists on these grounds.

4. See Thurow and Lucas [1972] for an application of this approach in the United States. It is also favored by sociologists such as Jencks et al. [1972].

wage, then the distribution problem boils down to determining the size of the surplus from production after wages are paid, and then deciding how to split it between capitalists' consumption and investment. This model underlies much of the current discussion about shadow prices for investment project analysis,[5] and has been used a bit in planning models. The key assumption— that employed labor consumes a bill of goods fixed in real terms and no more (e.g., at some "subsistence" level)—is easily phrased in linear programming terms. Some implications are discussed in section 5.

Section 6 gives our final observations and conclusions concerning appropriate modelling of these various human resource issues. Specific issues raised in the estimation of labor coefficients are reviewed in the appendix,[6] to this chapter.

## 2. EMPLOYMENT PROJECTION MODELS[7]

As already mentioned, early employment planning consisted primarily of projections based on independently predicted production levels. The linkage in these manpower or employment projection models is only one way: given output, employment is determined. From these projections and assumed labor supplies, unemployment forecasts can be made. The basic employment projection model is quite similar in spirit to input-output analysis. In input-output models, final demand determines gross output levels and, at least in dynamic versions, capital requirements as well. Similarly, it is assumed here that gross output determines employment levels.

Let us define some notation that will be utilized throughout this chapter. Let $e_{s,i}$ represent the employment, measured say in man-years,[8] of labor of type $s$ per unit of gross output in sector $i$. Gross output in sector $i$ is denoted by $X_i$, and total employment of labor type $s$ is defined as $E_s$. In the simplest form of the employment projection model, the labor-output ratios $e_{s,i}$ are taken as constant. That implies that

$$E_s = \sum_i e_{s,i} X_i \tag{2.1}$$

for all labor types $s$.

Just as with input-output analysis, some rather strong assumptions are being made here. In the first place, there is no scope for substitution among

---

5. The star exponents of the labor surplus shadow-pricing model are Little and Mirrlees [1969] and the team from UNIDO [1972].

6. The reader should also consult Chapter V for a discussion of how income distribution problems have been treated in multisectoral models.

7. Examples of employment projections models are Harbison and Myers [1965], Parnes [1962], and Jolly and Colcough [1972].

8. While, from the technical efficiency point of view, we want man-years, data often comes in the form of men employed. Especially when considering distribution issues, the distinction may be quite important. The model builder should be clear and consistent about which is being used.

the various labor skill types.[9] It is assumed that technology alone determines the relative mix of occupations in each sector; relative real wages have no role whatsoever in this process. Unfortunately, the neoclassical interpretation of observed nonshifting wages structures implies that there is considerable responsiveness of employment to relative real wages and scope for labor-skill substitution. (Blaug [1967], Bowles [1969, 1970], Dougherty [1972a], and Psacharopoulos and Hinchliffe [1972] all report results indicating very high values for elasticities of substitution between different labor skills.) This means that employment projections should allow for variation in the $e_{s,\,i}$ coefficients, as they respond to changes in relative factor costs along each sector's production function.

The second major assumption underlying equation (2.1) is that the average and marginal labor-output ratios are identical. There are several problems with this. In the first place, relative skill intensities hardly ever remain constant as output changes. Numerous examples of changing skill mix appear in a study prepared by Horowitz, Zymelman, and Herrnstadt [1966], in which international comparisons of employment and skill proportions, both cross section and time series, are made for nineteen countries. Secondly, it is clear from equation (2.1) that the total employment (across all skill types) coefficient for each sector $i$ is merely the sum, over $s$, of $e_{s,\,i}$. This constant coefficient implies that the employment elasticity with respect to gross output equals unity in each sector (as well as for each skill category). Empirical studies of incremental employment, such as Turnham and Jaeger [1971], definitely show that these elasticities, at least for total employment, are considerably less than one. However, the primary concern of the planner attempting to use employment projection methods is in projecting *changes* in employment levels and, through them, actual employment. With this shift in emphasis to incremental movements, it becomes possible to avoid constancy in average and even incremental employment-output levels.

One obvious approach goes along the lines of equation (2.1) except that it is formulated in incremental terms. Define $\Delta X_i$ as the increase in gross output in sector $i$ over some known base value $\bar{X}_i$, $\Delta E_s$ as the increase in employment of labor of type $s$ induced by $\Delta X_i$, and $e'_{s,\,i}$ as the increase in employment of labor of type $s$ associated with a unit increase in gross output of sector $i$. Then, $\Delta E_s$ can be written as the following linear homogeneous function of $\Delta X_i$:

$$\Delta E_s = \sum_i e'_{s,\,i}\Delta X_i, \qquad (2.2)$$

for all labor types $s$. Combining (2.1) and (2.2) yields the following linear non-

9. Capital-labor substitution is also neglected. However, since fixed production techniques are the standard assumptions made in most multisector planning models, they are better discussed in another context. In particular, see the relevant sections of Chapters III and XII.

homogeneous function for $E_s$ in terms of the planned-for increases in gross output:

$$E_s = \sum_i e_{s,i}\overline{X}_i + \sum_i e'_{s,i}\Delta X_i. \tag{2.3}$$

There are several obvious gains from formulating the projection model in terms of (2.2) or (2.3). In the first place, the average employment-gross output ratios are no longer constant or identical with the marginals. Therefore, employment elasticities can differ from unity, exceeding or falling short of one as the incremental coefficients, $e'_{s,i}$, are greater or less than the average ratios, $e_{s,i}$, for the base period. In addition, the employment elasticities can differ from labor type to labor type depending on the underlying assumptions concerning skill intensity on the margin as compared with existing production. This will, of course, lead to varying skill proportions in employment as a function of projected changes in output levels.

Although the above formulation allows for changes in skill proportions and nonunity employment elasticities, it retains the assumption of constant incremental employment-gross output ratios, $e'_{s,i}$. An alternative way of estimating changes in employment would be to estimate the elasticities associated with each skill and sector and then make projections under the assumption that they remain constant. Let the elasticity of employment of skill category $s$ with respect to gross output in sector $i$ be represented by $\varepsilon_{s,i}$. Holding these elasticities constant then implies:

$$\frac{\Delta E_s}{\overline{E}_s} = \sum_i \varepsilon_{s,i} \frac{\Delta X_i}{\overline{X}_i} a_{s,i}, \tag{2.4}$$

where $\overline{X}_i$ and $\overline{E}_s$ are the initial levels of gross output and employment, and $a_{s,i}$ is the initial proportion of type $s$ labor employed in sector $i$ (all known). With this formulation, we have nonconstant average and marginal employment output ratios, as well as varying skill proportions.

While both the constant incremental employment-gross output and the constant elasticity of employment approaches seem clearly superior to the simpler approach with which we started this discussion, it remains to be seen which is more practical in producing useful results for the planner.

Superficial comparison of equations (2.2) and (2.4) seems to imply that the constant elasticity approach is more general, since it relates the growth rates of employment and output rather than just increments. Even if actual employment levels are imperfectly known, as is often the case in developing countries, equation (2.4) still presumably says something about the growth of employment. However, consideration of the data requirements for estimating elasticities shows that this advantage is mostly illusory.[10] Elasticities must

10. More is said about data problems and estimation of labor demand coefficients in the appendix to this chapter.

usually be estimated from time series data on gross output and employment, exactly as with incremental employment-output coefficients, and the time series information alone will usually not contain enough variance to permit differentiation between the two hypotheses of constant incremental ratios and constant elasticities. This will be especially true whenever technological change is included (as is usually the case) in estimating the incremental coefficients.[11] Exactly the same problems occur if international comparisons are used as the data source. Since there is no easy way to determine which hypothesis best fits historical trends, we are left agnostic about which should be used in practice. The choice is not altogether academic; in testing large variations in planned output growth, the two hypotheses could give very different projections.[12]

No matter which sort of employment projection model is chosen, it seems clear that, if used at all, they should be used with utmost care and caution. The most important problem is that it is very difficult to project skill proportions under assumptions of no substitution possibilities between different categories of labor. In the real world, relative wages seem to matter and substitutions are made. As a consequence of the instability of the coefficients, actual applications of this method have not been entirely successful.[13] Unfortunately, such simple projection models may be all that are available to the planner. He may be able to hedge his guesses, but guesses must be made. In addition to the estimation problems which are discussed in the appendix to this chapter, several general guidelines seem appropriate. First, skill levels should not be too highly disaggregated. Past time series seem to indicate that substitution possibilities are reduced when the labor skill categories are more aggregative. Second, projections based on simple models with limited structural change are best used in estimating the effects of moderate changes in gross output levels. Therefore, manpower-based employment projections would seem better suited to periods of three to six years than longer planning horizons. For long-term planning, reliable results require more realistic assumptions and a more comprehensive model. In addition to the previously mentioned issue of the assumed insensitivity of employment to wage rate changes, we have not yet mentioned any supply considerations. In using manpower projection models, fixed supplies of each skill are assumed. This is especially dangerous for long-term forecasting when there is sufficient time for supplies to adjust to wage differentials through education and participation rate changes.

---

11. See Chapter VIII or Blitzer [1972] for a fuller development of this point.

12. Bruno [1968] demonstrates considerable shifts in Israeli comparative advantage in switching from one hypothesis to the other.

13. For critiques of employment projection models, see Blaug [1967], Bowles [1969, 1970], Dougherty [1972a], or Hollister [1967].

## 3. PRODUCTION PLANNING AND THE SUPPLY OF LABOR

A major weakness of employment projection models is that they contain no explicit supply linkages. Output growth is used for employment projections which can then be compared with independent supply projections to determine unemployment or manpower shortages. (More will be said in section 4 about this specification in connection with educational planning models.) The former determination is more common in developing countries, i.e., it usually turns out that surplus labor exists in most or all manpower categories.

This is, of course, the same as saying that the only binding constraints on the productive capacity of the economy are those related to physical capacity, foreign exchange availabilities, or institutional bottlenecks such as a government's inability to generate savings out of national income. It is not necessary to go over all the empirical evidence which concludes that this is not an entirely reasonable assumption in most planning situations. However, similar critiques could be made about almost any of the simplifying assumptions used in constructing numerical multisector planning models. The issue is not whether an assumption is entirely realistic but whether it is a useful simplification which allows the model to remain both understandable and empirically realistic. In the case of surplus labor, it is not altogether clear how important the biases are and which planning decisions are most affected.

For anyone even vaguely familiar with the published literature on multisector planning models, it would seem that surplus labor is a popular assumption. For example, of the seven planning models discussed in the well-known volume edited by Adelman and Thorbecke [1966], four have no labor constraints or employment projections whatsoever.[14] Part of the explanation lies with the difficulties involved in estimating labor coefficients. Part also lies in recognition of the instability of these coefficients, caused by substitution possibilities which are not well captured by the linear models. Moreover, employment problems were not given great importance in general—a point made very strongly in Chapter II. Apart from these reasons, there are analytical justifications for assuming surplus labor (but not for avoiding employment projections) based on a number of related theories about the process of economic development.

Although surplus labor theories of development have roots in both classical political economy and Keynesian analysis, writings of Lewis [1954] and Fei and Ranis [1964] led to their repopularization in the development context. Essentially, writers of this school maintain that the elasticity of supply of unskilled labor in a developing economy is high, due to the existence of a pool of workers employed in traditional activities at low or zero productivity

---

14. They are the model of Pakistan by Chenery and MacEwan, of Zambia by Seers, of India by Bergsman and Manne, and of Mexico by Manne. The models with labor constraints are for Colombia by Adelman and Sparrow, for Israel by Bruno, and for Argentina by Adelman.

(disguised unemployment). The employment problem, then, is perceived as one of generating sufficient growth in modern sectors of the economy to permit the ultimate liquidation of this labor surplus; as a corollary, production planning focuses its attention on the most binding constraints to modern sector growth, namely, physical capital and foreign exchange. As mentioned in section 5, the appropriate choice of technique in the modern sector to guarantee an optimal amount of investable surplus after payment of a subsistence wage has been discussed extensively.

Development experience has shown that all this is something of an over-simplification, although the alternative theoretical abstraction of a fully employed labor force in all sectors and regions also clearly leaves much to be desired. (A useful survey of some of the empirical evidence on these matters can be found in Healey [1972].) A number of neoclassical theorists attacked the surplus labor doctrine, maintaining that supplies of both labor and agricultural products to the urban-industrial sector may be fairly inelastic and that attention should be paid to investment and innovation in traditional agriculture as well. Of course, surplus labor enthusiasts counterattacked (particularly regarding the elasticity of supply of labor and its implications), and the debate continues.[15] It may never stop, for the discussion obviously involves more than simple empirical economic considerations. There are problems of definition regarding rural labor and employment in the context of village life and extended families. There are also sociological questions regarding motivation, nutrition, the changing role of women, and so on.[16] And finally, political persuasions of the participants in the debate have some influence—there is a clear positive correlation between generally "leftist" positions and adherence to surplus labor doctrines.

For our purposes, a few simple conclusions *can* be drawn. The most important is that for surplus labor to exist there must be rigidities in the economic system. These may take the form of a gap between the wages paid unskilled workers in the traditional and modern sectors; or they may stem from so-called uneconomic behavior of the traditional sector where objectives other than private profit maximization are pursued; or, there may be a lack of substitution possibilities in production techniques between physical capital and labor or between various labor categories.[17]

While these factors undoubtedly lead to excess supplies of unskilled labor in most developing countries, the same is not necessarily true for skilled workers. In fact, high level manpower is undoubtedly a limiting factor in at

---

15. For a sampling of these criticisms and analysis of the efficiency of traditional agriculture, see Jorgenson [1966, 1967] Schultz [1964], or Yotopoulos [1965, 1968]. Marglin [1966] and Dixit [1970a] show that many of the neoclassical allegations rest on restrictive premises, however.

16. A number of these issues are discussed by Myrdal [1968] and Leibenstein [1957].

17. On this point, the classic article is by Eckaus [1955].

least some parts of the Third World. Planners must take this into account when weighing the overall feasibility of a plan. In model-building practice, this has led to the incorporation of fixed-coefficient skilled labor constraints of the form of equation (2.1) or, in more sophisticated formulations, equation (2.3).[18] Thus, labor demand is handled in exactly the same way as demand for intermediate goods or physical capital. On the supply side, however, it is typical to assume fixed exogenous upper bounds. Since human capital formation is then outside the planning model, skilled labor acts as a primary factor of production. In algebraic form, a typical labor skill constraint is given by equation (3.1), where $\bar{E}_{s,t}$ is the exogenous projection of the supply of labor category $s$ in year $t$, and all other variables are defined as in section 2 (with the subscript $t$ representing time).

$$\sum_i e_{s,i,t} X_{i,t} \leq \bar{E}_{s,t} \tag{3.1}$$

The major improvement introduced by these constraints is in what programmers call primal feasibility. In other words, the output targets derived from models including restrictions such as (3.1) will be consistent with intermediate input demands, physical capital stock, and human capital availability. For planning exercises which focus attention on intersectoral consistencies, these skilled labor constraints will often add a dose of realism. In models which allow some choice in production specializations (i.e., optimizing models), these constraints can be very crucial to decisions about sectoral comparative advantage.[19] For example, results reported by Bruno [1966] and Blitzer [1972] indicate that optimal trade patterns are very sensitive to supplies of skilled labor. Process analysis models which allow for endogenous choice of techniques, also seem sensitive to labor skill assumptions.[20]

When dealing with choice, or optimizing models, one also has to consider the effect of labor supply on the shadow price system, or dual solution. As emphasized in Chapters III and VIII, acceptable primal results can often be obtained from a planning model only at the cost of elegance and/or stability in the dual. This appears to be the case when labor constraints of the above type are included in the specification. The shadow wages corresponding to these constraints frequently have unreasonable values and fluctuate widely in

---

18. Examples of well-known multisector models which have identical average and marginal labor coefficients include: Adelman and Sparrow [1966]; Bruno [1966]; Bruno, Dougherty, and Fraenkel [1970]; and Manne [1973a]. The marginal approach is used in Blitzer [1972].

19. This point is emphasized in Bruno [1966, 1968].

20. Westphal [1969] discusses a planning model for Korea with choice of techniques and economies of scale in certain sectors. Duloy and Norton [1973a] present a model of the agriculture sector in Mexico with very sophisticated labor supply and demand functions for different regions and months of the year.

response to small parametric changes in the statement of the planning problem. This undesirable behavior stems from both supply and demand aspects of the labor market specification.

Regarding the supply side, the assumption is that, before the upper bound on the right-hand side of (3.1) is reached, supply is completely elastic; but when the constraint binds supply, it is completely inelastic with respect to the shadow wage. Thus, there are no behavioral assumptions linking supply with the wage. This implies that the shadow wages are purely technocratic, unrelated to market wages or induced consumption demands. Therefore, it would be misleading to use these shadow wages as a guide to labor allocation in a largely market economy as long as workers do have a supply response to real wages.

This conclusion is reinforced by consideration of the labor demand relationship implicit in (3.1). The only labor substitution possibilities under this constraint are those resulting from shifts in the sectoral output pattern. This implies that labor demand will be very wage inelastic, which, together with inelastic supplies, can only lead to widely varying shadow wage levels. Once again, the plausibility of the dual solution suffers.

If more realistic dual variables are to be achieved, more flexibility must be introduced in demand, supply, or both. Three methods have been suggested: direct substitution of different labor types for one another in production, endogenous human capital formation, and the imposition of a fixed consumption level, or real wage, for employed workers.

To clarify the discussion of the first of these, assume for a moment that labor skills can be ranked in an order of skill intensity or human capital content. The various skill groups can then be numbered $s = 1, 2, \ldots, S$ where $s = 1$ represents the highest skill level and $s = S$ the lowest. In this case, it is reasonable to allow for downward substitution in production so that workers with more embodied human capital can substitute for those with less, on a one-for-one basis.[21]

Formally, this is most easily done by modifying supply aspects of the labor constraints. Let $LD_{s,t}$ represent the activity which downgrades a worker of skill $s$ to the skill level $s + 1$, $\overline{E}_{s,t}$ the exogenous supply of workers of skill $s$, and $E_{s,t}$ the total available supply in year $t$. We then have

$$E_{s,t} = \overline{E}_{s,t} - LD_{s,t} + LD_{s-1,t}. \tag{3.2}$$

Note that since (3.2) implies a "staircase" structure for the downgrading activities, successive downgrading permits any desired degree of downward

---

21. This assumption may be too strong in some situations, especially when there are many labor categories. Highly educated engineers may make very poor construction workers. All that can be said is that common sense should be used in the definition of the occupations fitting into each rung of the skill ladder.

substitution. The most important gain from introducing these activities is that the shadow wage for skill $s$ will never be less than that for skill $s + 1$.[22]

The logic which leads to downgrading also suggests the introduction of labor upgrading activities as well, which would put upper bounds on the difference between the shadow wage rates of any two skills. It is quite obvious that upgrading, unlike downgrading, cannot be done on a one-for-one basis; otherwise, it would not be necessary to have more than one skilled labor constraint. What makes this sort of procedure all but useless in practice is the lack of data about upward substitution parameters. The most readily available data would be market wages, but as long as these do not accurately reflect marginal productivity differences, they cannot be used. In addition, it is unlikely that the parameters of the upgrading activities would remain constant. It is much more probable that in the real world there are rising short-run marginal costs to upgrading. It is for these reasons that model builders who have experimented with upward substitution have been forced to drop the concept.[23]

Although the downgrading activities will produce some regularity in the shadow wage structure, they do nothing to reconcile it with labor supply functions or actual wage payments. Other ways of forcing shadow wages to be nearly in line with the market hinge on attempts to fill in linkages between production, income generation, and final demands. The following two sections discuss methods which have been proposed for doing this.

## 4. EDUCATIONAL PLANNING MODELS

Extending the planning model by making skill creation an endogenous activity is another means of preventing extreme or unstable values for shadow wages. This gives the model itself the option of choosing the appropriate changes in the supplies of labor skills, and helps tone down erratic wage behavior by fixing the relative production costs of each skill level.

Education sector planning models are now quite common and many examples, both for developed and developing countries, have been reported. Because of space limitations, we do not attempt any sort of systematic review of this literature.[24] A very brief look at the models' general nature will suffice to illustrate their advantages and disadvantages.

The education sector models come in two broad classifications. The first grew out of the employment projections manpower models discussed in section 2. The education model is given fixed requirements for each occupation

---

22. For proof of this assertion and more detail on this specification in general, see Blitzer [1972], or Keesing and Manne [1973].

23. See, for example, Keesing and Manne [1973]. If estimates are available of these non-linear rates of substitution, they can easily be introduced in the manner discussed in Chapter XII.

24. The most complete review of education planning is found in Blaug [1970].

in each time period and then meets these demands at minimum cost. The key weakness here is the rigidity of the labor requirements and the lack of any substitution possibilities on the demand side in response to relative cost. For example, the marginal social costs involved in educating one more skilled technician to meet a fixed demand may exceed the marginal social cost of not having his services available, but this cost information cannot be fed back into a demand generating model to reduce demands and rule out the apparent need to train him.

The second sort of education planning model, based on rate of return analysis, takes an opposite view of labor demand. In models of this type,[25] it is assumed that wages, either market wages or social marginal products, are given for each occupation. The model chooses the optimal supply of each skill category to maximize the return, social or private, to the education sector as a whole. This is done by equating the marginal costs of producing each occupation to its marginal value, or wage. In contrast with manpower requirements models in which there are no substitution possibilities between skills, rate of return models assume infinite substitution at rates reflected in the assumed wage structure.

Although the key difference between these two approaches is in their treatment of demand for skilled labor, there also may be differences in assumptions of how skill creation actually takes place. An education planner must decide how much choice there should be in linking occupations with education levels and how wide is the range of choice of techniques in setting up each school system. Both sorts of approaches can make rigid or flexible assumptions in these areas, but in general, manpower requirements models are identified with rather rigid substitution assumptions in these aspects as well.[26]

Problems such as these are typical in any partial equilibrium planning framework and the most direct way to allow for substitution is by embedding the education model in a multisector model, in the same way as, say, the agriculture sector.[27] Let us demonstrate how human capital formation could be included by means of a very simple model of education and skill formation.

Suppose that there is only one activity which can transform workers in each skill level $s + 1$ into workers of skill level $s$. Call these human capital forma-

---

25. For examples of rate of return models, see Bowles [1969], Carnoy [1967], and Thias and Carnoy [1969].

26. This is not necessarily so, however. Substitution in the creation of human capital is fully consistent with fixed exogenous requirements. Condos and Davis [1973a] provide a good example of a model based on fixed manpower requirements and choice of technique within the education sector.

27. If there is sufficient feedback between the economy-wide model and the education model, such as through demand curves for labor as a function of wages, then planning could be carried out in a multilevel manner. In Goreux and Manne [1973], such linkages are attempted between the economy-wide model and the agriculture and energy sectors. See Chapters XI and XII for further discussion of multilevel planning.

tion activities $ED_{s,t}$, where the time subscript $t$ denotes the period in which the education or training takes place. For simplicity, suppose that the only cost associated with human capital formation is the lost value from using workers in human capital creation activities rather than in the production of goods and services. Let $p_{j,s}$ denote the input into the education system of workers of skill category $j$ per unit of education activity $ED_{s,t}$ representing students and teachers. Defining $LE_{j,t}$ as the total allocation of skill level $j$ workers to the education sector in time period $t$, we have

$$LE_{j,t} = \sum_{s} p_{j,s} ED_{s,t}, \tag{4.1}$$

where the index $s$ covers all the various education activities.

If we also assume that each skill creation activity has a one period lag and that the units of the $ED_{s,t}$ activities are defined so that they represent new graduates available in year $t + 1$, we can rewrite the labor supply equation (3.2) as:

$$
\begin{bmatrix}
\text{Total avail-} \\
\text{ability of} \\
\text{manpower} \\
\text{of skill} \\
\text{level } s \text{ in} \\
\text{year } t
\end{bmatrix}
=
\begin{bmatrix}
\text{Exogenous} \\
\text{stock of} \\
\text{manpower} \\
\text{of skill} \\
\text{level } s \text{ in} \\
\text{year } t
\end{bmatrix}
+
\begin{bmatrix}
\text{Net gains or losses} \\
\text{through down-} \\
\text{grading}
\end{bmatrix}
+
\begin{bmatrix}
\text{Net creation, through} \\
\text{education activities,} \\
\text{between year 0 and} \\
\text{year } t
\end{bmatrix}
\tag{4.2}
$$

$$E_{s,t} = \bar{E}_{s,t} + [LD_{s-1,t} - LD_{s,t}] + \left[ \sum_{\tau=0}^{t-1} (ED_{s,\tau} - ED_{s-1,\tau}) \right] \cdot \tag{4.2$'$}$$

Note that there is still an exogenous term in the supply equation, $\bar{E}_{s,t}$. This could represent existing stocks as well as future increases which are already determined and therefore no longer subject to the planner's control.[28] The summation term represents the accumulation during the planning period of human capital formation of skill level $s$ and the loss through additional education of manpower trained for higher skills. Note, too, that if the $p_{j,s}$ coefficients call for more than one student per unit of education activity, this implies a certain dropout rate in the education process. Defining labor demands related to production as $L_{s,t}$, we can rewrite the labor supply constraints as

$$L_{s,t} + LE_{s,t} \leq E_{s,t}. \tag{4.3}$$

Similar formulations, although with more complex assumptions, have been tried with multisector dynamic planning models and seem to produce much more reasonable shadow wage structures than those resulting from models

---

28. See Keesing and Manne [1973] for a discussion of these so-called pipeline problems in education.

with fixed supplies of skilled labor.[29] Among the additional complexities which could be introduced easily are choice of techniques in the education activities, more complex lag structures, physical capital constraints on the school system, and intermediate current account costs.

While these extensions may be quite helpful in improving the shadow price structure of the planning model, it is not clear that they are very useful in the actual planning of the education sector. Just as with any other sector of the economy, in order to embed an education system into an economy-wide planning model, it is necessary to simplify enormously. Here the simplifications are complicated by problems of comparability between the skill levels, as represented in employment demand coefficients, and specific educational requirements. Therefore, even if the results for such a model indicate a need for accelerated investment in high level skills, the planner is given little guidance about whether more engineering or medical schools are required.[30] Nevertheless, even such broad guidelines might be useful in planning overall investment in education.

## 5. EMPLOYMENT, CONSUMPTION, AND SAVINGS

So far in this paper, we have been focusing on what might be described as the productive rather than the distributive side of multisector planning models. By the productive side, we mean the effects of labor skill supply considerations on the choice of consistent sectoral output levels as well as the creation of additional stocks of human capital. Distribution is then taken to mean the division of output between consumption and investment demands. In very simple input-output projection models, these final demands are exogenously set; then consistent sectoral outputs, foreign exchange requirements, and labor inputs are determined. In more sophisticated numerical exercises, the model itself decides on the optimal patterns of production and its distribution between consumption and investment. In particular, the shadow wage structure may have important feedback effects on the distribution decisions made in an optimizing model, which necessitate introducing explicit links between the productive and distributive sides of the model.[31]

In particular, one can expect unstable consumption patterns from a model without binding labor (or other primary factor) constraints. Models with complete surplus labor assumptions overstate the return to physical capital and thereby tend to produce unrealistically low consumption projections

---

29. For comparisons of shadow prices with and without endogenous skill creation activities, see Keesing and Manne [1973] or Blitzer [1972].

30. We have intentionally dodged the question of whether labor should be classified by occupations and professions or by level of educational attainment. If one recognizes the importance of apprenticeship or on-the-job training we see how difficult it is to map uniquely education with skill groups, to relate sector skill requirements to training.

31. This issue is also discussed in subsection 4.2 of Chapter III.

unless explicit linkages are introduced between employment and consumption levels. In order to improve these "primal" results, model builders have tended to introduce *arbitrary* constraints which produce smooth consumption paths. These have taken the form of either upper and lower bounds on consumption levels or upper bounds on the economy-wide marginal propensity to save. In effect, such constraints stabilize the model by acting as the missing primary factors.

The arbitrariness of most constraints imposed to stabilize the primal arises because they are not based on direct links between the economy's ability to generate savings and the production choices made by the model. General equilibrium theory indicates that production generates employment, which generates an income distribution, which generates demands for consumption and investment goods, which in turn generates production demands, and so forth, until an equilibrium is reached. As such, it seems desirable to derive endogenously the necessary savings bounds through the addition of at least some of these additional linkages.

In models for developing countries, the most appealing way to do this is to follow the surplus labor theories outlined in section 3 and assume that the supply of labor to the "modern" sector of the model is completely elastic at some wage $\bar{w}$. Also assume that workers spend their wage payments only on consumption. Formally, we add to the planning model constraints of the form of (5.1). Define the demand for labor in year $t$ as $L_t$; this will be a function of gross output levels. Next, assume that employed workers have a fixed proportions consumption basket in which $c_i$ is the per worker consumption demand for good $i$, and let $C_t$ be aggregate consumption in year $t$. Of course, $\sum_i c_i = \bar{w}$ is the institutionally fixed wage in base year prices. On these hypotheses, we derive the following lower bound on aggregate consumption:

$$C_t \geq \sum_i c_i L_t. \tag{5.1}$$

When binding, this constraint is equivalent to the key assumption of all labor surplus models that only workers consume and that investment is financed from what is left of profits after wages are paid.[32] Without this constraint, all value added, in shadow price terms, would be imputed to physical capital—the only scarce factor. But with (5.1) binding, the proportion allocated to consumption rather than investment will increase. This is because consumption is now subsidized in shadow price terms, raising (lowering) its marginal benefits (costs) relative to investment. This subsidy, the shadow price of constraint (5.1), represents the difference between the marginal value of consumption, as defined through an objective function which weights the relative social value of investment and consumption, and the marginal cost of consumption, which is defined by the budget shares and the individual shadow

---

32. We are also assuming that labor demand, $L_t$, does not exceed available supply.

prices for each good. The two will be equal only when constraints (5.1) are not binding.[33]

The shadow wage, which is defined as the marginal social cost of employing one more worker, now can be thought of as composed of two components. The first is associated with the supply constraints, equations (3.1), and represents the social marginal product of labor in scarce supply. This element will be zero whenever there is surplus labor. The second element corresponds to the consumption demand constraints (5.1) and will be positive when the objective function of the model, often together with surplus labor assumption indicates that, at the margin, investment activities are preferable to consumption.

Despite its simplicity and apparent relevance, the surplus labor consumption specification has not been adopted by builders of planning models. Perhaps the only disaggregated, *applied* study using surplus labor is CHAC—a sectoral model for Mexican agriculture developed by Duloy and Norton [1973a].

The major limitations in using this approach (and will be at least for the next few years) are once again data. Very little is known about consumption patterns by skill category. However, as more attention is paid to consumption and income distribution problems, this difficulty should be partially overcome. Although we have illustrated this method using extremely simple assumptions about consumption functions and the linkages between functional and personal income, more complex formulations are certainly possible.[34]

## 6. SUMMARY

The most obvious conclusion to be drawn from this survey is that, at least insofar as human resources are concerned, multisector planning models are in their infancy. Rigidities in model formulation, data availability, and incomplete theoretical conceptions have led to a large number of negative conclusions.

As the state of the art now stands, we have just begun to make proper use of labor supply constraints in determining consistent or optimal production plans. Since multisector planning models, so far, have been formulated with Leontief production functions, they are not useful vehicles for studying choice of techniques problems; such studies require knowledge of alternative techniques which utilize varying proportions of different occupations and physical capital stocks. Since future shifts in labor coefficients cannot be predicted with high degrees of accuracy, the employment projections derived from these models should be taken as indicative of general trends rather than as precise forecasts. Nevertheless, progress has been made. It seems evident

---

33. See Chapter VIII for a discussion of the implications for project selection of the shadow subsidy to consumption.

34. For example, the consumption functions need not be constant and could be linked to aggregate income through linearized Engel curves, as shown in subsection 2.4 of Chapter III.

from the studies mentioned in this survey that labor constraints do add to the reasonableness of the numerical results. Similarly, employment forecasts which are made consistent with other decisions and constraints in the economy, and vice versa, are less arbitrary than more simple approaches.

We have noted that rigid assumptions on the supply of skilled labor, whether infinite (surplus) or binding, usually will produce rather poor shadow price structures which are not particularly useful for the planner who might wish to use the dual results for investment planning. Until more is known about how to close planning models so that consumption demands are linked to production decisions through income distribution and demand for labor, only partial solutions to the shadow price problem are available. Endogenous human capital formation, in particular, seems to be useful in improving the shadow wage structure as well as in formulating education plans which are consistent with the rest of the planning exercise.

Therefore, the negative conclusions which have been made should be taken as similar to the warnings given in most of the other chapters about improper use of multisector planning models. In general, the recommendation is that supply and demand for labor be included, but in as careful and precise a way as possible. The more experience we have in including human resource problems in planning models, the greater the legacy left to planners of the future.

## Appendix on Estimating Labor Coefficients

The discussion here supplements that of section 2, where the employment projection methodology is sketched out. To use projection equations such as (2.1) it is necessary to estimate, in one way or another, average or marginal labor input coefficients. Although it is not our purpose to provide a cookbook on the derivation of such coefficients, some general guidelines are given which might be useful to practitioners.

The first step, as with other parts of a planning model, is to derive consistent base year data, i.e., actual employment levels, by sector and skill. Together with base year gross output levels, these give average employment – gross output ratios $e_{s,i,0}$. Employment data can come from several sources, but either a comprehensive census or large-scale survey is likely to be the basic one. To be representative, the census or survey must contain data on both large and small firms.[35] Also, sectoral definitions of the employment matrix must correspond with the definitions used in the rest of the planning model. Finally, note that if an input-output table is used, its base year will usually be different from the most recent year for which accurate sectoral-skill employment is known. Thus, even to derive consistent base year coefficients, assumptions have to be made about various rates of technical change, since it is unrealistic to assume time constant labor-output ratios.

While there are some analytically elegant methods for projecting changes in input-output matrices, heroic assumptions are almost always required to handle labor coefficients. For example, accurate values for average employment-output ratios may not be known for the base year 0, but for some previous year, say $-3$. This means that year 0 coefficients must be projected exactly like those for any other future period. Assuming constant rates of labor-saving technological change[36] for each skill employed in each sector, defined as $\alpha_{s,i}$, we have the following equation for the labor demand coefficients:

$$e_{s,i,t} = \bar{e}_{s,i,-3}/(1 + \alpha_{s,i})^{t+3} \tag{A.1}$$

The bar over the labor coefficient for period $-3$ means that number is known, while all others are projected. As anyone familiar with data difficulties knows, estimating all of these $\alpha_{s,i}$ would be a formidable task. Large-scale surveys or censuses are not done frequently, so that there is no real possibility for accurate time series estimates. As a compromise, one might assume that all workers in a category have identical productivity improvements, regardless of which sector employs them. Or one could assume identical productivity rates within

---

35. Frequently, the census of manufacturing is conducted only among firms above a certain minimum size.

36. Throughout, we assume Harrod-neutral technological change.

each sector. There is no correct procedure here; the planner will have to make the best of the data available.

A partial solution is suggested in cases where productivity surveys have been conducted on a small scale in some sectors. Typically, these cover the more modernized portions of the economy, often using data only from medium- and large-scale firms. If it is reasonable to assume that future output growth will be based on these techniques rather than more traditional ones,[37] then the planner might find it useful to separate partially marginal from average employment coefficients. There are a number of ways to do this, and we will go through one approach in detail.

First, assume that productivity changes can only be measured for each sector as a whole. Let $E_{i,t}$ represent total employment in sector $i$ during year $t$. Then,

$$E_{i,t} = e_{i,t}X_{i,t},\tag{A.2}$$

where $e_{i,t}$ is both the average and marginal total employment – gross output ratio for sector $i$. These coefficients are estimated using base year sectoral employment data and the assumed productivity rates. That is,

$$e_{i,t} = e_{i,0}(1 + \alpha_i)^{-t},\tag{A.3}$$

where $\alpha_i$ is the assumed productivity growth rate. In the next step of the derivation, total sectoral employment is broken down into its skill category proportions under the assumption that increases in output will have different proportions than those of the base year. Rewriting equation (A.2) as

$$E_{i,t} = e_{i,t}\overline{X}_{i,0} + e_{i,t}(X_{i,t} - \overline{X}_{i,0})$$
$$= E_{i,t}^1 + E_{i,t}^2\tag{A.4}$$

allows us to separate total employment into two categories, one a function of known base year output ($E_{i,t}^1$) and the other a function of output increases ($E_{i,t}^2$). Define $r_{s,i}^1$ and $r_{s,i}^2$ as the proportions of labor skill category $s$ per unit of employment $E_{i,t}^1$ and $E_{i,t}^2$, respectively. Sectoral employment can then be represented by skill categories as

$$E_{s,i,t} = r_{s,i}^1 E_{i,t}^1 + r_{s,i}^2 E_{i,t}^2\tag{A.5}$$

where $E_{s,i,t}$ is employment of skill $s$ in year $t$ by sector $i$. Substituting equation (A.4) into equation (A.5) yields,

$$E_{s,i,t} = (r_{s,i}^1 - r_{s,i}^2)e_{i,t}\overline{X}_{i,0} + r_{s,i}^2 e_{i,t}X_{i,t}.\tag{A.6}$$

It is clear from equation (A.6) that average and marginal coefficients are now different as long as the incremental proportions $r_{s,i}^2$, differ from the base year

---

37. We are here identifying traditional techniques with small firms. While it is not necessary that more modern techniques are socially optimal, multisector planning models are not generally built in a way to make such choice of techniques decisions. Rightly or wrongly, the standard assumption is to assign a given technique to each sector and let the model only choose the appropriate output mix among these.

proportions $r_{s,i}^1$.[38] While the base year proportions may be estimated from census or other comprehensive data, the incremental proportions could come from more selective studies of projected future technology. Using this approach, equation (2.1) would be replaced with the following equation derived from above.

$$E_{s,t} = \sum_i (r_{s,i}^1 - r_{s,i}^2)e_{i,0}(1 + \alpha_i)^{-t}\overline{X}_{i,0} + \sum_i r_{s,i}^2 e_{i,0}(1 + \alpha_i)^{-t}X_{i,t}. \quad (A.7)$$

Note that the first summation in equation (A.7) is independent of output forecasts and, for projection purposes, can be treated as an intercept term in the linear employment to output equation.

From the above discussion, it is clear that estimating reliable labor co-efficients is a difficult, time-consuming effort, requiring extensive manipulation of (often) unreliable data. Frequently, special productivity and employment studies for many sectors may be necessary. In terms of their effect on consistent production decisions, these efforts will be important only if labor availabilities really are a bottleneck to growth; i.e., at least some demand projections are likely to exceed supply. For countries with large-scale open unemployment in all labor skills, it is more appropriate to concentrate attention on the constraints that are producing low levels of employment rather than on the labor constraints themselves. For the same reasons, in those countries with large unemployment among low-skilled urban labor and low productivity or disguised unemployment in agriculture, the planner should put most of his efforts into estimating labor demand coefficients only for skilled labor.

Conceding that, from the viewpoint of production consistency, attention should be carefully focused on skilled labor, what is the appropriate level of disaggregation? Should skilled labor be treated as a homogeneous whole or divided into very precise classifications? On the one hand, since in the real world there are hundreds of occupations which are not at all perfect substitutes for each other, such as lathe operators and sanitary engineers, it would seem unrealistic to treat them as all homogeneous. On the other hand, the linear nature of our labor demand equations, allowing for no substitution at all between categories of workers, is also unrealistic and overly rigid. After all, tractor drivers can be trained to be bus drivers at very low cost. By combining occupation categories, the model builder can add a great deal of implicit substitutability. The nature of the examples above suggests the appropriate aggregation—namely, group occupations which are approximate substitutes, leaving several major skill categories (such as "technicians") separate. Among the multisector planning models reported in the literature, the number of different labor skill categories varies from one to six.[39]

---

38. Note that since the $r_{s,i}$ coefficients represent employment proportions, they will sum to unity. That is $\sum_s r_{s,i} = 1$.

39. The models with six labor skills are Adelman [1966] and Blitzer [1972].

Chapter VIII

# PLANNING MODELS, SHADOW PRICES, AND PROJECT EVALUATION

MICHAEL BRUNO

## 1. INTRODUCTION

This paper attempts to give a critical review of present planning model methodology in relation to the use of the "dual" of an optimizing framework and the derivation of shadow prices for decentralized decision making and the evaluation of investment projects. Being part of a survey volume, this discussion will naturally cover only one segment of planning methodology. Likewise, we shall not attempt to cover the wider area of the application of project evaluation methods, for which a considerable independent literature exists.[1] This topic will be discussed only to the extent that economy-wide planning methodology is considered.

A subject such as this cannot be discussed fruitfully if it is completely abstracted from any actual, or at least stylized, institutional setup. For our purpose it will be useful to distinguish between a hypothetical central planning office (CPO), which is in charge of the formulation and analysis of a macro-economic planning model, and a central office of project evaluation (COPE). While the former is in charge of the overall economy-wide framework, the latter is assumed to be responsible for the coordination of project evaluation methods, use of uniform prices, and so forth, on behalf of the various decentralized government investment allocation agencies. While in some countries (and perhaps ideally) the function of CPO and COPE would be located in one decision making unit, more often than not the two functions are institutionally divorced from each other (if they exist at all).[2] Ironically, such dichotomy also characterizes most of the literature on practical planning methodology.

Being part of an overall survey of economy-wide planning models, the role of prices[3] could have been approached here mainly from the CPO's vantage

---

1. For recent contributions, see the UNIDO [1972] and Little and Mirrlees [1969] volumes.

2. For many of the countries to which this volume is presumably addressed, a CPO already exists, as does a process of public investment allocation, with or without systematic reference to any common conceptual framework. Organizational and policy issues facing planners, especially macroplanners, are discussed at some length in Chapters I and II.

3. Throughout this chapter "prices" will generally refer to shadow prices. Reference to market prices will be explicit.

point—our models generate prices. What are they good for, if at all? Our answer to that question would be very mixed, as we shall see. The "dual" price system of an optimization framework should, first of all, be used to check the logic of the planning model itself. This is a limited but important, though often neglected, function of a computable price system. The advantage of this particular use of the dual, however, is that it can take place institutionally within the CPO itself. This first topic is taken up in section 2. The main "textbook" application of a centrally computed price system, however, is its use as COPE signals which decentralized public investment allocation agents could use instead of relying on market prices.

It would probably not be wrong to say that budding model builders often start off with the ideal, albeit naive, textbook image of the all-purpose economy-wide planning model in mind. Such a model would not only be expected to give answers to the main macro quantities (such as output by sector, consumption, investment, and trade) but might also be expected to provide estimates of shadow prices which the CPO could then send down to the lower echelons for use in day-to-day micro project decisions. In due course, even the model builder comes to learn that life is not that simple.

Shadow prices are being used increasingly in practice. Yet one cannot claim that, at the present state of the art, these prices are always derived or derivable from central economy-wide models. There is more than one reason for this. Sometimes it may be due to the simple fact of the administration of government functions in a diffuse and uncoordinated manner. Information derived from a CPO may not filter through to COPE (or its proxies) or to the actual investment allocators. Equally important is the fact that planning models may not have reached the stage in which their output ought to be fully trusted for such purposes, at least not as the single source of information. This problem, the reliability of price estimates derived from planning models, is discussed in section 3.

While the literature on empirical planning models usually stays rather quiet about the "top down" applicability of their price solutions to the evaluation of individual projects, the manuals on project evaluation criteria usually sin in the other direction. Relatively little is said about the methods by which a COPE should estimate or obtain what are sometimes called the "national parameters," e.g., nonmarket price information (such as the social discount rate, shadow wage and exchange rates, and so on).[4]

Instead of looking at prices from the point of view of a CPO, which is the subject of sections 2 and 3 of this paper, one could have started the discussion from the micro project evaluation side. Then we would ask what kind of

---

4. One should note that project evaluation is often helped by CPO-type information that is not necessarily confined to shadow prices, such as demand and growth projections of key sectors, balance of payments forecasts, distributional considerations, and so forth. This part of the macro-micro link, though very important in itself, will not be discussed here.

information, uniform price generating frameworks, and so on, should a COPE develop in the absence of a well-articulated central framework. Moreover, in the present context, how could the imperfect methods and rules of thumb used in project evaluation be improved upon as a result of planning model experience? Even if empirical planning models cannot be fully trusted at the moment, at least their *logical* structure could be used to organize "bottom up" information in a more systematic fashion. This is the main message in section 4, which concludes the paper.

## 2. THE ROLE OF THE DUAL AS A CHECKING DEVICE

The construction of a planning model usually starts with a detailed specification of a set of constraints on the quantity variables. In mathematical programming terminology, we would say that a planning framework is originally conceived in terms of the "primal" and not the "dual" problem. Yet an inspection of the dual is an almost essential prerequisite both for the full understanding of what a model does in terms of implied economic behavior and, no less than that, for the full understanding of its weaknesses and shortcomings.

Suppose $U(x)$ (aggregate consumption, national income, utility, and so on) is to be maximized with respect to the set of choice variables $x$ that are subject to $m$ constraints, say, $G_i(x) \leq R_i$ $(i = 1, 2, \ldots, m)$. Then the dual shadow price $p_i$ corresponding to any particular constraint $i$ can be interpreted, in economic terms, as the additional amount of the maximand $U$ that would be obtained through raising $R_i$ by one unit. The ratio of any *pair* of such shadow prices would correspond to the social marginal rate of substitution between the two $R_i$'s along the economy's social transformation frontier.

A word of qualification might be appropriate here. A planning model may often be no more than a simple consistency framework which is cast in algebraic terms only to use the computer device of parametric programming to work out alternative consistent and feasible solutions. If there is no real activity choice within the model, say, but only sets of lower or upper bounds on some quantity variables, a corresponding price solution may not have much to tell us about the workings of the model itself.[5]

An investigation of the associated set of prices will give us more mileage in understanding and checking the basic framework when there is considerable choice in the primal system and when more emphasis is put on *alternative* means of allocation of scarce resources. Once one penetrates the fog of numerous constraints and variables, most existing models lend themselves to relatively straightforward economic interpretation. In such an interpretation, prices naturally have a major role to play. Analogous to the competitive

---

5. Even in the case of a most rudimentary model, however, the model builder may be well advised to look at the dual if only to learn the limited nature of his imposed choice mechanism.

market mechanism, where prices actually perform the allocation role, in a simulated planning exercise the "as if" allocative role of shadow prices is important in itself. If the associated price system does not make economic sense, it is doubtful whether any real credence can be put in the results of the primal system, at least as far as its allocative or comparative advantage aspects are concerned.

As model builders find out sooner or later, the dual often consists of no more than a set of obvious relationships of the marginal cost-equals-price variety. Occasionally, however, inspection of such seemingly trivial relationships gives insights not easily gained from the original set of constraints. I shall give some rather simple examples based on a standard static open economy model.[6] Consider a primal model in which the main choice is among alternative trade activities and aggregate consumption ($C$) is being maximized subject to the following set of constraints:

(i) A Leontief production technology (given by an $n \times n$ input-output matrix for intermediate inputs, an $n \times n$ capital-output matrix and an $f \times n$ matrix of primary input coefficients);

(ii) Linearized consumption demand relationships;

(iii) A predetermined growth rate $h$ for all capital goods in the target year;[7]

(iv) Constraints on production or demand for tradable goods in the form of minimum and maximum bounds on individual linearized trade activities ($Z_i$) of the form,

$$\underline{Z}_i \leq Z_i \leq \overline{Z}_i, \quad i = 1, 2, \ldots, m. \tag{2.1}$$

(v) A linear overall balance of payments constraint. This model could, of course, be modified in several alternative directions,[8] but in this form it is sufficiently general for some practical applications. The main advantage of its simplicity lies in the fact that it can be contracted into a reduced form involving only the ($m + 1$) variables $C$ and $Z_i$ and the ($2m + f + 1$) primary input, balance of payments, and trade bound constraints (2.1).

The dual of the latter system can, after some manipulation, be written down in the following ($m + 1$) constraint form:[9]

$$l_0 w + m_0 q + h(l_0^k w + m_0^k q) = 1, \tag{2.2}$$

---

6. For reference to this model elsewhere in this volume, see Chapters III and VI. For the specific form in which it is used here, see Bruno [1967a] or the recent survey by Manne [1974a].

7. The factor $h$ is here assumed to be uniform for all capital goods, though this is not necessary.

8. One modification, to be mentioned again in section 4, is the addition of a separate domestic savings constraint. A dynamic version will also be taken up.

9. This is a slight modification of the formulation given in Bruno [1967a].

$$l_i w + m_i q + h(l_i^k w + m_i^k q) \gtreqless u_i q, \qquad (2.3)$$

or,

$$\frac{l_i + h l_i^k}{u_i - m_i - h m_i^k} \gtreqless \frac{q}{w}, \quad \text{for,} \quad Z_i = \underline{Z_i}$$

$$Z_i = \bar{Z}_i$$

$$\text{or} \quad \underline{Z_i} < Z_i < \bar{Z}_i.$$

Here: $w$ and $q$ are the shadow prices for the primary inputs and foreign exchange, respectively, in terms of aggregate consumption as numeraire; $w$ will be a vector or a scalar according to whether $f$ is greater than or equal to 1; and $l_0$ and $l_i$ are the total (direct and indirect) primary input coefficients in the production of $C$ and $Z_i$, respectively. Likewise, $m_0$ and $m_i$ are the corresponding total foreign exchange (import) coefficients. The same letters with a superscript $k$ denote the direct and indirect primary and foreign exchange components in the *capital* stock input. The marginal foreign exchange revenue for the $i$th trade activity is $u_i$, and $h$, as before, is the growth rate of the capital stock.

Equation (2.2) reads, simply, that the direct and indirect social cost of production of the numeraire good ($C$) must equal unity. Condition (2.3) implies that the social benefit from the $i$th trade activity will be greater than, less than, or equal to the direct and indirect costs of production according to whether $Z_i$ is at its maximum $\bar{Z}_i$ (intramarginal trade activity), at its minimum $\underline{Z_i}$ (unprofitable activity), or *between* the two bounds (*just* profitable, i.e., *at the margin*). In the case of a single primary labor input ($f = 1$),[10] (2.3) can be written in the simple form:

$$D_i = \frac{l_i + h l_i^k}{u_i - (m_i + h m_i^k)} \gtreqless \frac{q}{w}. \qquad (2.3')$$

In this case, all trade activities could be unambiguously ranked by the price-free ratio ($D_i$), which is a simple version of the real domestic resource cost (DRC).[11] If we know the economic or technical bounds on each trade activity and the total available foreign aid (i.e., the allowable trade deficit), we can arrange all activities in order of decreasing $D_i$ and determine the trade activity (or activities, if $f > 1$) which is *at the margin*, and thus solve for $w$ and $q$ from the respective equation(s) in (2.2) and (2.3). Later, we will apply this dual concept in another context, but for the moment we confine ourselves to its use as a checking device on the primal model.

Consider first some alternative fixed proportions production function

---

10. This might represent unskilled labor, with skilled manpower appearing as part of the endogenous embodied capital stock.

11. For a discussion of the concept, see Chapter VI.

specifications that could underlie this as well as many other types of planning models. Suppose one wants to estimate the unit labor coefficient for any activity on the basis of past statistical trend observations. Is labor productivity a function of time or a function of the scale of operation? Denote output by $X$, the labor input by $L$, and the other inputs by $K$. In the first case, the production function could take the form

$$X = Min[A_0e^{at}L, B(K)]. \tag{2.4}$$

In the second case, the production function might be

$$X = Min[C_0L^c, B(K)]. \tag{2.5}$$

The function (2.4) would underlie any standard time projection of labor coefficients, while formulation (2.5) corresponds to the Verdoorn [1956] model. Either one of these models might give a good interpretation of past time trends of labor productivity for the activity in question. Moreover, as long as we deal with extrapolations into the future for given expected $X$ levels, there is no basis for choosing between the two. Any choice of parameters $A_0$ and $a$ in (2.4) or $C_0$ and $c$ in (2.5) which are consistent with extrapolation from past time series observations would give the same point estimates of input use for a given future $X$ level.

The two basic production models would, however, give very different results when incorporated in a model in which there is choice between alternative production activities. In the case of model (2.4), at any point in time marginal and average labor coefficients are equal and constant, irrespective of the level of output. Intersectoral allocation will thus be based on *average* per unit labor use. In the case of model (2.5), on the other hand, average per unit labor input changes with the level of activity, and choice will be based on differential *marginal* labor unit costs.

Now consider the implications in terms of a dual framework such as equation (2.2) and (2.3). In the first case, the coefficients $l_0$ and $l_i$ will be average coefficients, while in the second they would be *marginal* coefficients. Obviously, the ranking and actual choice of activities, and the corresponding price solutions, may be very different for the two specifications.[12] The true implication of the production function specification becomes more apparent when one looks at the dual of the model.

My second example will be taken from a subject also discussed at some length in Chapter III—the implication of terminal conditions within a static model. The so-called stock-flow conversion factor is a device for tying capital

---

12. Equation (2.5) can be incorporated in a linear programming model in a linearized version (strictly speaking, this must be a mixed integer LP model). For an illustration of this as well as of different solution sets, see Bruno [1970]. Programming suggestions and computational techniques are given by Chapter XII.

stock variables, which outlive the planning horizon, to current investment, which by itself would give no intrahorizon capacity benefits, given long gestation periods. The way such conversion is formulated has important implications for the price system, however, and this in turn reflects back on the interpretation of the model's behavior patterns.

Consider the above model formulation in which the growth rate of capital stock in the terminal year is exogenously given, but both the capital stocks and the corresponding investment flows are to be endogenously determined. The real meaning of this particular specification becomes clear only when one looks at the dual framework (see, again, (2.2) and (2.3)) in which the implied *rate of return* on the capital stocks turns out to be the assumed growth rate, $h$, itself.[13] Once one remembers the Golden Rule interpretation of consumption maximization under fixed capital growth rates (i.e., choice from alternative, momentary, steady states), this result looks much more obvious. Yet, interpreting the assumption as an imposition of a given rate of return lends a different and quite plausible dimension to a seemingly innocuous computational device.

There are other examples that could be developed, including some using dynamic models, to show that the analysis of the associated dual ought to be a major component of the model builder's tool kit.[14]

## 3. RELIABILITY OF PRICE ESTIMATES DERIVED FROM MODELS

So far we have discussed the use of the price system only as an internal model checking device. We now turn to the more central question of whether shadow prices derived from economy-wide planning models can be used, at least in theory, as they were meant to be used—for public pricing policy and as signals for decentralized investment decisions. The frank truth is that the experience in this respect is as yet very limited and quite far from the idealized textbook picture.

To place the problem in its right perspective, one ought to point out from the outset that while some kind of shadow pricing procedure is implicit in almost any country's development policy,[15] only a few countries have any kind of experience with the construction of optimizing models. Furthermore, planners who have built optimizing frameworks have no tradition of incorporating such models into the methods by which price intervention or

---

13. Suppose we denoted the total capital/output ratios of $C$ and $Z_i$ by $k_0$ and $k_i$, respectively, and the rate of return by $r$, then we would expect to have for a unit cost of $C$: $1 = l_0 w + m_0 q + k_0 r$. Since $k_0 = l_0^k w + m_0^k q$ we must have $r = h$. Similarly, for individual trade activities in equation (2.3).

14. See also sections 4.1 and 4.2 of Chapter III and section 4 of the present paper.

15. One might go so far as to say that any government intervention in the form of indirect taxes, subsidies of exchange control, and so on, involves implicit "shadow" pricing, providing the economy is on some kind of efficiency frontier.

investment projects are determined.[16] As noted in Chapter II, it takes time and much experience before one can hope to achieve a better linking of the separate planning functions. But there is more to it than that. Even a very crude macromodel can give some reasonable estimates of the basic national accounts or the balance of payments totals. But it takes a much more refined model structure to be able to turn out shadow price estimates that are even remotely "reasonable," in terms of both magnitude and sensitivity to changes in exogenous variables.

We have already noted the fact that shadow price estimates may be very sensitive to alternative specifications of the underlying model or objective function. They ought to be sensitive, too, to the choice of policy, such as the intended speed of adjustment of the balance of payments deficit or government employment policy. This in itself is not to be deplored. After all, planning consists of a search for alternatives. What is worse is that models often turn out shadow prices that look unrealistic under any kind of test of "reasonableness." Dominance of linear relations, for the sake of computational simplicity, and artificial attempts to prevent the almost inevitable flip-flop behavior often cause jerky or otherwise unreasonable behavior of price solutions. Lack of sufficient factor or commodity substitution possibilities[17] (which would presumably be found in real life but not in the model) and too narrowly defined constraints are also contributing causes.[18]

With the further refinement of nonlinear models and with more empirically based information on substitution possibilities and alternative production and behavioral constraints, one might hope to overcome gradually some of these structural weaknesses of existing models. It is a very slow process and, given the enormous gaps in basic information existing for most countries, one cannot be overly optimistic at present.

The solution to the latter kind of problem is known, in principle, and has been tackled with some models and for some selected prices.[19] However, there are more inherent problems affecting the price system for which the existing methodology is in principle not very well suited. Two major issues come to mind.

The first general problem is the way in which "second best" restrictions, or

---

16. We are here mainly referring to the limited experience with economy-wide models. Models have been used successfully on a *sectoral* level to estimate shadow prices of factors that are more or less specific to the sector in question. Examples would be the planning of some public utilities (fuel, power), estimates of the shadow price of water in the agricultural sector, and so on.

17. Both substitution possibilities and nonlinearities are discussed in Chapter XII.

18. One example is that, under parametric variation of supplies, different kinds of labor skills jump discontinuously and may obtain either a zero shadow wage rate or relatively high values with no continuous spectrum of values in between. (See also Chapter VII.)

19. Reviews of models with more complete substitution possibilities are found in Chapter XII.

the assessment of the effective area of government control (see Sen [1972]), may alter the estimated shadow prices. Different agencies of the government affect the price system, often independently of each other, using a variety of policy tools (e.g., import licensing, tariffs, taxes, investment credit). What kind of "optimum" adjustment behavior can be imputed to the various parts of the government system itself when shadow prices and projects are to be evaluated? For example, should some or all potentially tradable inputs that are now domestically produced (due to excessive protection) be assumed importable and thus priced at their international prices in the future?[20] A correct specification of the underlying model would incorporate *all* realistic future restrictions in the parameters and constraints. Using the illustration of the previous model again, whether or not such restrictions exist may affect both the basic input coefficients of the various activities[21] as well as minimum and maximum bounds on these activities. Different restrictions will produce different resulting price solutions and optimal activity choice. In principle, one can directly incorporate second-best restrictions that affect the primal system and assess their effect on the resulting constrained equilibrium prices. In addition to the above examples, these could in practice take the form of capacity constraints, minimum consumption levels, maximum savings constraints, and so forth. However, with present techniques, it is much trickier to do anything with policy restrictions on the market price system itself, restrictions in the form of taxes, subsidies, minimum and maximum price constraints, and so on. One could use trial and error methods and various indirect devices, but there is still a long way to go before these can be systematically incorporated within an overall model structure.[22]

The second difficult issue, somewhat related to the first, arises from the fact that most economies are neither completely "planned" nor completely subject to free market behavior but are in a state of incomplete control. Previously we stressed the lack of full coordination within the government decision making mechanism itself, here the control area problem lies at the boundary between the public and the private sector. Thus, a government may want to push market prices in the direction of shadow prices but cannot do so completely or all at once. Projects chosen on the basis of shadow prices may fail in execution because the choice of inputs is done on the basis of *market* and not shadow prices. What is missing in all of our planning models is the

20. As shown in Sen [1972] and Dasgupta [1972], such assessment is a source of difference between the Little–Mirrlees and UNIDO project appraisal techniques. We will come back to that in the next section.

21. This will determine whether an indirect input will appear in the form of an $l_i$ (or $l_i^k$) in the numerator or an $m_i$ (or $m_i^k$) in the denominator of (2.3′) and may thus affect the ranking of different $Z_i$.

22. In the context of the balance of payments, empirical analyses of the effect on shadow prices of gradual tariff removal are being called for. An example is provided by Taylor and Black [1973].

feedback of quantity response to *actual* prices and the successive recalculation of shadow prices, given such private (or even public) sector response functions. Dasgupta and Stiglitz [1973] have analyzed conditions under which public sector efficiency may be required independently of private market behavior, but there are obviously many exceptions in practice.

Given so much criticism, is anything left to be said in favor of using planning models for actual shadow price estimation?[23] The first thing to be noted is that the competition is among very weak alternatives. In practice, shadow prices are often guessed at or else estimated by various indirect, partial equilibrium, methods which are not a priori superior to an intelligent use of a general equilibrium planning model (more on this in the next section). Secondly, to say that the overall shadow price solution often turns out to be unsatisfactory does not necessarily imply a uniformly low quality of results for each shadow price. For example, a low level of substitutability for different types of labor inputs may lead to strange or unrealistic estimates of wage rates but need not necessarily imply a similar low quality for the estimates of the shadow exchange rate. On the other hand, in a model in which exports are exogenously fixed and where the scope for import substitution is extremely limited, the shadow exchange rate estimate would be highly suspect. It would be much more reliable in a model in which there is considerable flexibility in the choice of foreign exchange producing (or saving) activities and where an attempt to incorporate second-best restrictions on trade has been made.

Can the reliability of individual shadow price estimates be tested at all? Unlike econometric forecasting models, planning models cannot be tested directly. However, one could compare solutions with other price estimates[24] or else perform simulated experiments in which *ex post* observations on exogenous variables are substituted into the model and the solutions are checked against observed market price behavior.[25] The problem with this is, of course, the supposition that one is observing an economy behaving "optimally," subject to a set of constraints that have been or can be correctly specified. Obviously, this whole area requires a great deal more work, both conceptual and empirical.

## 4. PARTIAL METHODS AND THE LOGIC OF PLANNING MODELS

We have so far mainly discussed the difficulties associated with the use of price information obtained from detailed planning models in a "top down"

---

23. Some of the above criticism is really more general and applies to the whole problem of using shadow prices for project evaluation, whether or not derived from an economy-wide model.

24. For example, comparison could be made with the existing rule of thumb project evaluation practice or else with correct market price estimates (e.g., the foreign exchange rate, corrected for effective protection).

25. E.g., I have made a very crude attempt to "check" Israeli estimates of the shadow exchange rate for a static LP model using *ex post* foreign trade figures.

approach to project evaluation. We shall now briefly take up the question of project evaluation as it appears from the point of view of a COPE operating in an economy in which there is no fully satisfactory overall model available. At the present state of the art, this may be the rule rather than the exception. Since this is not a study devoted to project evaluation, we do not go into the various problems of techniques and specific data gathering problems that are naturally the main subject matter of project evaluation manuals. It may often be the case, for example, that errors in the estimation of investment require-ments or future operating costs of any given project[26] might outweigh the inaccuracies or conceptual difficulties befalling the estimation of key shadow prices and other "national parameters" which project evaluators require. Yet our main emphasis here is on those signals and pieces of price information that help provide the required micro-macro links.

In the absence of a good "top down" link is there anything for a "bottom up" approach that can be learned from the *logic* of an economy-wide model or from the use of short-cut methods derivable from a macroplanning frame-work? The answer to that, I believe, is a qualified "Yes." Any reasonable project evaluation procedure must have as its background some conceptual macroframework which could be spelled out as an optimizing model. Any attempt to construct and work out even a rough shadow price generating model in quantitative terms can help a planner, in a particular country's empirical context, to understand the framework within which investment proj-ects are to be evaluated, as well as to suggest ways of organizing required information. Thus, writing down the dual price system for a hypothetical planning model for which the data do not fully exist may considerably improve one's way of organizing partial price information in a uniform and systematic fashion. It can also help point out restrictions on the degrees of freedom of choice of alternative price systems.

As an example consider equation (2.2), which is one of the basic cost-price equations appearing in the dual reduced form of many planning models. If each period's aggregate consumption appears in the maximand, then we know that the scalar product of primary factor prices (wage rate, interest rate, and foreign exchange) times the set of corresponding marginal (direct and indirect) primary factor coefficients (in producing the aggregate consumption basket) must equal unity.[27] In the absence of a complete model, we could use very rough input-output estimates of the breakdown of consumption by primary factor use to get one restriction on the set of prices. An equation like (2.2) helps us remember that we cannot arbitrarily choose both the shadow exchange rate and shadow wage without thereby automatically implying the rate of return.

---

26. This is not only the problem of objective uncertainty; there is often intentional mis-information on the part of interested parties.

27. Suppose, as before, all prices are measured in aggregate consumption units.

For further illustration consider the logic behind the complete static model mentioned in section 2. Even in the absence of a fully articulated model, individual project information relating to tradable goods can still be organized in a way suggested by the DRC ratio in equation (2.3′) for alternative estimates of the rate of return $h$.[28] Again what is required is an attempt to break down the cost structure of projects into direct and indirect primary and tradable inputs using full or partial input-output type calculations.[29]

Having done that, one can either use the *logic* of the model for the internal ranking of available projects or else use practioners' opinions as to what may be considered a "marginal project." A project $Z_i$ for which we can write equation (2.3′) with equality sign provides us with an estimate of $w/q$.[30] Together with a rough estimate of equation (2.2), this gives us the pair of prices $w, q$ for each assumed estimate of the rate of return $h$. We note, incidentally, that the ratio $w/q$ is a measure of the marginal productivity of labor in foreign exchange terms, so that no domestic numeraire appears. This is of some relevance to the interpretation of what underlies the project evaluation technique of Little–Mirrlees. They advocate use of border prices and spend considerable effort in stressing the role of the shadow wage, expressed at international prices. Having obtained the latter, their criterion is not basically different from that of DRC in (2.3′).[31]

A further illustration of the kinds of considerations we have in mind can be provided by investigating a dynamic version of the open economy planning model. Suppose we are looking for a modified version of project evaluation in a multiperiod context in which the economy may be assumed to maximize discounted aggregate consumption (with discount rate $r$). Had we written down a simple dynamic version of the previous model and derived its reduced form and dual, the following kind of allocation criterion for tradable goods would emerge:[32]

$$\sum_{t=0}^{T} \frac{u_{jt}q_t - (l_{jt}w_t + m_{jt}q_t)}{(1 + r)^t} - K_j \lessgtr 0 \qquad (4.1)$$

28. A corresponding statement can be applied to nontradables.

29. Note that this basic idea underlies all the main existing project evaluation techniques such as DRC, Little–Mirrlees (LM), or UNIDO. There is, of course, the problem mentioned before where to draw the line of direct versus indirect inputs, depending on one's assessment of the area of control. This issue is well discussed in Sen [1972].

30. More generally, we need as many such projects as there are primary inputs.

31. In their case the role of a separate savings constraint is also emphasized. This could be incorporated in the above framework without difficulty by noting that if savings or investment is the numeraire, the right-hand side of equation (2.2) would not be 1 but the shadow price of consumption in investment units (which would be less than 1). Also, a distinction would now have to be made between the discount rates of investment and consumption. See the discussion in Dasgupta [1972]. A similar point is taken up below in the context of the dynamic open economy model.

32. See Chapter III, section 5, and Bruno [1970]. The latter incorporates some refinements (such as externality effects derived from export growth constraints) which are abstracted here.

Here again $l_{jt}$ and $m_{jt}$ should be interpreted as expected total (direct and indirect) coefficients in period $t$ for project $j$. Again we should keep in mind control area considerations as to what can or cannot be considered potential importables; $w_t$ and $q_t$ are the respective shadow prices for primary factor(s) and foreign exchange, while $u_{jt}$ is the marginal foreign exchange revenue for good $j$ at time $t$.[33] $K_j$ denotes the required investment in the project, also evaluated at shadow prices. Suppose we decompose the latter into the form $K_j = m_j^k q_0 + l_j^k w_0$. Next we use some of the interdependences among shadow prices which come out of a full-fledged dynamic model of this kind.

Suppose foreign exchange can be transferred from one period to the next (borrowed or lent) at a fixed marginal interest rate $\rho$.[34] Optimal capital accumulation theory (or else common sense) tells us that the economy should be indifferent at the margin between investing or borrowing foreign exchange at a rate $\rho$ or a domestic resource at a rate $r$, corrected for capital gains due to a changing relative price $q$. This is reflected in the following intertemporal efficiency relationship:

$$\frac{q_{t+1}}{q_t} = \frac{1+r}{1+\rho}, \quad (t = 0, \dots, T). \tag{4.2}$$

From (4.2) it follows that

$$q_t = q_0 \left[\frac{1+r}{1+\rho}\right]^t.$$

Substituting for $q_t$ and for $K_j$, equation (4.1) can be transformed into the form:

$$\frac{\sum_{t=0}^{T} \dfrac{l_{jt} w_t}{(1+r)^t} + l_j^k w_0}{\sum_{t=0}^{T} \dfrac{(u_{jt} - m_{jt})}{(1+\rho)^t}} \gtreqless q_0. \tag{4.3}$$

This is a dynamic analog of the static criterion (2.3). Note that domestic primary resource costs are discounted at the rate $r$, whereas net foreign exchange benefits are discounted at $\rho$. Just as in a static framework, however, we should keep in mind that there is a further restriction on $w_t$ and $q_t$ of the type (2.2) which must hold in each time period $t$. Suppose, for simplicity, that this takes the form of a fixed expected rate of growth of the real wage, say, $w_t = w_0(1 + g)^t$. In that case, (4.2) can be further simplified into a price-free form which is an analog of (2.3'):

---

33. For a nontradable, one would have to write $p_{jt}$ instead of $u_{jt} q_t$.
34. The situation becomes more complicated if the interest rate is different for borrowing and lending and also if it changes with the amount borrowed. These problems can be tackled, in principle, but for simplicity are ignored here.

$$\frac{\sum_{t=0}^{T} l_{jt} \left(\frac{1+g}{1+r}\right)^t + l_{j0}^k}{\sum_{t=0}^{T} \frac{u_{jt} - m_{jt}}{(1+\rho)^t} - m_{j0}^k} \gtreqless \frac{q_0}{w_0}. \tag{4.3'}$$

If unit wage costs and other parameters are constant over time $l_{jt}(1+g)^t = l_j$ and the two interest rates are equal ($r = \rho$ and, thus, $q_t = q_0$), then (4.3') will simply degenerate into (2.3').

There is an intermediate case here which may be of practical interest. If all the above assumptions hold, except for the equality of interest rates (i.e., $q_t$ is expected to change over time), and if $T$ is large, (4.3') can be shown to degenerate into the following form:

$$\frac{l_j + r l_j^k}{(u_j - m_j) - \rho m_j^k} \gtreqless \left(\frac{r}{\rho}\right) \frac{q_0}{w_0},$$

which is a slight modification of (2.3').

The above analysis suggests an additional practical consideration for a COPE operating in an imperfect planning world. Equation (4.2) suggests a way of estimating the consumption rate of discount $r$ from observations on the marginal cost of foreign borrowing $\rho$ plus an estimate of the expected growth rate of $q_t$. The latter can be deduced from the speed at which the balance of payments is to be reduced in the future (a policy assumption), together with estimates of the supply response at the margin of tradables to a change in the tariff-cum-subsidy inclusive exchange rate.[35]

Here again we note that both the Little–Mirrlees as well as the UNIDO procedures can be shown to be very closely linked to the above type of framework, the main nuances being the way one would go about estimating $w$ or where the boundaries of the control area are drawn.[36]

Such considerations as the above serve to illustrate how project data together with partial methods based on the *logic* of economy-wide planning models can serve as substitutes for full-fledged textbook ideals. The information required for condition (2.3') or (4.3') is similar to what can be and is being collected by project evaluators in practice. All that is suggested here is an appropriate way for such information to be organized.

To sum up—our way of looking at things suggests that there is some preference for not viewing the problem of shadow price estimation within a planning system as a unified, well laid out computer program but rather as a process of information gathering from alternative sources. In this process, the

---

35. The possible use of the latter rate as a proxy for $q$ is discussed in Bacha and Taylor [1971]. Note that what is required here is the assumption that the growth *rates* of the two exchange rates are equal. This is a less problematic assumption.

36. Once the marginal project is known, the ratio $w_0/q_0$ in (4.3') is determined (for given $r$ and $\rho$). Conversely, if we know the shadow wage in foreign exchange terms, then (4.3') can determine the marginal project within a given project set.

output of a formal economy-wide model would be only one input which might give a *range* of shadow prices under alternative model experiments. This should be supplemented by guesses by experts, rule-of-thumb estimates, microproject information, and the like. The role of the overall model would be confined mainly to suggesting a common analytical framework or at least a loose frame of reference. In the absence of a common framework, heterogeneous information may be of little practical use. Moreover, complete reliance on partial methods cannot allow for analysis of interdependent projects, timing of linked projects, or assessing their effect on macropolicies.

Chapter IX

# PLANNING FOR MULTIPLE GOALS

## Daniel P. Loucks

---

## 1. Introduction

Planning occurs at many levels of any organization; though the scope of the plans differ, the process of planning at each level is generally the same. Goals are considered, information is gathered and processed, alternative choices are defined and evaluated, and—after a number of iterations that may modify the goals, information needs, and alternatives—a decision is made and a particular choice or plan is implemented. Often the process of planning continues, and plans may be modified after they have been put in action.

For the technician, it would be ideal if the choice of one economic policy over another could be evaluated in terms of a single goal that is well established, identified, and agreed upon. In fact, there are always many relevant planning objectives. These are often conflicting, and the importance of each one is rarely made precise before decisions are made. Public policy is often formulated on the basis of a mostly qualitative integration of numerous economic, political, social, and technological objectives. Explicit trade-offs between partially complementary and conflicting objectives are not always clear, leading to selection and implementation of plans which fail to meet many of the objectives to the extent originally envisioned.

Choice is further complicated by uncertainty in the outcome of any decision and by practical limits on simultaneous consideration of all relevant information. Even when supplemented by computers, the capacity of any group of planners is limited. (Games of perfect information such as chess are examples of this limitation.) They are usually forced to construct simplified mathematical representations of their problem to make efficient use of whatever information is available in order to predict and evaluate possible outcomes. Our objective is to review some of these mathematical modelling techniques and discuss methods for estimating the overall acceptability of specific policy alternatives.

While the emphasis here is on economy-wide models, the reader should be aware that not all of the techniques reviewed have in fact been used for development planning. Some of the most promising multiple objective methods have been proposed only recently and are still being discussed in the technical literature. Other methods have been applied to project evaluation problems, such as water resources development and environmental quality management,

but have not been applied to the analysis of multisector macroeconomic problems. Hence, this chapter is not primarily a review of the current state of the art but a look at what the future may be with regard to multiple objective planning models.

Mathematical models are usually restricted to those aspects of the evaluation process that are quantifiable, but the information derived from them may also significantly assist qualitative decision making. This is especially true where multiple objectives have been identified. In these situations, usually some alternatives are preferable when different objectives are examined. As the number of relevant objectives and alternatives increases, the ability of the decision making organization to grasp the complexities of its problem rapidly decreases. Here is where quantitative modelling techniques and those who know how to use them can be of considerable value as aids to, but not as substitutes for, the responsible political decision making process.

Before reviewing some quantitative techniques for assisting in planning for multiple objectives, it may be useful to outline some possible objectives that have been suggested for public investment policy and development planning. A partial list appears in Table 1.

**Table 1: Some Public Policy Goals and Possible Units of Measurement**

| Goal | Examples of Units of Measurement |
|---|---|
| (1) National Economic Growth | Discounted GNP, GDP, or terminal GNP, $; increase in total income, $; terminal capital stocks, $. |
| (2) Aggregate Consumption (standard of living) | Discounted consumption or utility of consumption, $. |
| (3) Income Distribution | Total weighted sum of logarithms of consumption of each income class, Gini coefficient, Theil coefficient, variance, coefficient of variation, relative mean deviation. |
| (4) Price Stability | Change in unit market or social price for various goods and services, $. |
| (5) Self Reliance | Balance of payments or trade deficit, $; employment of foreign labor, number or percent; discounted foreign exchange surplus, $; total imports, $. |
| (6) Educational Opportunity | School enrollments by grade, number or percent. |
| (7) Productive Capacity | Investments, $. |
| (8) Employment Level | Total unemployment or underemployment weighted by income groups, number or percent. |
| (9) Regional Development | Gross regional product or production, $; change in relative rates of aggregate or per capita growth in region, number or percent. |
| (10) Environmental Quality | Mass and energy residuals discharged in air, water, and land; weight, volume, concentration, temperature, decibel level. |
| (11) Social Mobility | Sum of weighted changes in employment by occupation, number or percent. |

Given any subset of the goals listed in Table 1, together with others that may be important, the problem is how to combine them into one simple measure of aggregate benefit. If this could be accomplished, it would be at least conceptually possible to find the policy that maximizes this total. Clearly it is not possible to add each objective value directly, even if each were expressed in the same terms, say dollars, for one dollar of national growth is not the same as one dollar of income redistribution. What needs to be defined is the minimum amount of one kind of benefit that must be given up in order to gain one unit of another kind of benefit.

To do this operationally, we must make several assumptions. The first is that public policy is rarely implemented to satisfy only a single economic objective. Often many very important objectives defy quantification, and these, together with the quantifiable objectives, must be considered in the planning and decision making processes.

The second assumption is that among the objectives that can be quantified, the parameters used to describe them need not be directly comparable. For example, there is no acceptable way of assigning a monetary value to environmental quality that is directly comparable to the monetary value of consumption or regional income and its distribution. Quantitative specification of many social-political goals (e.g., social mobility, enhanced educational and employment opportunities, productive capacity, reduced dependence on foreign capital and human resources) requires the analyst to take on the task of ascertaining the decision maker's welfare or utility function. This is usually done through finding out how he responds to the probable outcomes of various policy combinations.

The third major assumption is that selection of a policy that in turn *implies* the relative importance of each objective must take place in the political process. The relative weight given to each objective is ultimately based on political rather than solely on technical criteria. These weights are always conditional, depending in part on the decision maker's perception of: (i) his policy alternatives, (ii) how each alternative would be implemented if selected, and (iii) the likely outcomes. We assume that a distinguishing feature of public policy making is that the power to accept, reject, and implement plans rests only with public officials called policy or decision makers, and that "planners" only present possible alternatives to these decision makers. Preselection of policies to be discussed by technicians to reflect *their own* political desires is therefore ruled out.

We will first examine some methods that have been used for defining trade-offs among multiple objectives. The remainder of the discussion will then outline various approaches to planning and some corresponding modelling techniques that have been proposed to define the sets of solutions that satisfy, to the greatest extent possible, various weighted combinations of multiple noncommensurable but quantifiable objectives. A comparison of these

215

efficient solutions will indicate the relative sensitivity or importance of each objective in the overall plan or policy. Again, this information would be used to guide decisions rather than to determine them.

## 2. DEFINING TRADE-OFFS AMONG MULTIPLE OBJECTIVES

Consider the general public policy problem. Given a vector of decision or policy variables $\bar{X} = \{X_k : k = 1, 2, \ldots, K\}$, each component of which can assume a range of values defined by a number of constraints $g_i(\bar{X}) = 0$, the problem is to select the best policy vector $\bar{X}^*$. Single objective models assume that the decision makers' preferences are known and can be expressed as a single objective function $F(\bar{X})$ which, for a particular solution vector $\bar{X}$, expresses the utility of $\bar{X}$ to the decision maker. In these situations, the only computation required is to find the vector $\bar{X}^*$ which optimizes $F(\bar{X})$ subject to all constraints $g_i(\bar{X}) = 0$. Assuming only two policy variables, $X_1$ and $X_2$, and an objective $F(\bar{X})$ that is to be maximized, this problem is illustrated in Figure 1.

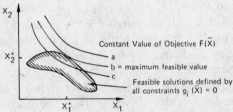

Figure 1. At Two-Variable Policy Program whose Optimal Solution is $X_1^*, X_2^*$

Most development or public investment analyses require comparison of various solution vectors $\bar{X}$ in light of numerous objectives or goals. Of the objectives that are quantifiable, each can be described by a function $F_j(\bar{X})$ that should be either maximized or minimized.[1] The task becomes one of trading off the value of one objective for another if by increasing one objective value, one or more other objective values decrease. Postponing for the moment the problem of estimating the optimal trade-off, we discuss here various methods for defining the feasible range of efficient trade-offs between objectives and means for determining the solution vector $\bar{X}$ associated with each set of efficient objective values.

A number of approaches can be used to examine the trade-offs between separate and noncomparable objectives. If there are only two or three objective functions $F_j(\bar{X})$, and a relatively few decision variables $X_k$ in the vector $\bar{X}$, then it may be possible to simulate all feasible combinations of decision variables $X_k$ in order to plot the values of each of the objective

---

1. In this discussion each $F_j(\bar{X})$ is assumed to be a superior objective, i.e., it is to be maximized. Obviously, any inferior objective can be changed to a superior one by multiplying by minus one.

functions associated with each vector $\overline{X}$. The envelope of these values would define the efficient vectors $\overline{X}$ and the trade-offs that are possible among these efficient combinations of $\overline{X}$. These concepts are illustrated for a two-objective problem in Figure 2.

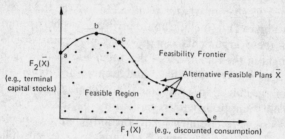

Figure 2.   Feasible Solutions for a Two-Objective Problem

Each point within the feasible region in Figure 2 represents a particular set of values for the decision variables $X_k$ in the vector $\overline{X}$ that satisfy a set of constraints $g_i(\overline{X}) = 0$, $i = 1, 2, \ldots, m$. The decision vectors that lie on the feasibility frontier,[2] curve *abcde*, are those that define the maximum value of objective $F_2(\overline{X})$ given a particular value of objective $F_1(\overline{X})$. Of interest to the planner and policy maker are the trade-offs defined by certain combinations of feasible and efficient decision vectors. Each decision vector on the *bcde* portion of the feasibility frontier is efficient in that there can be no increase in one objective value without a decrease in the other objective value. Solutions on the *ab* portion of the frontier are inferior solutions in that they are dominated by other solutions having higher values for each objective. Inferior solution vectors are of interest only if some of the objectives are inferior, i.e., they are to be minimized.[3] If all objectives are superior, then only the efficient superior solutions need be considered.

Clearly the use of simulation models as a means of defining the feasibility frontier and the corresponding trade-offs between each efficient decision vector becomes less attractive as the number of variables $(X_k)$ and objectives $(F_j(\overline{X}))$ increase. A simple graphic presentation of the trade-offs between objectives $F_j(\overline{X})$ becomes impossible as their number increases beyond three. For these reasons optimization techniques are usually suggested as a means of estimating feasible and efficient decision vectors $\overline{X}$.

It is appropriate here to mention that different models of the same decision problem could result in different feasibility frontiers. Also, simplifying assumptions and algorithmic, computer, data, or budget limitations add to the

---

2. For more discussion of this concept, see Chapter 3 of UNIDO [1972].

3. Such a situation would be indicated by a negative sloped decision maker's indifference curve.

uncertainty associated with the resulting feasibility frontier. This uncertainty might lead many to argue that the frontier is really a range of points, perhaps best represented by a probability distribution. Also, politicians whose aspirations exceed what appears to be feasible might suggest that one or more restrictions specified in the constraint set are really not constraints or that they are willing to give up what is required to enlarge the feasible region (as illustrated in Figure 1) to include an otherwise infeasible aspiration or target. While all of these arguments can be valid in certain situations, we will assume throughout the remainder of the discussion that the planning process can derive a reasonably well-defined and accurate feasibility frontier.

The use of optimization techniques for defining the feasibility frontier requires some assumptions with regard to the aggregation of each separate objective into a single, one-dimensional function defining a complete preference order. If the units of each objective $F_j(\overline{X})$ are the same, say dollars, then it is relatively easy to combine separate objectives into a single function. For example, MacEwan [1971] included in the same objective function the per capita increments to consumption in both West Pakistan and what was, at the time of his study, East Pakistan. These separate objectives were weighted relative to one another, permitting trade-offs between them to be obtained by varying the relative weights in an additive objective function maximizing the sum of the weighted individual objectives. Denoting the relative weight of each objective $F_j(\overline{X})$ by $W_j \geq 0$, such an objective function can be written

$$\text{Maximize} \quad \sum_j W_j F_j(\overline{X}), \qquad (2.1)$$

where the relative weights sum to 1 and the units of each objective $F_j(\overline{X})$ are the same. By varying the assumed relative weights, the noninferior convex portion of the feasibility frontier can be defined.[4] The trade-offs obtained by MacEwan for East and West Pakistan together with the relative weights used to define those trade-offs are illustrated in Figure 3.

The success of any attempted definition of the feasibility frontier through maximization of a weighted sum of various objectives depends critically on the assumption that the set of alternative combinations of different objectives is convex. A convex set of feasible alternatives has the property that a straight line segment between any two points in the set lies wholly within the interior of the set. For example, the portions *abc* and *de* of the feasibility frontier illustrated in Figure 2 are convex. If parts of the feasibility frontier are not convex (e.g., curve *cd*) or if they are convex but contain inferior points (e.g., curve *ab*), the maximization of weighted sums of individual objectives will not define all points on the frontier. In these situations, the feasibility frontier can be defined by constraining the values of some of the objectives while

---

4. For additional discussion of this procedure and some examples pertaining to a regional water quality management problem, see Dorfman, Jacoby, and Thomas [1972].

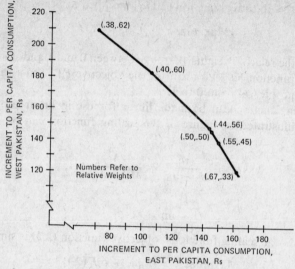

Figure 3. Regional Consumption Frontier from MacEwen [1971], p. 150

maximizing weighted combinations of the others—a tedious process, at best. More efficient adaptive search techniques have been proposed by Beeson and Miesel [1971].

The multiple objective problem becomes more complex when the objectives $F_j(\overline{X})$ are not all expressed in the same units. In these cases it is useful to define scaling functions $S_j(F_j(\overline{X}))$ to insure that each objective $F_j(\overline{X})$ ranges over the same set of numbers, e.g., between 0 and 1, as illustrated in Figure 4. The objective $F_j(\overline{X})$ in Figure 4 is assumed to range between its minimum value, $m_j$, and its maximum value, $M_j$.[5]

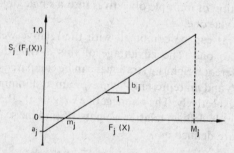

Figure 4. Scaling Objective Values

---

5. The maximum value, $M_j$, of objective $F_j(\overline{X})$ can be obtained from (2.1) by setting $W_j = J$ and all other weights to 0. The minimum value, $m_j$, can be obtained by setting $W_j = 0$ and selecting the minimum of all solutions $F_j(\overline{X})$ generated by various combinations of relative weights associated with the other objectives.

219

In this case, the objective function (2.1) is modified to become

$$\text{Maximize} \quad \sum_j W_j S_j(F_j(\bar{X})) \tag{2.2}$$

where again the relative weights $W_j$ range between 0 and 1 and sum to 1, and each scaling function $S_j(\ )$ transforms the objective $F_j(\bar{X})$ to a value within the convenient interval from 0 to 1.

The scaling function can be made linear for use in linear programming models. As illustrated in Figure 4, the scaling function can be defined as $a_j + b_j F_j(\bar{X})$, where

$$a_j = \frac{-m_j}{M_j - m_j} = \frac{-M_j}{M_j - m_j} + 1, \tag{2.3}$$

$$b_j = \frac{1}{M_j - m_j}. \tag{2.4}$$

Using these linear scaling functions, objective function (2.2) is simply

$$\text{Maximize} \quad \sum_j W_j[a_j + b_j F_j(\bar{X})] \tag{2.5}$$

where of course $\sum_j W_j \cdot a_j$ is a constant that can be ignored for the purpose of estimating the trade-offs between separate objectives $j$.

The aggregation of multiple objectives into a single function need not be additive, since nonlinear combinations can also be used to combine separate objectives. The difficulty is that nonlinear expressions usually increase the complexity of optimization algorithms required for solution. Whether or not it is proper to add together scaled objectives becomes important if the scaling reflects the utility of the objective in units common to each scaled objective. However, for determining only the trade-offs between separate objectives using varying relative weights, the problem of deciding on the appropriate means of aggregation of multiple objectives into a single objective function is purely a computional one.

The scaling terms can be combined with the relative weights so that together they sum to one. The advantage of this is that different solutions resulting from different weighting strategies can be compared easily. As before, let the value of $M_j$ and $m_j$ represent the maximum and minimum value of the objective $F_j(\bar{X})$, respectively. The nonnegative weights $\hat{W}_j$ that sum to one and include the previously defined relative weights $W_j$ and the scaling or normalizing constants $S_j$ are defined as

$$\hat{W}_j = \frac{W_j}{M_j - m_j} \bigg/ \sum_j \frac{W_j}{M_j - m_j}. \tag{2.6}$$

The objective function, equation (2.2), is then

$$\text{Maximize} \quad \sum_j \hat{W}_j F_j(\bar{X}). \tag{2.7}$$

Again, by varying the relative weights $W_j$ between 0 and 1 such that $\sum_j W_j = 1$, the trade-offs between each separate objective $F_j(\overline{X})$ can be defined.

These and other methods used to define the possible trade-offs between multiple objectives can result in a relatively large number of efficient alternative solutions. As the number of objectives increases, so does the number of alternative solutions required to define the possible trade-offs among these objectives. This in turn requires more computer time and expense. Perhaps more importantly, it also requires more of the decision maker's time to examine the numerous efficient solution vectors $\overline{X}$ that define the efficient trade-offs. Decision makers are not always willing to take the time to do this.

Considerable evidence suggests that, contrary to what would appear to be rational behavior, decision makers have typically not yearned for the opportunity to select what they judge to be the best from among a large number of alternative efficient solutions to a particular problem. They are more inclined to request from their staff or from an appropriate agency their single best solution and then either accept or reject it. This shifts the burden of finding trade-offs among values of conflicting objectives to the technicians. If their trade-offs are considered appropriate by the decision makers, their proposed policy will likely be accepted; otherwise it will probably be rejected. The iterative process of proposing a solution and having it accepted or rejected by the decision makers is one means of focusing in on the trade-offs that are considered acceptable, but not necessarily optimal, by the decision makers.

## 3. ALTERNATIVE PLANNING METHODS AND MODELS

The previous section was concerned mainly with techniques for generating efficient sets of solutions as a means of specifying trade-offs among multiple objectives. These methods involved the use of relative weights that could be varied by the analyst to map out an efficient trade-off or feasibility frontier. Now we consider selection of models for solution of the multiple objective planning problem. Such models must take into account the fact that an optimal set of relative weights is usually not known to the decision maker prior to the actual decision, so that final optimal weights may be imputed only after a decision is made. In addition, decision makers are reluctant to discuss in explicit terms the trade-offs they must make between a variety of conflicting objectives. Hence, for maximum effectiveness, any modeling technique must be capable of assisting the decision maker to identify feasible alternative solutions and to evaluate those solutions based on each of the applicable multiple objectives in terms that he can understand.

Here, we outline some planning approaches and corresponding models that have been proposed for solving multiple objective problems. These are classified into four groups: prediction planning, conventional planning, optimization planning, and compromise planning. Although it is not all-

encompassing, this classification scheme does isolate the major approaches to multiobjective planning.[6]

## 3.1 Prediction Planning

Some planners believe that given the existing conditions in an economy, its future development will be largely the same regardless of any development planning that may take place. They view planning as simply the process of forecasting or predicting future growth and identifying means of meeting the increased demands created by this growth. Their obvious interest is in models that can assist in the estimation of resource allocations that minimize the social cost of satisfying these future demands or requirements. Such planners rely heavily on econometric and statistical techniques for estimating future demands and long-run trends.

## 3.2 Conventional Planning

Another planning philosophy is based on the definition of a number of feasible plans from which one is selected that best meets a predetermined set of objectives articulated by the political leadership. This method of planning is rational and defensible if the resulting plans are internally consistent, if the data on which the plans are based are reasonably accurate and complete, if the implicit and explicit assumptions in the plans are correct, and if the targets adequately reflect the social needs or objectives of the decision makers.

This type of planning assumes that the targets of the decision maker are well defined prior to the planning exercise. If this is true, there are a variety of modeling techniques available to assist the decision making process. A number of studies (e.g., Charnes et al. [1970], Holt [1965], Holt et al. [1960], and Theil [1964, 1965]) have proposed models that minimize the loss, if any, in not meeting all targets. First the planner or analyst must specify the values $T_j$ of the targets that define the minimum acceptable level, if not the optimum value, of each objective $F_j(\bar{X})$. It is likely that these target values cannot all be satisfied simultaneously. Hence, a relative loss function $L_j$ for each target must be constructed so that the losses resulting from any deviation $D_j$ from a target $T_j$ (that is, $D_j = T_j - F_j(\bar{X})$) reflect the relative political importance of that deviation compared with the deviations from other targets. The problem is simply to find a solution $\bar{X}$ that minimizes the maximum loss; that is, planners seek to minimize:

$$\max_j L_j(D_j) \tag{3.1}$$

subject to

$$D_j = T_j - F_j(\bar{X}) \quad \text{for all } j, \tag{3.2}$$

and,

$$g_i(\bar{X}) = 0 \qquad \text{for all } i. \tag{3.3}$$

---

6. For more discussion, see the summary papers of MacGrimmon [1968], Roy [1971], Kornai [1969, 1970], and Waterston [1965].

As is well known, this problem can be rewritten for solution by convex programming techniques readily available at most computing facilities. The problem written in this format would be:
minimize

$$L \tag{3.4}$$

subject to, in addition to constraints (3.3),

$$D_j^+ - D_j^- = T_j - F_j(\bar{X}), \tag{3.5}$$

$$L \geq L_j^+(D_j^+), \tag{3.6}$$

$$L \geq L_j^-(D_j^-), \tag{3.7}$$

$$D_j^+, D_j^- \geq 0 \quad \text{for all } j. \tag{3.8}$$

The convex loss functions $L_j(D_j)$ defined in equation (3.1) are divided in two parts, one for deficit deviations $D_j^-$, and one for surplus deviations $D_j^+$.[7]

An alternative approach, called goal programming by Charnes et al. [1970], replaces the objective function (3.1) or (3.4) that minimizes the maximum loss by one that minimizes the absolute value of the losses.[8] Here the objective is:

$$\text{Minimize} \quad \sum_j |L_j(D_j)|. \tag{3.9}$$

Assuming linearity and positive loss coefficients $L_j^+$ and $L_j^-$, the problem can be rewritten, again for ease of solution as:

$$\text{Minimize} \quad \sum_j (L_j^+ D_j^+ + L_j^- D_j^-) \tag{3.10}$$

subject to (3.3), (3.5), and (3.8).[9]

The most difficult task in applying these techniques is clearly the definition of the appropriate targets and relative loss functions. Since the analyst is not likely to have an adequate knowledge of the decision makers' preferences before the final decision is made, the technician's best hope is to perform sensitivity analysis of various combinations of loss functions to estimate the relative importance of the objectives. In addition, it is also possible to test the relative accuracy of any set of loss functions by obtaining various solution vectors $\bar{X}$ that yield a specified value of the objective function and noting whether or not the solutions may realistically be regarded as equivalent. If

---

7. Theil [1964] discusses in detail the particular situation in which a quadratic loss function $\sum_j W_j(T_j - F_j(\bar{X}))^2$, the sum of weighted square deviations, is minimized.

8. For certain types of problems, Roy [1971] has proposed that objective functions (3.4) and (3.9) might be used sequentially to break ties if more than one optimal solution resulted using either one by itself.

9. A more general case of objective (3.10) would involve nonlinear nonnegative convex loss functions that could be approximated by piece-wise linear segments (see Chapter XII) if linear programming were to be used as a means of solving for the optimal solution.

they are not, either the loss functions or targets are poorly defined or the additivity assumptions are invalid.[10]

### 3.3 Optimization Planning

Optimization planning is a refinement of conventional planning in that both require a priori knowledge of the decision maker's preferences. To justify optimizations, one must assume that preferences are expressed as objectives rather than targets; planners then seek optimal solutions in light of these objectives, given the available resources. The optimal plan satisfies all feasibility constraints and is preferred to all other feasible plans.

Compared to conventional planning, optimization planning is more difficult, in a way that will not be resolved just by improved mathematical modelling techniques. The central problem is the inability of decision makers to know what they want prior to knowing what they can have, and even then being able only to guess at the outcomes of possible decisions concerning complex problems that have not been previously stated, let alone solved. This is a general criticism of all the applications of the optimization models based on normative economic theory that are suggested in the rest of this book.

### 3.4 Compromise Planning

Compromise planning is imperfect, but it is also realistic. It does not assume that the targets or the relative weights for each possible objective are known in advance of the planning exercise. Hence, the emphasis in this type of planning is on the generation of feasible but improving plans through the active involvement of the responsible decision maker in the planning process. Compromise planning explicitly assumes that the decision maker will consider and evaluate all the quantitative and qualitative factors that affect selection of plans. This strong assumption effectively summarizes the weaknesses and strengths of this planning philosophy. "Decision makers" *should* consider all possibilities and make their preferences clear, but who is to say that they will? Obfuscation is often the better part of political valor.

The distinguishing feature of these techniques is that no preference functions need be defined. Preferences are revealed only *ex post* by a process of selecting among pairs of efficient alternatives that are comparable, rather than by the *ex ante* construction of a preference function. We review here only a few of the many techniques proposed for this type of planning.

Two rather simple procedures called dominance and satisficing involve the comparison of alternative decision vectors $\overline{X}_i$ and do not require the decision

---

10. Additive forms of a deterministic objective function, e.g.,

$$Z = V[F_1(\overline{X}), \ldots, F_j(\overline{X}), \ldots] = V[F_1(\overline{X})] + V[F_2(\overline{X})] + \ldots + V[F_j(\overline{X})] + \ldots$$

are valid if the substitution rate between any two objectives $F_j(\overline{X})$ does not depend on the values of the other objectives. Although this condition appears rather restrictive, in practice, substitution rates are frequently independent enough to imply additivity.

maker to specify how much more of one objective he must have in order to compensate for a loss of another. Dominance exists if one alternative results in an equal or higher value for all objectives than do all other alternatives, and if at least one objective has a strictly higher value. Perhaps more importantly, if one alternative results in all objective values being equal to or less than the corresponding objective values of all other alternatives, then clearly it is dominated by those alternatives and can be dropped from further consideration.

While dominance can be a useful method for reducing the size of some decision problems, it is not a very effective method for making the final decision when a number of alternatives remain. For example, all alternatives $\overline{X}_i$ that are on the noninferior portion *bcde* of the feasibility frontier in Figure 2 are not dominated, i.e., there exist no other alternatives that have equal or higher values for each of the objectives. Since the formal studies of dominance by Pareto, these nondominated alternatives have often been called Pareto optimal (or Pareto admissible). As implied in Figure 2, there are usually many Pareto optimal alternatives and each has an objective value that is higher than that of all other alternatives. Although dominance has reduced the number of alternatives from all those that are feasible to those that define the feasibility frontier, the problem of choice among these efficient alternatives remains.

One method of further reducing the number of alternatives is called satisficing. As described by Simon [1955], the decision maker supplies the minimal values he will accept for each objective. Alternatives that do not yield these objective targets or values are dropped from further consideration. Those that do are again screened after increasing the minimal acceptable values of one or more objectives. When used in an iterative fashion, the number of alternatives can be reduced to a single choice. Like dominance, satisficing requires no numerical values for each objective. Nor is any special credit given to alternatives having relatively high values of one or more objectives.

These two techniques, while simple and requiring relatively little information, have a number of limitations. To overcome some of these, other more complex evaluation techniques have been proposed, necessarily requiring more information and assumptions.

Within a mathematical programming framework, Benayoun et al. [1971] have proposed a sequential iteration and exploration technique that involves the decision maker. The process "teaches" the decision maker to recognize what he considers as good solutions and important objectives. The final solution selected by the decision maker represents his "best" compromise among conflicting objectives. Assuming that preferences do not change during the decision making process, the final compromise is achieved in relatively few iterations, depending on the number of objectives being considered.

225

Clearly, most planning situations are dynamic and involve changing preferences and planning environments. In these situations, the final compromise is more a function of the time available for planning than of the number of objectives. The authors have labeled their approach STEM (step method).[11]

STEM assumes that the decision maker is initially unable to define the relative importance of the separate objectives $F_j(\overline{X})$. To teach him, a number of calculation and decision making iterations are required involving conversation between technician and decision maker. During the decision making phase of each iteration, the decision maker examines the results of the calculation phase and develops new insights and information about his objectives. This information, in turn, is used in the calculation phase of the next iteration, thereby providing a guide for the search of the best compromise.

The essence of the calculation phase of STEM is a payoff matrix as illustrated in Table 2. This matrix depicts the value of all separate objectives $F_j(\overline{X})$ for feasible solution vectors $\overline{X}$ that maximize each of those separate objectives. Each column $j$ in the payoff matrix corresponds to the values of each objective for the solution vector $\overline{X}$ that maximizes the objective function $F_j(\overline{X})$ subject to constraints $g_i(\overline{X}) = 0$. The maximum values $M_j$ of all objectives $F_j(\overline{X})$ are the values along the main diagonal of the matrix. All other values, denoted by $Z_{lj}$, are the values of objective $F_i(\overline{X})$ when $F_j(\overline{X})$ $(j \neq l)$ equals its maximum value $M_j$.

**Table 2: Pay-off Matrix for STEM**

| Objective | $F_1(\overline{X})$ | $F_2(\overline{X})$ | $\ldots$ | $F_j(\overline{X})$ |
|---|---|---|---|---|
| $F_1(\overline{X})$ | $M_1$ | $Z_{12}$ | $\ldots$ | $Z_{1J}$ |
| $F_2(\overline{X})$ | $Z_{21}$ | $M_2$ | $\ldots$ | $Z_{2J}$ |
| $\vdots$ | $\vdots$ | $\vdots$ | $\ldots$ | $\vdots$ |
| | | | $\ldots$ | |
| $F_J(\overline{X})$ | $Z_{J1}$ | $Z_{J2}$ | $\ldots$ | $M_J$ |

The ideal solution vector $\tilde{X}$ would result in a maximum value for each objective $F_j(\overline{X})$, i.e., a $J$-vector $\tilde{Z}$ of values $M_j$. It is assumed that no such feasible solution vector exists, otherwise there would be no need to compromise between objectives. Referring back to Figure 2, for example, one cannot have $F_1(\overline{X}) = M_1 = e$, and $F_2(\overline{X}) = M_2 = b$, their maximum values, simultaneously. Some compromise must be made along the feasibility frontier between $M_1$ and $M_2$.

In each calculation phase, a feasible solution is sought that is the nearest,

---

11. STEM was specifically adapted for linear programming. This description of the STEM procedure is somewhat modified, indicating that it can be adapted to any convex programming problem.

in the minimax sense, to the ideal solution $\tilde{Z}$.[12] Defining $D_j$ as the difference between objective $F_j(\bar{X})$ and its maximum value, $M_j$, and $D$ as the maximum of all the weighted differences $W_j D_j$, the problem in each calculation phase is to minimize this maximum difference. That is, choose $\bar{X}$ to:

$$\text{Minimize} \quad D \tag{3.11}$$

subject to (3.3) and

$$D \geq W_j\{M_j - F_j(\bar{X})\} \quad \text{for all } j. \tag{3.12}$$

Constraints (3.12) simply insure that $D$ is no less than each weighted difference between the maximum and existing value of each objective and, as before, the set (3.3) represents all the other constraints specific to the problem being solved. The weights $W_j$ indicate the relative magnitude or significance of the deviations from the optimum. These weights can include scaling or normalizing terms. Denoting $m_j$ as the minimum value assumed by objective $F_j(\bar{X})$ in the payoff matrix, i.e., $m_j = \min_l Z_{jl}$, the weights $W_j$ can be defined as the quotient of a sensitivity parameter $\gamma_j$ and a scaling parameter $\alpha_j$.

$$W_j = \gamma_j/\alpha_j. \tag{3.13}$$

The numerator,

$$\gamma_j = \begin{cases} \dfrac{M_j - m_j}{M_j} & \text{if } M_j > 0 \\ \dfrac{m_j - M_j}{m_j} & \text{if } M_j \leq 0 \end{cases} \tag{3.14}$$

indicates the relative range of the values assumed by objective $F_j(\bar{X})$. If, for various solution vectors $\bar{X}$, the value of $F_j(\bar{X})$ does not vary much from the optimum solution $M_j$, the objective is not sensitive to a variation in the weighting values $W_j$, and therefore a relatively small weight can be assigned to this objective. As the variation in $F_j(\bar{X})$ becomes larger with changes in the decision vector $\bar{X}$, the weight $W_j$ will become correspondingly greater.

The denominator, or $\alpha_j$ term of (3.13), is used to scale each objective and insure that the sum of the relative weights $W_j$ equals 1. Initially, these are set as

$$\alpha_j = (M_j + K)\{\sum_i \gamma_i/(M_i + K)\}, \tag{3.15}$$

where, if any $M_j \leq 0$, $K = 1 - \min_j M_j$; otherwise $K = 0$. On succeeding iterations the relative weights associated with objectives whose values are satisfactory to the decision maker are set to zero and $\alpha$ is changed accordingly by summing only over those objectives whose values are unsatisfactory. By normalizing the values of each objective and insuring that the relative weights

---

12. The minimax criterion is only one of many that could be used to define the "best" compromise solution. See, for example, the discussion by Milnor [1954].

sum to one, different solutions obtained from different sets of relative weights can be easily compared.

The initial solution $\bar{X}_0$ resulting from the calculation phase is presented to the decision maker, who compares its objective vector $\bar{Z}_0$ with the "ideal" objective vector $\check{Z}$. If the values of some components of $\bar{Z}_0$ are satisfactory and others are not, the decision maker must accept a certain reduction in the value of one or more satisfactory objectives in order to improve the unsatisfactory ones in the next computation phase; i.e., in the decision phase he identifies the objective values $F_j^*(\bar{X}_0)$ that can be reduced and the permissible amount of the reduction $\Delta F_j^*$.

Prior to the next iteration, three changes are made to the model: (i) the relative weights $W_j^*$ of the satisfactory objectives are set equal to 0, (ii) the feasible region is modified by additional constraints that limit the reduction of each satisfactory objective value to no more than the permissible reduction and insure that the unsatisfactory objective values do not decrease,

$$F_j^*(\bar{X}) \geq F_j^*(\bar{X}_0) - \Delta F_j^*, \quad \text{for all } j^* \tag{3.16}$$

$$F_j(\bar{X}) \geq F_j(\bar{X}_0), \quad \text{for all } j \neq j^* \tag{3.17}$$

and (iii) the $\alpha_j$ term used in equation (3.13) is adjusted, as previously described, to insure that the relative weights of the nonsatisfactory objectives sum to 1.

The next iteration begins with the solution of the modified programming problem and ends with a further adjustment in the relative weights and constraint set. This sequence of iterations continues until either all or none of the components of the objective vector $\bar{Z}$ are satisfactory. If all of the components are satisfactory, the decision vector $\bar{X}$ represents a good compromise. If none of the components are satisfactory, there is no solution to the problem.

If there are $J$-objectives, the total number of iterations required to obtain either a best compromise solution, or no solution, is no more than $J$ provided the decision maker does not change his preferences during the iterative process. This latter assumption, of course, is rather heroic, but its violation would not detract significantly from the potential usefulness that an iterative procedure similar to STEM might have in the decision making process.

The analyst using STEM can further assist the decision maker by presenting the results of a sensitivity analysis on the different objective functions in the neighborhood of the solution $\bar{X}$ for each iteration. Also, during each calculation phase, several discrete reductions between zero and the maximum acceptable reduction $\Delta F_j^*$ of each satisfactory objective can be evaluated.[13]

---

13. When the best compromise solution has been obtained, the relative weights that would yield this solution can be calculated a posteriori, if desired, by the simultaneous solution of equations (3.18) and (3.19):

$$\text{Constant} = W_j(M_j - F_j(\bar{X})) \quad \text{for all } j, \tag{3.18}$$

and

$$\sum_j W_j = 1 \tag{3.19}$$

This iterative STEM procedure can be illustrated by a simple numerical example. Following, in part, MacEwan's [1971] example, suppose there are two distinct regions in a country, the first containing half the population of the second. For planning purposes, three objectives are identified: the maximization of the increase in per capita consumption, $C_r$, in each of the two regions $r$, and in the country as a whole, $C_1 + 2C_2$. These three objectives:

$$F_1: \text{maximize } C_1,$$
$$F_2: \text{maximize } C_2,$$
$$F_3: \text{maximize } (C_1 + 2C_2),$$

are subject to a variety of constraints $g_i(C_1, C_2) = 0$, that define all feasible combinations of $C_1$ and $C_2$. These feasible combinations are illustrated by the shaded area in Figure 5(a). Also illustrated are the maximum values of each of the three objectives. Clearly not all objectives can be maximized simultaneously, hence it is necessary to calculate the payoff matrix of $Z_{1j}$'s, the values of the $l$th objective when the $j$th objective is maximized. In this case, these values can be observed from Figure 5(a).

|  |  | Objective $F_j$ | | |
|---|---|---|---|---|
|  | $l$ | $j$ | | |
|  |  | 1 | 2 | 3 |
|  | 1 | 30 | −5 | 15 |
| Objective $F_l$ | 2 | −10 | 16 | 10 |
|  | 3 | 10 | 27 | 35 |

Using the values in the payoff matrix, the weights $W_j$ defined by equations (3.13), (3.14), and (3.15) for each of the three objectives $j$ are 0.24, 0.63, and 0.13, respectively. If these weights are used in constraints (3.12), the values of $C_1$ and $C_2$ that minimize the maximum weighted deficit are 14.6 and 10.1, respectively. This solution is then given to the decision maker.

Suppose that the decision maker is not satisfied with this solution because of the difference in increased consumption between the two regions. He must then specify how much, if any, he is willing to reduce the increase in consumption of region 1, $C_1$, in order to increase the consumption in region 2. Assuming this permissible reduction of $C_1$ is 4, the possible values of $C_1$ and $C_2$, defined by all constraints $g_i(C_1, C_2) = 0$ and the additional constraints (3.16) and (3.17),

$$C_1 \geq 14.6 - 4 = 10.6,$$
$$C_2 \geq 10.1$$
$$C_1 + 2C_2 \geq (14.6 - 4) + 2(10.1) = 30.8,$$

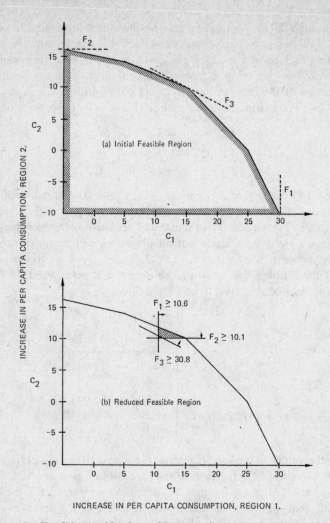

Figure 5. Feasible Combinations of Increases in Per Capita Consumption

are those contained in the shaded region illustrated in Figure 5(b). Note that in this example, if a reduction in $C_1$ is allowed, it is reflected in all objectives containing $C_1$—i.e., $F_1$ and $F_3$. Recalculating the weights $W_j$, this time only for objectives $F_2$ and $F_3$, yields 0.83 and 0.17, respectively. The relative weight for the objective $F_1$ that was reduced is set equal to 0. Using these weights in constraints (3.12), the values of $C_1$ and $C_2$ that minimize the maximum weighted deficit are 10.6 and 11.8.

Let us assume that the decision maker is satisfied with this solution. The

relative weights that would have given us this solution immediately can be obtained from the simultaneous solution of equations (3.18) and (3.19),

$$\pi = W_1(30 - 10.6),$$
$$\pi = W_2(16 - 11.8),$$
$$\pi = W_3(35 - 34.2),$$
$$W_1 + W_2 + W_3 = 1,$$

which yields 0.033, 0.155, 0.812 for $W_1$, $W_2$, and $W_3$, respectively.

The STEM algorithm just discussed corresponds to an educational process that leads to a compromise. The process involves the reduction of some objective values in order to achieve more acceptable values of other objectives. A number of other deterministic approaches for solving multiple objective problems have been proposed.[14] Rather than review more of these, we will now turn very briefly to procedures that are probabilistic, i.e., that explicitly define the uncertainty inherent in the decision makers' trade-offs and preferences.

In a political setting, establishing preferences or making choices is, at least partially, an unpredictable or random process. There is uncertainty about the effects of decisions and the wishes of those who make or are affected by the decisions. Predictions of each decision maker's preferences among various objectives, or of his future choices among possible vectors of objective values, are obviously not known with certainty. Therefore, it can be argued that any procedure used to define a politically optimal solution of a multiobjective problem should capture the inherently probabilistic nature of the decision making process.[15]

Uncertainty is often handled either by game theory or decision theory. If the uncertainty is due to events controlled by other decision makers, then a variety of game theoretic models can be applied (Luce and Raiffa [1957]). When the uncertainty is not due to events controlled by a decision maker, and the required probability distributions can be derived from historical data, then mathematical programming, simulation, and decision theoretic models can be used (Raiffa [1968], Savage [1954]).

Decision theory is also applicable when only subjective probabilities are available. Using subjective probabilities, alternative solutions can be ranked in terms of their political feasibility (i.e., the desirability of each solution to those responsible for decision making). To illustrate this procedure, it will be useful to review a deterministic method proposed by Raiffa [1968] for comparing two mutually exclusive alternatives where there are two objectives $F_1(\overline{X})$ and $F_2(\overline{X})$.

14. See, for example, Freimer and Yu [1972], MacGrimmon [1968], Raiffa [1969], Russell, Spofford, and Haefele [1972], Sapit [1966], and Stankard et al. [1968].
15. See Costello [1970] and Luch [1959].

231

A decision maker is to select one of two alternative solutions $\bar{X}_1$ or $\bar{X}_2$ having objective values $\{F_1(\bar{X}_1), F_2(\bar{X}_1)\}$ and $\{F_1(\bar{X}_2), F_2(\bar{X}_2)\}$, respectively. For each alternative $i$, an arbitrary reference value $F_2^*$ is selected for objective $F_2(\bar{X}_1)$. The decision maker is then asked to specify a value of $F_1(\bar{X}_i)$, say $F_{1i}$, such that he will be indifferent between the original alternative $\bar{X}_i$ having objective values $\{F_1(\bar{X}_i), F_2(\bar{X}_i)\}$ and some alternative having objective values $\{F_{1i}, F_2^*\}$. For the two alternatives $i = 1, 2$, the decision maker is indifferent between $\{F_{1i}, F_2^*\}$ and $\{F_1(\bar{X}_i), F_2(\bar{X}_i)\}$. Since $\{F_{1i}, F_2^*\}$ and $\{F_{12}, F_2^*\}$ differ only in the value of objective $F_1(\bar{X})$, it can be concluded that alternative $\bar{X}_1$ is preferred to alternative $\bar{X}_2$ if $F_{11} > F_{12}$, and $\bar{X}_2$ is preferred to $\bar{X}_1$ if $F_{11} < F_{12}$, assuming that $F_1(\bar{X})$ is a superior objective. Haith [1971] has extended this technique to include more than two objectives and also the uncertainty of the decision makers' preferences.

## 4. Discussion and Conclusions

The methodologies that have been reviewed in this paper represent only a few of a relatively large class of procedures designed to assist in the definition and evaluation of multiple-objective policies. Each one, to a greater or lesser extent, provides a mechanism for estimating the trade-offs between conflicting objectives. Some go beyond this to predict what the politically optimal trade-offs may be, at least from the point of view of the abstract "decision makers" who are supposed to represent the best interests of society.

Of course, it must be recognized that real political decision makers are often reluctant to learn the methodology of policy analysis and evaluation or to spend the time answering seemingly "academic" questions that would eventually lead to a set of well-defined relative weights. This often occurs because political leaders rely on the support of distinct interest groups that are in conflict with one another. In such situations, it is obviously to their advantage not to be too explicit in quantifying political value judgments regarding trade-offs between conflicting objectives. Technicians, of course, all too often encourage politicians not to intervene in making value judgments in areas they consider themselves competent. But it is precisely in these areas that they themselves have bias or special interests.

It is clear that what is needed is a methodology that does not require explicit intervention by the political decision makers, yet makes use of value judgments that must come from them alone. The assumptions underlying all the methods discussed here is that decision makers will please the technicians by accepting responsibility for the assignment of values to the relative weights of various objectives, and that the technicians must devote more time to acquiring the skills necessary to articulate those objective values in advance of specific decision making. If the decision makers could indicate even a reasonable range of appropriate values for the relative weights of each

objective, planners could present them with policy alternatives reflecting only these ranges of politically determined weights between various public goals.

In the meantime, perhaps the best procedure for politically unbiased planners (if they exist) to follow is to consider the relative weights as unknown, to identify the values of the weights that make significant differences in the values of the objectives, and to define the policies that are efficient for different ranges of weights. These alternative policies together with their policy implications can then be submitted to the responsible decision makers. Such a planning procedure might insure that the political leadership is aware of the relevant alternatives and the efficient trade-offs among multiple goals. At the same time, it would stress the importance of the politician's role in the assignment of relative priorities and in the definition of the best compromise solution. Finally, such a procedure would form the basis for a systematic determination of the relative priorities among various goals by the political process, perhaps leading to a time when they will be at least approximately specified in advance of particular policy formulation and evaluation. Through the further development and use of analytical planning techniques similar to those reviewed in this discussion, technicians can begin to enlighten those who would suggest that public policy evaluation and analyses should not be political.

Chapter X

# INTERINDUSTRY PLANNING MODELS FOR A MULTIREGIONAL ECONOMY

MRINAL K. DATTA-CHAUDHURI

## 1. INTRODUCTION

This chapter is devoted to an exploration of the possibilities of using linear interindustry planning models for formulating the regional allocation strategy of a multiregional economy.

Even though the interindustry planning models are cast in the economy-wide framework of production and exchange, and their structural similarities with general equilibrium analysis gives an impression of completeness, these models, at the current state of the art, cannot help policy planners much beyond exploring systematically certain implications of broad development strategies. Their level of aggregation in practice and the levels of simplicity with which they incorporate various technological, behavioral, and institutional relationships make it almost impossible to derive the details of specific policy conclusions. For the latter purpose, more detailed partial studies are indispensable. But economy-wide interindustry models can provide useful guides to the policy planners by delimiting the more promising areas for detailed investigations.

So far, research in interindustry planning has been directed mainly toward determining the sectoral composition of an investment program; sometimes problems of technological choice also have been studied. In other words, the focus of attention has been the problems of choice relating to domestic production versus foreign trade and technological alternatives in a production program. The problems of choice relating to alternative regional allocations have remained relatively neglected, partly because of their complexity (and dimensionality) and partly because of the inevitable political sensitivities associated with them.[1]

---

1. In Indian planning, for example, one finds repeated assertions in all planning documents over the last twenty years that "balanced" regional development is the policy goal of the system. But during all those years, there was never an attempt to examine even the meaning of "balanced" growth. One can almost detect a systematic attempt on the part of the Central Government and the Planning Commission to pretend that the problem of regional choice does not exist. Given the group-sociological and political tensions among the constituent states of the Indian Union, the sensitiveness of the Planning Commission in analyzing the problem of regional choice openly and rationally is understandable; but the economic significance of this problem remains extremely important for the economy.

During the past twenty years, significant steps have been made in extending interindustry analysis in the direction of regional planning. Methodological studies have been stimulated by empirical work on pressing regional development problems. Since we deal here mainly with methodological issues, we shall not try to survey the entire literature on the subject. We shall try, however, to develop a number of models which seek to answer specific strategy questions.

Nor shall we go into a related and highly important area—policy models for determining industrial locations. The usual linear models built for interindustry studies are not suitable for the analysis of these location problems where the economies of scale and the complexities of the transportation network are important. (Some methods of attacking this class of problems via integer programming are discussed in section 3 of Chapter XI.)

Interindustry models of regional analysis fall into two broad categories. The first includes models built in order to determine the allocations among the different regions of an economy. The second consists of purely one-region models, where it is usually assumed that the flow of resources in (and from) the other regions of the economy will be adjusted automatically in response to the development strategy of the region modelled. If the first type has structural similarities with general equilibrium analysis, the second type, even though they are interindustry models, has certain parallels with Keynesian multiplier analysis. In this chapter, we shall first develop the interregional models and later go into the regional models.

In the literature on regional planning, there is a great deal of work on defining the concept of a region. These are attempts at identifying homogeneity characteristics with respect to which contiguous geographical areas can be demarcated for the purpose of convenient physical planning. Here we shall not discuss these issues at all, having assumed that the purpose of building planning models is to help the decision making apparatus of the country in choosing a consistent (and rational) development strategy. Therefore, the regional units defined in the political and administrative setup of the economy are the relevant units for our purposes. A regional unit of this type normally will have established political institutions for administrative decisions, and for bargaining with the Central Planning Office, and will usually have shared cultural and sociological traits.

## 2. EXTENSION OF INPUT-OUTPUT ANALYSIS TO A MULTIREGIONAL FRAMEWORK

Input-output analysis was extended to the case of a multiregional economy in the early fifties by Moses [1955] and Isard [1953, 1960]. In the spirit of the basic Leontief model, in these extensions where technological choice is ruled out by postulating only one fixed coefficient production technique in each industry, choice among alternative sources for interregional trade is also ruled

out by assuming that each region purchases its requirements for every good according to a fixed regional supply pattern. Let $Z_i^\delta$ be the total requirement of the $i$th good in the $\delta$th region. The static Leontief model of commodity flows within the region can be described as

$$Z_i^\delta = \sum_{j=1}^{n} X_{ij}^\delta + F_i^\delta \quad i, j = 1, 2, \ldots, n \qquad (2.1)$$

where $X_{ij}^\delta$ is the amount of $i$th good used as a current input in the $j$th industry of the $\delta$th region; and $F_i^\delta$ is the final demand for the $i$th good in the $\delta$th region.

In the usual input-output analysis for a closed economy, two conditions are imposed. The first is that of fixed coefficient technology:

$$X_{ij}^\delta = a_{ij}^\delta X_i^\delta \qquad (2.2)$$

where $X_i^\delta$ is the production of the $j$th good in the $\delta$th region and $a_{ij}^\delta$ is the amount of $i$th good required for the production of one unit of the $j$th commodity in the $\delta$th region. The second condition, of course, is that demand should equal supply (production):

$$Z_i^\delta = X_i^\delta. \qquad (2.3)$$

But in the multiregional economy, equation (2.3) would imply that each regional economy functions as an autarchy. To allow for interregional trade (in fixed proportions) it is postulated that

$$X_i^\delta = \sum_{\mu=1}^{s} t_i^{\delta\mu} Z_i^\mu \qquad (2.3')$$

where $t_i^{\delta\mu}$ is the proportion of the $\mu$th region's total requirements of the $i$th good met out of the production of the $\delta$th region. Of course,

$$\sum_{\delta=1}^{s} t_i^{\delta\mu} = 1 \quad \text{for all } i = 1, 2, \ldots, n, \qquad (2.4)$$
$$\mu = 1, 2, \ldots, s,$$

and there are $s$ regions in the economy.[2] In matrix notation:

Let $X^\delta$ = an $n$-dimensional vector of the $\delta$th region's production

$\quad Z^\delta$ = an $n$-dimensional vector of the $\delta$th region's gross requirements

$\quad F^\delta$ = an $n$-dimensional vector of the $\delta$th region's final demands

$\quad A^\delta$ = an $n$x$n$ dimensional input-output coefficient matrix for the $\delta$th region

$\quad T_i$ = an $s$x$s$ trade coefficient matrix for the $i$th commodity

---

2. For generality, all models in this chapter are set up in multiregional form. However, in practice sometimes this can be reduced to two regions; i.e., when a country has only a "north–south" problem. The reader may wish to explore for himself the ways in which the complexities of many-region analysis partially simplify in this case.

$X_i$ = an $s$-dimensional vector of the production of the $i$th commodity in the different regions

$Z_i$ = an $s$-dimensional vector of the total demands for the $i$th good in the different regions.

Then the structural relations defining the commodity flows in this multi-regional economy can be described as

$$Z^\delta = A^\delta X^\delta + F^\delta \qquad \delta = 1, 2, \ldots, s \qquad (2.5)$$

and

$$X_i = T_i Z_i \qquad i = 1, 2, \ldots, n. \qquad (2.6)$$

To solve for the gross demands, from these equations (2.5) and (2.6) let us define new vectors and matrices in $ns$ dimensional space.

$X = (X^1, X^2, \ldots, X^s), Z = (Z^1, Z^2, \ldots, Z^s), F = (F^1, F^2, \ldots, F^s),$

$\bar{X} = (X_1, X_2, \ldots, X_n), \bar{Z} = (Z_1, Z_2, \ldots, Z_n),$

$A = \text{diagonal } (A^1, A^2, \ldots, A^s),$

$T = \text{diagonal } (T_1, T_2, \ldots, T_n).$

Let $E$ be the $ns \times ns$ permutation matrix which converts $\bar{X}$ and $\bar{Z}$ into $X$ and $Z$ respectively, such that $X = E\bar{X}$ and $Z = E\bar{Z}$. Then the system of equations (2.6) can be rewritten as

$$X = ETE^{-1}Z$$
$$= T^*Z, \quad \text{where } T^* = ETE^{-1}. \qquad (2.7)$$

Equation (2.5) can be rewritten as

$$Z = AX + F. \qquad (2.8)$$

Premultiplying by $T^*$, we have,

$$X = T^*AX + T^*F. \qquad (2.9)$$

Under the usual assumption of nonsingularity of the $T^*A$ matrix, one can solve for the required structure of commodity production in the economy as

$$X = (1 - T^*A)^{-1} T^*F. \qquad (2.10)$$

Since the elements of any column of $T$, $E$ and $E^{-1}$ add up to one, the existence and nonnegativity of $(1 - T^*A)^{-1}$ is assured by the usual requirements imposed on the input-output matrices in a Leontief system.

It is also easy to extend this analysis to the case analogous to the dynamic input-output analysis by introducing capital coefficient matrices ($B^\delta$ and $B$), where $B^\delta$ is the $n \times n$ capital coefficient matrix for the $\delta$th region and

$$B = \text{diagonal } (B^1, B^2, \ldots, B^s).$$

Then the corresponding dynamic system can be characterized as

$$X(t) = T^* \cdot [AX(t) + B\dot{X}(t) + F(t)], \qquad (2.11)$$

where $X(t)$ and $F(t)$ are the gross output and final demand vectors at time $t$, where $\dot{X}(t)$ is the vector of incremental outputs.

Such an input-output system can be used to construct a consistency model for planning in a multiregional economy, similar to the one discussed by Chakravarty and Eckaus [1964] for the case without regional disaggregation. If the vector of final demands is specified, under the twin assumptions of fixed technological and trade coefficients, one can work out the production targets as well as the investments for the various sectors of the different regions. But the question is whether this can be described as a reasonably good planning method. The assumption of fixed technology for each industry in input-output analysis is often justified on the supposedly factual ground that technological alternatives at the relevant range of factor prices are, indeed, few. Therefore, the facts of available technology make the problem of choice unimportant.

A similar argument cannot be made for locational choice; geographical space is continuous and, except in the case of a country with a unique geographical distribution of natural resources, the problem of location is real and relevant.

The argument for retaining the assumption of a fixed interregional trading (and production) pattern is often advanced, therefore, on grounds of political and group-sociological considerations. The basis of this argument is real. Each region would naturally want to protect and further its own economic interests, and such conflicts of interest are usually reflected in the political process of the country. But the basic regional interests are, or at least ought to be, expressed in terms of consumption, employment, and incomes. Retaining the existing trading and production pattern is not the only way of balancing regional interests; in fact, it may be a highly irrational and wasteful strategy. Whatever may be the distributional judgment of the central planning authorities, or whatever may be the institutional mechanism of resource allocation among the regions, the need for mapping out the various feasible allocation strategies remains. Any planning model that fails to perform this important task cannot help planners in choosing a rational and nonwasteful development strategy.

It is in this context that the role of optimizing planning models becomes important. Enthusiastic programmers sometimes justify their optimization models as exercises in simulating the process of competitive equilibrium for the economy. But any model that wants to generate a realistic pattern of interregional trade endogenously will have to be built on an extremely fine commodity classification (and also small geographical aggregates), since the fundamental reason for trade and exchange lies in differentiation among

commodities and markets. Later, in section 5, we shall discuss methods of correcting for underestimation of aggregate volume of interregional trade in optimization models. But at this stage it is useful to present the structure of a general interindustry optimization model for a multiregional economy. The purpose of these models, as indicated earlier, is to explore the efficient alternative allocation strategies by using the parametric methods of programming.

## 3. OPTIMIZATION MODELS

Several authors[3] have used the linear programming framework to construct interregional optimization models for determining the pattern of production, trade, and transportation in a multiregional economy. These models differ from one another in several characteristics: in the specification of the objective function, in the assumptions regarding symmetry among the different economic activities, in the treatment of interregional flows and transportation, and in many other minor details. We shall not go into a survey of these models to bring out their comparative merits, since none of them can be recommended for universal application by planners. However, they serve the useful purpose of bringing out the technological interdependence among the production and transport activities in a multiregional economy and, therefore, provide guidelines for constructing less ambitious but usable models as guides to policy formulation. In the present state of the art, usable models have been limited to optimization over the choice of interregional production and transport activities for a limited number of highly interdependent sectors of an economy, keeping the remaining sectors exogenous to the model.[4]

However, in one important respect these optimization models fall into two distinct classes, according to whether they maximize some measure of welfare or minimize costs. For partial optimization exercises, cost minimization has an obvious appeal, but Mennes, Tinbergen, and Waardenburg [1969], for example, have constructed economy-wide planning models where overall production and transport costs are minimized. These models can be used for planning only if the exogenous cost information has been generated by some other (simpler) economy-wide optimization model or by assuming that (possibly corrected) market information can be used for the purpose. In order to retain comparability with the usual type of interindustry planning models, the multiregional optimization model presented below will be "welfare maximizing." It can be considered a generalization of the Chakravarty–

---

3. A few examples of distinct approaches can be found in the following works: Beckmann and Marschak [1955]; Lefeber [1959]; Isard [1953]; Moses [1955]; Mennes, Tinbergen and Waardenburg [1969]. This is by no means an exhaustive list of important works in this field.

4. A few of the examples of this kind of partial optimization models used in empirical work are: Heady and Hall [1969]; Vietorisz and Manne [1963]; Isard, Schooler, and Vietorisz [1959]; Kendrick [1967b]; and Datta–Chaudhuri [1967]. This, again, is just a small, and not necessarily representative, sample of such studies.

Lefeber [1965] or Eckaus–Parikh [1968] type of interindustry planning model. Thus, it is an intertemporal optimization model with a fixed time horizon, capital stocks (production capabilities) for the various industries given in the initial as well as the post-terminal periods, and the maximand is the discounted present value of aggregate consumption. The commodity composition of consumption baskets is fixed. For the sake of notational simplicity, technological choice (which could have been in the form of linear activities) is ruled out, and the investment-output lag is taken to be uniform—one period for every industry. For simplicity, the assumption of unlimited supply of each category of labor is assumed; this can, of course, be relaxed by introducing linear labor constraints as shown in Chapter VII of this volume.

## 4. A MULTIREGIONAL OPTIMIZATION MODEL

Assume there are $s$ regions in the economy and $n$ sectors of commodity production. The $(s + 1)$th region in our notation is the rest of the world with which our economy has trading possibilities. The $(n + 1)$th sector is the interregional transport activity. Intraregional transport is assumed to be distinctly different from interregional transport and is included in the $n$ sectors of commodity production in a region.

The initial conditions of the model are specified as given capital stocks in the base period for every industry in each region as well as for the interregional transport sector.

$$K_i^\delta(0) = \bar{K}_i^\delta(0), \qquad i = 1, 2, \ldots, n, \qquad (4.1a)$$
$$\delta = 1, 2, \ldots, s$$

$$K_{n+1}(0) = \bar{K}_{n+1}(0). \qquad (4.1b)$$

The maximum output of a sector bears a fixed coefficient relationship with the corresponding capital stock, although the coefficient may vary from region to region.

$$X_i^\delta(t) \leq \beta_i^\delta \cdot K_i^\delta(t) \qquad i = 1, 2, \ldots, n \qquad (4.2a)$$
$$\delta = 1, 2, \ldots, s$$
$$t = 0, 1, \ldots, T - 1$$

$$X_{n+1}(t) < \beta_{n+1} K_{n+1}(t). \qquad (4.2b)$$

The production of a commodity requires current inputs in fixed proportions. The input-output coefficients may, again, show regional variations

$$X_i^\delta(t) = \text{Min} \; [X_{1i}^\delta/A_{1i}^\delta, \; X_{2i}^\delta/A_{2i}^\delta, \; \ldots, \; X_{ni}^\delta/A_{ni}^\delta],$$

or

$$X_{ji}^\delta(t) \geq A_{ji}^\delta X_i^\delta(t), \quad j, i = 1, 2, \ldots, n \qquad (4.3a)$$
$$\delta = 1, 2, \ldots, s$$
$$t = 0, 1, \ldots, T - 1.$$

241

Interregional transportation $X_{n+1}(t)$ also requires current inputs in fixed proportions, but it is indifferent as to the region from which it gets its supplies:[5]

$$X_{n+1}(t) = \text{Min} \left[ \sum_{\delta} X_{1,n+1}^{\delta}/A_{1,n+1}, \sum_{\delta} X_{2,n+1}^{\delta}/A_{2,n+1}, \ldots, \right.$$
$$\left. \sum_{\delta} X_{n,n+1}^{\delta}/A_{n,n+1} \right]$$

or

$$\sum_{\delta} X_{1,n+1}^{\delta}(t) \geq A_{i,n+1} X_{n+1}(t), \quad i = 1, 2, \ldots, n \tag{4.3b}$$
$$t = 0, 1, \ldots, T - 1.$$

Supply-demand inequalities for each commodity in every region should be specified. Sources of supply are imports from other regions as well as from the outside world. The categories of demand are: (i) interindustry demand for current inputs $X_{ij}^{\delta}(t)$; (ii) investment demands by various industries $I_{ij}^{\delta}(t)$; (iii) household consumption demands $C_i^{\delta}(t)$; (iv) government demands $G_i^{\delta}(t)$; and, (v) export demands from other regions and the rest of the world. Thus,

$$X_i^{\delta}(t) + \sum_{\mu=1}^{s+1} X_i^{\delta\mu}(t) \geq \sum_{j=1}^{n+1} X_{ij}^{\delta}(t) + C_i^{\delta}(t) + \sum_{j=1}^{n+1} I_{ij}^{\delta}(t) + G_i^{\delta}(t)$$
$$+ \sum_{\mu=1}^{s+1} X_i^{\delta\mu}(t), \quad i = 1, 2, \ldots, n \tag{4.4a}$$
$$\delta = 1, 2, \ldots, s$$
$$t = 0, 1, \ldots, T - 1.$$

The supply of interregional transportation $X_{n+1}(t)$ must, of course, be met by domestic production. The demands come from: (i) household consumption $C_{n+1}^{\delta}(t)$; (ii) government consumption $G_{n+1}^{\delta}(t)$; and, (iii) for commodity movement: a unit of $i$th commodity moved from the $\delta$th region to the $\mu$th region requires a constant amount $\Theta^{\delta\mu}$ of $X_{n+1}$. Thus,

$$X_{n+1}(t) \geq \sum_{\delta=1}^{s} [C_{n+1}^{\delta}(t) + G_{n+1}^{\delta}(t)] + \sum_{\delta \neq \mu = 1}^{s+1} \sum_{i=1}^{n} \Theta_i^{\delta\mu} X_i^{\delta\mu}(t)$$
$$t = 0, 1, \ldots, T - 1. \tag{4.4b}$$

As is usually done, government demand can be exogenously specified

$$G_i^{\delta}(t) = \bar{G}_i^{\delta}(t), \quad i = 1, 2, \ldots, n + 1 \tag{4.5}$$
$$\delta = 1, 2, \ldots, s$$
$$t = 0, 1, \ldots, T - 1.$$

---

5. Since the details of geography are not introduced in these models, there does not seem to be any easy way of relaxing this rather unrealistic assumption that, in effect, the transport sector can costlessly move its own inputs within the network as needed.

The specification of foreign trade within the bounds of a linear model presents the usual difficulties. Following the methods outlined in Chapters III and VI, we shall assume that the supply of importables in each period is constrained by the sum of exogenously specified demands for the exports of the country and the net inflow of foreign assistance. The economy, of course, has the full freedom to choose the regional supply source for exports and to use imports anywhere it likes.[6] The foreign trade balance inequality is expressed in some standard foreign currency. Export and import prices $\bar{P}_i$ and $P_i$ (expressed in foreign currency) are given

$$\sum_\delta X_i^{\delta, s+1}(t) \geq \bar{E}_i(t), \quad i = 1, 2, \ldots, n, \tag{4.6a}$$

$$\bar{A}(t) + \sum_{i=1}^n \bar{P}_i \bar{E}_i(t) \geq \sum_{i=1}^n P_i \sum_{\delta=1}^s X_i^{s+1, \delta}. \tag{4.6b}$$

As stated earlier, new capacities in every industry can be created with one year's uniform gestation lag. Furthermore, if we assume an "exponential decay" variety of depreciation rule, then

$$K_i^\delta(t + 1) = (1 - d_i^\delta)K_i^\delta(t) + \Delta K_i^\delta(t), \quad i = 1, 2, \ldots, n \tag{4.7a}$$
$$\delta = 1, 2, \ldots, s$$
$$t = 0, 1, \ldots, T - 1,$$

$$K_{n+1}(t) = (1 - d_{n+1})K_{n+1}(t) + \Delta K_{n+1}(t), \quad t = 0, 1, \ldots, T - 1. \tag{4.7b}$$

Like current production, capacity creation is also assumed to be subject to fixed coefficient technology so that

$$\Delta K_i^\delta(t) = \text{Min} \ [I_{1i}^\delta(t)/b_{1i}^\delta, \ I_{2i}^\delta(t)/b_{2i}^\delta, \ \ldots, \ I_{ni}^\delta(t)/b_{ni}^\delta]$$

or

$$I_{ij}^\delta(t) \geq b_{ij}^\delta X_j^\delta(t), \quad i, j = 1, 2, \ldots, n \tag{4.8a}$$
$$\delta = 1, 2, \ldots, s$$
$$t = 0, 1, \ldots, T - 1.$$

$$\sum_\delta I_{i,n+1}^\delta(t) \geq b_{i,n+1} X_{n+1}(t), \quad i = 1, 2, \ldots, n, \tag{4.8b}$$
$$t = 0, 1, \ldots, T - 1.$$

This optimization model will be complete if we specify the terminal conditions and the objective function. Given the structure of the model, the rational way of specifying the terminal conditions would be in terms of terminal capital stocks. But with fixed coefficient production functions, these

---

6. In linear models (see Weisskopf [1967]), a distinction is sometimes made between competitive and noncompetitive imports. Although it is easy to introduce this dichotomy in the model, we have not done so. See Chapter VI for further discussion on how this can be done.

inequalities could easily be translated into relationships involving employment or gross outputs. The objective functions can be defined in terms of the intertemporal and interregional distribution of private consumption. In the literature of dynamic linear programming models for investment planning, various ways of specifying the terminal capital stock have been discussed.[7] But the problem becomes even more complicated in the case of a multiregional model with distributional objectives regarding regional allocation. In this case, the specification of the various kinds of capital stocks in the different regions needs to be consistent not only with an acceptable post-terminal growth strategy of the economy but also with the regional distribution of incomes and employment in the long run. Obviously, there is no perfect way of arriving at a satisfactory specification in this respect. In what follows, three alternative ways of closing the optimization model with terminal conditions and an objective function are discussed.[8]

The simplest way of closing the model is to ignore the possibility of any separate treatment of the regional distributional goals in the specification of the terminal stocks. Here, the terminal stocks are specified only in accordance with the long-run growth strategy of the overall national economy. But the objective function (defined in terms of intertemporal consumption during the planning period) can include the distributional judgments of the policy maker. Therefore, terminal capital stocks are specified in terms of national aggregates as:

$$\sum_{\delta=1}^{s} K_i^{\delta}(t) \geq \bar{K}_i(T), \quad i = 1, 2, \ldots, n \tag{4.9a}$$

and

$$K_{n+1}(T) \geq \bar{K}_{n+1}(t), \tag{4.9b}$$

where $\bar{K}_i(T)$ and $\bar{K}_{n+1}(T)$ reflect the post-terminal growth strategy of the economy. Now, to define the objective function in terms of the consumption of the various regions during the different periods within the planning horizon, let us define an aggregate consumption basket for the $\delta$th region as

$$C^{\delta}(t) = \text{Min} \ [C_1^{\delta}(t)/m_1^{\delta}, \ C_2^{\delta}(t)/m_2^{\delta}, \ \ldots, \ C_{n+1}^{\delta}/m_{n+1}^{\delta}]$$

or

$$C_i^{\delta}(t) \geq m_i^{\delta} \cdot C^{\delta}(t), \quad i = 1, 2, \ldots, n + 1 \tag{4.10}$$
$$\delta = 1, 2, \ldots, s$$
$$t = 0, 1, \ldots, T - 1.$$

---

7. The problems of specifying terminal stocks in multisectoral economy-wide models (without regional dimensions) have been extensively discussed in Chapter III. What is required is to get some insights into the post-terminal development of the economy from some simpler framework and build these into the requirements of terminal capital stocks.

8. All three are discussed, although in a different manner, in section 5 and the appendix of Chapter III.

Given the relative backwardness of the different regions, a set of distributional weights $W^\delta$ can be used to define the social value of consumption during any period of time.

$$C(t) = \sum_{\delta=1}^{s} W^\delta C^\delta(t), \quad t = 0, 1, \ldots, T - 1 \qquad (4.11\text{a})$$

and the maximand is then defined as the discounted present value of social consumption during the entire planning period.

$$\text{Maximand} = \sum_{t=0}^{T-1} 1/(1 + r)^t \, C(t) \qquad (4.11\text{b})$$

It is worth noting that if a sufficient degree of interregional distributional objective is built into the maximand, then, in the actual solution of the model, the regional distribution of capital stocks in the terminal period will also tend to reflect it, even though the terminal constraints do not include any distributional judgment explicitly.

Another way of closing the model is to define the objective function in terms of terminal year targets and to specify exogenously the consumption requirements of the various regions for the different periods of time. This turns out to work rather well, because the optimization model has been constructed around an *open* Leontief system and, as such, consumption demands are not linked through behavior with the process of income generation. Moreover, it may be easier to make realistic (and politically feasible) projections of consumption levels during the planning period and to formulate the development objective of the society in terms of the long-term growth in outputs or employment. In that case we specify the constraints and the maximand as

$$K_{n+1}(T) \geq \bar{K}_{n+1}(T) \qquad (4.9')$$

$$C_i^\delta(t) \geq \bar{C}_i^\delta(t), \quad i = 1, 2, \ldots, n + 1 \qquad (4.10')$$
$$\delta = 1, 2, \ldots, s$$
$$t = 0, 1, \ldots, T - 1$$

and

$$\text{Maximand} = \sum_{\delta=1}^{s} W^\delta \sum_{i=1}^{n} \lambda_i^\delta K_i^\delta(T) \qquad (4.11')$$

where $\lambda_i^\delta$ is the employment generated by one unit of the $i$th type of capital in the $\delta$th region, and $W^\delta$ 's are the socially specified set of weights to measure the social willingness-to-pay for generating employment at the end of the plan in the different regions.

A third way of closing the model is to define the objective function both in

terms of consumption within the plan horizon and the terminal stock of capital.

$$K_{n+1}(t) \geq \bar{K}_{n+1}(T) \tag{4.9''}$$

and

$$\text{Maximand} = \sum_{t=0}^{T-1} 1/(1+r)^t \sum_{\delta=1}^{s} W^\delta C^\delta(t) + \Psi \sum_{\delta=1}^{s} W^\delta \sum_{i=1}^{n} K_i^\delta(T). \tag{4.11''}$$

This way of incorporating both the short-run and the long-run objectives of the society into one objective function has the obvious difficulty of having to pre-assign a tradeoff between terminal capital stock and the current level of consumption—the parameter $\Psi$ in (4.11''). The only way of arriving at an approximate value of $\Psi$ is by solving an aggregative infinite horizon optimum growth model. But even then it remains highly unsatisfactory. However, one advantage of this formulation is the possibility of using this programming framework parametrically to map out the various feasible options open to the multiregional economy.

## 5. THE PROBLEMS OF ENDOGENOUS INTERREGIONAL TRADE

We have already mentioned the main difficulty in generating interregional commodity flows from a full optimization model, namely that the commodity classification would have to be extremely fine. Therefore, in constructing realistic computable models, one may have to give up the claims of generating within the model a set of efficient interregional trade flows, and introduce "behavioral" relationships to explain the trade flows $X_i^{\delta\mu}$. Such behavioral relationships may be introduced for trade flows in all sectors. Or, in some cases, one might still want to look for efficient flow patterns at least for sectors which are defined in terms of individual homogeneous bulk commodities (cement, pig iron, and the like), while introducing behavioral relationships in the case of more aggregate sectors.

In the literature there are three commonly used estimation procedures for interregional trade flows. The first is based on the "location quotient" (LQ) method developed by Florence [1962]. The location quotient for the $i$th industry in the $\delta$th region is computed by dividing the region's share of employment of the economy. An industry with a location quotient greater than one is classified as an exporting industry for the region, while those with value less than one are characterized as importing activities. Isard [1960] has listed assumptions under which this classification would be valid; these include the similarities of per capita income and sectoral distribution of expenditures in the different regions. The estimation of a region's exports (or imports) of a product can be done by applying the location quotient to the corresponding per capita gross output figure. This procedure of estimation, however, makes the implicit assumption that the multiregional economy is an autarchy, i.e., that net production and consumption vectors of the whole

economy are equal. Moreover, the experiences of using this method in constructing the balance of regional trade statistics show that regions often export products of industries with less than unity LQ and import products of industries with LQ greater than one, and, as such, this method seems to consistently underestimate the overall volume of interregional trade in an economy.

The second common estimation procedure is the "minimum requirement" (MR) method introduced by Ullman and Darcey [1960]. In this method, the first step is to determine what proportion of the total employment in an industry of a region is engaged in production for the local market. If all regions are the same size, then one takes the region with the lowest percentage of its total employment in an industry as the minimum requirement for the local market. The excess of employment over this minimum is taken as the measure of the extent to which regions export this commodity. If the regions are of unequal size, one can normalize the regional employment data according to any particular measure of size to derive the measures of minimum requirements. Applying these MR measures on the gross output/employment ratios is supposed to provide the estimates of a region's exports and imports. It is easy to see that this method would result in overestimation of the overall volume of interregional trade.

Recently, Stilwell and Boatwright [1971] have suggested a combination of these two estimation methods. Their estimate of the net export of the $i$th product from the $i$th region is

$$\frac{E_i^\delta Q_i}{\sum_\delta E_i^\delta} = \frac{\sum_\delta E_i^\delta (Q_i - X_i + M_i)}{\sum_\delta \sum_i E_i^\delta}, \tag{5.1}$$

where $E_i^\delta$ = employment in the $i$th industry of the $\delta$th region,

$Q_i$ = the gross output of the $i$th product from the economy,

$X_i$ = value of exports of the $i$th product from the economy,

$M_i$ = value of imports of the $i$th product into the economy.

The third estimation formula often suggested in the literature is the so-called "gravity method," where the volume of the flow of the $i$th commodity from the $\delta$th to the $\mu$th region is supposed to be proportional to

$$\frac{(Q_i^\delta)^\alpha \cdot (D_i^\mu)^\beta}{(d^{\delta\mu})^\gamma}, \tag{5.2}$$

where $Q_i^\delta$ is the output of the $\delta$th region, $D_i^\mu$ is the gross demands of the $\mu$th region and $d^{\delta\mu}$ is some measure of the distance of the two regions and $\alpha$, $\beta$, and $\gamma$ are structural parameters. This formula seems to be a construction by analogy with Newtonian mechanics, although various probabilistic models of

247

a commuter's movement in a city are given to provide theoretical justification.[9] In any case, we do not need to provide any detailed discussion of this theory, because this type of nonlinear relationship has not been tested yet within the structure of linear models.[10]

## 6. LEONTIEF'S BALANCED GROWTH MODEL

The difficulties of generating reasonable interregional commodity flows, either from efficiency considerations or from the production and demand variables, has led researchers to construct models where interregional trade variables need not be introduced explicitly. The original work in this direction stems from Leontief [1953]. Since Leontief constructed his "Balanced Intranational" model and Isard [1953] tried to apply it to United States data, this line of approach has been used with increasing sophistication by others, notably the researchers in the Netherlands School of Economics. The latter group of economists is more interested in purely regional (as against interregional or intranational) development models, and we shall discuss their models—"Attraction Models" as they call them—after presenting the structure of the original Leontief static model.

Leontief postulates a certain asymmetry among the different commodities with respect to ability to enter interregional trade. In his simplest model, the $n$ commodities are classified into two groups: $h$ of them are regional commodities $(R)$ and the remaining $(n - h)$ national commodities $(N)$, so that the vector of gross output $X$ and final demands $F$ as well as the input-output matrix can be partitioned as

$$X = \begin{bmatrix} X_R \\ X_N \end{bmatrix}, \qquad F = \begin{bmatrix} F_R \\ F_N \end{bmatrix}, \qquad A = \begin{bmatrix} A_{RR} & A_{RN} \\ A_{NR} & A_{NN} \end{bmatrix}.$$

The balance equation for the economy as a whole can then be written as

$$X = AX + F. \tag{6.1}$$

Now, it is assumed that the national commodities need only to be balanced nationally, whereas the production-consumption balance must be struck on a regional basis for the regional commodities. In other words, the national commodities are perfectly mobile but the regional commodities are perfectly immobile between regions. With this assumption, the balance equations for the regional commodities in the $\delta$th region can be written as:

$$\begin{bmatrix} X_R^\delta \\ X_N^\delta \end{bmatrix} = [A_{RR}\ A_{RN}] \begin{bmatrix} X_R^\delta \\ X_N^\delta \end{bmatrix} + F_R^\delta, \tag{6.2}$$

9. For detailed discussion of the gravity model, see Isard [1960], pages 493–566.

10. The appendix of Chapter XII discusses a method by which a formulation such as (5.2) can be introduced at low cost into a linear programming model. Such an application of the gravity model would be most welcome research.

or

$$[I - A_{RR}]X_R^\delta - A_{RN}X_N^\delta = F_R^\delta; \tag{6.2'}$$

and solving for $X_R^\delta$, we have:

$$X_R^\delta = [I - A_{RR}]^{-1} F_R^\delta + [I - A_{RR}]^{-1} A_{RN}X_N^\delta. \tag{6.3}$$

The second assumption is that the proportion of the regional outputs of the national goods are given. These proportions may be derived from the existing ones, in which commodity production in the economy is distributed among regions, along with the assumption that the proportions remain stable over time. Or these proportions may reflect the prior judgment of the planner regarding the desirable pattern of regional allocation. Anyway, we are given, for each region $\delta$, an $(n - h) \times (n - h)$ diagonal matrix $R^\delta$; the $i$th diagonal element gives the proportion of the $i$th commodity produced in the $\delta$th region. Needless to add, this sum of the allocation matrices of all regions is the identity matrix

$$\sum_\delta R^\delta = I \tag{6.4}$$

and by assumption

$$X_N^\delta = R^\delta X_N. \tag{6.5}$$

Substituting (6.4) and (6.5) in (6.3) yields

$$X_R^\delta = [I - A_{RR}]^{-1} [F_R^\delta + A_{RN}R^\delta \overline{A}_N F] \tag{6.6}$$

where $\overline{A}_N$ is the matrix formed by the lower $(n - h)$ rows of $[I - A]^{-1}$.

This scheme of a simple dichotomy in the commodity space is easily extendable to a more complicated structure of a hierarchy of groups and a corresponding hierarchy of regions with national commodities perfectly mobile within the economy, state commodities perfectly mobile within a state but immobile between the states, district commodities immobile outside the districts, and so on. It is a matter of factual judgment whether such a complete classification of commodities with respect to the degree of mobility can be applied in the real world; but even if one could do that, the "relevant region" for a commodity need not coincide with the administrative boundaries of given regional units, around which statistics collection is normally built. It may not be easy to collect production and demand data with the required pattern of regional aggregation. Moreover, models of extensive levels of classification are obviously not designed to help in the formulation of a "desirable" regional allocation policy; whatever may be their value as a forecasting device, they are not of great help to the planners.

## 7. CHENERY'S "REGIONAL MODEL" FOR (SOUTH) ITALY

The "Regional model" constructed by Chenery [1953, 1956] in connection with the studies relating to the development problems of South Italy in the

early fifties, is basically regional—as against "interregional"—in character. Even though Chenery's framework can be used for constructing an input-output model for a multiregional economy, the model itself should be considered as a multisectoral generalization of regional multiplier analysis. The type of question the model seeks to answer is as follows: What would be the impact on the outputs, employment, and income of South Italy in response to a specific change in demands somewhere in the economic system? With standard macroeconomic analysis, one would require demand functions of various kinds, including a consumption function, (induced) investment function, and import demand function. Chenery rightly rejected a purely macroeconomic analysis for this underdeveloped region, where specific supply bottlenecks can be serious. He uses an interindustry framework so that capacity constraints in certain sectors may be explicitly introduced.

Chenery's regional input-output model is constructed through an expansion of the internal trade sector of a typical "national" input-output model. The vector of gross supplies is, of course, the sum of the domestic production and imports vectors. Domestic production of a commodity is assumed to be a fixed proportion of the gross demand for that commodity. The import of the commodity into the region can be either from the other regions of the economy or from abroad. The ratio of the amount supplied from each region to the total demand in one region is called the "regional supply coefficient." Thus, the corresponding interregional model consists of a linear system of different input-output matrices linked together by regional supply coefficients.

Since the purpose of the model is to predict the effects of an exogenous increase in some specified pattern of demands on regional income and employment, household consumption needs to be endogenous to the model. In a linear model this is done by introducing a new set of coefficients denoting the marginal propensities to consume the products of the different sectors. For the purpose of predicting the short-term impact of any public investment program on the pattern of regional outputs and employment, this is indeed a powerful model. The needs of public policy do not generally extend beyond this point. However, a model builder with the ambition of determining the rational pattern of resource use in a multiregional economy cannot afford to expect any set of "regional supplies coefficients" as given parameters.

## 8. ATTRACTION MODELS

The notion of "regional supply coefficients" introduced by Chenery has been generalized by a group of Dutch economists into the concept of "attraction coefficients." The "supply coefficients" operate on interregional trade and, through trade, on the levels of current production in the region's economy. The "attraction coefficients" are supposed to operate through the investment activities and determine the effects of a change in the pattern of demand on the location of new activities as well as on the levels of produc-

tion. Since, in the attraction models, one tries to measure directly induced investment effects (or new capacity creation) these models are explicitly regional—rather than interregional. The best presentations of the structure of the Attraction Model can be found in Klaasen [1972], Klaasen and van Wickeren [1969] and van Wickeren and Smit [1971]. The Attraction Model works with the assumption of asymmetry among different products with respect to their mobility, as in the models of Leontief, Isard, or Chenery. In principle, each product is supposed to have its market area of a particular size, or what is called "the relevant region." As we have seen earlier, if we cannot redefine regional classification according to these characteristics of the commodity space and have to work with politically and historically given regional units, then the problem boils down to seeing how far one can construct an operationally meaningful sector classification of this sort corresponding to the given regional hierarchy.

For simplicity, let us assume only a two-level regional hierarch—the nation and the regions. Then the sectors for which the "relevant regions" are smaller than the size of the given region are classified as "regional sectors." The other sectors, the products of which go into interregional or international trade are called "national sectors."

For simplicity, take the simplest version of the Attraction Model where there are no interindustry relations between the two sets of sectors, regional and national. The interindustry relations for the economy of the region can be written down as

$$X_R = A_R X_R + F_R \tag{8.1}$$

and

$$X_N = A_N X_N + F_N + E_N - M_N \tag{8.2}$$

where $X_R$ and $X_N$ are vectors of gross outputs of the regional and the national sectors respectively. $F_R$ and $F_N$ are the corresponding final demands, $A_R$ and $A_N$ are the input-output matrices, and $E_N$ and $M_N$ are vectors of exports and imports of the region, which are, by assumption, for the national sectors only.

The Attraction Theory further assumes that the gross outputs of the national sectors in the region are determined by two sets of attraction coefficients—one relating to the attraction due to demands and the other, that due to supply, so that

$$X_N = \lambda[X_N + M_N - E_N] + (L\alpha) \cdot X_N \tag{8.3}$$

where $\lambda$ is a diagonal matrix of demand attraction coefficients operating on the gross commodity demands of the region $(X_N + M_N - E_N)$ and $(L\alpha)$ is a matrix whose elements are products of supply attraction coefficients and allocation coefficients. The last equation can be rewritten as

$$X_N = \lambda[A_N X_N + F_N] + (L\alpha)X_N \tag{8.4}$$

251

Let $\lambda A_N = \bar{A}_N$ and $F_N = \bar{F}_N$ where $\bar{A}_N$ is the matrix of purely regional input coefficients and $\bar{F}_N$ is the vector of that part of final demands for $N$-goods which is met from regional sources. Then (8.4) can be written as

$$X_N = \bar{A}X_N + \bar{F}_N + (L\alpha)\cdot X_N. \qquad (8.5)$$

Furthermore, if the purely regional subsystems of national products can be written as

$$X_N = \bar{A}X_N + F_N + \bar{E}_N, \qquad (8.6)$$

where $\bar{E}_N$ is the vector of true exports of the region (excluding the transit trade), then one can see that

$$\bar{E}_N = (L\alpha)X_N. \qquad (8.7)$$

In other words, the supply-attraction effects can be defined in terms of the exports of the region.

This model can be made more sophisticated by introducing interindustry relations among all sectors as well as by introducing explicit dynamics, as has been done by van Wickeren and Smit [1971]. But the real problem lies in the estimation of the attraction coefficients. These coefficients, obviously, are supposed to summarize all information about the locational advantages of the region. The authors of the model recommend that these coefficients should be statistically estimated "by applying least squares or other estimating methods . . . on a (cross-section) sample of comparable regions."[11]

But there are real problems with trying to apply this methodology to a developing country. In the first place, it is not realistic to assume that such a cross-section would exist among the administrative regions of a country. Even more importantly, data attraction coefficients are normally supposed to depend directly or indirectly on endowments of natural resources. But the Attraction Model rules out the possibility. For some highly industrialized countries with easy transport and communications, this may be an acceptable framework, but for underdeveloped countries, it could be quite wrong.

## 9. USE OF INPUT-OUTPUT FRAMEWORK FOR SPECIAL TYPES OF REGIONAL DEVELOPMENT PROBLEMS

We have seen in the preceding sections that there are both analytical and statistical difficulties in constructing a complete interindustry model for regional planning. Nonetheless, the framework of input-output analysis can be extremely useful in measuring production linkages among different economic activities. Therefore, whenever one needs to measure certain categories of interindustry linkages in order to formulate regional development strategies, input-output analysis will be helpful. In the field of regional

---

11. Van Wickeren and Smit [1971], pp. 90–91.

development policy, economists and geographers have used concepts such as "central place" and "growth poles" to designate geographical centers which need support in order to grow and to promote economic growth for the surrounding region. Application of input-output coefficients can be useful in quantifying some of the relationships implied in these theories, thus helping formulate more precise policy conclusions.

The notion of a "central place" is inherent in the process of orderly development of an essentially agricultural region. The agricultural development of a region requires supplies of nonagricultural inputs, access to wider markets for final commodities or processing industries, access to financial or other commercial institutions, and so forth. Unlike agriculture, which is a rural activity making heavy use of land, these nonagricultural activities grow typically in urban centers, using relatively little land. Such an urban center, or a "central place," is necessary for the growth of agriculture. An inadequate urban center may act as a barrier to progress for the agricultural activities of the surrounding area. Moreover, health, education, and other public services require central places to capture the economies of scale of running hospitals, schools, judiciary, and other administrative services.

Now suppose a new area is opened to agricultural development, with the help of extension services and a settlement scheme. One would like to know how to plan for the development of a central place in the new area. What activities, input supplies, and processing would come to this urban center or what other activities could be made to come there in response to feasible incentives? Obviously, two sets of information are needed: first, technological linkages among industries; and second, attraction coefficients measuring the transport, communication, and other cost advantages for attracting economic activity. Input-output coefficients provide measures of production linkages. But true attraction coefficients for any particular region are difficult to estimate. As mentioned previously, the Attraction theorists suggest that these coefficients be estimated by regression analysis on a sample of similar regions or cities. We have discussed earlier why this procedure may be unsatisfactory. But in formulating development policies for an actual region, it may be possible to use simple location theory analysis—on the basis of estimated transport and production cost advantages for the region itself—to measure the attractive power of the central place vis-à-vis the rest of the economy.

The "growth pole" theory is developed around the supposed external economies and the economies of scale in the growth process of nonagricultural activities like manufacturing and services. Interindustry linkages and indivisibilities in the supply of urban infrastructure provide, in this theory, the basic reasons for the phenomenon of concentrated growth in cities. In promoting regional development through modern industries and services, there is a need to identify the industrial complex most suitable for a potential growth pole. Klaasen [1972] has demonstrated the possibilities of using input-output

analysis to identify these activities for a regional center. The problem is to identify the "nonbasic" or tradable goods sectors first, and then to plan for the development of basic, or essentially nontradable, sectors which will sustain the growth of the former. Klaasen's model is basically an attraction model, relying on regression analysis to estimate attraction coefficients.

## 10. INTERREGIONAL PLANNING MODELS AND REGIONAL ECONOMIC POLICY

From the point of view of policy formulation in a multiregional economy, the planning authorities would expect the model builders to help them decide what category of investment should be made in which region, and how to plan for the required transportation of the interregional commodity flows. Ideally, this would require solution of an optimizing model of the kind described in section 4 to determine location of economic activities and required transportation flows. However, as discussed earlier, today's computational technology does not permit simultaneous solution of all choice problems facing the national planning authorities. One way out is to ignore certain kinds of choices. For example, in sections 6 and 7, we discussed models where interregional commodity flows were estimated in terms of their past behavior rather than solved endogenously. But this is obviously unsatisfactory because one cannot explore rational locational patterns once the pattern of trade is fixed.

A more promising approach, possibly, is to try to decompose the overall choice problems of national planning into a system of interrelated suboptimization problems tied together in a framework of multilevel planning.[12] Purely analytical results in the field of decentralized planning (based on certain decomposition algorithms) are not yet rich enough to give clear-cut procedural rules for formulating a multilevel planning system. Therefore, judgments and intuitions of model builders are indispensable in the actual development of such a system.

In this connection, the multilevel planning system built for the Mexican economy by Goreux, Manne [1973] and their associates is highly instructive. In particular, the agricultural subsystem constructed by Duloy and Norton[13] deserves special attention by regional planners. This is an optimization model with 2,345 cropping activities for 33 crops of Mexican agriculture. The agricultural economy is divided into 4 regions and 20 districts. Some of the production inputs are constrained by availability within districts, others by availability within regions, and some by availability within the entire agricultural economy of Mexico. On the demand side, the domestic market is characterized by downward sloping price elastic demand curves whereas

---

12. Various aspects of multilevel planning are discussed in Chapters XI and XII.
13. See Duloy and Norton [1973a].

foreign markets are assumed to be perfectly elastic. The maximand of the model is the sum of producers' and consumers' surpluses.

If such a framework of interconnected models is available to a planning authority, it is possible to pose specific choice problems in an adequate partial framework. For example, it is possible to map out realistic investment alternatives for a district by specifying its relations with the rest of the economy at realistic levels. It is also possible to measure the economic impact of, say, a large multipurpose river development scheme—a typical investment program designed to give a big push to a regional economy.

## 11. REGIONAL ECONOMIC POLICY AND INCOME REDISTRIBUTION

Regional development policy is often linked with the objective of income redistribution. In the context of a short-run incomes policy, increased government spending in depressed areas is a commonly accepted policy prescription. For investment planning, however, mobility of labor, wherever feasible, is an alternative to investment within the region. Only when mobility is restricted does the question of a trade-off between the objectives of efficiency and equity come up. An economist's normal response to a decision problem involving multiple objectives is defined by a socially acceptable trade-off between the two goals in the objective function of the planning model.[14] But the main trouble is that the planning models (particularly, interindustry models) are constructed on commodity flows and "domestic products," whereas for a proper specification of the distributional goal (in terms of rich and poor segments of population), one needs information regarding income flows and "regional incomes." The assumption that the "regional income" and the "domestic product of the region" are identical may be highly unrealistic in many cases. One may often find that the main beneficiaries of a large investment program in a backward region are asset owners from outside the region.

Moreover, a properly specified distributional objective should include the distribution of income within a region. The demand for higher allocations for a backward region often comes from the better off people within that region, who are themselves mobile but want to use the backwardness of the region in order to improve their own relative position vis-à-vis the rich people elsewhere in the economy. In a situation of this kind, one may find that an increased allocation to a backward region may worsen the relative income distribution within the region.

This does not mean that a depressed region never deserves higher investment allocations on the grounds of distributional equity, but that the problem of distributional equity often cannot be posed meaningfully in the context of an interindustry model.

---

14. For discussion of noneconomic approaches to multiple objectives, see Chapter IX.

## 12. CONCLUSIONS

Our brief survey of the interindustry models for multiregional economies seems to lead to a few broad summary conclusions regarding their usability:

(i) These models are not yet very useful as practical guides to making rational choice with respect to the regional allocation of resources, at least in the context of today's computational technology. In the judgment of the present author, regional or locational choice is extremely important for geographically large and culturally diverse countries, and the possibilities of savings in resource use by making rational choice in this area are significant. But the construction of meaningful computable models seems to be beyond our scope today.

(ii) For short-run forecasting problems we do have usable models. But these models are constructed on assumptions of the stability of the interregional trading coefficients and/or attraction coefficients, in addition to the usual ones regarding the fixity of technological coefficients. This makes them unreliable for use in the long-run planning context—particularly in underdeveloped countries where the marginal changes are likely to be significant compared with existing averages.

(iii) Interindustry analysis can be used imaginatively in a partial context in formulating development strategy for a particular region or an urban center. But it is difficult to formulate such partial models that will have general applicability in many different situations. However, measurement of interindustry linkages is essential for formulating viable regional development programs. Input-output analysis provides the obvious framework for posing these policy problems.

Chapter XI

# PLANNING WITH ECONOMIES OF SCALE

### LARRY E. WESTPHAL

---

## 1. INTRODUCTION

Economies of scale are particularly significant in developing economies where market size is often much smaller than the scale at which increasing returns are exhausted within single plants. Because the coordination implicit in the communication of price signals is not sufficient where there are significant economies of scale, investment decisions require explicit coordination to achieve efficient resource allocation. Recognition of this fact, among others, has led to numerous special theories and intuitive suggestions to guide investment decisions in developing economies. Among the best known are Rosenstein–Rodan's theory of the Big Push [1943, 1961], the theories of Balanced Growth of Lewis [1955] and Nurkse [1953, 1961], Leibenstein's concept of Critical Minimum Effort [1957], Hirschman's theory of Unbalanced Growth [1958], and the attempts of authors such as Fleming [1955], Lipton [1962], Scitovsky [1959], Streeten [1959], and Sutcliffe [1964] to reconcile some of the conflicting conclusions. These theories lack clear and precise operational content and each assumes a particular set of circumstances which may or may not be valid for a specific economy.

In principle, at least, a more efficacious vehicle to guide the requisite coordination would be a mathematical programming model based on a more precise description of economic structure and articulation of policy objectives. And, indeed, several "demonstration" planning models with economies of scale have been constructed to indicate the utility of a mathematical programming approach which can simultaneously embrace many of the elements stressed by these authors and determine the significance of each within a particular setting.[1]

Few *applied* increasing returns planning models have been constructed, however, for the art of planning with economies of scale has only recently passed beyond its infancy. Ten years ago it was prohibitively expensive to obtain globally optimal solutions to planning models that specified increasing returns in a number of activities. Today it is practical to solve models of modest size, and the cost of computation is still falling rapidly as major advances continue to be made. But computation is only part of the art. Pertinent empirical information regarding the significance of various types of

---

1. See Haldi [1960] and Chenery and Westphal [1969].

scale economies is lacking, and many theoretical issues regarding resource allocation under increasing returns remain largely unexplored. Economies of scale are best understood at the micro level, particularly with respect to direct production activity. But there is, at present, no satisfactory theoretical or empirical basis on which to aggregate over micro activities characterized by increasing returns. Consequently, there are no applied economy-wide planning models in which scale economies are specified for aggregate sector activities.[2] The ultimate goal of incorporating economies of scale within applied economy-wide planning models remains unrealized.

Applied increasing returns planning models have focused on programming the timing, location, and scale of investments within individual sectors, and they have been quite disaggregated in their attention to technological detail. In this chapter we shall focus on these sector models with increasing returns. They have a substantial advantage over traditional project appraisal, for they are able to incorporate interdependencies among highly interrelated activities—between similar activities conducted at different points in time and space and those stemming from input-output relationships and joint production.

The reader might question why a chapter dealing with partial equilibrium (i.e., sector) models is included in a volume on economy-wide planning. The answer is that planners at the center must often focus a disproportionate share of their attention on investment projects having economies of scale, for the coordination of investment is particularly important in these cases. An economy-wide model is not necessarily mandatory to achieve efficient co-ordination. Coordination problems between levels of planning are discussed in section 6.

This chapter's organization is as follows: We will, in section 2, review the empirical literature on economies of scale. Section 3 examines several models for planning investments in individual production processes characterized by increasing returns, dealing separately with the questions of timing and location. In section 4, we take up multiprocess models which span a number of interrelated activities having economies of scale. Section 5 presents an evaluation of the models surveyed, while the linkages between sector and economy-wide planning and the policy implications of increasing returns are reviewed in section 6.

## 2. EMPIRICAL ESTIMATES

There are economies of scale (or, equivalently, increasing returns) if average production cost declines with increases in the volume of capacity,

---

2. One applied economy-wide, increasing returns planning model is known to the author; however, economies of scale are specified at the plant level in this model. See Westphal [1969].

where capacity is measured in units of output per unit of time.[3] Average cost at a particular scale is calculated on the basis of that choice of production technique which minimizes total production costs with respect to given input prices. Measured economies of scale thus depend upon input prices as well as the technology set. Economies of scale may be measured with respect to the scale of a plant, firm, or industry. Here we are concerned largely with economies of scale internal to the plant. Economies of scale internal to the firm are most often either pecuniary economies arising out of the greater bargaining strength of large firms or economies in management and associated overhead services provided by the firm. The former are not *real* economies and, therefore, should be neglected in planning resource allocation to maximize social objectives. Estimates of the latter are highly tenuous and unreliable. Economies of scale for the industry, and external to the firms within it, can generally be traced to scale economies internal to plants supplying the industry; to this extent such economies are dealt with here and in the multiprocess model developed in section 4.

The degree of increasing returns is generally expressed by the elasticity of total cost with respect to scale. A "scale elasticity" less than 1.0 implies falling average costs; the smaller the elasticity, the faster is the fall in average costs with rising scale. It is generally assumed, and with ample justification for plants in most industries, that there are economies of scale in production cost up to a certain scale, the "minimum efficient scale," beyond which there are constant or decreasing returns. If we neglect trade, the significance of economies of scale in an industry serving a given market (regional or national) is roughly indicated by the number of minimum efficient scale plants needed to satisfy demand. Economies of scale are most significant where the capacity of a single minimum efficient scale plant exceeds demand at a price equal to minimum average cost; they are insignificant if the market can support a large number of such plants.[4] This much having been said, it would seem relatively easy to obtain empirical estimates of the degree of increasing returns internal to plants within an industry and to assess their significance with respect to a given market. Such is not the case, however, since very few plants produce a homogeneous, single-product output.[5]

Plants in most industries produce a variety of products. This is true even in electricity generation, where, at a minimum, it is necessary to distinguish between peak and average power requirements.[6] Furthermore, most industrial

---

3. Distribution costs, and especially transportation costs, are dealt with separately in most investment planning exercises.

4. See Bain [1956], Chapter 3.

5. Furthermore, as defined, "minimum efficient scale" has no prescriptive relevance for investment planning since it omits considerations of alternative sources of supply, demand growth over time, and distribution costs. These aspects of the investment planning problem are of critical importance as indicated in section 3.

6. See Anderson [1972].

products go through a series of processing stages, and each stage often employs specialized equipment and labor. In the remainder of this survey, we refer to the specialized equipment used at a particular processing stage by the term "process element," and we implicitly assume that production techniques are embodied in these process elements. The steel industry provides a good example: An integrated steel mill produces a wide range of finished products (e.g., plate, hot and cold rolled sheet, tin plate—each in various dimensions) in its rolling mill using numerous distinct process elements. The basic raw materials are iron ore and coke, from which pig iron is made; the pig iron is processed into steel ingots, which are further processed into finished products. In addition, a variety of conveying and materials preparation equipment is used between production processing stages and forms a large share of the plant's capital cost.[7] To complicate matters further, not all of the processing stages required to transform an industry's basic raw materials into its finished products need be carried out in the same plant, for particular process stages may be subcontracted out to other plants. Subcontracting to plants that specialize in particular processes (e.g., casting or forging) is particularly prevalent in the mechanical engineering industry. To summarize: multi-product, multiprocess production technology is highly complex and may be organized at the plant level in countless ways, which results in a tremendous diversity among plants within any given industry. All of this means that a unidimensional measure of capacity is insufficient to analyze economies of scale.

Pratten and Dean [1965], in a very careful analysis of several industries, distinguish several interrelated dimensions of scale that must be considered in addition to the total output capacity of the plant: (i) the number of distinct products produced; (ii) the range of processing operations (or stages) carried out in the plant; (iii) the capacity of each process element; (iv) the length of each individual production run; and (v) where different products partially or completely share various process elements, as in petroleum refining, the various permutations of output levels that are possible (the plant's flexibility with respect to output mix). Economies of scale with respect to total output capacity are affected by variations in each of these elements.

Economies of scale internal to plant operations may be traced to one of several factors. *Indivisibilities* lead to cost elements which are more or less independent of the scale of output. "First copy" costs, or the research and development costs associated with the introduction of a new product, are important in most industries. Spreading these costs over a greater volume of output obviously reduces their contribution to average cost. "First copy" costs have not been introduced into investment planning models, for it seems doubtful that these models could deal adequately with such highly specific phenomena.

---

7. See Kendrick [1967b], appendix A for further details.

Another indivisibility, separate from but similar to "first copies," is associated with setting up a production run at a particular processing stage. For many products, demand is insufficient to justify continuous, year-round production. Instead, a number of production runs are made in the course of a year; the number of runs and the "lot size" of each depends primarily upon the volume of demand and inventory carrying costs. Indivisible costs in the form of labor inputs and idle equipment are associated with setting up a process element for each individual run, and economies may be realized by spreading these costs over larger lot sizes.[8]

The last important indivisibility is that of capital equipment. Though they may be available in units of varying (sometimes discretely varying) capacity, most process elements have a fixed minimum capacity. Economies are associated with both specialization and increased dimensions. *Specialization* of both capital equipment and labor inputs increases with greater volumes of output. Specialization takes place through the introduction of different production techniques (i.e., process elements) which have lower average costs at higher levels of capacity. Economies of *increased dimensions* mean that the cost of capital equipment often increases less rapidly than its capacity, even when the technique (i.e., design of process element) is held fixed. The most frequently cited reason is that capacity is generally determined by a volume measure, whereas cost is proportional to surface area. The clearest examples are found in the spheres, cylinders, pipes, and other geometrical configurations present in chemical plants, for which a doubling of surface area leads to an approximate tripling of volume. This is expressed in the "0.6 rule" of chemical engineering, which states that the scale elasticity of process elements is approximately 0.6.[9]

Economies of scale over a wide range of capacity are found in the use of capital equipment and labor in plants producing published matter, cement, chemicals, petrochemicals, petroleum, refined metals, machine tools, and bicycles, to name but a few of the products produced under increasing returns.[10]

---

8. The determination of optimal lot size is a familiar problem in inventory control and production scheduling. Lot size phenomena also lead to economies in the use of material inputs, for the optimal lot size and thus optimal inventory levels expand less than in proportion to annual output. See, for example, Buffa and Taubert [1972], Chapter 3.

9. See Moore [1959].

10. Bain [1956] has compiled engineering estimates for 20 manufacturing industries in the United States. Moore [1959], Haldi and Whitcomb [1967], and Silberston [1972] provide surveys of a number of other engineering studies. Econometric estimates of scale elasticities estimated from data for the United States are reviewed by Jorgenson [1972], who concludes that "the elasticity of substitution and the degree of returns to scale may be taken to be equal to unity" (p. 246). As Jorgenson observes in reference to Bain's estimates, these results are consistent with there being economies of scale up to the minimum efficient plant size, because the optimal plant size is small in relation to total industry capacity in the United States. However, this obviously does not imply that optimal plant sizes are small in relation to industry demand in developing countries.

Empirical studies of these industries have demonstrated that the elasticity of total plant investment cost with respect to plant capacity is constant over a large range of capacity, frequently being between 0.6 and 0.8. In these cases, doubling plant size increases investment costs by approximately 60 to 80 percent. These elasticities refer to the construction of complete plants, not to the expansion of capacity by eliminating one or more limiting bottlenecks (i.e., capacity at particular processing stage) within an existing plant. Depending on the industry, economies of scale in the use of labor may be even greater. Increasing returns are sometimes also found in the use of raw materials, although these are generally less important than the economies associated with capital and labor use.

Pratten and Dean found that,

> "apart from the spreading of indivisible first copy costs over a larger output as scale increases, the main sources of economies of scale for large plants are the use of larger capacity equipment, the use of more specialized equipment and personnel, and the greater utilization of specialized resources by improving the balance of operations."[11]

With respect to the last factor, an increase in the total output capacity of a plant generally makes it possible to secure greater balance among the capacities of its process elements such that each is more nearly utilized to full capacity.[12] The economies of scale that may be achieved through capacity balancing are particularly important in industries producing a wide range of differentiated products involving a great many separate process operations. The footwear, book printing, and mechanical engineering industries are good examples. The use of distinct process elements in production also gives rise to an important dynamic element in investment planning, for it makes possible the time phased installation of process elements in a manner that permits total production capacity to grow more closely in step with anticipated demand. For example, in the cement industry, a single rotary kiln might be installed in the first phase of a plant's construction along with sufficient capacity in ancillary units (e.g., slurry basin and smokestack) to permit the addition of another kiln in a second, later phase.[13]

A few words are also in order regarding sources of data to estimate scale economies. Plant scale economies can be estimated from *ex post* historical accounting records or from *ex ante* engineering analysis. The use of *ex post* data in econometric estimation has many pitfalls. It is difficult, if not impossible, to isolate plants producing identical product mixes and to insure that all of the observations pertain to the construction and operation of balanced plants. To obtain a sufficiently large sample size, it is necessary to incorporate data for plants built at different locations and points in time, perhaps in

---

11. Pratten and Dean [1965], p. 102.

12. In a single product plant, complete balance occurs when output is a common multiple of each process element's capacity.

13. Example taken from Manne [1967a].

piecemeal fashion. Differences in capital goods' prices and technology must therefore be reckoned with. The most reliable estimates are thus *ex ante* engineering estimates based on the design of balanced plants and on equipment suppliers' catalogs for equipment prices. These are also the most relevant to planning present and future investments. From the manner in which they are obtained, the most trustworthy estimates of scale elasticities are those relating to the costs associated with individual process elements; the least trustworthy, those relating to entire plants.[14]

The foregoing brief review demonstrates that planning in the presence of significant scale economies must often go below the plant level to choose the optimal configuration of process elements within individual plants. Where subcontracting relationships among plants offer potentially important resource savings, it may also be desirable to plan the design of plants so as to maximize the gains from such relationships. Finally, it is important to investigate the time-phased construction of individual large-scale plants, which avoids the excess capacity that results from concentrating each plant's construction in a single period and substitutes for the staggered construction of a larger number of small plants.[15]

However, we hasten to add that it is sometimes legitimate, in view of the questions being asked and the technology of the particular industry, to assume that plants produce a single product employing a single (integrated) processing operation. This is most legitimate in the process industries such as chemicals production, metals refining, and cement production, where a steady flow of individually undifferentiated inputs is continuously transformed into a steady flow of undifferentiated output. In the next section, we discuss models appropriate to planning the construction timing of balanced plants which produce a single principal output. To highlight their principal assumption, we have characterized these models as "single-process models." Section 4 develops the "multiprocess model" which may be used to specify subplant investment choices within a sector planning framework.

## 3. SINGLE-PROCESS MODELS

The simplest analytical tool applicable to investment decisions under economies of scale is "break-even" analysis. It is appropriate only where market boundaries are well defined and demand is stationary through time. Tradable commodities either can be produced or imported; this leads to a

---

14. Moore [1959], Haldi and Whitcomb [1967], and Silberston [1972] give excellent capsule summaries of the problems of estimation and cite additional references.

15. Because of differences in plant design, the phased construction of a single plant is generally somewhat more expensive than the single-stage construction of a balanced plant having the same capacity. In the cement plant example, two rotary kilns cost more than a single kiln having the same capacity. Thus, it is not merely a question of optimal time phasing but also of choosing among process elements of different capacity and design.

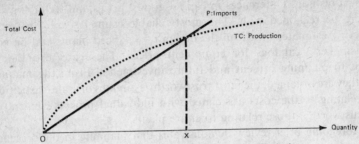

Figure 1.   Single-process Break-even Analysis

"make-buy" choice regarding the source of supply of such commodities. Figure 1, taken from Manne [1967a], illustrates break-even analysis of the make-buy choice for a particular commodity. The $TC$ curve is the long-run total cost curve for production. We suppose that plant construction is characterized by economies of scale, so the total cost curve is concave. The total cost of imports, shown by the curve $P$, is strictly proportional to the quantity imported, for the unit price of imports is assumed constant (infinite supply elasticity). Efficient resource allocation requires that the total cost of meeting the given demand be minimized. Let $X$ denote the quantity at which the total cost of imports equals the total cost of domestic production. This is the "break-even" point. If the actual quantity demanded falls short of $X$, the commodity should be supplied through imports; if it exceeds $X$, the commodity should be produced. It can be verified easily that this condition is equivalent to saying that the long run *average* cost of production at the quantity demanded must be less than or equal to the import price if the commodity is optimally to be produced.[16]

Note the all or nothing character of the optimal policy: either all of the product is imported or all of it is produced. This particular prescription will shortly be seen to be incorrect where demand grows through time. However, one insight from the make-buy diagram is correct. The "minimum optimal scale plant" is determined by relative prices as well as by technology and factor productivity. In Figure 1, $X$ is the capacity of the minimum optimal scale plant, since production in a smaller plant would be more expensive than importing. It is easily seen that a fall in the price of imports would increase the scale of the minimum optimal scale plant, whereas a price increase would reduce the minimum optimal scale. The price of imports may change either because of changed supply conditions abroad or because of a change in the

16. Boon [1964, 1965–66, 1969] has made extensive use of break-even analysis to explore the interrelationship between capital-labor substitution and economies of scale in a number of processing activities, primarily in metal working. His model incorporates both the indivisibility of individual machines and lot size phenomena. Economies of scale are specified through the use of a fixed charge cost function.

exchange rate. Apart from the fact that there may not be a finite capacity at which average production costs are minimized, it really makes no economic sense to identify the minimum optimal scale with the capacity that minimizes average cost. Nor does it make sense to equate the minimum optimal size plant with the scale of the largest and newest plants being built in developed economies.

Another insight can also be gleaned from this simple construct. Let us change the interpretation of the $P$ curve to that of a total revenue curve. This would be valid were it possible to export the commodity at a constant world market price. Given that the total cost curve does not have an inflection point at which marginal costs begin rising, the net revenue maximizing level of production must be infinite. But this is clearly absurd. To avoid such extreme conclusions, either the demand for exports must be properly specified to be less than infinitely elastic with respect to price, or average costs must begin rising beyond some scale of output. In the absence of hard facts both about export demand elasticities and the precise shape of the long-run total cost curve, most modelers of increasing returns prefer to take at least the level of export demand as exogenously specified and completely price inelastic. The sensitivity of the optimal investment policy to the exogenous export forecast may be tested easily with this specification.

Break-even analysis is easy to do and is extremely useful for determining whether there is sufficient demand to justify production. One may conclude that plant construction would not be optimal in the near future if demand were anticipated to fall well below the break-even point. But where demand is near the break-even level and is growing rapidly or where the geographical market is very large, simple break-even analysis errs by neglecting significant *intraprocess* interdependence. Increasing returns lead to interdependence between decisions to build plants using the identical technology to produce the same product at different points in time and different locations in space.[17] To evaluate the trade-offs between gaining the advantages of large-scale production on the one hand and incurring the costs of excess capacity and transportation on the other, it is necessary to evaluate not single projects but alternative investment *programs* defined over time and space. We will deal with the temporal and spatial dimensions separately.

## 3.1  Temporal Interdependence

Chenery [1952] was apparently the first to state the dynamic investment planning problem for a single process model incorporating the trade-off between the cost of carrying excess capacity and the lower unit production

---

17. This is not to suggest that there is not also interdependence between investment projects to build plants producing similar, substitutable products or using different technologies. Here, we merely wish to focus on the smallest domain in which economies of scale lead to interdependence.

costs permitted by building ahead of demand. Demand growth and resource costs are specified exogenously and a capacity cost function with a constant elasticity is used; the objective is to minimize the cost of producing at the level of demand over an infinite horizon. Chenery demonstrated that total costs would be minimized by investment in overcapacity. The optimal amount of overinvestment at each point of capacity installation varies inversely with the discount rate and the scale elasticity.

Manne [1961, 1967a] extended the model to include stochastic demand growth and the choice between domestic production and imports. We shall discuss in some detail the model in which imports (but not exports) are possible, the growth of demand is linear, and plants are assumed to have infinite lives.[18] Figure 2 may help the reader to visualize the problem and

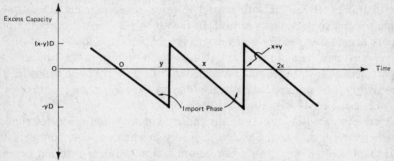

Figure 2. Time Path of Excess Capacity and Imports

interpret the notation. Let time equal to zero denote a point at which there are neither excess capacity nor imports. The growth of demand after time zero is satisfied through imports up to time $y$, at which point a plant of capacity $xD$ is constructed to replace imports and satisfy the growth of demand up to time $x$; $D$ is the annual increment in demand and $x$ is the time at which the new plant first produces at full capacity. The notation is summarized below:

$D$ = annual increase in demand, where it is assumed that demand grows at a constant *arithmetic* rate;

$x$ = the time interval between the construction of successive plants; thus $xD$ is the size of plant constructed;

$k(xD)^a$ = capacity cost function for a single plant of size $xD$, where $k$ is a constant of proportionality and $a$ is the scale elasticity;

$p$ = import penalty cost, defined as the unit import price less the average current input cost of domestic production, and assumed to be positive;

$r$ = the annual discount rate; and

---

18. This case is comprehensively discussed in Chapters 2 and 10 of Manne [1967a].

$y$ = the duration of the temporary import phase; i.e., the elapsed time between the point at which full capacity is reached in all plants and the point at which the next plant is built.

Given that the objective is to minimize the total discounted cost of meeting demand over an infinite horizon, it is not immediately obvious that this notation is correct, since it assumes that successive plants are constructed at constant cycles of $x$ units of time and that the temporary import phase will have the same duration in each construction cycle. It can be shown (for any capacity cost function exhibiting economies of scale) that these assumptions characterize the optimal phasing policy when the annual increment in demand is constant.[19]

The trick to obtaining an explicitly solvable mathematical statement of the optimization problem is in writing down the proper recursive equation. Looked at from time zero, the optimization problem is to

$$\text{Minimize} \quad C(x, y) = \int_{t=0}^{y} p(tD)\, e^{-rt}\, dt + e^{-ry}\, k(xD)^{a} + e^{-rx}\, C(x, y). \quad (3.1)$$

The first two terms to the right of the equals sign pertain to the first import-construction cycle: the first term is the total discounted penalty for imports purchased during the temporary import phase; the second term is the discounted cost of constructing a new plant at the end of the import phase. The third term is the present value of the costs incurred in future cycles. Since the same import-construction cycle will be continually repeated over the entire infinite horizon (again, given a constant value for each parameter through time), the infinite horizon cost of a given policy is the same, except for a discount factor, at each point where full capacity is reached. Current (or variable) production input costs have not been neglected, as it may appear, for the import penalty is defined to be the import price less average current input costs. By virtue of this definition, and the additional assumption of constant average current costs, we may disregard current input costs, for their discounted sum is a constant that is unaffected by the policy chosen. The minimum cost policy is found by solving equation (3.1) through numerical methods.

The principal qualitative conclusion from this model is that there are definite gains to temporary imports and to building ahead of demand, for these permit larger plants to be built. Infinite horizon cost is not very sensitive to errors in policy over a relatively wide range of plant scales. In Manne's illustrative example, the construction of plants of half and double the optimal scale leads to proportional cost increases of 5.5 and 7.7 percent, respectively.[20]

---

19. Constant cycle times are also optimal if demand grows geometrically so long as the constant scale elasticity capacity cost function is used and temporary imports are excluded.

20. In this example, $a$ equals 0.7, the discount rate is 10 percent, and imports are not a feasible alternative supply source (i.e., the import penalty is infinite).

The same conclusion emerges from sensitivity tests with other increasing returns planning models: the proportional loss, measured either in terms of cost at shadow prices or welfare, is generally far less than the proportional error in the parameter whose misestimation would result in the choice of incorrect policy. However, while this means that model prescriptions are insensitive to modest errors in parameter estimates, it does not imply that current government policies are necessarily close to the optimum. In India, for example, Manne [1967a, Chapter 8] finds that the construction of plants that are too small has increased infinite horizon costs (evaluated at shadow prices) by between 15 and 20 percent for aluminum, caustic soda, and cement.

Manne [1967a] and his associates have extended the model to other time paths of demand and discuss the effects of incorporating depreciation (i.e., plant replacement) and economies of scale in plant operating costs. The solution technique used with all the model variants is dynamic programming, which Manne [1967a] has also applied to models that incorporate the spatial dimension by distinguishing multiple producing and consuming regions. Locational models are used to examine the trade-off between increased transportation cost and the gains from building bigger plants that will serve larger market areas. Rather than examine a dynamic programming formulation of the spatial model, we will illustrate its essential features using a mixed integer programming (MIP) formulation.[21]

By virtue of its adaptability to model a wide variety of relationships involving increasing returns, MIP is an extremely valuable tool for planning with economies of scale.[22] Furthermore, MIP is often the only possible means of solving a nonconvex model. We will therefore concentrate on MIP formulations in the remainder of this survey. MIP requires functions that are at least piecewise linear, and so we digress momentarily to discuss linear approximations to the constant elasticity cost function.

## 3.2 A Digression: Linear Approximation

A "fixed charge" cost function can be used to approximate any constant elasticity cost function exhibiting increasing returns. Its statement in a programming model is

$$\text{Total cost} = Fp + Vc, \tag{3.2}$$
$$Cp - c \geq 0, \tag{3.3}$$

and
$$p = 0 \text{ or } 1.0, \tag{3.4}$$

where $p$ = zero-one variable associated with the fixed charge;
$c$ = capacity of the plant constructed;
$F$ = the fixed charge or fixed cost associated with plant construction;

21. For an early statement of this type of model, see Vietorisz and Manne [1963]; we will take up further examples below.
22. See Dantzig [1963].

$V =$ the variable cost associated with plant construction; and

$C =$ an upper bound (positive) on the capacity of plant.

Equation (3.2) is the fixed charge cost function; equations (3.3) and (3.4) are required to insure that the fixed charge is incurred if any capacity whatsoever is built. Consider equation (3.3): If $c$ is greater than zero, then so, too, must $p$ be greater than zero; but by equation (3.4), if $p$ is greater than zero, then it must be 1.0. On the other hand, if $c$ is equal to zero, then $p$ equal to zero satisfies all of the constraints. Thus, the entire fixed charge $F$ is incurred if a plant, regardless of scale, is built, but the fixed charge is not incurred if no plant is built. The parameter $C$ may represent a technologically determined upper bound to plant capacity or it may indicate the scale at which average capacity construction cost is a minimum; otherwise it is a purely fictitious parameter set to a sufficiently large value to insure that equation (3.3) would never be binding were a plant built. Regardless, equation (3.3) is required to link the fixed charge variable $p$ to the amount of capacity constructed. No particular meaning is ascribed to the fixed charge itself in most practical applications, for it is merely used to obtain the approximation. The key point is that the fixed charge approximation may be applied to any concave total cost function.

Figure 3 illustrates that the fixed charge cost function closely approximates the constant elasticity cost function over a fairly wide range of plant scales. Large errors of cost estimation will not be made as long as capacity expansion is confined to this range.[23] The optimal solution to an MIP model employing

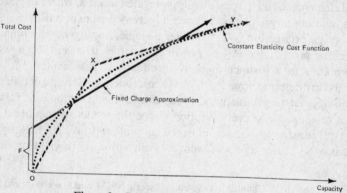

Figure 3.   Process Capacity Cost Functions

23. In practice, there are a number of ways to choose $F$ and $V$ once the constant elasticity cost function is given. They may be chosen so that the two cost curves coincide at the plant scale thought a priori to be optimal, or they may be estimated through a least squares regression over points for a particular interval along the constant elasticity cost function. Stoutjesdijk et al. [1973] discuss the latter approach.

269

the fixed charge approximation will not necessarily be identical to that for a model which differs only in using the constant elasticity cost function. This is true even if the optimal plant scale in the former is such that the approximation is exact.

The fixed charge approximation is a close relative to a family of piecewise linear approximations to a concave function. A member of that family having two linear segments is illustrated by $OXY$ in Figure 3. Specification of piecewise linear concave function in an MIP model requires the use of a number of integer variables equal to one less than the number of linear segments.[24, 25] These integers are needed to insure that the variables associated with each linear segment are entered into the basis in the correct order; without them, these variables would be entered in reverse order since marginal cost is higher, the closer a segment is to the origin.[26] A single integer variable is required for either approximation pictured in Figure 3. Since an approximation using two linear segments will be closer to the "true" function, it is somewhat surprising that most MIP increasing returns planning models employ the fixed charge approximation. Perhaps it has been mistakenly thought that it is easier to interpret solutions if the latter is used, since there is then a unique marginal cost along a given cost function. However, intuitive insights based on the use of the fixed charge approximation carry over to the use of the piecewise linear approximation as well.

## 3.3 Spatial Interdependence

Manne's [1964] model of plant location under economies of scale gives the essential elements found in spatially disaggregated models, where the trade-off through building larger plants is between increased transportation costs and lower average production cost. Consider a single, homogeneous commodity which can be produced at any of $I$ distinct locations to meet the known and fixed demands in $J$ distinct markets. Production costs exhibit increasing returns and are described by a fixed charge cost function. Because of differences in technology, factor productivity, or input prices, production cost functions need not be the same in every location. Since the model spans only a single year, plant construction costs must be annualized through the use of a capital recovery factor and then added to current costs to yield production

---

24. See the appendix to Chapter XII as well as Dantzig [1963], and Markowitz and Manne [1957]. We are here assuming that the concave function appears as a cost function in a minimizing problem.

25. A recently developed and computationally superior alternative omits the zero-one variables and applies a branch and bound method directly to the piecewise linear problem. See Tomlin [1970] and Erlenkotter [1971].

26. Alternatively, if one were to use the convex combination approach that is discussed in the Chapter XII appendix, failure to employ integers would yield an optimal solution with convex combinations of zero and the extreme cost-capacity combination.

costs.[27] The objective is to minimize the costs of meeting the fixed demands in all markets.

The notation follows:

$c_{ij}$ = annual production at location $i$ destined for market $j$;

$p_i$ = zero-one variable associated with production at location $i$;

$V_{ij}$ = the variable charge component of production cost at location $i$ plus the constant transportation cost per unit produced at $i$ and shipped to $j$;

$F_i$ = the fixed charge component of production cost at location $i$;

$D_j$ = annual demand at location $j$.

One may interpret the model's failure to distinguish between production and capacity in one of two ways: either the model is used to plan capacity installation and it is assumed that there will be no excess capacity, or the model is used to plan production and it is assumed that capacity is already in place at each location (in amount $C_i$). In the latter case, capital costs are omitted from the objective function and current inputs are assumed to have increasing returns.

The programming model is:

$$\text{Minimize total system costs} = \sum_i F_i p_i + \sum_i \sum_j V_{ij} c_{ij} \tag{3.5}$$

Subject to:

$$\sum_i c_{ij} = D_j, \quad j = 1, \ldots, J; \tag{3.6}$$

$$C_i p_i - \sum_j c_{ij} \geq 0, \quad i = 1, \ldots, I; \tag{3.7}$$

and

$$p_i = 0 \text{ or } 1.0, \quad i = 1, \ldots, I, \tag{3.8}$$

where the definition of $C_i$ remains as before and it is implicitly understood that all continuous, noninteger variables are bounded from below by zero. Equation (3.6) requires that all demands be met; equations (3.7) and (3.8) are associated with the fixed charge approximation. This model resembles the standard transportation programming model except that production costs are included and exhibit increasing returns. The model neglects imports from outside the producing regions $J$; however, such imports could easily be incorporated into the specification.

---

27. The capital recovery factor states the fraction of a capital good's purchase price that must be set aside into a depreciation reserve in each year of its life in order to have accumulated the original purchase price by the end of its life. It is a function of the interest rate at which the depreciation reserve is accumulated and of the lifetime of the capital good. See Oakford [1970], pp. 19–21, for the algebra.

A dynamic single-region model and a static spatial model have now been developed. Either model's prescriptions are likely to be misleading—the former because it neglects the spatial dimension of demand and would therefore prescribe plants that are too large when too great an area is taken as the unit for projecting demand; the latter because it neglects the growth of demand over time and would therefore prescribe plants that are too small. Of course, it may not be necessary to introduce spatial disaggregation if the costs of transporting the finished product are sufficiently small. Conversely, the location of plants may be predetermined by the location of raw materials if the cost of transporting raw materials is high relative to that of shipping the finished product. But there is nothing to suggest that building ahead of demand *within the producing region* is ever likely to be suboptimal. This by no means implies that spatial interdependence may be neglected in a dynamic model. Where a separate analysis is conducted for each region (however defined), the failure to recognize trading possibilities between producing regions will generate too much excess capacity. The proper time phasing of plant construction within the various regions makes it possible, at least in part, to use plant capacities in excess of regional demands in some areas to satisfy temporarily the growth of demand in other areas where demand exceeds regional production capacity. This can lead to a substantial reduction in system-wide excess capacity and a large savings in cost. The key trade-off in a dynamic, spatial increasing returns model is, therefore, between transportation costs and excess capacity; the trade-offs are not merely between transportation costs and average production costs or between foregone investment opportunities (i.e., excess capacity) and average production costs.

We will not state a formal model of the single-process, dynamic, spatial investment planning model, for the principal features of such a model should be apparent. Readers wishing a more complete exposition should consult Manne [1967a]. We next take up multiprocess models with scale economies.

## 4. Multiprocess Models

Single-process models assume a given time path of demand and exogenous input prices. They may therefore neglect significant *interprocess* interdependencies, for intermediate input supply and demand relationships make it necessary to coordinate investments in related processes. This has been the theme of a number of important articles within the development literature; in our context, the most notable is Chenery's [1959] article on the interdependence of investment decisions. We will use a simplified version of his model to explore the meaning of interdependence among processes.

### 4.1 An Illustrative Model

Consider two interrelated processes that are both characterized by economies of scale. To lend an element of reality to our discussion, assume

that the first produces machinery while the second produces steel.[28] Following Chenery and the conventional design of multiprocess planning models, we suppose that the objective of the planning exercise is to minimize the cost of meeting exogenously stated demands for steel and machinery. The exogenous demand for steel includes all demand *except* the intermediate demand from machinery production.[29] All demand for machinery is exogenous, for the model is static and thereby neglects the interdependence arising out of the demand for machinery to produce steel.[30] The model thus focuses on the interdependence stemming from the use of steel to make machinery. Two alternative sources of supply for each product are investigated: production and imports. Export demand is exogenous, and locational considerations are neglected.

The notation follows:

$i$ = product index: 1 for machinery, 2 for steel;

$c_i$ = the amount of the $i$th product produced;

$p_i$ = the zero-one variable associated with production of the $i$th product;

$m_i$ = the amount of imports of the $i$th product;

$F_i$ = the fixed cost coefficient for production of the $i$th product;

$V_i$ = the variable cost coefficient for production of the $i$th product;

$C_i$ = an upper bound on $c_i$ needed to specify the fixed charge cost function;

$W_i$ = the unit import price (domestic currency equivalent) of product $i$;

$D_i$ = the exogenously specified demand for the $i$th product; and

$A$ = an input-output coefficient stating the required amount of steel to make one unit of machinery.

The model is stated below:

$$\text{Minimize total cost} = F_1 p_1 + V_1 c_1 + F_2 p_2 + V_2 c_2 + W_1 m_1 + W_2 m_2, \quad (4.1)$$

Subject to:

$$c_1 + m_1 = D_1; \quad (4.2)$$

$$-Ac_1 + c_2 + m_2 = D_2; \quad (4.3)$$

$$C_i p_i - c_i \geq 0, \quad i = 1, 2; \quad (4.4)$$

and

$$p_i = 0 \quad \text{or} \quad 1.0, \quad i = 1, 2. \quad (4.5)$$

28. A number of other paired identifications would be possible.

29. Other intermediate uses of steel, for example to produce automobiles, are reflected in the exogenous demand estimate. Depending on the circumstances, one might wish to make this and other major intermediate uses of steel endogenous in an applied model.

30. Alternatively, the production of steel producing machinery may be excluded altogether from the overall planning exercise, it having been a priori determined that steel producing machinery would be imported in any event.

Equations (4.2) and (4.3) are, respectively, the material balance equations for machinery and steel. Equations (4.4) are required to specify the fixed charge cost function, and equations (4.5) state that each integer variable may assume only the values zero and one.[31] The long-run total cost equation for steel production is $F_2 + V_2 c_2$, where $c_2 > 0$; the long-run average and marginal costs of steel production are therefore $V_2 + (F_2/c_2)$ and $V_2$, respectively. The long-run cost equation $F_1 + V_1 c_1$ for machinery production is not quite the total cost equation, for it *excludes* the cost of intermediate steel inputs. The cost of steel inputs is endogenously determined and is charged through the appearance of the intermediate input coefficient in the material balance equation (4.3) for steel.[32]

Break-even analysis may be used to solve this illustrative model.[33] Production of either product is optimal only if the demand for it equals or exceeds the output at which average cost equals the price of imports. Because of interdependence between the processes, there are now two break-even points *with respect to the exogenous demand* for each commodity, depending upon whether the other commodity is being produced or imported.

*Machinery Break-Even Points:* Starting first with machinery ($i = 1$), the break-even level of exogenous demand is found by equating total domestic production cost to the total cost of imports. Two break-even points must be distinguished, one if steel is imported and another if steel is produced.

If steel is imported:

$$F_1 + V_1 D_1^* + A W_2 D_1^* = W_1 D_1^*; \tag{4.6}$$

thus,

$$D_1^* = F_1/(W_1 - V_1 - A W_2). \tag{4.7}$$

If steel is produced:

$$F_1 + V_1 D_1^0 + A V_2 D_1^0 = W_1 D_1^0; \tag{4.8}$$

thus,

$$D_1^0 = F_1/(W_1 - V_1 - A V_2). \tag{4.9}$$

Equations (4.7) and (4.9) state the break-even condition. $D_1^*$ is the break-even level of exogenous demand when steel inputs must be imported; $D_1^0$ is the break-even level when steel is produced. Note that the expressions for $D_1^*$ and $D_1^0$ differ only in the last term of the denominator. In the former case, steel is priced at its import cost; in the latter, at its marginal cost of production.

---

31. We suppose that the upper bounds $C_i$ are such that constraints (4.4) would not be binding were a plant operated in either sector.

32. Let $q_2$ be the shadow price of steel (i.e., the dual variable associated with (4.3)), then the marginal cost of producing machinery is $V_1 + A q_2$.

33. Rhee and Westphal [1973b] use break-even analysis to explore the implications of various types of interdependence in addition to that arising from intermediate input relationships.

(We discuss the rationale for pricing produced intermediate inputs at marginal rather than average cost in subsection 4.3.) The denominator of each expression is the marginal savings of domestic production over import cost.[34] The break-even point is such that the total marginal savings over import cost just offsets the fixed cost. Assuming that the marginal cost of steel production is less than its import price ($V_2 < W_2$), we have that $D_1^0$ is less than $D_1^*$.

*Steel Break-Even Points:* Break-even points for steel production are found in a similar fashion:

If machinery is imported:

$$F_2 + V_2 D_2^* = W_2 D_2^*; \qquad (4.10)$$

thus,

$$D_2^* = F_2/(W_2 - V_2). \qquad (4.11)$$

If machinery is produced:

$$F_2 + V_2(D_2^0 + AD_1) = W_2(D_2^0 + AD_1); \qquad (4.12)$$

thus,

$$D_2^0 = [F_2/(W_2 - V_2)] - AD_1. \qquad (4.13)$$

Equations (4.11) and (4.13) express the break-even condition. $D_2^*$ is the break-even level of exogenous demand for steel when machinery is imported; $D_2^0$ is the break-even level when machinery is produced. Simultaneous production of both products does not change the marginal cost of production in the case of steel as it does in the case of machinery. However, simultaneous production increases the demand for steel and thereby lowers the level of exogenous demand at which steel production is competitive with imports (compare equations (4.11) and (4.13)).

The break-even boundaries are graphed in Figure 4, where the axes measure the exogenous demand for each product. To compare market allocations with optimal solutions for various exogenous demand levels, let us assume a decentralized market economy in which producers are required to sell at marginal cost and receive a subsidy for each unit sold equal to the difference between import price and marginal cost. We will further assume that there is no initial capacity in either sector. If the exogenous demand for machinery exceeds $D_1^*$, then it should be produced rather than imported, and it would be produced in the market economy. Similarly for steel and $D_2^*$. However, if the exogenous demand for one of the products, say, $i$, exceeds $D_i^*$, while that for the other, $j$, falls between $D_j^0$ and $D_j^*$, then the phasing of initial production in the market economy will be suboptimal.

Consider the region bounded by *JBIL*. Production of steel would be initiated immediately, and it also would be optimal to initiate the production of

---

34. We assume that this magnitude is positive.

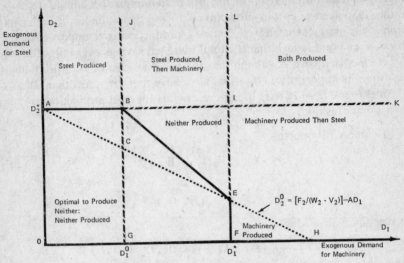

Figure 4.  Two-process Break-even Analysis

machinery simultaneously. However, in the absence of perfect foresight concerning future market prices, machinery production would not commence in the market economy until steel was being produced and sold at marginal cost. In this case, the timing of plant construction in the market economy is suboptimal and, in the absence of perfect foresight concerning future steel demand, the initial steel mill would not be big enough. Two smaller steel mills would be built rather than a single larger one, resulting in efficiency losses throughout the lives of these plants.[35] Were steel produced under constant returns, the efficiency losses resulting from delayed machinery production would be only temporary, for average steel production costs would be unaffected by the scale of the plants built. Thus, the costs of imperfect coordination are higher where there are economies of scale in the supplying processes.

The timing of plant construction in the market economy would be reversed were the exogenous demand levels in the region bounded by *KIEH*. The start-up of machinery production would increase the demand for steel beyond its break-even point. Here the efficiency losses are only temporary, for construction of the steel mill is delayed until after the quantity demanded for use in machinery production has been revealed.

Neither commodity would be produced in the market economy were exogenous demands in the region bounded by *BCEI*, where the exogenous demands lie between respective break-even points. There would be no incentive to produce machinery unless steel could be purchased at its marginal

---

35. Note that the second steel mill would actually be built only if the intermediate demand for steel to produce machinery exceeded the break-even level.

276

production cost, and steel production would not be expected to break even unless the potential intermediate demand from machinery production were correctly anticipated. However, it is optimal to produce both machinery and steel if the exogenous demand levels fall in the triangle *BEI*, where

$$F_1 + F_2 + V_1 D_1 + V_2(D_2 + A D_1) \leq W_1 D_1 + W_2 D_2; \qquad (4.14)$$

i.e., where the total cost of producing both products is less than or equal to the total cost of importing both.[36] Lack of coordination precludes plant construction even though both products should be produced if demands fall in this region. This is the region of "maximum interdependence," for it is the only region in which the market economy would not ultimately produce what optimally ought to be produced. However, too much significance should not be attached to this case. In reality, the growth of demand for both products would eventually lead to exogenous demand levels outside the triangle; therefore, under conditions of growing demand, efficiency losses may once again be considered to result from delaying plant construction.

We have assumed marginal cost pricing of domestic production in the market economy. What if average cost pricing or pricing at import cost is assumed? Following the line of reasoning employed above, one can demonstrate that market allocations would be further from the optimal solution than when marginal cost pricing is employed. For example, assume that the exogenous demand for steel only slightly exceeded $D_2^*$, while that for machinery fell between $D_1^0$ and $D_1^*$. The average cost of steel production would then be only slightly less than its import cost. Under these conditions, it would not appear profitable to produce machinery in a decentralized market economy, even though it is optimal since the exogenous demand for steel is alone sufficient to justify incurring the fixed charge for its production. This is but an illustration of the well-known principle that marginal cost pricing is required for efficient resource allocation, even in the presence of economies of scale.

To summarize: Interdependence from intermediate input use runs in two directions—there is a price dimension on the using sector side and a quantity dimension on the supplying sector side. Price interdependence primarily affects the make-buy choice with respect to higher stage products and is significant when plant construction is delayed beyond the optimal date. In the extreme case (illustrated by region *BEI* in our example), price interdependence

---

36. The condition just stated is independent of the sectoral break-even conditions and is more limiting than their combination derived under the assumption of simultaneous production. It is the requirement that the system as a whole break even. One can easily verify that points $B$ (i.e., $D_1^0, D_2^*$) and $E$ (i.e., $D_1^*, D_2^0$) lie on the boundary given by (4.14), and that the boundary is a straight line. Note that the system break-even condition is a necessary but not sufficient condition for the optimality of producing both products; sufficiency also requires that each plant break even separately.

also affects the make-buy choice with respect to lower order, intermediate products. It is of greater potential significance the larger is the intermediate input-output coefficient and the greater is the difference between the import price and the marginal cost of producing the intermediate input. Quantity interdependence affects the scale decision in supplying sectors and remains significant even where price interdependence is insignificant. Consider the region bounded by *LIK* in Figure 4, where the exogenous demand for both products exceeds the break-even point for independent production. Market decisions would here correctly lead to the production of both products. However, the steel mill would be of suboptimal scale unless a correct forecast were made of the intermediate demand from machinery production.

Lack of coordination may thus lead to suboptimal timing of plant construction and will almost certainly lead to suboptimal scales for the plants constructed to supply intermediate inputs. The policy implication is clearly that there is a need for coordination among investment plans in interdependent sectors. We have illustrated interdependence with respect to the make-buy choice.[37] Decisions in other types of circumstances may be equally affected by interdependence. These circumstances include all those where true opportunity costs cannot be determined independently of the optimal allocation of resources. Market prices are not then adequate to evaluate investment projects.

## 4.2 Outline of a Complete Model

To achieve *intraprocess* as well as *interprocess* coordination, it is necessary to turn to a mathematical programming model that is simultaneously dynamic, spatially disaggregated, and multiprocess. We omit a mathematical statement of the complete multiprocess model, for there exist several excellent discussions of its specification and numerical implementation.[38] We will, however, state a static, one-region *MIP* formulation to outline the complete model's basic structure and to indicate the data required to implement a multiprocess model. The model outlined below is a general formulation which contains the essential elements found in any multiprocess model. While specific applied models differ from it in particular details of specification, their basic logic is the same.

The first step in constructing a multiprocess model is to establish its boundaries by distinguishing between endogenous and exogenous products. The former are those products for which production processes appear in the model; production activities for the latter do not appear explicitly. Corresponding to the division between endogenous and exogenous products is a division between endogenous and exogenous activities. The exogenous products and activities comprise the rest of the economy that is omitted from

---

37. It should be obvious that the same analysis applies if there is initial, pre-existing capacity and decisions concern expanding existing plants or building new plants.

38. See Kendrick [1967b] and Stoutjesdijk et al. [1973].

the model. The interface between endogenous and exogenous activities is in the model's objective function and right hand side parameter values. The costs of factor inputs and exogenous products required as intermediate inputs to endogenous production processes enter the objective function, and exogenous activities determine the stated demands that must be met over and above the intermediate demands from the endogenous production processes. Labor wages by skill category, prices of capital goods, and prices of exogenous intermediate inputs must be determined outside the multiprocess model, as must the interest rate and foreign exchange rate. It is generally assumed that exogenous inputs are supplied to the endogenous activities along infinitely elastic supply schedules. Exogenous demand estimates are also required; here, it is usually assumed that exogenous demand is perfectly price inelastic.[39] This description should make it clear that a multiprocess model neglects those interdependencies which cross the interface between exogenous and endogenous activities. It is necessary, therefore, to exercise considerable care in establishing the boundaries defining endogenous products and activities; significant interdependencies should not be omitted.[40]

The model set out below is similar to the illustrative model discussed above, though it also includes the interdependence that arises out of joint production. Joint production refers to the production of more than one product in a given modular component of capacity, or process element. Joint products sometimes occur as natural by-products of processes designed to obtain a single principal output; the by-product is generally of secondary value or, as in the case of mineral slag, has a positive disposal cost. In other cases, however, where larger capacity leads to lower average costs, plants are designed to maximize the cost savings that result from sharing capacity among several processes that could otherwise be carried out independently. Capacity sharing in this sense is extremely important, for example, in the mechanical engineering industries.[41]

As noted in section 2, it is frequently necessary to go below the plant level to achieve a proper specification of technology and investment choices. This is the case where significant savings are possible through the phased expansion of an individual plant's capacity or where plants produce multiple products. In most applications, therefore, the process elements distinguished in a model will refer to individual pieces of capital equipment or separate integrated production lines or shops, though they may also represent entire plants. The

---

39. There is nothing, in principle, to preclude the specification of upward sloping supply schedules for exogenous inputs and downward sloping demand schedules for net outputs; however, problems of parameter estimation and the possibility of sensitivity analysis have led to the specification described in the text.

40. We will return to this point in the conclusion.

41. Rhee and Westphal [1973a] discuss a model for planning investments in the mechanical engineering industries which focuses on capacity sharing phenomena.

specific division of processing facilities into process elements depends upon the sector and the specific questions addressed by the model.[42]

Our target year model has four distinct sets of activities:

$s_j$ = level of operation of the $j$th production process, $j = 1, \ldots, J$;

$m_i$ = imports of the $i$th product, $i = 1, \ldots, I$;

$c_k$ = new capacity of the $k$th type of process element, $k = 1, \ldots, K$;

$p_k$ = zero-one variable associated with new capacity in the $k$th type of process element, $k = 1, \ldots, K$.

The number of production processes $J$ need not equal the number of products $I$, since a single process may produce more than one product or the model may incorporate choices among production techniques so that a single product is producible by more than one production process. Likewise, the number of process elements $K$ need not equal the number of either production processes or products. In a simple make-buy model without choice of technique, capacity sharing and by-product production would lead to fewer process elements than processes; on the other hand, individual production processes may require capacity in several process elements. These relationships again depend upon how the model is built up from an engineering description of the technology being modelled. Note that two variables are required for each process element in order to specify a fixed charge cost function for processing capacity.

*Objective Function:* The objective function is to minimize the cost of meeting stated exogenous demands:

$$\text{Minimize} \quad \sum_{k=1}^{K} (F_k p_k + V_k c_k) + \sum_{j=1}^{J} E_j s_j + \sum_{i=1}^{I} W_i m_i, \qquad (4.15)$$

where $F_k$ = the fixed cost coefficient for capacity in the $k$th type of process element;

$V_k$ = the variable cost coefficient for capacity in the $k$th type of process element;

$E_j$ = the exogenous cost per unit of operation of the $j$th process; and

$W_i$ = the unit import price (domestic currency equivalent) of product $i$.

*Material Balance Constraints:* Four distinct sets of constraints appear in the model. There is, first, a material balance constraint for each product stating that the sum of production plus imports must equal the sum of exogenous demands plus the endogenously generated demand for its use as an intermediate input in production elsewhere:

$$\sum_{j=1}^{J} A_{ij} s_j + m_i \geq D_i, \quad i = 1, \ldots, I, \qquad (4.16)$$

---

42. The methodology of decomposing production facilities into process elements within the format of a multiprocess model is discussed in Nam et al. [1973].

where $A_{ij}$ = intermediate input-output coefficient: if positive, the output of the $i$th product per unit level of operation of the $j$th process; if negative, the input of the $i$th product per unit level of operation of the $j$th process; and,

$D_i$ = the exogenous demand for the $i$th product.

*Capacity Balance Constraints:* For each type of process element, there is a constraint requiring that total capacity be at least equal to the processing requirements generated by the production processes:

$$c_k - \sum_{j=1}^{J} B_{kj}s_j \geq -c_k^0, \quad k = 1, \ldots, K, \qquad (4.17)$$

where $B_{kj}$ = capacity input-output coefficient: the amount of capacity required in a process element of type $k$ per unit level of operation of the $j$th process; and,

$c_k^0$ = existing initial capacity in process elements of type $k$.

*Fixed Cost Constraints:* The third set of constraints requires that the fixed cost associated with a given process element be incurred if a new unit of that process element is required:

$$C_k p_k - c_k \geq 0, \quad k = 1, \ldots, K, \qquad (4.18)$$

where $C_k$ = an upper bound on $c_k$, needed to specify the fixed charge cost function.

*Zero-One Constraints:* Finally, the fourth set of constraints requires that the variables associated with the fixed costs be either zero or one.

$$p_k = 0 \quad \text{or} \quad 1.0, \quad k = 1, \ldots, K. \qquad (4.19)$$

If there is a technologically determined upper bound to the scale of a single process element of a given type, demand may be such that operation of more than one element is optimal.[43] The variable $p_k$ must then be permitted to assume integer values greater than 1.0. One can easily compute the maximum total capacity that might be required for any type of process element from the exogenous demands and the assumption that all demands are met by production using processes that require the maximum unit input of capacity in that type of process element. The appropriate change in the model's statement of the relevant feasible range for the associated $p_k$ variable can be made on the basis of this calculation.

The three way classification of production cost is a central feature of the

---

43. Recall that the technologically determined upper bound may be given by the scale at which average capacity cost is a minimum.

model. The costs of endogenous intermediate inputs are endogenously determined and are charged through the material balance constraints. Processing costs are also endogenously determined and are charged through the capacity balance constraints. These include at least an annualized capital charge reflecting the investment cost of constructing *new* capacity.[44] Labor costs may be included in the processing cost coefficients $F_k$ and $V_k$ or may appear in the exogenous cost parameters directly associated with individual production processes $E_j$. The former course can be followed in a static model to specify economies of scale in labor use.[45] (This specification would not be correct in a dynamic model if at least some labor costs are a function of process element operating rates rather than capacity, for temporary excess capacity may be optimal in a dynamic model.) The third cost element, $E_j$, incorporates at least the cost of exogenous intermediate inputs, including those which are assumed a priori to be imported as well as those assumed to be domestically produced even though they are exogenous to the model. In a dynamic model, economies of scale in labor costs (as well as material inputs) related to process element operating rates may be specified through a fixed charge cost function for the exogenous cost elements $E_j$, which then include these labor costs.[46]

The exogenous demand parameters $D_i$ state demand requirements from activities exogenous to the model. Some of this demand may be for intermediate inputs used in production activities that are exogenous to the model. Other exogenous demands include final demands for investment and consumption use. Exogenous demand for some endogenous products may be zero, if these products are intermediate inputs required only for endogenous production activities. Material balance constraints for these products are required, nonetheless, to reflect the interdependence between their production and that of other, related products.[47]

44. In a target year model such as this, the capital charge is usually determined by applying a capital recovery factor to the investment cost figure. The same basic method (i.e., the conversion of capital costs to an equivalent uniform payment series with payments being charged only within the model's horizon) is used in dynamic models to avoid the problems associated with a finite horizon. See Chapter III for a more complete discussion of the terminal problem.

45. But see the following footnote.

46. Separate parameterization of capacity (i.e., capital) and labor costs may also be necessary in a static model if there are differences in the proportions between capacity and labor inputs used to process different products that may share capacity in the same process element.

47. However, if the model contains only a single production activity for each such product, these products may be "netted out" by using their material balance constraints to solve for their production levels as functions of the remaining activities. In the derived reduced form, the capacity utilization coefficients for the remaining activities then include the total indirect capacity requirements needed to produce the omitted intermediate inputs used by these activities. The reduction thereby achieved in the number of constraints can be substantial, particularly in a spatial model. The model constructed by Kendrick [1967b], for

It should be obvious that interdependence enters the model through the material and capacity balance constraints, and that the model's use to explore or capture the effects of interdependence is limited to that among endogenous products and processes. Capacity sharing gives rise to a new type of interdependence, since break-even points for individual process elements can no longer be computed with respect to single production activities.

Assume, for example, that there are no endogenous intermediate inputs, that there is no choice of technique, that each process produces a single output, that each process requires only a single process element, but that there is capacity sharing. By the second and third assumptions, products and processes may be ordered so that the same index, $j$, applies to both. The break-even condition in a simple make-buy model for operating a single process element $k$ becomes:

$$F_k + \sum_{j \in J_k} (V_k B_{kj} + E_j) D_j \leq \sum_{j \in J_k} W_j D_j, \qquad (4.20)$$

where $J_k$ denotes the set of production processes (products) that may share capacity in the $k$th capacity element. This break-even condition may be satisfied for all of the products in $J_k$ taken together, even though the demand for each single product within the set is below the break-even point for production without sharing. The calculation of break-even boundaries becomes far more complicated (if not impossible) where endogenous intermediate inputs are present, choice among techniques is specified, and individual production processes require capacity in several process elements such that a number of production processes may jointly share some process elements but not others.[48] Break-even analysis is then not a feasible method of solution, and MIP must be used.

Our statement of the model omits two types of activities frequently present in multiprocess models. The first are endogenous export activities, which have a single $-1.0$ coefficient in the appropriate material balance constraint and minus the export price in the objective function.[49] Export revenues thus reduce total system costs. Each export activity must be bounded from above or else the marginal revenue from exporting a given product must decline with the volume exported. Otherwise, unless there is a constraint limiting the system's total volume of production or capacity, the optimal solution will be to export an infinite amount of at least one commodity for which marginal

---

example, omits all material balance constraints except those pertaining to the delivery of final products to each market destination; this reduced form is achieved by "netting out" *all* of the production activities in the original, complete statement of the model.

48. The shortcomings of break-even analysis in these cases are discussed in Rhee and Westphal [1973b].

49. Export demand may be exogenous if it is a priori known that the product will be produced and exported and the central question concerns the process or location of production.

production cost is less than unit export revenue.[50] The other additional activities represent by-product sales. By-products are said to occur when a single production process has more than one output.[51] Since by-products are produced in fixed proportions, it may be optimal to produce in excess of the demand for individual by-products. This is why the material balances must be stated as inequality constraints.[52] To describe more clearly the interface between endogenous and exogenous activity, by-product demands are sometimes specified endogenously in a similar fashion to export demands. For by-products that have a disposal *cost*, the objective function coefficient of the by-product "sales" activity is positive and the corresponding slack or free disposal activity is omitted.

Sensitivity analysis is generally performed with respect to the foreign exchange rate, the interest rate, the wage rates of various grades of labor, and the prices of key exogenous intermediate inputs, as well as the exogenous demand parameters. Sensitivity analysis with respect to cost parameters requires knowledge of the breakdown of exogenous production costs into (i) those denominated in foreign exchange (expressed in their domestic currency equivalent), (ii) capital costs, (iii) labor costs by skill class, and (iv) costs associated with major exogenous intermediate inputs. Whether a given exogenous intermediate input is to be imported or produced locally must be determined outside the model by a partitioning of exogenous inputs into those that are respectively imported and domestically supplied.[53]

While ideally necessary, it is difficult to maintain consistency among forecasts of the various exogenous cost elements. A change in the assumed exchange rate, interest rate, or wage rates logically implies a revision in the domestic production cost forecasts for exogenous inputs. At an even lower level, to the extent that the cost of a given exogenous intermediate or capital input is jointly determined with the costs of other exogenous inputs, an independent change in its assumed supply price implies the need for similar revisions. In addition to affecting directly the forecasted supply prices of imported inputs, a change in the assumed exchange rate implies a possible

---

50. The optimal solution will be characterized by extreme specialization if unbounded, constant marginal revenue export activities are specified along with a constraint on total activity.

51. This is to be distinguished from capacity sharing, where several production processes share a single process element and there are not predetermined, fixed proportions among the joint products.

52. The capacity balance constraints need be inequalities only where *existing* process element capacity may not be fully utilized in the optimal solution.

53. In addition, a model covering a particular sector will generally not include production processes for all products falling under that sector. A preliminary cost-benefit or break-even analysis will have determined that the growth of demand for some of these products would more than likely be met by imports over the medium-term future. The use of "preselection" to limit the model's focus to those processes where greater information is required is discussed in Vietorisz [1963].

revision in the partitioning of exogenous inputs as between those that are, respectively, imported and produced domestically.[54] A change in any other exogenous price parameter also indirectly implies the same possibility. Unless supplemented by forecasting outside the model, therefore, standard sensitivity analysis picks up only the direct effects of exogenous price parameter changes and not the indirect effects due to induced changes in the supply costs of exogenous inputs. These indirect effects may be (and generally are) neglected where expected to be small.

We now sketch the additions required to make the model dynamic. The objective function in the multiperiod model is total discounted cost over the horizon period. Each activity appearing in the static model must be subscripted by time period, for the same set of activities appears in each period in the dynamic model. The cost elements appearing for each period are the same as those present in the static model, the only difference being that the cost associated with capacity constructed in a given period is equal to the (discounted) sum of the annual rentals that must be paid over the remaining periods within the horizon. The interval between periods is generally fixed to be at least as great as the realistic gestation period for new capacity.[55] However, gestation lags appear explicitly only if both the production and the use of capital goods are endogenous. A set of material balance constraints is required for each period; thus, the time path of exogenous demand must be forecasted over the model's horizon. A set of capacity balance constraints is also required for each period; available capacity is equal to that remaining from initial capacity in the base period plus that endogenously constructed in the previous periods. Finally, a dynamic model requires sets of fixed cost and zero-one constraints for the new capacity that may be constructed in each period.

There is a very significant difference between the properties of the static and dynamic models. Newly constructed capacity will be fully utilized in the static model, but in the dynamic model it will generally be optimal to over-invest in anticipation of demand growth within the model's horizon.[56]

---

54. The exchange rate assumed to obtain the partitioning must, of course, equal that used to estimate the production cost of exogenous, domestically supplied inputs.

55. It is not meant to suggest that this must be the case. The choice of period length, interval between periods, and time horizon are critical decisions both with respect to relevance and computational feasibility. Space limitations preclude a discussion of these issues here; the reader is referred to the relevant parts of Chapter III and to Hopkins [1969]. See also the following footnote.

56. The problems arising from the use of a finite horizon are more severe in the case of increasing returns than under constant or decreasing returns. Because a fixed horizon model neglects demand growth beyond the terminal period, the prescribed scales for plants built in the later periods are likely to be too small. A relatively long horizon is needed to insure that omission of post-terminal demand growth does not unduly affect prescriptions for the scale of plants constructed early in the plan period. With respect to scale decisions then, the validity of the model's prescriptions is greatest for the initial periods.

This difference makes the dynamic the far more attractive model.

A multiregional model again has the same basic structure, but activities, capacity, and exogenous demands must be subscripted by region and transport activities, for interregional trade flows must be added to the model. A new element, transportation cost, enters the objective function. A set of material balance constraints is required for each region; total supply includes local production plus imports from other producing regions and the rest of the world. Exports to other demanding regions must be added to endogenous demand. Exogenous demand estimates are required for each demanding region. Initial capacity estimates are needed for each producing region, since a set of capacity balance constraints is now required for each producing region. Finally, sets of fixed cost and zero-one constraints must be distinguished for each producing region. A very significant difference again exists between the properties of the single- and multi-region models. The implicit exogenous demand schedule for a given product produced in a particular region is piecewise linear and downward sloping in the latter case, since unit transportation costs are an increasing function of distance.[57]

The data required to implement a multiprocess model include exogenous demand forecasts, estimates of existing capacity, exogenous cost parameters, and technical intermediate and capacity input-output coefficients. The latter are generally engineering estimates stated in physical terms; thus, the units employed to measure supply, demand, and capacity are physical rather than monetary. These data requirements may appear excessively burdensome; however, compendia of engineering estimates of input coefficients and capacity cost functions are available for some industries and are in preparation for others.[58] These rarely will yield all the data that are required, but they should often provide a great deal of relevant information.

---

57. This statement implicitly assumes that production cost functions are identical in all producing regions. However, the implicit demand schedules will be downward sloping even if they are not; the only difference, then, is that the rank order of destinations by net sales price will not coincide with the rank order of destinations by unit transport cost from the producing region.

58. See Vietorisz [1968a] for a general bibliography. Manne [1967b] and Isard et al. [1959] provide technical norms for petroleum and petrochemicals production. The Special Topics Division of the World Bank's Development Research Center has compiled up-to-date technical norms for a number of industries, including fertilizers, steel, pulp and paper, and cement. One should also consult reports on previously constructed multiprocess models and the engineering and trade press for the particular industries being studied. As a general rule, there are more readily available and useable data for the process industries, like cement, metal refining, and chemicals, which produce a continuous and undifferentiated output stream, than there are for those industries which produce products in individual units. An example of the latter type of industry is the mechanical engineering sector. The Special Topics Division of the World Bank's Development Research Center is also active in obtaining technical norms for processes within this sector. However, the wholesale transfer of technical

### 4.3 Properties of Mixed Integer Programming

Mixed integer programming is less widely known than is linear programming and so we devote this section to a brief discussion of MIP. In matrix notation, the MIP multiprocess model given above may be stated as follows:

$$\text{Minimize} \quad Fp + Vc + Es + Wm \tag{4.21}$$

Subject to:

$$As + Im \geq D \tag{4.22}$$

$$Ic - Bs \geq -c^0 \tag{4.23}$$

$$Cp - Ic \geq 0 \tag{4.24}$$

$$p_k = 0 \quad \text{or} \quad 1.0, \quad k = 1, \ldots, K: \tag{4.25}$$

where lower case letters denote vectors of unknown activity levels, upper case letters denote vectors or matrices of exogenous parameters,[59] $c^0$ is a vector of initial capacities, and $I$ is the identity matrix.

If each zero-one variable is assigned a value $p_k^*$ equal to either zero or one, then the vector of zero-one variables may be moved to the right hand side of the problem. This yields the following linear programming (LP) problem:

$$\text{Minimize} \quad Vc + Es + Wm + Fp^*, \tag{4.26}$$

Subject to:

$$As + Im \geq D, \tag{4.27}$$

$$Ic - Bs \geq -c^0, \tag{4.28}$$

$$-Ic \geq -Cp^*. \tag{4.29}$$

The elements on the right of the above expressions (including $Fp^*$) are exogenous.

One way to solve the MIP problem for the global optimum is to solve $2^K$ LP problems, one LP problem being associated with each possible combination of values for the zero-one variables. The optimal solution to the MIP problem is that associated with the combination of zero-one values yielding the lowest LP objective function value. This solution method is called complete enumeration; it is expensive, for it requires the solution of many LP problems. A more efficient procedure is obviously desirable. Research into MIP algorithms is widely and actively being conducted; see Balinski [1965, 1967], and Geoffrion and Marsten [1972] for recent surveys.

Most of the suggested algorithms proceed by using shadow price information to estimate lower bounds on the objective function value that would be

---

norms estimated for one region or country to other locales is subject to much greater difficulty in the case of nonprocess industries.

59. Note that $C$ is a diagonal matrix.

realized for various zero-one combinations; if a solution satisfying the zero-one constraints is found that has an objective function value less than that of every combination that has been explicitly enumerated *and* less than lower bound on the objective function value for every combination not explicitly enumerated, then it is known to be the optimal solution. The savings in such "branch and bound" algorithms result from not having to solve the LP problems associated with those zero-one combinations having lower bounds on their objective function values that exceed the objective function value for the best known solution satisfying the zero-one constraints.[60]

Even these algorithms are expensive to employ. Thus, a solution strategy that is often the most satisfactory is, first, to use a standard MIP algorithm to obtain upper and lower bounds to within a predetermined degree of approximation of the globally optimal objective function value. This is followed by an exploration, through partial enumeration, of alternative investment patterns (or construction phasings) determined by the analyst and generated by exogenously setting the zero-one variables.[61] Each solution so obtained is a known local optimum. The best of these solutions, however, is not necessarily the globally optimal solution. But, given the uncertainty regarding parameter estimates, the exclusion of various important considerations from the model, and the relative insensitivity of the objective function value to minor deviations from the globally optimal investment pattern, too much importance should not be attached to the global optimum. The knowledge gained about the system being modeled through comparing alternative investment patterns is far more important than the single globally optimal solution.

The shadow prices obtained from the multi-process MIP model are marginal costs (or revenues) in the same sense as shadow prices from a pure LP model. Consider, for example, the shadow prices associated with the material balance constraints. Let $q_i$ denote the shadow price of the $i$th product. For expositional ease only, assume that each production process produces a single output, there is no choice of technique, there is no initial capacity, and the process element capacity bounds $C_k$ are not binding; then the shadow price of the $i_1$th product, if it is produced, may be shown to be given by

$$q_{i_1} = [E_{i_1} + \sum_{i \neq i_1} A_{ii_1} q_i + \sum_{k=1}^{K} B_{ki_1} V_k]/A_{i_1 i_1}. \qquad (4.30)$$

The expression on the right is the marginal cost of producing the $i_1$th product: the first term is the exogenous input cost, the second is the total endogenous

---

60. Seemingly effective algorithms of this type are discussed in Efroymson and Ray [1966] and Davis and Ray [1969]. For economic interpretations of two different algorithms, see Manne [1973c] and Westphal [1971], Chapter 3.

61. A combination of values for the zero-one variables implies a particular plan of capacity construction, since there is a zero-one variable associated with each capacity element. In a dynamic model, the phasing of capacity construction is also implied.

intermediate input cost, and the third is the marginal cost of capacity in process elements. If the $i_1$th product is not optimally produced, then it is seen easily that its shadow price is its unit import cost.

Shadow prices from an MIP model do not have all of the properties of LP shadow prices, however.[62] The minimum value of system total cost will *exceed* the maximum value of total net sales revenue evaluated at shadow prices by the total shadow cost of the zero-one activities that are operated at the unit level in the optimal solution.[63] In addition, the shadow prices depend on the

---

62. A simple graphical illustration is given in subsection 4.4 below.

63. This is because sales revenues are valued at marginal cost prices rather than average cost prices in the dual. The primal problem may be restated as follows:

$$\text{Minimize} \quad \text{minimum} \quad Fp + Vc + Es + Wm,$$

$$\text{Subject to} \quad p^* \quad p, c, s, m$$
$$As + Im \geq D$$
$$Ic - Bs \quad \geq -c^0$$
$$Cp - Ic \quad \geq 0$$
$$Ip \quad = i^*$$

where we have separated the problem into its two logically separable components: (i) selection of a set of values for the zero-one variables (optimization over $p^*$), and (ii) solution of the LP problem associated with the selected combination of zero-one values (optimization over $p, c, s, m$). The MIP dual problem is

$$\text{Minimize} \quad \text{maximum} \quad D'q - c^{0\prime}r + p^{*\prime}v,$$

$$\text{Subject to} \quad p^* \quad q, r, u, v$$
$$Iv + C'u \leq F'$$
$$Ir \quad - Iu \leq V'$$
$$A'q - B'r \quad \leq E'$$
$$Iq \quad \leq W',$$

where "$'$" denotes the matrix transpose and $q$, $r$, $u$, and $v$ are respectively the vectors of shadow prices associated with the constraints in the primal. (Note that $v_k$ may be positive or negative since it is associated with an equality constraint; $q$, $r$, and $u$ must be non-negative.)

Let "$-$" over a variable denote the globally optimal solution value. The minimum value of system total cost is then $F\bar{p} + V\bar{c} + E\bar{s} + W\bar{m}$; total net sales revenue as it would appear in a strict LP cost minimization model is $D'\bar{q} - c^{0\prime}\bar{r}$. The difference between these values is $\bar{p}^{*\prime}\bar{v}$, for

$$F\bar{p} + V\bar{c} + E\bar{s} + W\bar{m} = D'\bar{q} - c^{0\prime}\bar{r} + \bar{p}^{*\prime}\bar{v}$$

by the duality properties of linear programming. If the fixed cost constraints are not binding, then $\bar{v}_k = F_k$ for $k$, such that $\bar{p}_k^* = 1.0$, and the difference between system cost and net revenue is the cost of the zero-one activities operated at the unit level. However, if the fixed cost constraint is binding for some $k$ such that $\bar{p}_k^* = 1.0$, then $\bar{v}_k < F_k$, and the minimum value of total system cost exceeds the maximum value of total net sales revenue by something *less* than the actual cost of the zero-one activities undertaken (i.e., a positive rental is associated with process element upper bounds that are binding).

An additional result needs to be made explicit. The MIP dual defined above yields the same values for the shadow price vectors $q$, $r$, and $u$ as does the dual to the LP given by equations (4.26) through (4.29) that is associated with the optimal set of integer values. Westphal [1971], Chapter 3, discusses these relationships in detail for an analogous maximization problem. (Westphal's assertion there that the nonconvex dual associates the same optimal shadow prices with a given pattern of investment as does the dual to the LP for the same pattern is correct; however, the proof is in error.)

pattern of investment followed. Shadow prices at the optimum thus *cannot* be used to yield necessary conditions for determining whether a new continuous activity, not present in the original statement of the model, would be in the optimal solution if introduced into the model. Even if the activity could not be profitably introduced into the previous optimal solution, its introduction into a previously suboptimal solution associated with a different pattern of investment might lead to a lower value for the objective function than that originally obtained. Neither can shadow prices be used to yield necessary conditions that are generally valid for the inclusion or exclusion of integer variables (at level 1.0) in the optimal solution. The usefulness of the marginal cost (or revenue) property of MIP shadow prices is limited therefore. Nonetheless, certain investment patterns can generally be excluded legitimately on the basis of marginal cost calculations. Pre-analysis, using marginal costs, can often be accomplished by hand and yields important insights.[64]

MIP applied to the multiprocess model has an interesting economic interpretation. General equilibrium analysis teaches that a two-step procedure is required to evaluate investment projects having increasing returns to scale:[65] first, the plant's scale must be such that the demand for its output, when priced at marginal cost, is just satisfied; second, the "total surplus" afforded purchasers of the output by virtue of their buying at a price equal to marginal cost must be compared with the "project loss" equal to total production cost at that scale less total sales receipts from sales at marginal cost.[66] Let the term "net surplus" denote total surplus less project loss. A plant of the scale so determined should be established only if net surplus is nonnegative; otherwise, no plant should be built. This is illustrated in Figure 5, where we temporarily assume that imports are not possible. Under the (extreme) circumstances pictured, there is no quantity for which demand at a uniform supply price will yield total revenues equal to or in excess of total costs; even with average cost pricing, the plant would operate at a loss. Nonetheless, the plant's establishment at the scale $J$ is profitable to the economy as a whole, since the total surplus, measured by $AGH$, exceeds the project loss $DFHG$ by the difference between the triangular areas $ADE$ and $EFH$; this difference is the net surplus and is given by the shaded area $AKLD$.[67]

Evaluation becomes somewhat more complex when it is possible to substitute among alternative sources of supply. Consider the case when imports

64. See Meeraus and Stoutjesdijk [1973], Rhee and Westphal [1973a & b], and Westphal [1971].

65. See Hotelling [1938] and Oort [1958].

66. The project's total surplus is the sum of the producers' surpluses on purchases of the output as investment and/or current inputs to production elsewhere and the consumers' surpluses on purchases of the output as consumption goods. In a dynamic setting, the total surplus and project loss must be computed for each point in time and then summed at the assumed discount rate to yield present values.

67. We are here making the conventional assumptions of this type of analysis.

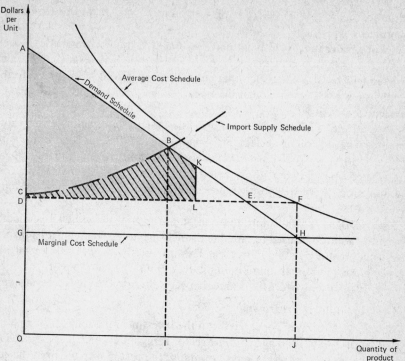

Figure 5. The Net Surplus Criterion

constitute an additional supply source. The optimal supply under imports is
$I$.[68] It might appear that the product should therefore be imported since
average production cost exceeds unit import price at this quantity. But this is
incorrect, because domestic production would entail an expansion of the
amount supplied, and the evaluation must be based on a comparison of the
sum of the consumers' and producers' surpluses and losses under the two
alternatives.[69] Relative to having no supply of the commodity whatsoever,
were the commodity produced in amount $J$, the additional welfare is still
measured by the area $AKLD$; this exceeds the area $ABC$, which measures the
gain were the commodity imported in amount $I$. The net surplus is measured

---

68. The import supply curve shows that the unit cost in domestic currency increases as
more is supplied; this follows from assuming that activity in the rest of the economy is
adjusted to the given level of imports so that equilibrium is maintained at each point on the
curve. In this case, the supply curve for imports may rise even if the world market price of
the commodity remains constant, for the equilibrium exchange rate may increase as adjustments are made in the rest of the economy.

69. This example, therefore, further illustrates the errors that result from the neglect of
interdependence in break-even analysis, which assumes that the quantity to be supplied is
independent of the supply price.

by the hatched area *CBKLD*. (The project's total surplus in this case is *CBHG*; its project loss remains the same.)

Now consider the globally optimal solution to a multiprocess MIP model. Given the marginal cost property of MIP shadow prices, any plant constructed will be of a scale such that production meets all the demand forthcoming at a price equal to marginal cost.[70] The "net surplus" of a plant's construction at a particular point in time is given by the difference between the overall globally optimal solution value and the optimal solution value obtained when the opposite decision is made regarding the plant's construction in that period. So defined, net surplus must be nonnegative if a plant is to be constructed optimally in a given period, and it is negative otherwise. In a cost minimization problem, positive net surplus implies a reduction in total system cost.

Thus, MIP here is no more than an application of well known economic principles and can be used to estimate the net surplus associated with a plant's construction at a given point in time. This provides only little help in solving for the globally optimal solution, but it does give a clear interpretation for the difference in objective function values between alternative investment patterns.

### 4.4 Mixed Integer Programming in Economy-Wide Models

So far, we have been concerned with the investment planning problem as it would appear to a "manager" of the sector being modelled. He is assumed to buy resources at fixed prices and to minimize the cost of meeting fixed outside demands. The investment planning problem appears in a somewhat different form to the economy-wide planner who is trying to maximize welfare under given resource constraints. He cannot assume fixed resource prices and, thus, cannot work within a construct that minimizes cost.

We may illustrate the difference between these two, dual, perspectives with respect to the choice of technique problem. Consider first the problem as it would appear to the economy-wide planner. We will work with a simple model in which there is a choice between two techniques, $x_1$ and $x_2$, each with increasing returns. Labor and capital are the only inputs required in each technique, and there are economies of scale in the use of both inputs. A fixed endowment of capital and labor is available; the problem is to choose the technique or combination of techniques, and their associated production levels, that maximize output:

$$\text{Maximize} \quad x_1 + x_2, \tag{4.31}$$

subject to:

Labor constraint: $\qquad \bar{N}_1 y_1 + N_1 x_1 + \bar{N}_2 y_2 + N_2 x_2 \leq N,$ (4.32)

Capital constraint: $\qquad \bar{K}_1 y_1 + K_1 x_1 + \bar{K}_2 y_2 + K_2 x_2 \leq K,$ (4.33)

---

70. This statement loses some of its validity to the extent that exogenous demand is (mistakenly) assumed to be price inelastic. Nonetheless, endogenously generated intermediate demands *are* price elastic within the model.

Fixed charge constraint: $X_i y_i - x_i \geq 0, \quad i = 1, 2,$ (4.34)

Zero-one constraint: $y_i = 0 \quad \text{or} \quad 1.0, \quad i = 1, 2.$ (4.35)

The variable $x_i$ is the level of production using the $i$th technique, $y_i$ is the associated zero-one variable, and $X_i$ is the parameter linking the zero-one and continuous variables. The parameters $N$ and $K$ denote the amounts of labor and capital, respectively, available to produce the product in question. (In reality, the economy-wide planner would embed this choice in an economy-wide model that would not distinguish among factor allocations to particular sectors; we pose the problem in this somewhat fictitious way to simplify the exposition.)

The isoquant for $x_1 + x_2 = D$ is graphed in Figure 6; it is the piece-wise linear "curve" labeled *ABCDEF*. The process rays emanate not from the origin but from points given by the fixed charge input requirements. In order to move from a point on a process ray to a point that combines production by both activities, it is necessary to incur the fixed charge input requirements associated with the other production activity. For example, to substitute production via the second technique for production by the first, starting at point *B*, it is first necessary to incur the second technique's fixed input requirements and move to point *J*. Points *J* and *H* are not efficient. However, the segment *CD* between these points is efficient. One clear implication of the nonconvexity of production isoquants under economies of scale is that the aggregation problem is much more severe than it would be in a constant or decreasing returns world. As Figure 6 illustrates, simple weighted averages of input requirements for individual techniques are not feasible where there are increasing returns.[71]

The choice of technique problem from the sector planner's perspective is to

$$\text{Minimize} \quad \bar{C}_1 y_1 + C_1 x_1 + \bar{C}_2 y_2 + C_2 x_2 \tag{4.36}$$

subject to:

$$\text{Material balance constraint:} \quad x_1 + x_2 = D, \tag{4.37}$$

and the fixed charge constraints (4.34) and zero-one constraints (4.35), where $D$ is the fixed demand that must be met and $\bar{C}_i = w\bar{N}_i + r\bar{K}_i$ and $C_i = wN_i + rK_i$, $w$ and $r$ being the fixed wage and capital rental rates, respectively.

Now suppose that the optimal allocation from the economy-wide perspective involves production at point *P* along the segment *CD*. The ratio of the shadow rental to the shadow wage would then be given by the slope of the segment *CD*. *C'D'* is an isocost line having the same slope; thus, the sector planner's optimal choice of technique, when confronted with these shadow prices, is to specialize using technique 2. This simple example illustrates the fact that dual perspectives of the same planning problem need not yield the same choice

71. Specifically, a weighted average of *B* and *E* does not yield a feasible resource input allocation to achieve *D* units of output.

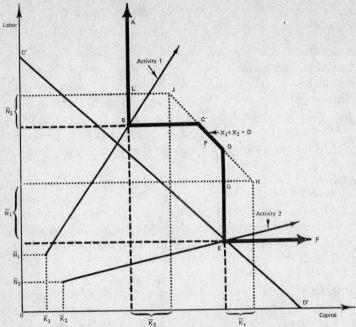

Figure 6.  Isoquant Under Increasing Returns

where increasing returns are involved.[72] Cost minimization leads to specialization under increasing returns. It follows that decentralized planning through communication of prices from the center will not and cannot reveal large portions (the segment $BCDE$ in our example) of a sector's feasible production set.[73]

Given that the economy-wide perspective yields the truly optimal allocation and choice of technique, these results suggest that the optimal investment patterns obtained from multiprocess sector planning models may in fact be suboptimal in the economy-wide context and that an economy-wide planning model is required to program investments if there are economies of scale in *any* activities within the economy. This is no doubt theoretically correct, but an adequate description of technology in the presence of increasing returns is far too disaggregated for it to be embedded, without aggregation, in an economy-wide model. Sufficient disaggregation *is* possible in a multiprocess sector model, however. Thus, the choice between perspectives is not clearcut, for it also involves the issue of aggregation. And we do not yet know how to aggregate over activities having economies of scale in order to achieve the

72. Except for the problem of degeneracy, the dual perspectives do lead to the same solution if technology is linear—a well-known theorem in linear programming.

73. Observe that points other than $B$ and $E$ will *not* be cost minimizing for *any* combination of positive prices for capital and labor. An excellent discussion of the problems of decentralized planning under economies of scale is given by Vietorisz [1968b].

appropriate specification of an economy-wide model at a higher level of aggregation. At least for the present, the planner must be content with multi-process models of the form described in section 4.2. The aggregation problem under increasing returns is clearly an area where further research is needed.

## 5. EVALUATION

What are we to conclude about the practical relevance and utility of planning models with increasing returns? The first point is that models like those discussed here have been, and increasingly are being, applied to practical planning. The single process models, both dynamic and spatial, applied by Manne [1967a] to several industries in India are relatively simple to apply and, judging from the results of that application, yield policy prescriptions that may result in substantial cost savings over the policies arrived at through conventional methods. Given estimates of the relevant scale elasticities, the data requirements of a single process model are no more severe than those of a carefully conducted project appraisal. Manne's book provides a number of tables and simple formulas that can be used to obtain solutions without the aid of computers. All of this constitutes a very strong argument for applying single process models where there are economies of scale.

Dynamic, multiregional, multiprocess increasing returns planning models have also been employed in a number of instances. Recent, well-documented applications include planning investments in the Brazilian steel industry (Kendrick [1967b]), the East African fertilizer industry (Stoutjesdijk et al. [1973]), a major part of the Indian electricity generating sector (Gately [1971]), and the Mexican energy sector (de la Garza and Manne [1973]).[74]

Several additional, interesting features of these models will be summarized here. Known opportunities for expanding the output of existing plants through adding modular components of capacity can be evaluated within the model. Kendrick, for example, analyzes the gains from adding roughing mills and a tinning line to existing steel mills in order to increase their capacity for producing semifinished output. The East African fertilizer model is dis-aggregated below the plant level to permit the evaluation of alternative construction phasings for each individual plant through the successive addition of individual process elements.

Indivisible projects of fixed scale and design can also be specified by the use of zero-one variables not directly coupled to continuous capacity variables. Gately's model, for example, evaluates different scales and designs for hydro-electric generating dams at particular locations. In this case, it is necessary to add mutual exclusivity constraints stating that no more than a single dam may be constructed at a given location. An interesting application of the model is to multinational planning among several countries. Here, the model is used to

---

74. There have also been numerous industrial applications, particularly in England, the United States, and the USSR.

explore possible regional cooperation schemes involving the location of plants in several countries and trade in the products produced. While political considerations are likely to have a strong influence on the eventual location of plants, the model can be of great value in indicating potential gains from regional cooperation. Game theory results involving the concept of the "core" have been used to identify these gains and indicate their possible distribution among participating countries.[75]

The data requirements to implement a multiprocess model may appear to be quite severe. However, virtually the same data are required for a careful, process-by-process cost-benefit project *design and evaluation* exercise. Project evaluation exercises that employ less data cannot address the most important questions that can be examined in a multiprocess model. Nor can even the most comprehensive benefit-cost type of project design and evaluation exercise properly take into account interdependence or dynamic and locational choices, which are of the utmost significance in planning investments with increasing returns. Numerous choices are involved in planning investments within a sector: choice between production and imports, choice among techniques (i.e., process elements that accomplish the same processing activity), choice among time phasings of investment at the plant and subplant levels, and choice among plant locations and interregional trade patterns. The possible combinations of choices that might be made often run into the tens and hundreds of thousands. In this light, a multiprocess model is no more than an efficient mechanism to explore these choices and select an optimal or near-optimal combination.[76] However, the recognition of interdependence among activities within a multiprocess model makes it more than merely an efficient vehicle for carrying out standard cost-benefit analysis where the number of possible choices is large.[77]

Computation is the principal difficulty in implementing planning models with economies of scale. In the past, such models have been solved in one of three mathematical modes: dynamic programming, mixed integer programming, and simulation. Dynamic programming appears to be superior for single process models. However, it requires a particularized solution algorithm tailored to the precise specification of the model (or vice versa depending upon one's starting point), and at present it cannot be applied to obtain optimal solutions unless the dimensionality—time horizon and number of regions—

75. See Kendrick [1967a], Gately [1971], Erlenkotter [1972b], Stoutjesdijk et al. [1973], and Mennes [1973].

76. For a clear exposition along these lines, see Wein and Sreedharen [1968].

77. Recognition of interdependence leads to the choice of more efficient allocations. One estimate of the efficiency gains to be realized by using multiprocess analysis rather than project appraisal appears in Stoutjesdijk et al. [1973]. A particular project having an attractive benefit-cost ratio under project appraisal was found to be unattractive in a multiprocess analysis where it was estimated that the increase in discounted total system costs over the horizon would be approximately 2 percent if the project were undertaken.

of the model is limited. With respect to single location models, Manne and Veinott (in Manne [1967a]) provide a general technique for obtaining solutions for any concave capacity cost function and any arbitrary time path of demand when the time horizon is finite. Optimal solutions to the infinite horizon model have so far been obtained only under rather restrictive assumptions.[78]

The solutions obtained via dynamic programming for multiregion, single process models have generally been approximate; that is, global optimality is not assured.[79] Nonetheless, such approximate solution methods have been shown to improve appreciably on the construction phasing policies obtained under more naive methods, and they have been applied to quite large problems; Erlenkotter [1972a], for example, reports solutions to a finite horizon (20 years) model having 21 supplying and 45 demanding locations.

Dynamic programming has not been extensively applied to multiprocess models. In the one example that has been found in the literature, Sreedharen and Wein [1967] determine the optimal installation timing for individual process elements within a single, multi-product plant where demand is stochastic, there is no choice of technique, and the sequence of process element installation (but not its precise timing) is predetermined. The pre-specification of installation sequence is, of course, a rather severe restriction of the model.[80] On the other hand, their model permits separate make-buy choices with respect to each product. It was applied to the design of an integrated iron and steel mill making semifinished products.

The major attraction of mixed integer programming is the flexibility it permits in model specification, for it can be used to model a wide range of technological relationships and trade-offs. This and the availability of general-purpose computer software packages explain its superiority, at least for the present, over dynamic programming for modelling interdependent multiple processes. As with dynamic programming, the chief drawback to MIP is computational expense, which rises rapidly with a model's dimensionality. To obtain globally optimal solutions at reasonable expense, a model must generally have no more than 100 integer variables, and most applications have far fewer than this.[81] As a consequence, there is a definite trade-off among the

---

78. These are (i) any concave capacity cost function and arithmetic demand growth and (ii) the constant scale elasticity capacity cost function and geometric demand growth. In both cases, plant lives are assumed infinite.

79. Erlenkotter [1972b] discusses procedures that yield global optimality for problems of relatively small size. Manne [1967a] gives an excellent discussion of approximate procedures.

80. However, the model can be adapted to determine the optimal sequence and/or choice among techniques by exploring all possible combinations through complete enumeration. See Wein and Sreedharen [1968].

81. As an example: a proven globally optimal solution to the East Africa fertilizer model was never obtained, though *several hours* of computer time (on a CDC 6600) were spent looking for the optimal solution. The full model contains around 100 integer variables.

number of time periods, regions, and processes with increasing returns that may appear in a computationally feasible model. However, two factors make this objection less serious than it might appear. First, as was outlined in subsection 4.3, it is possible, without solving for the global optimum, to use an MIP model to explore the consequences of alternative investment programs; a great deal can be learned thereby which cannot be comprehended through traditional project appraisal techniques. Second, the state of the art is progressing very rapidly and may be expected to continue to do so.[82]

There have been several simulation models applied to investment planning problems.[83] While simulation permits the specification of more exact non-linear functional relationships, mixed integer programming permits explicit solution for the globally optimal solution and provides production cost estimates in the form of the shadow prices associated with the primal solution. With regard to the choice between MIP and simulation models, each type of model has its unique advantages. The most fruitful planning strategy appears to be the use of an MIP model as a screening device to identify the most attractive investment patterns, followed by the use of a more accurately specified nonlinear simulation model to analyze these prospects in greater detail. According to Anderson [1972], the planning of investments in electricity generation has followed this strategy in some countries.

For the present, the principal utility of the *multiprocess* approach appears to be the perspective given by its logic. This perspective yields a format for the assembly of data on related projects which allows simple calculations to increase significantly the knowledge brought to bear in planning interrelated investments. There is not space here to discuss the details of this approach—the reader is referred to Isard et al. [1959], Meeraus and Stoutjesdijk [1973], and Rhee and Westphal [1973a]. These calculations largely involve computing break-even boundaries, checking marginal and average production costs against import cost, and finding decompositions that will reduce a large model into submodels of the most highly interrelated processes. For planning in most developing countries, the computer-assisted complete solution of large-scale models must await further advances in associated computer software.[84]

---

82. It is very important that potential users of MIP communicate with those active in the field to find out the latest advances before proceeding to duplicate work already done. Journals of operations research, mathematical programming, and mathematical economics may be consulted to learn of recent advances, but articles in these journals generally lag two to three years behind current research. Those active in MIP communicate among themselves on an informal, as well as formal, basis.

83. For a survey of applications to planning investments in electricity generation, see Anderson [1972]. A recent specific application is reported in Jacoby [1967].

84. Software includes not only solution algorithms but also matrix generators for structured data processing to set up the MIP model and report generators for structured data processing to yield easily readable solution information.

But we would stress that these advances may be expected within the next few years.

## 6. MULTILEVEL LINKAGES AND POLICY

Multiprocess or sector investment planning models occupy an intermediate position within the overall planning process, coming between economy-wide planning models and detailed, microanalytic project design and evaluation. Sector planning, like project evaluation, takes certain prices and demands as exogenously given. These must be consistent with economy-wide projections. On the other hand, economy-wide quantity and shadow price forecasts must be based on an adequate description of technology at the sectoral level. How are proper linkages among these different planning levels to be achieved?

A number of "well defined," formal decentralized planning procedures have been proposed which rely on the communication of various price and quantity signals between two (economy-wide and project) or more levels.[85] Nearly all of these procedures assume that technology exhibits constant or diminishing returns.[86] Well-defined procedures have never been formally applied in national economic planning, though they have been indirectly applied in an informal, ad hoc manner to design organized information flows between levels.[87] We will outline an informal procedure for linking sector planning to economy-wide and project planning, but it is important to recognize that this or any other informal decentralized planning procedure can do no more than assure a "reasonable" degree of *consistency* among various levels of planning. In particular, we will not deal directly with the problem raised in the discussion of Figure 6.

The purpose of linking the various planning levels is to arrive at a mutually consistent set of quantitative allocations and shadow prices. Thus, the shadow prices of central resources (e.g., foreign exchange, investment funds, labor) and exogenous inputs are not taken as given in a decentralized planning exercise, though they are in any particular solution of a multiprocess model. The flow of information from economy-wide to sector planning would consist of (i) shadow prices for central resources and major exogenous inputs and (ii) aggregate quantity projections (production, consumption, investment, and so forth, broken down by major sectors) to be used, respectively, to estimate exogenous cost and demand parameters in a multiprocess model.[88] The flow

---

85. For the definition of "well defined" and for several examples of such procedures, see Malinvaud [1967]. Geoffrion [1970] surveys some sixty decomposition methods which are analogous to formal decentralized planning procedures.

86. Heal [1969] gives a well-defined decentralized planning procedure under increasing returns to scale. His procedure, however, is not guaranteed to lead to the global optimum.

87. Kornai [1973] discusses the issues involved here.

88. Chapter VIII discusses the use of shadow prices derived from multisector models and rightly suggests a number of reservations regarding their use in project planning.

in the reverse direction would consist of technological parameters aggregated from the solutions of a multiprocess model. Multilevel planning proceeds by iteratively up-dating the technological coefficients in the multisector model based on the technological choices and process element scales found to be optimal in the sector planning model under the latest set of aggregate price and quantity estimates. As a first approximation, average technological coefficients can be used in the multisector model rather than an increasing returns specification. To check the sensitivity of the economy-wide plan to process choices within the sector, several alternative technology vectors can be passed simultaneously from the sector model to the economy-wide model; each vector would correspond to the sector model's solution under a different set of assumptions regarding central resource shadow prices.[89]

The most serious practical difficulty in communicating between the economy-wide and sector levels is the difference in aggregation and data bases. Models at the former level are generally input-output models in which technological coefficients are stated in value terms; models at the latter level are generally specified at a much greater level of disaggregation, using physical units of measurement. These differences between models at the two levels are among the factors precluding the direct use of well-defined decentralized planning procedures.

The procedure outlined above will lead to a reasonably efficient resource allocation if two conditions are satisfied: (i) the choice of processes within the sector does not significantly influence the shadow prices of central resources; and (ii) the exogenous demands stipulated in the sector model are consistent with the product shadow prices obtained in the sector model solution. Essentially, these conditions state that there must not be significant interdependencies between activity endogenous to the sector model and that in the rest of the economy. Project choices should be embedded in a model whose scope is sufficiently broad that significant interdependencies do not cross its boundaries. In some cases, this may even require that project choices be evaluated at the economy-wide level. Westphal [1969] found, for example, that each of two large-scale import substituting projects proposed in Korea, a steel mill and petrochemicals complex, required such a large fraction[90] of available investment resources and had such an enormous impact on the foreign exchange balance that the timing of the implementation of either project would have an identifiable impact on the shadow prices of investment and foreign exchange. Plans for project implementation thus had to be evaluated in an economy-wide model that specified increasing returns in the technology of both projects.

---

89. See Chapters III.3 and IV.6 in Goreux and Manne [1973] for a description of experiments along this line based on LP models at the sectoral level.

90. Together, the construction of these plants would have required 5 percent of the total investment expected over the Second Five Year Plan.

In subsection 4.1, we noted that there are two sides to interdependence. On the price side this affects both the timing and scale of investment decisions, while, on the quantity side, it affects only scale decisions. Quantity interdependencies are easily identified from a detailed knowledge of input-output relationships and can be handled without great difficulty as long as substitution possibilities are limited. Price interdependencies arising out of competition for scarce resources, input-output relationships, and joint production are more difficult to deal with. However, the mere presence of one or more of these elements need not imply *significant* interdependence, the neglect of which would lead to allocations that are far from optimum. Given that it takes time and planning resources to build models that incorporate interdependence, it is obviously desirable to have criteria that would determine the conditions under which there is significant interdependence. Unfortunately, such criteria have not been developed. The present state of the art is such that significant interdependence can only be identified *ex post* by comparing solutions to partial and more comprehensive planning models to determine whether an extension of the planning boundaries affects the choices being modeled.[91]

However, several rules of thumb emerge from the observation that significant interdependence is due to the sensitivity of shadow prices to alternative resource allocation decisions. Significant price interdependencies are highly unlikely in a competitive economy that engages in free international trade (where each commodity's import and export prices lie close to one another), for then relative commodity shadow prices must lie within narrow bounds. Although changes in technology that affect product prices could lead to significant interdependence, it is generally true that significant price interdependencies are far more likely in highly protected, inward-looking economies. Likewise, they are more probable in developing economies which have not yet experienced much structural transformation. Given the degree of protectionist policy (including discrimination against exports) and the level of per capita income, significant interdependencies caused by economies of scale are more likely in small, rather than in large, economies.[92]

These rules of thumb suggest that multiprocess models are most clearly needed to plan activities which cannot be evaluated at present market prices because these prices do not closely approximate present or future opportunity costs. To determine the optimal design, scale, and phasing of an investment project, the analysis should simultaneously consider (i) capacity expansion and production activities for its major inputs whose present market prices do not equal future opportunity costs, and (ii) capacity expansion and production activities for the major users of its output if the shadow price of the output

91. See Manne [1973c], p. 496, and Rhee and Westphal [1973a] for elaborations of this point.
92. See Rothenberg [1960].

depends upon project decisions. Activities of the first type determine the price of the project's operating inputs; the scale of the project in turn determines, at least in part, the intermediate demand for the output of these activities. The relationships between the project and activities of the second type run in the opposite direction.

In addition to these criteria for determining the boundaries of a multi-process planning model, we may state another: the larger a project is, either in relation to the markets for its inputs and output(s) or in relation to its use of available investment resources, the more far-reaching will be the effects of its implementation. At the limit, as in the cases of the steel mill and petro-chemicals complex cited above, the Aswan High Dam in Egypt, and the Tarbella Dam in Pakistan (to cite but a few examples), the economy-wide effects are very significant.[93]

One implication of the foregoing discussion is that the interdependencies associated with a given project will be quite different depending upon the economy in which it is implemented. Given the same level of per capita income, the construction of a steel mill, for example, in a small, protected economy is likely to have more far-reaching effects than the construction of the same steel mill in a large, unprotected economy. The absolute size of the economy (measured, say, by real GNP) may be the most important determinant of a given project's impact on relative shadow prices. For example, there is a big difference between building the first steel mill in Korea, the fourth or fifth in India, or the fiftieth in the United States. Adequate planning of the steel mill may require an economy-wide model in Korea, a sector model in India, and no more than project appraisal in the United States. To summarize: What must be planned at the economy-wide or regional level in some countries may be equally well planned at the sector or enterprise level in other countries; the levels at which similar investment decisions are evaluated certainly should be expected to be quite different under different circumstances.[94]

The flow of information between multiprocess models and detailed project design and evaluation at the micro level is relatively straightforward because both employ the same data base, making aggregation relationships quite straightforward. Multiprocess models omit numerous specific details and thereby provide a mechanism capable of dealing with the combinatorial problem encountered when planning a set of interrelated projects that are defined over time, space, alternative processes, and products. Focusing on a single project obviously precludes the ability to deal with interdependence, but it is necessary to permit attention to the very detailed aspects of project design and operation. This perspective is obviously indispensible, while a

93. Multisector models to explore these effects need not have a large number of zero-one variables. Westphal's [1969] model for Korea includes three time periods and has only six zero-one variables.

94. Bain's [1956] discussion of the conditions of entry has a number of highly relevant insights into this issue.

302

multiprocess model is required only where there are potentially significant interdependencies among a set of projects.

The flow of information from the project level to the sector level would consist of technical information regarding production processes; the flow in the reverse direction is an investment program stating the time phasing and location of particular projects, the techniques (process elements) to be employed, and the scales to be implemented. The information flow generally would not stop with a single iteration. In the first iteration, the model may be used as a screening device to isolate project combinations that appear to be most attractive. Detailed engineering can then be concentrated on these projects. Furthermore, a microanalytic evaluation of the optimal program at each iteration by engineers and sector specialists may reveal that certain factors were omitted from the multiprocess model whose inclusion would change the optimal investment program. Planners often do not become aware of a significant factor until confronted with the implications of its omission.

In this regard, it is important to point out that neither economists nor engineers, working alone, are qualified to exploit the full value of a multiprocess model. The solution to a multiprocess model is optimal only with respect to the alternatives explicitly appearing within it, and economists are insufficiently familiar with technology to specify the relevant choices. Engineers are needed to suggest the formal specification of technology within the model, to identify appropriate technologies and technological parameters, to propose possible investment programs (particularly in the expansion or modernization of existing plants), and to interpret and evaluate the solutions obtained. Economists are needed to implement the linkages between planning levels and to suggest criteria for identifying appropriate production technologies at the project level. There have been few joint efforts at sector planning by economists and engineers; as more take place, we may expect multiprocess models to become increasingly useful.

The major policy implication of significant interdependence is obvious: interdependent activities must be planned simultaneously. We have seen that this is necessary to achieve efficient allocation where there is significant price interdependence. While make-buy and choice of technique decisions need not be made simultaneously if significant price interdependence is absent, quantity interdependence always leads to the need for consistent forecasts of demand, and, therefore, at least, to indicative planning. Suboptimal scale decisions are otherwise likely to be made; and the welfare losses from such decisions are not temporary where there are economies of scale.

The policy tools to achieve a properly coordinated investment program include investment licensing and various industrial incentives policies. Multiprocess models can be used to determine which investment projects (*at what scales*) ought to be licensed and to obtain consistent demand forecasts based

on a given investment program; however, the models built to date do not provide much information relevant to establishing industrial incentives policies that will lead market decisions to the optimal investment program. In fact, the MIP models are poorly specified to investigate or forecast *market behavior*, because they implicitly assume marginal cost pricing and costless financing of the resulting deficits. These assumptions may appear appropriate for government-owned and -operated enterprises, but they neglect the second-best considerations arising because the financing of enterprise deficits may introduce distortions from the first-best optimum elsewhere in the economy. The models also fail to consider the social costs of the possible creation of monopolistic or oligopolistic industries where economies of scale are exploited without regard to the resulting effects on market structure and behavior. Therefore, at least with respect to some environments, there are significant policy issues concerning pricing and market structure which are not adequately dealt with in the models constructed to date.

These criticisms suggest several important directions for research into the design of increasing returns planning models. There is an urgent need for criteria to identify significant interdependencies *ex ante* prior to the specification and solution of a multiprocess model. Research on aggregation under economies of scale is also needed, for it will not be possible to explore thoroughly the implications of economies of scale within economy-wide planning models until such aggregation principles are developed. Empirical information regarding economies of scale, presented in a manner that permits specification within planning models, needs to be extended further. Agglomeration phenomena, closely linked to questions of aggregation, are not sufficiently well understood. This is particularly true with respect to the firm's nondirect overhead costs, both internal and external. Increasing returns to lot size for both capital and labor resulting from fixed setup costs are an important source of declining average costs in many nonprocess industries, but only recently has there been any attempt to incorporate lot size phenomena into multi-process increasing returns planning models—and these attempts are at the very micro level.[95]

Uncertainty has been neglected in most models built to date, but it is clearly an important factor to consider before resources are committed to a large-scale project. Uncertainty exists with regard to future domestic and export demand levels, future competitive import prices and exogenous input prices, technological parameters, and the future development of superior techniques. Only the consequences of demand uncertainty within single process models appear to have been formally investigated. Building on the model discussed in subsection 3.1, Manne [1961] has demonstrated that

---

95. See Vietorisz [1973] and Nam et al. [1973]. Scale economies in labor use within the process industries arise primarily out of indivisibility rather than lot size phenomena.

greater uncertainty (i.e., higher variance) of demand leads to *larger* optimal plant sizes. Garg [1974], working with a simplified MIP model, reached the somewhat different conclusion that the optimal plant size should be such that the probabilities of over- and under-capacity are in inverse proportion to their respective penalties. If the interest costs of carrying excess capacity are sufficiently high, Garg's result thus calls for a smaller plant than were the expected level of demand certain to be achieved. Garg's investigation also suggests that the explicit introduction of uncertainty should lead to the delay of investment where the passage of time leads to continuously improved information.

The introduction of uncertainty into models incorporating choice among techniques and multiple processes would also have pronounced effects upon their prescriptions.[96] To minimize the adverse effects of uncertainty requires that plants be designed to operate flexibly in response to changing circumstances. This has two major implications. First, the realization of economies of scale very often results in a much higher proportion of fixed to total annual production costs.[97] This contradicts a principal requirement of operating flexibility, which is to have a high proportion of variable to total production costs, so that losses from operating below capacity may be reduced. Second, flexibility in output mix (and, where possible, input streams) is desirable where demands (and input prices) cannot be forecast with perfect certainty. Attaining product mix flexibility often requires the sacrifice of some scale economies.

Other factors need to be introduced where very large scale plants are concerned. The decision to build a mammoth plant means that there will be few potential bidders on its construction, for the number of suppliers with the technological know-how and experience required to build large plants is generally quite limited. As a rule, the degree of competition among suppliers to construct a plant declines with the scale of plant to be built.[98] There is also the question of reliability and unscheduled downtime. The larger the scale of an individual plant, the greater is its proportion of total industry capacity. The detrimental effects of an unscheduled shutdown of 20 or 30 percent of an industry's capacity are obviously far more serious than those of a temporary loss of 5 or 10 percent.

---

96. For more on uncertainty, see Chapter VI. For a possible method of incorporating uncertainty, see Kornai [1967], Chapters 12–14; Sengupta [1972] provides a survey of stochastic programming.

97. Under the fixed charge cost function specified in subsection 3.2, the proportion of fixed to total annual production costs declines with scale. However, this will generally not be the case when there is a choice among techniques, each technique being represented by a fixed charge cost function.

98. See, for example, Cilingiroglu's [1969] discussion of market structure in heavy electrical equipment.

Finally, solution algorithms and associated computer software require a great deal of further development. Clearly, we have a lot to learn about economies of scale and how they may be meaningfully specified in readily solvable models at various planning levels. Given the empirically documented prevalence of increasing returns and the importance of coordinated decisions where they appear, further research into planning with economies of scale should have a high payoff.

Chapter XII

# SUBSTITUTION AND NONLINEARITIES IN PLANNING MODELS

JOHN H. DULOY AND PETER B. R. HAZELL

## 1. INTRODUCTION

Typically, linear multisector planning models of the types discussed in this volume offer very limited substitution possibilities in production, factor supply, or final demands. In fact, as shown in section 2, they often assume pure complementarity among inputs and among products, and fixed supplies of primary factors. Such rigid specifications are not likely to be realistic. In econometric studies of aggregate consumption and sectoral or national production functions, for example, it is usual to take the opposite view and assume neoclassically continuous marginal rates of substitution. This is generally a more realistic view of substitution in demand, but, in practice, substitution among inputs in production varies by sectors and even with the individual production process. These processes are probably better described by alternative but discrete ways of mixing inputs. This chapter reviews how such substitution possibilities can be introduced into multisector models without departing from the computational advantages of a linear structure.

Introducing possibilities for substitution in multisector models also leads to a number of desirable model features (in addition to greater realism) which have been mentioned in other chapters. Included among these (with chapter references in parentheses) are:

(i) It helps to avoid artificial bottlenecks in model solutions. For example, a labor constraint may be more binding than necessary if capital/labor substitution is ignored. (Chapters III, VI, and VII);

(ii) It assists exploration of policies for full utilization of key resources. A topical example is full employment in labor surplus economies. Suitable policies are likely to be found only if possibilities of labor substituting for other factors are taken into account. (Chapters V and VII);

(iii) It leads to more plausible dual values, which are less prone to large variations in response to small changes in factor supplies. (Chapters III and VIII);

(iv) It can lead to greater product diversification in the model solutions without addition of artificial constraints. (Chapters III, V, and VI).

There are a number of different possible substitution relationships. Here we will follow Chenery and Raduchel [1971] and distinguish between direct

307

and indirect substitution, but with a slightly narrower focus in interpretation. Direct substitution pertains to flexibilities in the technology set. It may involve transformations of one basic resource into another (for example, upgrading labor skills through education) and the possibility of mixing factors (both intermediate and basic) in different proportions in the production process. Indirect substitution, on the other hand, is based on the trading possibilities of the "market." Thus, foreign trade allows a country to specialize its factor usage in those products for which it has a comparative advantage, implicitly and indirectly expanding its substitution possibilities. Similarly, consumers change their relative purchases in response to price signals, thus further expanding the economy's overall possibilities frontier. Typically, linear economy-wide models have taken marginal consumption shares as fixed and unresponsive to relative prices. However, substitution through foreign trade has been more extensively analyzed and we do not attempt to add much to the discussions of Chapters III and VI.

The general approach to modeling all these substitution possibilities that we adopt here is of process analysis in an optimizing framework. This means, for example, that alternative production possibilities are specified as fixed-proportion technology vectors, and optimization is used to choose the combination of these activities which maximizes production or minimizes costs. This approach contrasts to the more neoclassical specifications discussed in section 6 of Chapter III and may well be more relevant for developing countries (as we hope to demonstrate below).

The substantive part of the Chapter begins in the next section, where we define more precisely the principal substitution problems faced by builders of multisector planning models. Section 3 is devoted to techniques for introducing direct substitution, while indirect substitution is discussed in section 4. In the last section are our general conclusions. Finally, an appendix reviews a precise, low-cost method for approximating some nonlinear functions in a linear model.

## 2. ALTERNATIVE FORMS OF SUBSTITUTION AND MODELING CONSIDERATIONS

With a Leontief production structure, gross output levels in each time period (repeated in a dynamic model) are determined by levels of final demands. Defining gross output as the vector $X$, final demands as $Y$, and the input-output matrix as $A$, we have:

$$X = (I - A)^{-1}Y. \qquad (2.1)$$

Similarly, the demands for primary factors $K^1$ are derived as a linear function of gross output levels as:

$$K = FX, \qquad (2.2)$$

---

1. Factors that could enter the vector $K$ include various types of physical and human capital, unskilled labor, concessionary foreign loans, and so forth.

where $F$ is the matrix of factor demands.[2]

The technology associated with the production of $X$ can be summarized, therefore, by the partitioned matrix

$$\begin{bmatrix} I - A \\ F \end{bmatrix}$$

where the rows of $I - A$ contain requirements for intermediate factors and the rows of $F$ contain requirements for primary factors. Now, if there is only a single column associated with each product (or sector), then the implied production function has isoquants of the form shown in Figure 1(a). The isoquants depict the combinations of factor inputs (intermediate or basic) which lead to fixed levels of output $X_j$, and the form shown implies that, in this case, the inputs are pure complements. That is, there is only one possible way of combining the inputs in the production of $X_j$.

Possibilities for direct substitution in transforming factors into products require the introduction of isoquants of the types shown in Figures 1(b) or 1(c) (for a two-factor system). These illustrate that factors can be combined in variable proportions to produce the same output. The crucial difference between the isoquants in Figures 1(b) and 1(c) is that the former is completely nonlinear or neoclassical, while the latter is of process analysis form, being made up of combinations of fixed-proportions technologies. In fact, there are two possible degrees of substitution implicit in Figure 1(c). On the one hand, discrete packages of factor inputs (depicted by the vertices $X_1$, $X_2$, and $X_3$) might be combined linearly, so that any point on the segmented isoquants can also be attained; on the other, the alternative input packages may be mutually exclusive so that intermediate points between the vertices are not attainable. Choice among these alternative specifications has important computational implications. Smooth, or neoclassical, substitution, as depicted in the isoquants in Figure 1(b), require nonlinear programming techniques to solve. However, the more discrete process analysis approach leads to linear models, which can be solved by conventional linear programming when linear combinations of the alternative input mixes are possible but require mixed integer programming techniques to solve when the alternative input mixes are mutually exclusive. While such computational considerations are obviously important in empirical work, the choice of specification should also be tolerably realistic.

The neoclassical approach can often lead to models with more attractive price structures, and it does permit direct entry of specific formulations for the

---

2. Unless we are dealing with a programming model, there is no guarantee that primary factor demands will be consistent with their supplies. This problem is discussed in some detail in Chapter V.

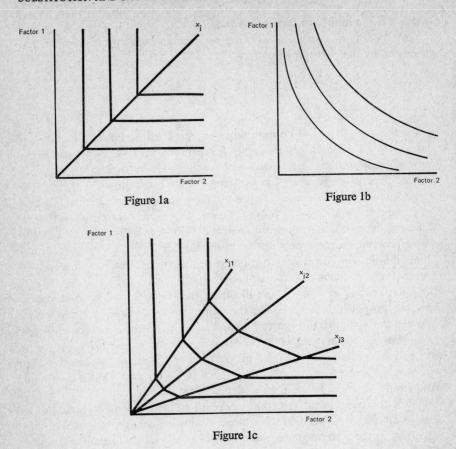

Figure 1a

Figure 1b

Figure 1c

production function.[3] However, except in the case of highly aggregated models (of the kind used in econometric studies), the process analysis specification is probably more descriptive of developing countries. This is clearly the case in the engineering and energy sectors, where there are very limited technological alternatives; but, even in agriculture, cross-country and time-series data indicate a distinctly discrete set of technology and factor mixes. Clearly, these alternative packages of technology and factor mixes may be mutually exclusive at the very micro level, but they can be combined at the sector and economy-wide level. For example, the technology choices in building a single electricity generating plant are mutually exclusive (hydro, coal, oil, or nuclear powered), but when considering the electricity sector in aggregate, alternative types of plants can be combined in varying proportions. Again, while

---

3. See section 6, Chapter III, for a review of these types of models, especially the models by Johansen [1960, 1968] and Chenery and Raduchel [1971].

technology choices at the farm level tend to be mutually exclusive, there are obvious combinations at the agricultural sector level. This is particularly evident in the coexistence of traditional and modern modes of agricultural production in most developing countries. Consequently, we propose to adhere to a process analysis approach in this chapter and, more particularly, to a specification in which the alternative packages of technology and input mixes can be combined in a linear way. However, readers with incurable neoclassic syndromes may view this treatment simply as a linear approximation to a continuous world (that is, the isoquants in Figure 1(c) can be viewed as linear approximations to the isoquants in Figure 1(b)).

Possibilities for direct substitution in transforming one factor into another are illustrated in Figure 2 for the two-product, two-factor case. The production structure defined by equation (2.2) defines a fixed production possibility frontier *abc* in the primary factors *L*. However, if transformations are permitted among the components of *L*, then this effectively blurs the frontier and allows both the shape and location of the frontier to be determined in a variety of ways, providing the sum of resources used remains feasible. One possibility is illustrated in Figure 2 by the dotted frontier *efg*, which results from transforming $\Delta A$ units of factor *A* into additional $\Delta B$ units of factor *B*. Clearly, transformations of this kind are equivalent to substitution in factor mixes in terms of expanding the production possibilities of an economy.

Numerous substitution problems arise in the determination of final invest-

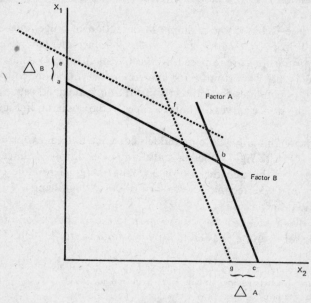

Figure 2

ment demands. However, in the standard multisector formulation, investment demands usually are determined through a strict accelerator relationship which links capacity expansion in each sector to demands for specific investment goods from the capital goods producing sectors. Letting $J(t)$ represent investment demands by sector of origin in year $t$, $B$ the matrix of capital coefficients, and $k$ the diagonal matrix of incremental capital-output ratios,[4] demands for investment are expressed as:

$$J(t) = Bk(X(t + 1) - X(t)).$$ (2.3)

Here, too, direct substitution implies introducing isoquants of the forms depicted in Figures 1(b) or 1(c) to allow alternative usages of investment goods for each sector. We will again adopt the process analysis approach and assume isoquants of the type in Figure 1(c).

Final demands for domestic consumption are typically determined in the objective function in linear programming models[5] but are forecast exogenously in input-output models. However, in both cases the underlying demand structure is usually taken as:

$$\frac{C_i(t)}{N(t)} = \Phi_i \left[ \frac{C_T(t)}{N(t)} \right]^{\varepsilon_i},$$ (2.4)

where $C_T(t)$ denotes total consumption expenditure, $N(t)$ is population size, $\varepsilon_i$ is the Engel elasticity for the $i$th product, and $\Phi_i$ is a constant. Adjustments must be made to insure that the $C_i(t)$ add up to $C_T(t)$ (see Chapter III, section 2.4).

This structure is based on a simple linearization of Engel curves which enforces fixed proportions among commodities in incremental consumption. These fixed proportions are imposed irrespective of changes in relative prices; hence, there is no opportunity for indirect substitution in consumption demand. The possibilities for indirect substitution in demand requires introduction of indifference curves of similar shapes to the isoquants in Figures 1(b) and 1(c).

Finally, although many planning models continue to treat export demands as fixed or subject to rigid upper bounds, a number of models have allowed some substitution through the use of a falling marginal revenue curve for certain exports. These techniques are well discussed in Chapter VI and will not be repeated here.

With this much background, we now turn to the mechanics of introducing more flexible substitution possibilities in linear multisector models. The scope

---

4. When possibilities for substituting other factors for capital are introduced into the model, then the coefficients in $k$ ought to be adjusted to reflect changes in the capital intensity of production.

5. See sections 4 and 5 of Chapter III for discussion of alternative objective functions.

for doing this in input-output models is very limited—partly because the *A* and *B* matrices must be square if the system is to be solved, but, more importantly, because there is no optimization procedure to determine choices among alternative possibilities. Consequently, the most that can be done in empirical work is to update these matrix coefficients over the planning period on the basis of exogenous forecasts. Methods for doing so are reviewed in Chapters III, IV, and V. Indirect substitution in final domestic demand is also difficult to manage, because demand forecasts are exogenous to the model. For these reasons, we shall focus our attention on substitution relations in linear programming models.

To simplify the presentation, we shall concentrate on single-period models, with the understanding that the extensions to dynamic models follow largely on a period by period basis. Special considerations in dynamic models will be mentioned as they arise.

## 3. DIRECT SUBSTITUTION

### 3.1 Substitution in the Technology Set

Introduction of isoquants of the form depicted in Figure 1(c) can be accomplished by adding other vectors for each product (or sector) into the

$$\begin{bmatrix} I - A \\ F \end{bmatrix}$$

matrix. The *A* and *F* matrices will no longer be square, but this is immaterial in a linear programming model. The additional vectors reflect alternative ways of mixing inputs (the vertices in Figure 1(c)); linear combinations (the lines connecting vertices) are also feasible. Thus, introducing additional columns amounts to introducing segmented linear isoquants. Note that, when the technology set is convex (as is usual), no more than two (adjacent) activities will be at positive levels in any efficient solution.

The technique is nothing more than the conventional process analysis widely used in linear programming models of individual firms.[6] Why, then, has this form of specification not been utilized more widely in empirical planning models? One problem is that additional columns add to computing costs. However, with modern computing equipment and the advent of highly efficient revised simplex packages, the increment to costs would be small except in the largest of multiperiod models. A more important problem is in the estimation of the alternative technology vectors. In principle, these can be estimated and specified in the Manne and Markowitz [1963] process analysis framework, which can yield not only the coefficients for primary resource requirements but also those for intermediate inputs. In practice, however, difficulties arise on account of aggregation, because alternative technologies

6. Process analysis, at the firm level, is discussed in Chapter XI.

that allow factor substitution possibilities occur at the level of the individual product, narrowly defined, or even at the level of the industrial or agricultural process.[7] This means that the rows and columns of the technology set must be considerably disaggregated, usually to the extent that the model becomes a conglomerate of highly detailed sector models. Computational problems then require use of some method of decomposition, and aggregation procedures must be established to enable communication between different sector models when defined at different levels of aggregation. We will return to these problems in subsection 3.3.

To simplify these problems, it is appealing to consider restricting substitution possibilities to the primary resource requirements in the $F$ matrix, as Chenery and Raduchel [1971] do in the context of a nonlinear programming model. However, this may not be widely applicable. For example, substitution of capital for labor in agriculture also involves many changes in the requirements per unit of output of other factors such as land and foreign exchange, and such intermediate inputs as petroleum, machinery, construction, and chemicals. To capture these changes brings us back to a process analysis approach.

There are several empirical multisector models incorporating alternative technologies directly into the technology set which illustrate these points. In the framework of a static model of Hungary, Kornai [1969] reflects capital-labor substitution possibilities through alternative mixes of outputs from three vintages of equipment: old, modernized, and new, for each of 491 products. Duloy and Norton [1973c] modified Manne's [1973a] fifteen-sector, six-period model of Mexico (DINAMICO), by replacing the single vector in each period for agriculture with twenty-four vectors reflecting a range of substitution possibilities. These vectors were derived from a self-contained agriculture sector model (CHAC).[8] Lastly, in a four-period, seventy-sector model of the Ivory Coast, Goreux [1973] included alternative vectors for agriculture and education, as well as for investments in those sectors.

## 3.2 Substitution in Factor Supply

Analogous to the way in which factor demands can be varied, supply variations for factors can be introduced. This involves introducing a vector of transformation activities $Z$ which implicitly combine some factors into other factors in much the same way as the production activities $X$ combine factors and some products into other products. Letting the vector $K$ represent the total supplies of each factor (after transformation activities) and $\bar{K}$ the existing fixed stock of each factor, we have the following equality:

$$K = \bar{K} + QZ. \tag{3.1}$$

---

7. On this point see Nam, Rhee, and Westphal [1973] and Bassoco and Rendon [1973], as well as Chapter XI.

8. See Duloy and Norton [1973a].

Here $Q$ is a matrix whose elements $q_{ij}$ define the technology of factor substitution. For example, if $Z_1$, the first activity in $Z$, costlessly downgrades labor of skill class 1 to a lower skill class 2, the corresponding coefficients would be $q_{11} = -1$ and $q_{21} = +1$.

This formulation can be very flexible. For example, on the labor side it allows substitution among labor skills with or without a loss of efficiency; it allows the incorporation of an educational submatrix into the model which, at a cost, transforms lower grade skills in one period to higher grade skills in a subsequent period through education;[9] it permits migration from the agricultural labor force to the urban, which can be assumed to be at a cost in terms of increased urban services; and it can permit substitution of capital for labor.

Again, the main difficulty with this approach is that a fairly detailed disaggregation of the primary factors is likely to be required, and alternative columns may be needed for each transformation (for example, education) to enable substitution among alternative mixes of intermediate goods required in the transformation process. Models all too soon become large and unwieldy. Adelman's [1966] model for Argentina, Manne's [1973a] DINAMICO model, Goreux's [1973] Ivory Coast model, and Blitzer's [1972] Turkey model illustrate these points. They all incorporate labor transformations through education and/or migration.

Another way of introducing greater flexibility in the primary resource constraints ought to be mentioned, even though it is not strictly a substitution relation. This involves replacing the fixed coefficients in $F$ by stepped factor supply functions, so that additional units of the resources can be obtained at an increasing cost. For example, this technique is used in DINAMICO to handle two sources of foreign capital—namely, exogenous inflows of capital on concessional terms and endogenously determined inflows of direct foreign private investment funds at a higher cost. In this example, the supply functions had two steps, though additional steps could easily have been included.

## 3.3 Decomposition and Model Linkages

A basic problem in introducing direct substitution relations is that it requires considerable sector disaggregation in order to identify meaningful technological alternatives. This detail is typically found only in sector models, which usually differ in their definition of coverage, degree of disaggregation by product, and in their objective functions, both from each other and from economy-wide models. Other differences may include sector specific resource constraints (such as land and water in the agricultural sector); disaggregation of time (seasonal changes are important for production in agriculture and for demand in the power sector); different lengths of planning periods to handle particular structures of sectoral gestation lags; and disaggregation over space

---

9. For details on this, see Chapter VII and the pioneering work of Adelman [1966].

(a model of the agricultural sector should typically be disaggregated by regions defined by ecological criteria).

Such differences lead to aggregation problems in linking the sectoral models in an economy-wide model. Even when this is accomplished, the final structure may be too large and unwieldy to solve as a single linear program. These problems are so important in practice that we deviate temporarily from the main theme of development to consider them more fully.

Disaggregation by sectors leads to economy-wide models that have a block diagonal structure in part of the constraint set. Consequently, computational problems can be solved in principle by application of the Dantzig and Wolfe [1960, 1961] decomposition algorithm. This algorithm involves decomposing the large model into a "central" model and a set of "peripheral" models, and then following rules for iterative information flows among the components of the decomposed system. As a solution algorithm for large models, to be used as an alternative to brute force application of the simplex method, the procedure does not involve any loss of information. It converges to the optimal solution. However, in practice, the number of iterations required to achieve this optimal solution can be immense, and the algorithm can rarely be regarded as a practical computational procedure. Consequently, practitioners must seek alternative and more "informal"[10] ways of linking sector and economy-wide models, which, typically, do involve some information loss.

Procedures for doing this are based on an idea first proposed by Kornai [1969]: to obtain parametric solutions of the sectoral models for a range of combinations of shadow prices or quantitative allocations of economy-wide resources employed in the sector. The solution vectors so obtained are then incorporated into the economy-wide model by augmenting the technology set in the manner described in subsection 3.1. If the entire set of possible basic solution vectors were included, corresponding to all possible combinations of the central resource shadow prices, then the procedure would not involve any information loss. In practice, however, unless the number of basic solutions is very limited, only a subset of the possible vectors can be included. Thus, some judgment is clearly needed in the choice of the shadow price combinations considered.[11]

One problem with this approach is that the number of shadow prices to be considered in the sector models can be very large (it will include the shadow prices for both primary and intermediate production inputs). Manne and Weisskopf [1970], Goreux [1973] and others have shown how the number of intermediate goods balances can be reduced when some of the sectors supply-

---

10. The term "informal" is used to distinguish these procedures from "formal" algorithmic methods of linking models, such as the Dantzig–Wolfe algorithm.

11. This task is somewhat eased if additional vectors can be added on an iterative basis by solving the economy-wide model and observing the shadow prices obtained.

ing them are modeled without resource substitution possibilities; that is, for these sectors, the $A$ and $F$ matrices in (2.1) and (2.2) are square.

One example of the approach is to transform the demands for the outputs of these sectors into terms of the primary factors $K$ required in their production. This is achieved through a transformation of the form

$$D = F^*(I - A^*)^{-1}H, \tag{3.2}$$

where: $A^*$ = the input-output matrix for these sectors,

    $H$ = a matrix of final demands, which in its simplest form, would contain the vectors of final demands for consumption, investment and exports,[12]

and    $F^*$ = a matrix which contains the requirements of primary factors $K$ for each sector in $A^*$. It is part of the $F$ matrix in equation (2.2).

The columns of the $D$ matrix then express the requirements of primary factors necessary to meet one unit of the final demand which appears in the corresponding column of $H$. Incorporating the $D$ matrix into the economy-wide model in place of $F^*$ eliminates the need to keep track of intermediate flows of the goods produced by the sectors in $A^*$.[13] That is, $A^*$ can be omitted from the economy-wide model.

Intermediate requirements by other sectors for goods produced in $A^*$ are merely transformed, using the $D$ matrix, so that they are also expressed in terms of the primary factors. Goreux applied this procedure to his Ivory Coast model, where the urban sector conformed to $A^*$, and agricultural and education sector models are linked to the urban sector through an appropriate $D$ matrix transformation. One added attraction of this technique is that it can lead to significant reductions in the row size of the economy-wide model. The $D$ matrix has, at most, as many rows as there are basic resources in the economy-wide model, and this typically will be much smaller than the dimension of $A^*$.

Aggregation problems in linking models must be overcome by establishing rules for mapping sectoral definitions into the definitions of the economy-wide model. Thus, for example, a quantity index might be used to aggregate the products of a process analysis model of the mechanical engineering sector, which can then be communicated to a more aggregate central model. These rules are often necessarily quite informal and serve to highlight the need for adhering to as consistent a set of definitions as possible when building the individual models. (For more on this, see Kornai [1973].)

An attempt at an informal linkage with empirical planning models for Mexico was made by Duloy and Norton [1973c]. They linked a static model of

12. In formulation (2.1), $H$ was summed across columns to form vector $Y$.
13. They can be calculated *ex post*.

the agricultural sector (CHAC) to the dynamic multisectoral model DINAMICO constructed by Manne [1973a]. Twenty-four alternative technology vectors from solutions of the sectoral model were generated for combinations of the prices of three economy-wide resources. The inclusion of these vectors led to an increase in the annual growth rate of GNP from 6.92 percent to 7.27 percent; to substantial changes in some shadow prices (particularly of labor and foreign exchange); to an increase in the growth rate of employment in agriculture; and to a shift in comparative advantage at the margin from manufacturing toward agriculture.

## 4. INCORPORATING INDIRECT SUBSTITUTION IN CONSUMPTION

Proper introduction of price-induced substitution in final domestic demand really requires specification of a utility, or social welfare, function. This approach has the advantage of allowing decreasing marginal utility in aggregate consumption to be introduced, and, in dynamic models, enables more satisfactory handling of investment patterns over time without requiring recourse to accelerator structures. We begin, however, with a review of more partial solutions to the problem.

### 4.1 Partial Solutions

Modifying the demand structure for the $i$th commodity in equation (2.4) to assure $\sum_i C_i(t) = C_T(t)$ (see equation (2.16) in Chapter III), we can reformulate (2.4) as

$$C_i(t) = \varepsilon_i \lambda_i C_T(t) + \bar{C}_i(t), \tag{4.1}$$

where

$$\bar{C}_i(t) = \frac{N(t)}{N(0)} C_i(0)(1 - \varepsilon_i),$$

and

$$\lambda_i = \frac{C_i(0)}{C_T(0)}.$$

Note that all $\bar{C}_i(t)$ and $\lambda_i$ are constants. The fixed proportions implicit in this linearized Engel function can be partly relaxed when maximizing $\sum_i C_i(t)$ by replacing (4.1) with upper and lower bound constraints:

$$C_i(t) \leq (1 + k)\varepsilon_i \lambda_i C_T(t) + (1 + k)\bar{C}_i(t), \tag{4.2}$$

and

$$C_i(t) \geq (1 - k)\varepsilon_i \lambda_i C_T(t) + (1 - k)\bar{C}_i(t), \tag{4.3}$$

where $k$ is the percentage departure allowed from (2.4). This is the approach taken by Sandee [1960] and Bruno [1966], and it did result in some responsiveness of consumption patterns to relative factor scarcities. It does, however, introduce additional constraints in the model and, consequently, additional shadow prices when these are binding. These shadow prices, as pointed out in

Chapter III, can be interpreted as taxes or subsidies on the corresponding consumption goods. However, this interpretation would seem to be of little practical significance; few planners would recommend the implementation of a set of taxes and subsidies generated by an essentially arbitrary device to overcome one of the major sources of rigidity in a linear programming model.

A rather more elaborate device to achieve the same ends has been proposed by Duloy and Norton [1973b]. This involves grouping commodities such that the marginal rate of substitution is zero between all groups and constant within each group.[14] A group may consist of one or more commodities, and limits are defined on the variability of the commodity mix within each group.

The relevant portions of the indifference surface with respect to two commodities in a group are illustrated for the two-commodity case in Figure 3, where the rays $OC$ and $OD$ define the limits on the composition of the commodity bundle. This structure readily can be incorporated into a linear programming model; in fact, additional linear segments representing different marginal rates of substitution can also be introduced. Clearly, the technique is approximate, but it does lead to fewer constraints than the upper- and lower-bound constraint approach and, hence, to fewer dual variables to interpret. However, this approach has yet to be applied to economy-wide models whose commodities are already highly aggregated.

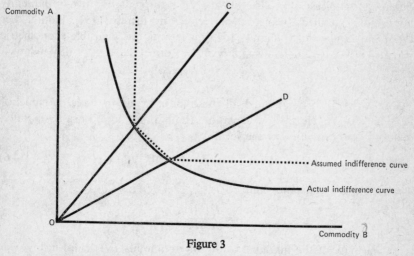

**Figure 3**

## 4.2 Complete Solutions

Moving beyond essentially arbitrary devices to overcome rigid consumption behavior requires the specification of cardinal utility functions. The resurrection of cardinalism and its usefulness in theoretical and empirical studies is eloquently argued by Manne [1974a] and will not be discussed here.

---

14. The rates of marginal substitution were fixed at base year relative prices.

Carter [1967] demonstrated the usefulness of the cardinal utility approach by reformulating Sandee's [1960] model to remove the upper and lower bounds on each consumption good. He incorporated a log-linear objective function of the Stone–Geary form

$$U(t) = \sum_i \alpha_i \log \left[ C_i(t) - C_i(0) \right], \tag{4.4}$$

where the $\alpha_i$ coefficients are marginal expenditure shares.[15] This formulation allows relative prices and quantities to vary in response to factor scarcities. The nonlinear objective function was approximated linearly using the approach outlined in the appendix to this chapter.

So far, we have dealt with basically static formulations to incorporate substitution in demand. However, an important strength of the cardinal utility approach lies with dynamic models which generate optimal paths for consumption, savings, and investment over time. In particular, investment and the growth of capital stocks can be made endogenous in a dynamic model, removing the need for accelerator structures and the consequent problem of adjusting capital-output ratios to reflect resource substitution.

The main developments in this area stem from Ramsey's [1928] pioneering work on intertemporal choice. He assumed an additive separable utility function over time for a single-commodity economy. However, inter-commodity choices may also be analyzed through additive separability assumptions—termed "want independence" by Frisch [1959]. Houthakker [1960] and Lluch and Williams [1973] have obtained plausible econometric estimates of the parameters $a_i$ and $b_i$ in the "direct addilog" utility index

$$U(t) = \sum_i a_i (C_i(t))^{b_i}. \tag{4.5}$$

Goreux [1973] has combined all these ideas in his multisector model of the Ivory Coast. He used a separable (both inter- and intra-temporally) isoelastic utility function of the form:[16]

$$U(t) = \sum_i \alpha_i C_i(t)^{[1 + (1/w_i)]}, \tag{4.6}$$

where the $\alpha_i$ are constants, and

$$\frac{1}{\omega_i} = \frac{d^2 U_i(t)}{dC_i(t)^2} \frac{C_i(t)}{U_i(t)}$$

is the elasticity of the marginal utility of commodity $i$. To sum utility over time he used a social discount rate, and he used a linear approximation to the

---

15. A useful, up-to-date review of consumer demand theory is given by Brown and Deaton [1972]. Their section 4 discusses complete systems of demand equations derived from maximization of specific utility indexes. The functions appearing in equations (4.4) and (4.5) are well-known members of this class.

16. To ensure additivity in total consumption, Goreux actually modifies (4.6) to allow $\omega_i$ to change with income effects. This procedure is too complicated to report here.

resultant function as the objective function in his four-period, twenty-year planning horizon model. Apart from the usual commodity balance rows, the levels of consumption, savings, and investment were not directly constrained, and yet, in the solutions, these variables followed very plausible and smooth time paths. The dual variables also were very reasonable and well behaved. This model is particularly encouraging; it highlights the value of introducing, in a comprehensive way, the types of substitution relations discussed in the chapter.

## 5. CONCLUSIONS

This chapter has taken a narrow focus; we have reviewed modifications that can be made to incorporate substitution possibilities and nonlinearities into otherwise rigid linear programming models. In particular, we have discussed ways of introducing substitution among factors in production and investment, of allowing transformations to convert basic resources from one factor input to another, and of permitting price-responsive substitution in demand. These flexibilities can all be handled within a linear programming framework, thus greatly enhancing the usefulness of linear models but without requiring special algorithms to solve.

The main difficulty in applying these ideas is that considerable model disaggregation is usually necessary to identify meaningful technological alternatives. This leads to problems in computation and in establishing linkages between sectors of differing degrees of aggregation. In practice, these problems can be handled only on an informal basis, but enough empirical studies have now been undertaken to indicate that the effort can be very worthwhile.

## APPENDIX ON SEPARABLE NONLINEAR FUNCTIONS IN LINEAR PROGRAMMING

In section 4.2 of this chapter we introduced nonlinear utility functions as the most complete way of handling substitution in demand. However, if the resultant model is to be solved by linear programming, then linear approximating procedures are required. Similar problems can arise in the constraint set. For example, in section 3.2 we mentioned the possibility of introducing increasing cost functions for the supply of some basic resources. This appendix reviews ways of handling such nonlinear functions.

We confine our discussion to functions which are separable; that is, they can be written in the form $y = \sum_j f_j(x_j)$. We further assume that nonlinear functions appearing in the objective function are concave (convex) if the problem is one of maximization (minimization), while those in the constraint set are of opposite curvature. These assumptions eliminate the possibility of local optimal solutions which cannot be handled with conventional linear programming computer codes.[17] Finally, and without any loss in generality, we shall focus on approximating non-linear concave functions which appear in the objective function of a maximizing problem.

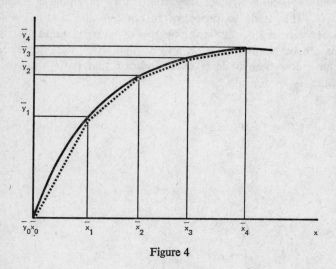

Figure 4

The best-known procedure for linearizing a nonlinear function $y = f(x)$ is illustrated in Figure 4. The function $f(x)$ is approximated by a series of linear segments (the dotted lines) which are defined over intervals $\bar{x}_i - \bar{x}_{i-1}$ on the

---

17. Problems of nonconvexity, in the context of increasing returns to scale, are discussed in Chapter XI.

$x$ axis, and corresponding intervals $\bar{y}_i - \bar{y}_{i-1}$ on the $y$ axis. Let $s_i$ denote the slope of the linear segment in the $i$th interval, that is,

$$s_i = \frac{\bar{y}_i - \bar{y}_{i-1}}{\bar{x}_i - \bar{x}_{i-1}},$$

and define $v_i$ as variables which measure the value of $x$ over the corresponding $i$th interval, such that $0 \le v_i \le \bar{x}_i - \bar{x}_{i-1}$. That is, $v_i$ ranges from zero to the length of the $i$th interval. Now, since $y = f(x)$ is to be maximized, then the following equation system:

$$\text{Max } y^* = \sum_i v_i s_i, \qquad\qquad (A.1)$$
$$x$$

subject to

$$x = \sum_i v_i, \qquad\qquad (A.2)$$

$$0 \le v_i \le \bar{x}_i - \bar{x}_{i-1}, \quad \text{all } i, \qquad\qquad (A.3)$$

will provide a linear approximation to $y$. Note that since the slope coefficients $s_i$ decrease in value as $x$ increases (because the function is concave), then the $v_i$ variables will always enter the solution in sequential order from left to right, and no modifications in the simplex method are required to insure this.

Equations (A.1) through (A.3) can easily be incorporated into a linear programming model. Equation (A.2) is purely definitional and could be eliminated, if desired, by substituting $\sum_i v_i$ for $x$ whenever this occurs in the programming problem. Clearly, the degree of accuracy of the approximation depends on the number of segments introduced, but the associated cost is an extra column ($v_i$) and upper bound row for each segment. While extra columns add little to computational costs with modern linear programming computer codes, extra rows are expensive. Consequently, the cost of introducing many nonlinear approximations would soon become prohibitively expensive if this were the most efficient approach.

A more efficient method, from the computational point of view, is to work with $f(x)$ directly rather than with approximations to its slope. Define new variables $w_i$ for each interval in Figure 4, such that $0 \le w_i \le 1$. These variables should be viewed as weights rather than as values of $x$. A linear approximation to $y = f(x)$, under the maximization assumption, is then given by:

$$\text{Max } y^* = \sum_i \bar{y}_i w_i, \qquad\qquad (A.4)$$
$$x$$

subject to

$$\sum_i w_i \le 1, \qquad\qquad (A.5)$$

$$x = \sum_i w_i \bar{x}_i, \qquad\qquad\qquad\qquad (A.6)$$

and

$$w_i \geq 0.$$

In this case, only *one* "real" constraint, equation (A.5), is added independently of the number of segments (hence, columns) introduced.[18] Again, the definitional equation (A.6) can be eliminated by substitution.

This formulation is identical to the first—that is, the values of $y^*$ obtained always lie on the segmented function in Figure 4.[19] This is trivially true when one $w_i$ is equal to 1 (say, $w_3$) and all the others are zero, since in this case $y^* = w_3 \bar{y}_3 = \bar{y}_3$, which is a corner point on the segmented function, as seen in Figure 4. The equivalence is less obvious when the value of $y^*$ selected lies intermediate between two boundary points, and, in fact, $y^*$ will only lie on the segmented function if it is a simple linear combination of the two adjacent $\bar{y}_i$ and $\bar{y}_{i+1}$ boundary points (that is, when $w_i$ and $w_{i+1}$ are positive and all other $w$'s are zero). However, this will always be true, given equation system (A.4) to (A.6), since any linear combination of three or more $w_i$'s will lead to a value of $y^*$ which lies interior to the segmented function (Figure 5). Clearly, the same value of $y^*$ can then be achieved with a smaller value of $x$ (a savings of $\Delta x$ in Figure 5), and this alternative will always be preferred when $y^*$ is maximized.

Linear approximating techniques of the kinds discussed here have been used in a number of empirical studies: Carter [1967] and Goreux [1973] linearized

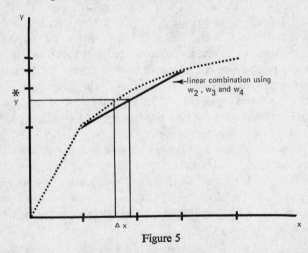

Figure 5

---

18. Despite the greater computational efficiency of this approach, it has received scant attention by planning economists. Notable exceptions are Duloy and Norton [1973b] and Goreux [1973].

19. A mathematical demonstration of the equivalence of equations (A.1) to (A.3) and (A.4) to (A.6) is quite straightforward and is left to the interested reader.

separable utility functions (see subsection 4.2) in the objective functions of their economy-wide models, and Duloy and Norton [1973a] linearized the sum of producers' and consumers' surplus in the objective function of an agricultural sector model.[20] A further application is considered in section 2 of Chapter VI, where a revenue function of export earnings is linearized.

---

20. This particular objective function was used to obtain competitive equilibria in product markets for fixed demand structures.

# SELECTED ADDITIONAL READINGS

## CHAPTER I:

There are, by now, many general works describing the development process and methods to hopefully accelerate it. Some of these works are cited in the chapter; additional ones would include Tinbergen [1967] and Griffin and Enos [1970]. Both of the latter texts are oriented toward the problems of development planning and contain elementary expositions of some of the methods used. Adelman [1969], especially the first three chapters, describes how some of the procedures and models used in development planning were actually developed in South Korea. A history of the models developed for Israel and their actual use is provided by Halevi [1969]. Gunnar Myrdal provides an excellent critique of some of the currently accepted theories of underdevelopment, as well as a description of some of his own theories, in appendix 2 of Myrdal [1968]. And lastly, several of the important readings on development planning are provided, in an edited form, in sections 8 and 9 of Meier [1970].

## CHAPTER II:

About the only published works dealing explicitly with the notion of dialogue in the planning process are two articles in the *Economics of Planning*, Kornai [1969a, 1970]. But these ideas are implicitly given in several descriptions of the planning process as it has actually been carried out. The example of several developed countries is given in Dunlop and Fedorenko [1969]; see especially the article in that volume on French and Belgian planning by Jean Waelbroeck. Several input-output based models have been developed and actually used in Norway. Several of these models and their use are described in a special issue of the *Economics of Planning* (no. 1–2, vol. 8, 1969). For descriptions of how planning procedures were actually carried out in developing countries in the 1950's and early 1960's, see Hagen [1963]. Finally, the chapter by Lee Hee Il in Adelman [1969] provides a description of a committee system which was set up in South Korea to evaluate projects and to facilitate communication between model-builders, government officials, and industrialists during the Second Five Year Plan.

## CHAPTER III:

Several books and articles describe the methodology used in formulating input-output and linear programming models. At an introductory level, see Todaro [1971], Heesterman [1970a, 1970b], and Chenery and Clark [1959]. At a more advanced level, see Kendrick [1972c], Manne [1974a], and Tinbergen and Bos [1962]. India provides an example of how a series of models

was developed, starting with simple Harrod–Domar and ending with inter-temporal, multisectoral linear programming models. The models became more complex as newer methods made them possible and as data became available. A description is given in Bhagwati and Chakravarty [1969]. A critique on the use of quantitative planning methods, and in particular on the use of capital-output ratios, is given in appendix 3 of Myrdal [1968].

## Chapter IV:

An introduction to national income accounting as well as an illustration of some elementary analytical operations possible with national income accounts is given in Richard and Giovanna Stone [1972]. A companion work on social accounts based on an input-output framework is Richard Stone and Giovanna Croft-Murry [1959]. The relationships to national income accounts and elementary analytical operations feasible in this social accounting framework are discussed. The most complete description of the new United Nations' System of National Accounts (SNA) is provided in the official manual, United Nations [1968]. A description of the basic structure and philosophy of the new SNA is given in Stone [1968b]. Other standard texts on national income accounting are two by Ruggles and Ruggles [1956, 1970]. The United Nations issues many manuals on methodology in gathering and using statistics; for input-output analysis, see United Nations [1966]. Gathering capital coefficients suitable for use in input-output studies can be extremely difficult; a description of the problems encountered and their resolution in the case of the United States is provided in Grosse [1953a, 1953b]. Finally, see Stolper [1966] on the possibilities of planning in cases where statistics are not available and Morgenstern [1963] on whether one should believe the statistics in any case.

## Chapter V:

Illustrations are provided in Stone [1966, 1967, 1968a] of how consistency models built around input-output relations can be used in the analysis of national economic systems. Chapter V pointed out that India has also used a consistency oriented methodology in drawing up the Fifth Five Year Plan. A brief description of the model can be found in Krishnan [1973]. An illustration of how an optimizing model can be used to map the production frontier of an economy and thus provide consistent trade-offs between policy variables is given in Clark and Foxley [1973].

## Chapter VI:

International trade theory is covered in several texts and review articles, including Negishi [1972] and the three articles of Chipman [1965a, 1965b, 1966]. For more current developments and applications, see recent issues of the *Journal of International Economics*.

## CHAPTER VII:

The chapter cites the major multisectoral studies which have tried to plan the development of the educational system simultaneously with the development of the rest of the economy. Another such study would be that for France described in Benard [1970]. There have been many more studies which have taken the future development of the economy as exogenously given and have then tried to plan the education sector. General texts or articles which review this latter methodology include Coombs [1970], Correa [1969], Davis [1966], and Sen [1970]. Collections of studies done in this framework include Organization for Economic Cooperation and Development [1965, 1967] and Ahamad and Blaug [1972].

## CHAPTER VIII:

The notion of interpreting the dual values attained from optimizing models as prices has been discussed extensively in the theoretical economics literature. At an introductory level, see Chapters 5–8 of Baumol [1972], and at a more advanced level, Balinski and Baumol [1968]. The argument for using the dual variables from optimizing models for project evaluation has been made by Tinbergen [1958]. A description of how the dual variables calculate the total cost to the economy of a major development project is shown in Chapter 8 of Clark [1970] and also in Clark, Foxley, and Jul [1973]. A theoretical discussion of the use of price-guided decentralizing procedures in development is given in Heal [1973].

## CHAPTER IX:

The chapter describes one of the methods by which a linear programming model may be applied iteratively to a government official to obtain the implicit weights given to alternative, competing objectives. Another is given in Pekelman and Sen [1974], who also review much of the literature in this area. Discussions of the relevance of Kenneth Arrow's General Impossibility Theorem to economic planning are given in Chapter 2 of Heal [1973] and in Johansen [1969].

## CHAPTER X:

Regional planners have created a completely separate body of literature on regional planning methods and problems from which development planners can draw. General works dealing with regional planning include Isard [1960], Meyer [1963], Brown [1969], and Kendrick [1971]. The use of input-output methods to analyze interregional problems began with Leontief [1953]; a review of input-output methods for regional systems is given in Richardson [1972]. Polenske [1972] and Mathur [1972] provide recent examples of its use.

The use of linear programming in studying locational decisions is illustrated in Vietorisz [1967], Lefeber [1959], Ghosh and A. Chakravarti [1970], and Takayama and Judge [1971]. Finally, an example of how to balance alternative regional growth objectives in a national linear programming model is provided in MacEwan [1971].

# BIBLIOGRAPHY

Adelman, Irma [1966]. "A Linear Programming Model for Educational Planning: A Case Study of Argentina." In I. Adelman and E. Thorbecke, eds. *The Theory and Design of Economic Development*. Baltimore: Johns Hopkins University Press.

———— ed. [1969]. *Practical Approaches to Development Planning: Korea's Second Five-Year Plan*. Baltimore: Johns Hopkins University Press.

Adelman, Irma; David C. Cole; Roger Norton; and Lee Kee Jung [1969]. "The Korean Sectoral Model." In I. Adelman, ed. *Practical Approaches to Development Planning: Korea's Second Five-Year Plan*. Baltimore: Johns Hopkins University Press.

Adelman, Irma, and Sherman Robinson [1973]. "A Non-Linear, Dynamic, Micro-Economic Model of Korea: Factors Affecting the Distribution of Income in the Short Run." Discussion Paper no. 36, Research Program in Economic Development, Princeton University.

Adelman, Irma, and Frederick T. Sparrow [1966]. "Experiments with Linear and Piece-Wise Linear Dynamic Programming Models." In I. Adelman and E. Thorbecke, eds. *The Theory and Design of Economic Development*. Baltimore: Johns Hopkins University Press.

Adelman, Irma, and Erik Thorbecke, eds. [1966]. *The Theory and Design of Economic Development*. Baltimore: Johns Hopkins University Press.

Adelman, Irma, and Laura D'Andrea Tyson [1973]. "A Regional Micro-Economic Model of Yugoslavia: Factors Affecting the Distribution of Income in the Short Run." Mimeographed. Development Research Center, International Bank for Reconstruction and Development.

Agarwala, A. N., and S. P. Singh, eds. [1958]. *The Economics of Underdevelopment*. London: Oxford University Press.

Ahamad, B., and M. Blaug, eds. [1972]. *The Practice of Manpower Forecasting*. Amsterdam: North-Holland.

Almon, Clopper [1963]. "Consistent Forecasting in a Dynamic Multi-Sector Model." *Review of Economics and Statistics* 45: 148–62.

———— [1970]. "Investment in Input-Output Models and the Treatment of Secondary Products." In A. P. Carter and A. Brody, eds. *Applications of Input-Output Analysis*. Amsterdam: North-Holland.

Anderson, D. [1972]. "Models for Determining Least-Cost Investments in Electricity Supply." *The Bell Journal of Economics and Management Science* 3: 267–99.

Arrow, Kenneth J. [1954]. "Import Substitution in Leontief Models." *Econometrica* 22: 481–92.

Arrow, Kenneth J., and Frank H. Hahn [1971]. *General Competitive Analysis*. San Francisco: Holden-Day.

Arrow, Kenneth J., and M. Hoffenberg [1959]. *A Time Series Analysis of Inter-Industry Demands*. Amsterdam: North-Holland.

Arrow, Kenneth J., and Mordecai Kurz [1970]. *Public Investment, the Rate of Return, and Optimal Fiscal Policy*. Baltimore: Johns Hopkins University Press.

Atkinson, A. B., and J. E. Stiglitz [1972]. "The Structure of Taxation and Economic Efficiency." *Journal of Public Economics* 1: 97–119.

Bacha, Edmar, and Lance Taylor [1971]. "Foreign Exchange Shadow Prices: A Critical Review of Current Theories." *Quarterly Journal of Economics* 85: 197–224.

331

———— [1974]. "The Unequalizing Spiral: A First Growth Model for Belindia." Mimeographed. Development Research Group, Center for International Affairs, Harvard University.

Bacharach, M. [1970]. *Biproportional Matrices and Input-Output Change*. Cambridge: At the University Press.

Bain, J. S. [1956]. *Barriers to New Competition*. Cambridge, Mass.: Harvard University Press.

Balassa, Bela [1973]. "Just How Misleading are Official Exchange Rate Conversions? A Comment." *Economic Journal* 83: 1258–67.

Balinski, M. L. [1965]. "Integer Programming: Methods, Uses, Computation." *Management Science* 12: 253–313.

———— [1967]. "Some General Methods in Integer Programming." In J. Abadie, ed. *Methods of Nonlinear Programming*. Amsterdam: North-Holland.

Balinski, M. L., and W. J. Baumol [1968]. "The Dual in Nonlinear Programming and its Economic Interpretation." *Review of Economic Studies* 35: 237–56.

Ball, R. J., ed. [1973]. *The International Linkage of National Economic Models*. Amsterdam: North-Holland.

Bardhan, Pranab K. [1973]. "Planning Models and Income Distribution with Special Reference to India." Mimeographed. Indian Statistical Institute.

Barr, James K., and Alan S. Manne [1967]. "Numerical Experiments with a Finite-Horizon Planning Model." *Indian Economic Review* 11: 1–31.

Bassoco, Luz María, and Teresa Rendón [1973]. "The Technology Set and Data Base of CHAC." In L. M. Goreux and Alan S. Manne, eds. *Multi-Level Planning: Case Studies in Mexico*. Amsterdam: North-Holland.

Bauchet, Pierre [1964]. *Economic Planning: The French Experience*, translated by Daphne Woodward. New York: Praeger.

Baumol, William J. [1972]. *Economic Theory and Operations Analysis*. 3rd edition. Englewood Cliffs, N.J.: Prentice-Hall.

Beckmann, Martin J., and Thomas A. Marschak [1955]. "An Activity Analysis Approach to Location Theory." *Kyklos* 8: 125–41.

Beeson, R. M., and W. S. Miesel [1971]. "The Optimization of Complex Systems with Respect to Multiple Criteria." *Proceedings of the 1971 Systems, Man and Cybernetics Conference; Joint National Conference on Major Systems*, October 25–29, 1971, Anaheim, California.

Behrman, Jere R. [1972]. "Short-Run Flexibility in a Developing Economy." *Journal of Political Economy* 80: 292–313.

Benard, Jean [1970]. "Intersectoral Optimization and Development in the Educational System." In A. P. Carter and A. Brody, eds. *Contributions to Input-Output Analysis*. Amsterdam: North-Holland.

Benayoun, R.; J. deMontgolfier; J. Tergny; and O. Laritchev [1971]. "Linear Programming with Multiple Objective Functions: Step Method (STEM)." *Mathematical Programming* 1: 336–75.

Bergendorff, Hans; Charles R. Blitzer; and Han K. Kim [1973]. "Applications of Control Theory to a Leontief-Type Planning Model." Paper presented to the 8th International Symposium on Mathematical Programming, August 27–31, 1973, Stanford, California. Mimeographed. Development Research Center, International Bank for Reconstruction and Development.

Bergendorff, Hans, and Peter B. Clark [1973]. "Chile: An Experimental Model for Testing Consumption Redistribution." Mimeographed. Development Research Center, International Bank for Reconstruction and Development.

Bergendorff, Hans; Peter B. Clark; and Lance Taylor [1973]. "Welfare Gains From

Optimization in Dynamic Planning Models." Mimeographed. Development Research Center, International Bank for Reconstruction and Development.

Bergsman, Joel, and Alan S. Manne [1966]. "An Almost Consistent Intertemporal Model for India's Fourth and Fifth Plans." In I. Adelman and E. Thorbecke, eds. *The Theory and Design of Economic Development*. Baltimore: Johns Hopkins University Press.

Bergson, Abram [1964]. *The Economics of Soviet Planning*. New Haven: Yale University Press.

Bhagwati, Jagdish N., and Sukhamoy Chakravarty [1969]. "Contributions to Indian Economic Analysis: A Survey." *American Economic Review* 59: Supplement to No. 4.

Bhagwati, Jagdish N., and Richard S. Eckaus, eds. [1970]. *Foreign Aid: Selected Readings*. Harmondsworth, England: Penguin Books.

Blaug, Mark [1967]. "Approaches to Educational Planning." *Economic Journal* 77: 262–87.

——— [1970]. *An Introduction to the Economics of Education*. Harmondsworth, England: Penguin Books.

Blitzer, Charles R. [1972]. "A Perspective Planning Model for Turkey: 1969–84." Mimeographed. Development Research Center, International Bank for Reconstruction and Development.

Blitzer, Charles R.; Hikmet Cetin; and Alan S. Manne [1970]. "A Dynamic Five-Sector Model for Turkey, 1967–82." *Papers and Proceedings of the American Economic Association* 60: 70–75.

Blitzer, Charles R., and Alan S. Manne [1974]. "Employment, Income Distribution and Shadow Prices in a Dualistic Economy." Mimeographed. Development Research Center, International Bank for Reconstruction and Development.

Boon, Gerard K. [1964]. *Economic Choice of Human and Physical Factors in Production*. Amsterdam: North-Holland.

——— [1965–66]. "Optimal Capital Intensity in Metal Chipping Processes." Progress Reports 1 and 2, Institute of Engineering Economic Systems, Stanford University.

——— [1969]. "Decision Rules for Equipment Investments in Metal-Product Industries with Special Reference to Metal-Chipping and Metal-Cutting Machines." In UNIDO, *Development of Metalworking Industries in Developing Countries*. New York: United Nations (ID/6).

Bowles, Samuel [1969]. *Planning Educational Systems for Economic Growth*. Cambridge, Mass.: Harvard University Press.

——— [1970]. "Aggregation of Labor Inputs in the Economics of Growth and Planning: Experiments with a Two-Level CES Function." *Journal of Political Economy* 78: 68–81.

Brown, A. J. [1968]. "Regional Problems and Regional Policy." *National Institute Economic Review* 46: 42–51.

——— [1969]. "Surveys of Applied Economics: Regional Economics, with Special Reference to the United Kingdom." *Economic Journal* 79: 759–96.

Brown, Alan, and Angus Deaton [1972]. "Models of Consumer Behaviour: A Survey." *Economic Journal* 82: 1145–1236.

Bruno, Michael [1962]. *Interdependence, Resource Use and Structural Change in Israel*. Jerusalem: Bank of Israel.

——— [1966]. "A Programming Model for Israel." In I. Adelman and E. Thorbecke, eds. *The Theory and Design of Economic Development*. Baltimore: Johns Hopkins University Press.

——— [1967a]. "Optimal Patterns of Trade and Development." *Review of Economics and Statistics* 49: 545–54.

——— [1967b]. "The Optimal Selection of Import-Substituting and Export-Promoting Projects." In *Planning the External Sector: Techniques, Problems and Policies*. New York: United Nations (ST/TAO/SER.C/91).

333

—— [1968]. "Estimation of Factor Contribution to Growth Under Structural Disequilibrium." *International Economic Review* 9: 49–62.

—— [1969]. "Fundamental Duality Relationships in the Pure Theory of Capital and Growth." *Review of Economics and Statistics* 36: 39–53.

—— [1970]. "Development Policy and Dynamic Comparative Advantage." In R. Vernon, ed. *The Technology Factor in International Trade*. New York: Columbia University Press for National Bureau of Economic Research.

—— [1972a]. "Domestic Resource Costs and Effective Protection: Clarification and Synthesis." *Journal of Political Economy* 80: 16–33.

—— [1972b]. "Resource Allocation Over Time and the Real Exchange Rate." Mimeographed. Hebrew University and Falk Institute.

—— [1974]. "Structural Change and the Dynamics of the Real Exchange Rate." Mimeographed. Hebrew University and Falk Institute.

Bruno, Michael; Christopher Dougherty; and Mordecai Fraenkel [1970]. "Dynamic Input-Output, Trade and Development." In A. Carter and A. Brody, eds. *Applications of Input-Output Analysis*. Amsterdam: North-Holland.

Buffa, E. S., and W. H. Taubert [1972]. *Production-Inventory Systems: Planning and Control*. Homewood, Ill.: Richard D. Irwin.

Burmeister, Edwin, and A. Rodney Dobell [1970]. *Mathematical Theories of Economic Growth*. New York: Macmillan.

Cardwell, Lucy A. [1973]. "Tariff Reform in a Linear Programming Model of Chile." Ph.D. dissertation, Massachusetts Institute of Technology.

Carnoy, Martin [1967]. "Rates of Return to Schooling in Latin America." *Journal of Human Resources* 2: 359–74.

Carrothers, Gerald A. P. [1956]. "An Historical Review of the Gravity and Potential Concepts of Human Interaction." *Journal of the American Institute of Planners* 22: 94–102.

Carter, Anne [1970]. *Structural Change in the American Economy*. Cambridge, Mass.: Harvard University Press.

Carter, Anne, and A. Brody, eds. [1970a]. *Contributions to Input-Output Analysis*. Amsterdam: North-Holland.

—— [1970b]. *Applications of Input-Output Analysis*. Amsterdam: North-Holland.

Carter, Nicholas G. [1967]. "A New Look at the Sandee Model." In K. Shell, ed. *Essays on the Theory of Optimal Economic Growth*. Cambridge, Mass.: MIT Press.

Cauas, Jorge [1972]. "Short-Term Economic Theory and Policy—The Chilean Case, 1964–70." Mimeographed. Development Research Center, International Bank for Reconstruction and Development.

Celasun, Merih [1972]. "Perspectives of Economic Growth in Turkey: 1973–1977: Experiments with Three Macroeconomic Models." Graduate Program in Operations Research, Middle East Technical University, Ankara.

Chakravarty, Sukhamoy [1969]. *Capital and Development Planning*. Cambridge, Mass.: MIT Press.

Chakravarty, Sukhamoy, and Richard S. Eckaus [1964]. "An Approach to a Multi-Sectoral Intertemporal Planning Model." In P. N. Rosenstein-Rodan, ed. *Capital Formation and Economic Development*. Cambridge, Mass.: MIT Press.

Chakravarty, Sukhamoy, and Louis Lefeber [1965]. "An Optimizing Planning Model." *Economic Weekly* 17: 237–52.

Charnes, A.; W. Cooper; M. A. Keane; E. T. Snow; and A. S. Walters [1970]. "A Mixed Goal Programming Model for PPBS in a Consumer Protection Regulatory Agency." Paper presented at the 7th Mathematical Programming Symposium, The Hague.

Chenery, Hollis B. [1952]. "Overcapacity and the Acceleration Principle." *Econometrica* 20: 1–28.

———— [1953]. "Regional Analysis." In H. B. Chenery, P. G. Clark, and V. Cao-Pinna, *The Structure and Growth of the Italian Economy*. Rome: U.S. Mutual Security Agency.

———— [1955]. "The Role of Industrialization in Development Programs." *Papers and Proceedings of the American Economic Association* 45: 40–57.

———— [1956]. "Inter-regional and International Input-Output Analysis." In T. Barna, ed. *The Structural Interdependence of the Economy*. New York: John Wiley and Sons.

———— [1959]. "The Interdependence of Investment Decisions." In M. Abramovitz et al., *The Allocation of Economic Resources*. Stanford: Stanford University Press.

———— [1960]. "Patterns of Industrial Growth." *American Economic Review* 50: 624–54.

———— [1961]. "Comparative Advantage and Development Policy." *American Economic Review* 51: 18–51.

Chenery, Hollis B., and Associates [1974]. *Redistribution with Growth*. London: Oxford University Press.

Chenery, Hollis B., and Michael Bruno [1962]. "Development Alternatives in an Open Economy." *Economic Journal* 72: 79–103.

Chenery, Hollis B., and Paul G. Clark [1959]. *Interindustry Economics*. New York: John Wiley and Sons.

Chenery, Hollis B.; Paul G. Clark; and Vera Cao-Pinna [1953]. *The Structure and Growth of the Italian Economy*. Rome: U.S. Mutual Security Agency.

Chenery, Hollis B., and W. Ginsburg [1969]. "Simulating the Process of Industrialization." Economic Development Report no. 147, Development Research Group, Harvard University.

Chenery, Hollis B., and K. Kretschmer [1956]. "Resource Allocation for Economic Development." *Econometrica* 24: 365–99.

Chenery, Hollis B., and Arthur MacEwan [1966]. "Optimal Patterns of Growth and Aid: The Case of Pakistan." In I. Adelman and E. Thorbecke, eds. *The Theory and Design of Economic Development*. Baltimore: Johns Hopkins University Press.

Chenery, Hollis B., and William J. Raduchel [1971]. "Substitution in Planning Models." In H. B. Chenery, ed. *Studies in Development Planning*. Cambridge, Mass.: Harvard University Press.

Chenery, Hollis B.; Shuntaro Shishido; and Tsunehiko Watanabe [1962]. "The Pattern of Japanese Growth, 1914–1954." *Econometrica* 30: 98–139.

Chenery, Hollis B., and Alan Strout [1966]. "Foreign Assistance and Economic Development." *American Economic Review* 56: 679–733.

———— [1968]. "Foreign Assistance and Economic Development: Reply to Fei and Ranis Comment." *American Economic Review* 58: 912–16.

Chenery, Hollis B., and Moshe Syrquin [1975]. *Patterns of Development: 1950–1970*, London: Oxford University Press.

Chenery, Hollis B., and Lance Taylor [1968]. "Development Patterns: Among Countries and Over Time." *Review of Economics and Statistics* 50: 391–416.

Chenery, Hollis B., and Hirofumi Uzawa [1958]. "Non-linear Programming and Economic Development." In K. J. Arrow, L. Hurwicz, and H. Uzawa, eds. *Studies in Linear and Non-Linear Programming*. Stanford: Stanford University Press.

Chenery, Hollis B., and Larry E. Westphal [1969]. "Economies of Scale and Investment Over Time." In J. Margolis and H. Guitton, eds. *Public Economics*. London: Macmillan.

Chile, Government of, ODEPLAN [1971]. *Plan Nacional, 1971–76*. Santiago.

Chipman John S. [1965a]. "A Survey of the Theory of International Trade, Part 1: The Classical Theory." *Econometrica* 33: 477–519.

———— [1965b]. "A Survey of the Theory of International Trade, Part 2: The Neo-Classical Theory." *Econometrica* 33: 685–760.

———— [1966]. "A Survey of the Theory of International Trade, Part 3: The Modern Theory." *Econometrica* 34: 18–76.

Çilingiroğlu, Ayhan [1969]. *Manufacture of Heavy Electrical Equipment in Developing Countries.* World Bank Staff Occasional Papers no. 9. Baltimore: Johns Hopkins University Press.

Clark, Peter Bentley [1970]. *Planning Import Substitution.* Amsterdam: North-Holland.

Clark, Peter Bentley, and Alejandro Foxley [1973]. "Target Shooting with a Multisectoral Model." In R. Eckaus and P. N. Rosenstein-Rodan, eds. *Analysis of Development Problems: Studies of the Chilean Economy.* Amsterdam: North-Holland.

Clark, Peter Bentley; Alejandro Foxley; and Ana Maria Jul [1973]. "Project Evaluation within a Macroeconomic Framework." In R. S. Eckaus and P. N. Rosenstein-Rodan, eds. *Analysis of Development Problems: Studies of the Chilean Economy.* Amsterdam: North-Holland.

Clark, Peter Bentley, and Lance Taylor [1971]. "Dynamic Input-Output Planning with Optimal End Conditions: The Case of Chile." *Economics of Planning* 11: 10–30.

Cline, William R. [1972]. *Potential Effects of Income Redistribution of Economic Growth: Latin American Cases.* New York: Praeger.

Cohen, S. C. [1969]. *Modern Capitalist Planning: The French Model.* Cambridge, Mass.: Harvard University Press.

Cole, David C., and Princeton Lyman [1971]. *Korean Development: The Interplay of Politics and Economics.* Cambridge, Mass.: Harvard University Press.

Condos, Apostolos, and Penny S. Davis [1973a]. "Ivory Coast Research Project: A Dynamic Linear Programming Model of the Education Sector of the Ivory Coast." Mimeographed. Development Research Center, International Bank for Reconstruction and Development.

―――― [1973b]. "Ivory Coast Research Project: A Dynamic Linear Programming Model of the Urban Sector of the Ivory Coast." Mimeographed. Development Research Center, International Bank for Reconstruction and Development.

Coombs, Philip H. [1970]. *What is Educational Planning?* Paris: International Institute for Educational Planning, UNESCO.

Corden, Max [1971]. *Theory of Protection.* Oxford: Clarendon Press.

Correa, Hector [1969]. *Quantitative Methods for Educational Planning.* Scranton, Penna.: International Textbook.

Costello, Timothy W. [1970]. "Psychological Aspects: The Soft Side of Policy Formulation." *Policy Sciences* 1: 161–67.

Dantzig, George B. [1963]. *Linear Programming and Extensions.* Princeton: Princeton University Press.

Dantzig, George B., and Philip Wolfe [1960]. 'Decomposition Principle for Linear Programming." *Operations Research* 8: 101–11.

―――― [1961]. "The Decomposition Algorithm for Linear Programs." *Econometrica* 29: 767–78.

Dasgupta, Partha [1972]. "A Comparative Analysis of the UNIDO Guidelines and the OECD Manual." *Bulletin of the Oxford University Institute of Economics and Statistics* 34: 33–51.

Dasgupta, Partha, and J. E. Stiglitz [1974]. "Benefit-Cost Analysis and Trade Policies." *Journal of Political Economy* 82: 1–33.

Datta-Chaudhuri, Mrinal K. [1967]. "Regional Specialization in Metallurgical and Machine-Building Industries in India in the Framework of a Planning Model for Optimum Use of National Resources." *Indian Economic Review* 2 (new series): 219–70.

David, Paul A. [1972]. "Just How Misleading are Official Exchange Rate Conversions?" *Economic Journal* 82: 979–90.

―――― [1973]. "A Reply to Professor Balassa." *Economic Journal* 83: 1267–76.

Davis, P. S. and T. L. Ray [1969]. "A Branch-Bound Algorithm for the Capacitated Facilities Location Problem." *Naval Research Logistics Quarterly* 16: 331–43.

Davis, Russell G. [1966]. *Planning Human Resource Development: Educational Models and Schemata*. Chicago: Rand McNally.

Diamond, Peter A., and James A. Mirrlees [1971]. "Optimal Taxation and Public Production: I—Production Efficiency." *American Economic Review* 61: 8–27.

Dixit, Avinash [1970a]. "Growth Patterns in a Dual Economy." *Oxford Economic Papers* 22: 229–34.

———— [1970b]. "On the Optimum Structure of Commodity Taxes." *American Economic Review* 60: 295–301.

Dorfman, Robert [1969]. "An Economic Interpretation of Optimal Control Theory." *American Economic Review* 59: 817–31.

Dorfman, Robert; J. D. Jacoby; and H. A. Thomas, Jr. [1972]. *Models for Managing Regional Water Quality*. Cambridge, Mass.: Harvard University Press.

Dorfman, Robert; Paul A. Samuelson; and Robert Solow [1958]. *Linear Programming and Economic Analysis*. New York: McGraw-Hill.

Dorfman, Robert and Richard Thoreson [1969]. "Optimal Patterns of Growth and Aid with Diminishing Returns to Investment and Consumption." Economic Development Report no. 142, Development Research Group, Harvard University.

Dougherty, Christopher R. S. [1972a]. "Substitution and the Structure of the Labour Force." *Economic Journal* 82: 170–82.

———— [1972b]. "Estimates of Labor Aggregation Functions." *Journal of Political Economy* 80: 1101–19.

Duloy, John H., and Roger D. Norton [1973a]. "CHAC, a Programming Model of Mexican Agriculture." In L. M. Goreux and A. S. Manne, eds. *Multi-Level Planning: Case Studies in Mexico*. Amsterdam: North-Holland.

———— [1973b]. "Competitive and Noncompetitive Demand Structures in Linear Programming Models." Discussion Paper no. 3, Development Research Center, International Bank for Reconstruction and Development.

———— [1973c]. "Linking the Agricultural Model and the Economy-Wide Model." In L. M. Goreux and A. S. Manne, eds. *Multi-Level Planning: Case Studies in Mexico*. Amsterdam: North-Holland.

Dunlop, John T. and Nikolay P. Fedorenko, eds. [1969]. *Planning and Markets: Modern Trends in Various Economic Systems*. New York: McGraw-Hill.

Eckaus, Richard S. [1955]. "The Factor-Proportions Problem in Underdeveloped Areas." *American Economic Review* 45: 539–65.

———— [1973]. "Absorptive Capacity as a Constraint Due to Maturation Processes." In J. N. Bhagwati and R. S. Eckaus, eds. *Development and Planning: Essays in Honour of Paul Rosenstein-Rodan*. Cambridge: MIT Press.

Eckaus, Richard S., and Kirit S. Parikh [1968]. *Planning for Growth: Multisectoral, Intertemporal Models Applied to India*. Cambridge, Mass.: MIT Press.

Efroymson, M. A., and T. L. Ray [1966]. "A Branch-Bound Algorithm for Plant Location." *Operations Research* 14: 361–68.

Erlenkotter, Donald [1967]. "Optimal Plant Size with Time-Phased Imports." In A. S. Manne, ed. *Investments for Capacity Expansion: Size, Location, and Time-Phasing*. London: George Allen and Unwin.

———— [1971]. "Nonconvex Programming and Capital Budgeting with Continuous Project Scale." Discussion Paper no. 16, Operations Research Study Center, Graduate School of Management, University of California at Los Angeles.

———— [1972a]. "Capacity Planning for Large Multilocation Systems: Approximate and Incomplete Dynamic Programming Approaches." Mimeographed. Operations Research Study Center, Graduate School of Management, University of California at Los Angeles.

———— [1972b]. "Economic Integration and Dynamic Location Planning." *Swedish Journal of Economics* 74: 8–18.

337

Evans, H. David [1972]. *A General Equilibrium Analysis of Protection: The Effects of Protection in Australia*. Amsterdam: North-Holland.

Fei, John C. H., and Gustav Ranis [1964]. *Development of the Labor Surplus Economy: Theory and Policy*. Homewood, Ill.: Richard D. Irwin.

Fleming, J. Marcus [1955]. "External Economies and the Doctrine of Balanced Growth." *Economic Journal* 65: 241–56.

Florence, P. Sargant [1962]. *Post-War Investment, Location and Size of Plant*. Cambridge: At the University Press for the National Institute of Economic and Social Research.

Foxley, Alejandro [1973]. "Redistribucion del Consumo: Efectos Sobre la Produccion y el Empleo." Presented at the International Conference of ECIEL on Consumption, Income, and Prices, October 1–3, 1973, Hamburg, Germany.

Foxley, Alejandro; Peter Bentley Clark; and Ana Maria Jul [1973]. "Projecting the Optimal Level of Copper Production in Chile." In R. S. Eckaus and P. N. Rosenstein-Rodan, eds. *Analysis of Development Problems: Studies of the Chilean Economy*. Amsterdam: North-Holland.

Freimer, M., and P. L. Yu [1972]. "An Approach Toward Decision Problems with Multi-Objectives." CSS 72–03, University of Rochester.

Friedmann, Santiago [1968]. "An Algorithm for Dynamic Programming of Economic Growth." Mimeograph. Center for Research in Management Science, University of California at Berkeley.

Frisch, Ragnar [1959]. "A Complete Scheme for Computing All Direct and Cross Demand Elasticities in a Model with Many Sectors." *Econometrica* 27: 117–96.

——— [1960]. *Planning for India: Selected Explorations in Methodology*. Bombay: Asia Publishing House.

Gale, David [1960]. *The Theory of Linear Economic Models*. New York: McGraw-Hill.

de la Garza, Guillermo Fernandez, and Alan S. Manne [1973]. "ENERGETICOS, A Process Analysis of the Energy Sectors." In L. M. Goreux and A. S. Manne, eds. *Multi-Level Planning: Case Studies in Mexico*. Amsterdam: North-Holland.

Garg, Prem C. [1974]. "Investment Planning Under Economies of Scale and Uncertainty." Mimeographed. Development Research Center, International Bank for Reconstruction and Development.

Gately, T. Dermot [1971]. "Investment Planning for the Electric Power Industry: A Mixed-Integer Programming Approach, with Applications to Southern India." Ph.D. dissertation, Princeton University.

Geoffrion, Arthur M. [1970]. "Elements of Large-Scale Mathematical Programming, Parts I and II." *Management Science* 16: 652–91.

Geoffrion, Arthur M., and R. E. Marsten [1972]. "Integer Programming Algorithms: A Framework and State-of-the-Art Survey." *Management Science* 18: 465–491.

Ghosh, A., and A. Chakravarti [1970]. "The Problem of Location of an Industrial Complex." In A. P. Carter and A. Brody, eds. *Contributions to Input-Output Analysis*. Amsterdam: North-Holland.

Gilbert, Milton, and Irving Kravis [1954]. *An International Comparison of National Products and the Purchasing Power of Currencies*. Paris: Organization for European Economic Cooperation.

Ginsburgh, V., and J. Waelbroeck [1974]. "Linear Programming Models and General Equilibrium Theory." Mimeographed. Department of Economics, University of British Columbia.

Goreux, Louis M. [1973]. "Ivory Coast Research Project: An Outline of the Central Model." Mimeographed. Development Research Center, International Bank for Reconstruction and Development.

Goreux, Louis M., and Alan S. Manne, eds. [1973]. *Multi-Level Planning: Case Studies in Mexico*. Amsterdam: North-Holland.

Griffin, K. B., and J. L. Enos [1970]. *Planning Development*. London: Addison-Wesley.

Griliches, Zvi, and V. Ringstad [1971]. *Economies of Scale and the Form of the Production Function*. Amsterdam: North-Holland.

Grosse, Robert N. [1953a]. *Capital Requirements for the Expansion of Industrial Capacity*. Washington, D.C.: U.S. Bureau of the Budget.

—— [1953b]. "The Structure of Capital." In W. Leontief, ed. *Studies in the Structure of the American Economy*. New York: Oxford University Press.

Grubel, Herbert G., and Harry G. Johnson, eds. [1971]. *Effective Tariff Protection*. Proceedings of a conference sponsored by the General Agreement on Tariffs and Trade and the Graduate Institute of International Studies, December 17–20, 1971, Geneva.

Hagen, Everett E., ed. [1963]. *Planning Economic Development*. Homewood, Ill.: Richard D. Irwin.

Hagen, Everett E. [1968]. *The Economics of Development*. Homewood, Ill.: Richard D. Irwin.

Haith, D. A. [1971]. "An Approach for Evaluating Alternative Water-Resource Plans." Ph.D. dissertation, Cornell University.

Haldi, John [1960]. "Economies of Scale in Economic Development." Memorandum no. E-7, Project for Quantitative Research in Economic Development, Stanford University.

Haldi, John, and Donald Whitcomb [1967]. "Economies of Scale in Industrial Plants." *Journal of Political Economy* 75: 373–85.

Halevi, Nadov [1969]. "Economic Policy Discussion and Research in Israel." *American Economic Review* 59: Supplement to No. 4.

Harberger, Arnold [1968]. "Survey of Literature on Cost-Benefit Analysis for Industrial Project Evaluation." In *Evaluation of Industrial Projects*. Vol. 1. New York: United Nations (ID/Ser. N/1).

Harbison, Frederick, and Charles A. Myers, eds. [1965]. *Manpower and Education: Country Studies in Economic Development*. New York: McGraw-Hill.

Harvard Economic Research Project [1953]. "Estimates of the Capital Structure of American Industries, 1947." Mimeographed. Harvard University.

Hatanaka, Michio [1960]. *The Workability of Input-Output Analysis*. Ludwigshafen am Rhein: Fachverlag für Wirtschaftstheorie und Ökonometrie.

Heady, Earl O., and Harry H. Hall [1969]. "Application of Linear and Nonlinear Programming Models in Specifying Land Use, Spatial Equilibrium and Prices for Agriculture." In K. A. Fox, J. K. Sengupta, and G. V. L. Narasimham, eds. *Economic Models, Estimation and Risk Programming*. Heidelberg: Springer-Verlag.

Heal, G. M. [1969]. "Planning Without Prices." *Review of Economics and Statistics* 36: 347–62.

—— [1973]. *The Theory of Economic Planning*. Amsterdam: North-Holland.

Healey, Derek T. [1972]. "Development Policy: New Thinking About an Interpretation." *Journal of Economic Literature* 10: 757–97.

Heesterman, A. R. G. [1970a]. *Allocation Models for National Economic Planning*. Dordrecht, Holland: D. Reidel.

—— [1970b]. *Forecasting Models for National Economic Planning*. Dordrecht, Holland: D. Reidel.

Higgins, Benjamin [1968]. *Economic Development: Principles, Problems, and Policies*. Revised edition. New York: W. W. Norton.

Hildebrand, Francis B. [1968]. *Finite Difference Equations and Simulations*. Englewood Cliffs, N.J.: Prentice-Hall.

Hirschman, Albert O. [1958]. *The Strategy of Economic Development*. New Haven: Yale University Press.

Holland, Edward P., and Robert W. Gillespie [1963]. *Experiments on a Simulated Under-developed Economy: Development Plans and Balance of Payments Policies.* Cambridge, Mass.: MIT Press.

Hollister, R. G. [1967]. "A Technical Evaluation of the O.E.C.D.'s Mediterranean Regional Project and Conclusions." In J. A. Lauwerys, G. Z. Bereday, and M. Blaug, eds. *The World Year Book of Education: 1967. Educational Planning.* London: Evans Brothers.

Holt, Charles C. [1965]. "Quantitative Decision Analysis and National Policy: How Can We Bridge the Gap?" In Bert G. Hickman, ed. *Quantitative Planning of Economic Policy.* Washington, D.C.: The Brookings Institution.

Holt, Charles C.; Franco Modigliani; John G. Muth; and Herbert Simon [1960]. *Planning Production, Inventories, and Work Force.* Englewood Cliffs, N.J.: Prentice-Hall.

Hopkins, David S. P. [1969]. "Sufficient Conditions for Optimality in Infinite Horizon Linear Economic Models." Technical Report no. 69–3, Operations Research House, Stanford University.

Horowitz, Morris; Manuel Zymelman; and Irwin L. Herrnstadt [1966]. *Manpower Requirements for Planning: An International Comparison Approach.* Two vols. Department of Economics, Northeastern University.

Hotelling, Harold [1938]. "The General Welfare in Relation to Problems of Taxation and of Railway and Utility Rates." *Econometrica* 6: 242–69.

Houthakker, Hendrik S. [1957]. "An International Comparison of Household Expenditure Patterns, Commemorating the Centenary of Engel's Law." *Econometrica* 25: 532–51.

—— [1960]. "Additive Preferences." *Econometrica* 28: 244–57.

—— [1965]. "New Evidence on Demand Elasticities." *Econometrica* 33: 277–88.

India, Government of, Planning Commission, Perspective Planning Division [1964]. *Notes on Perspective Development, India: 1960–61 to 1975–76.* New Delhi.

—— [1973]. *A Technical Note on the Approach to the Fifth Five-Year Plan of India.* New Delhi.

International Labour Organisation [1970]. *Towards Full Employment: A Programme for Colombia.* Report of the employment study mission. Geneva.

—— [1971]. *Matching Employment Opportunities and Expectations: A Programme of Action for Ceylon.* Report of the employment study mission. Geneva.

Intriligator, Michael D. [1971]. *Mathematical Optimization and Economic Theory.* Englewood Cliffs, N.J.: Prentice-Hall.

Isard, Walter [1953]. "Some Empirical Results and Problems of Regional Input-Output Analysis." In W. Leontief, ed. *Studies in the Structure of the American Economy.* New York: Oxford University Press.

—— [1956]. *Location and Space Economy.* New York: John Wiley and Sons.

—— [1960]. *Methods of Regional Analysis.* Cambridge, Mass.: MIT Press.

Isard, Walter; Eugene W. Schooler; and Thomas Vietorisz [1959]. *Industrial Complex Analysis and Regional Development.* Cambridge, Mass.: MIT Press.

Jacoby, Henry Donnan [1967]. "Analysis of Investment in Electric Power." Economic Development Report no. 162, Development Research Group, Harvard University.

Japan, Council of Industry Planning [1958]. *Capital Structure of the Japanese Economy.* Tokyo.

Japan, Government of, Economic Planning Agency [1965a]. *Econometric Models for Medium-Term Economic Plan, 1964–1968.* Tokyo.

—— [1965b]. *Medium-Term Economic Plan, 1964–1968.* Tokyo.

Jencks, Christopher et al. [1972]. *Inequality: A Reassessment of the Effect of Family and Schooling in America.* New York: Basic Books.

Jo, S. H., and S. Y. Park, eds. [1972]. *Basic Documents and Selected Papers on Korea's Third Five Year Economic Development Plan (1972–76).* Sogang University, Seoul.

Johansen, Leif [1960]. *A Multi-Sectoral Study of Economic Growth*. Amsterdam: North-Holland.

—— [1968]. "Explorations in Long-Term Projections for the Norwegian Economy." *Economics of Planning* 8: 70–117.

—— [1969]. "An Examination of the Relevance of Kenneth Arrow's General Possibility Theorem for Economic Planning." *Economics of Planning* 9: 5–42.

—— [1972]. "The Rate of Growth in Dynamic Input-Output Models: Some Observations Along Lines Suggested by O. Lange and A. Brody." Mimeographed. Institute of Economics, University of Oslo.

Johnson, Harry G. [1966]. "Factor Market Distortions and the Shape of the Transformation Curve." *Econometrica* 34: 686–98.

Jolly, Richard, and C. Colcough [1972]. "African Manpower Plans: an Evaluation." *International Labour Review* 106: 207–64.

Jorgenson, Dale W. [1960]. "A Dual Stability Theorem." *Econometrica* 28: 892–99.

—— [1961]. "The Structure of Multi-Sector Dynamic Models." *International Economic Review* 2: 276–93.

—— [1966]. "Testing Alternative Theories of the Development of a Dual Economy." In I. Adelman and E. Thorbecke, eds. *The Theory and Design of Economic Development*. Baltimore: Johns Hopkins University Press.

—— [1967]. "Surplus Agricultural Labor and the Development of a Dual Economy." *Oxford Economic Papers* 19: 288–312.

—— [1971]. "The Economic Theory of Replacement and Depreciation." Mimeographed. Harvard Institute of Economic Research, Harvard University.

—— [1972]. "Investment Behavior and the Production Function." *Bell Journal of Economics and Management Science* 3: 220–51.

Keesing, Donald B., and Alan S. Manne [1973]. "Manpower Projections." In L. M. Goreux and Alan S. Manne, eds. *Multi-Level Planning: Case Studies in Mexico*. Amsterdam: North-Holland.

Kelley, A. J.; J. G. Williamson; and R. J. Cheetham [1972]. *Economic Dualism in Theory and History*. Chicago: University of Chicago Press.

Kendrick, David [1967a]. "Investment Planning and Economic Integration." *Economics of Planning* 7: 40–72.

—— [1967b]. *Programming Investment in the Process Industries: An Approach to Sectoral Planning*. Cambridge, Mass.: MIT Press.

—— [1970]. "Mathematical Models in Economic Planning." Mimeographed. Department of Economics, University of Texas, Austin, Texas. To be published by Holden-Day.

—— [1971]. "Mathematical Models for Regional Planning." *Regional and Urban Economics* 1: 247–87.

—— [1972a]. "Numerical Models for Urban Planning." *Swedish Journal of Economics* 74: 45–67.

—— [1972b]. "On the Leontief Dynamic Inverse." *Quarterly Journal of Economics* 86: 693–96.

—— [1972c]. "Systems Problems in Economic Development." In J. M. English, ed. *Economics of Engineering and Social Systems*. New York: Wiley-Interscience.

Kendrick, David A., and Lance Taylor [1970]. "Numerical Solution of Nonlinear Planning Models." *Econometrica* 38: 453–67.

—— [1971]. "Numerical Methods and Nonlinear Optimizing Models for Economic Planning." In H. B. Chenery, ed. *Studies in Development Planning*. Cambridge, Mass.: Harvard University Press.

Klaasen, Leo H. [1972]. "Growth Poles Theory." In A. R. Kuklinski and R. Petrella, eds. *Growth Poles and Regional Policies*. The Hague: Mouton.

341

Klaasen, Leo H., and Alfred C. van Wickeren [1969]. "Interindustry Relations, An Attraction Model: A Progress Report." In H. C. Bos, ed. *Towards Balanced International Growth*. Amsterdam: North-Holland.

Klein, Lawrence R. [1953]. "On the Interpretation of Professor Leontief's System." *Review of Economics and Statistics* 20: 131–36.

Koopmans, Tjalling C. [1964]. "Economic Growth at a Maximal Rate." *Quarterly Journal of Economics* 78: 355–94.

Kornai, Janos [1959]. *Overcentralization in Economic Administration*. Translated by John Knapp. London: Oxford University Press.

———— [1967]. *Mathematical Planning of Structural Decisions*. Amsterdam: North-Holland.

———— [1969a]. "Man-Machine Planning." *Economics of Planning* 9: 209–34.

———— [1969b]. "Multi-Level Programming: A First Report on the Model and on the Experimental Computations." *European Economic Review* 1: 134–91.

———— [1970]. "A General Descriptive Model of Planning Processes." *Economics of Planning* 10: 1–19.

———— [1971]. *Anti-Equilibrium*. Amsterdam: North-Holland.

———— [1972]. *Rush Versus Harmonic Growth*. Amsterdam: North-Holland.

———— [1973]. "Thoughts on Multi-Level Planning Systems." In L. M. Goreux and A. S. Manne, eds. *Multi-Level Planning: Case Studies in Mexico*. Amsterdam: North-Holland.

———— [1974]. *Mathematical Planning of Structural Decisions*, 2nd edition. Amsterdam: North-Holland.

Kresge, David T. [1971]. "The Macroeconomic Model." In D. T. Kresge and P. O. Roberts, eds. *Systems Analysis and Simulation Models*. Washington, D.C.: The Brookings Institution.

Krishnan, T. N. [1973]. "The Fifth Five-Year Plan Model." *Economic and Political Weekly* 8: special number, 1445–56.

Krueger, Anne O. [1966]. "Some Economic Costs of Exchange Control: The Turkish Case." *Journal of Political Economy* 74: 466–80.

———— [1972]. "Evaluating Restrictionist Trade Regimes: Theory and Measurement." *Journal of Political Economy* 80: 48–62.

Kurtz, E. B. [1930]. *Life Expectancy of Physical Property Based on Mortality Laws*. New York: Ronald Press.

Kuznets, Simon [1971]. *Economic Growth of Nations: Total Output and Production Structure*. Cambridge, Mass.: Harvard University Press.

Lage, G. M. [1970]. "A Linear Programming Analysis of Tariff Protection." *Western Economic Journal* 8: 167–85.

Leeman, Wayne A., ed. [1963]. *Capitalism, Market Socialism, and Central Planning*. Boston: Houghton Mifflin.

Lefeber, Louis [1959]. *Allocation in Space: Production, Transport and Industrial Location*. Amsterdam: North-Holland.

———— [1966]. "Comment on: 'An Almost Consistent Intertemporal Model for India's Fourth and Fifth Plans' by Joel Bergsman and Alan S. Manne." In I. Adelman and E. Thorbecke, eds. *The Theory and Design of Economic Development*. Baltimore: Johns Hopkins University Press.

———— [1968]. "Planning in a Surplus Labor Economy." *American Economic Review* 58: 343–73.

Leibenstein, Harvey [1957]. *Economic Backwardness and Economic Growth*. New York: John Wiley and Sons.

Leontief, Wassily [1953]. "Interregional Theory." In W. Leontief, ed. *Studies in the Structure of the American Economy*. New York: Oxford University Press.

———— [1970]. "The Dynamic Inverse." In A. Carter and A. Brody, ed. *Contributions to Input-Output Analysis*. Amsterdam: North-Holland.

Lewis, W. Arthur [1954]. "Economic Development with Unlimited Supplies of Labor." *The Manchester School of Economic and Social Studies* 22: 139–91.

——— [1955]. *The Theory of Economic Growth.* London: George Allen and Unwin.

——— [1966]. *Development Planning: The Essentials of Economic Policy.* New York: Harper and Row.

Lindbeck, Assar [1971]. *The Political Economy of the New Left: An Outsider's Viewpoint.* New York: Harper and Row.

Lipton, Michael [1962]. "Balanced and Unbalanced Growth in Under-developed Countries." *Economic Journal* 72: 641–57.

Little, Ian M. D., and James A. Mirrlees [1969]. *Manual of Industrial Project Analysis in Developing Countries: Social Cost-Benefit Analysis.* Paris: Organization for Economic Cooperation and Development.

Lluch, Constantino, and Alan Powell [1973]. "International Comparisons of Expenditure and Saving Patterns." Mimeographed. Development Research Center, International Bank for Reconstruction and Development.

Lluch, Constantino, and Ross Williams [1973]. "Cross-Country Demand and Saving Patterns: An Application of the Extended Linear Expenditure System." Mimeographed. Development Research Center, International Bank for Reconstruction and Development.

Lopes, F. L. [1972]. "Inequality Planning in the Developing Economy." Ph.D. dissertation, Harvard University.

Lubell, Harold [1947]. "Effects of Redistribution of Income on Consumers' Expenditures." *American Economic Review* 37: 157–70.

Luce, R. Duncan, and Howard Raiffa [1957]. *Games and Decisions.* New York: John Wiley and Sons.

Luch, R. D. [1959]. *Individual Choice Behavior: A Theoretical Analysis.* New York: John Wiley and Sons.

Luft, Harold S. [1968]. "The Use of a Long Range Simulation Model for Policy Planning in a Developing Country: The Colombian Experience." Senior honors thesis, Harvard University.

MacEwan, Arthur [1971]. *Development Alternatives in Pakistan: A Multisectoral and Regional Analysis of Planning Problems.* Cambridge, Mass.: Harvard University Press.

MacGrimmon, K. R. [1968]. "Decision Making Among Multiple-Attribute Alternatives: A Survey and Consolidated Approach." Memorandum RM–4823–ARPA, Rand Corporation.

Malinvaud, Edmond [1967]. "Decentralized Procedures for Planning." In E. Malinvaud and M. O. L. Bacharach, *Activity Analysis in the Theory of Growth and Planning.* London: Macmillan.

Manne, Alan S. [1961]. "Capacity Expansion and Probabilistic Growth." *Econometrica* 24: 632–49.

——— [1963]. "Key Sectors of the Mexican Economy: 1960–70." In A. S. Manne and H. M. Markowitz, eds. *Studies in Process Analysis.* New York: John Wiley and Sons.

——— [1964]. "Plant Location Under Economies-of-Scale: Decentralization and Computation." *Management Science* 11: 213–35.

——— [1966]. "Key Sectors of the Mexican Economy, 1962–72." In I. Adelman and E. Thorbecke, eds. *The Theory and Design of Economic Development.* Baltimore: Johns Hopkins University Press.

——— ed. [1967a]. *Investments for Capacity Expansion: Size, Location, and Time-Phasing.* Cambridge, Mass.: MIT Press.

——— [1967b]. "Programming Data for the Petroleum Refining Industry." *Industrialization and Productivity.* Bulletin 10, 57–73. New York: United Nations.

——— [1970]. "Sufficient Conditions for Optimality in an Infinite Horizon Development Plan." *Econometrica* 38: 18–38.

———— [1973a]. "DINAMICO, A Dynamic Multi-Sector, Multi-Skill Model." In L. M. Goreux and A. S. Manne, eds. *Multi-Level Planning: Case Studies in Mexico.* Amsterdam, North-Holland.

———— [1973b]. "Economic Alternatives for Mexico: a Quantitative Analysis." In L. M. Goreux and A. S. Manne, eds. *Multi-Level Planning: Case Studies in Mexico.* Amsterdam: North-Holland

———— [1973c]. "A Mixed Integer Algorithm for Project Evaluation." In L. M. Goreux and A. S. Manne, eds. *Multi-Level Planning: Case Studies in Mexico.* Amsterdam: North-Holland.

———— [1974a]. "Multi-Sectoral Models for Development Planning: A Survey." *Journal of Development Economics* 1: 43–69.

———— [1974b]. "On the Efficiency Price of Capital in a Dual Economy." *Quarterly Journal of Economics* 88: 574–95.

Manne, Alan S., and Harry M. Markowitz, eds. [1963]. *Studies in Process Analysis: Economy-Wide Production Capabilities.* New York: John Wiley and Sons.

Manne, Alan S., and Ashok Rudra [1965]. "A Consistency Model of India's Fourth Plan." *Sankhya* series B, 27: 57–144.

Manne, Alan S., and Thomas E. Weisskopf [1970]. "A Dynamic Multi-Sectoral Model for India, 1967–75." In A. Carter and A. Brody, eds. *Applications of Input-Output Analysis.* Amsterdam: North-Holland.

Marglin, Stephen A. [1966]. "Comment on 'Testing Alternative Theories of the Development of a Dual Economy' by Dale Jorgenson." In I. Adelman and E. Thorbecke, eds. *The Theory and Design of Economic Development.* Baltimore: Johns Hopkins University Press.

———— [1967]. *Public Investment Criteria.* Cambridge, Mass.: MIT Press.

———— [1974]. *Value and Price in the Labor-Surplus Economy,* forthcoming.

Markowitz, Harry M., and Alan S. Manne [1957]. "On the Solution of Discrete Programming Problems." *Econometrica* 25: 84–110.

Marston, A.; R. Winfrey; and J. C. Hempstead [1953]. *Engineering Evaluation and Depreciation.* 2nd edition. New York: McGraw-Hill.

Martens, Andre, and Robert S. Pindyck [1973]. "An Application of Optimal Control to Investment Allocation for Development Planning." International Institute for Quantitative Economics, Sir George Williams University.

Mathur, P. N. [1972]. "Multiregional Analysis in a Dynamic Input-Output Framework." In A. Brody and A. P. Carter, eds. *Input-Output Techniques.* Amsterdam: North-Holland.

Meeraus, Alex, and Ardy Stoutjesdijk [1973]. "The Solution of Industrial Process Analysis Models." Mimeographed. Development Research Center, International Bank for Reconstruction and Development.

Meier, Gerald M., ed. [1970]. *Leading Issues in Economic Development: Studies in International Poverty.* New York: Oxford University Press.

Meier, Gerald M., and Robert E. Baldwin [1957]. *Economic Development: Theory, History, Policy.* New York: John Wiley and Sons.

Mennes, L. B. M. [1973]. *Planning Economic Integration Among Developing Countries.* Rotterdam: Rotterdam University Press.

Mennes, L. B. M.; Jan Tinbergen; and J. G. Waardenburg [1969]. *The Element of Space in Development Planning.* Amsterdam: North-Holland.

Meyer, J. R. [1963]. "Regional Economics: A Survey." *American Economic Review* 53: 19–54.

Milnor, J. [1954]. "Games Against Nature." In R. M. Thrall, E. H. Coombs, and R. L. Davis, eds. *Decision Processes.* New York: John Wiley and Sons.

Mirrlees, James A. [1967]. "Optimal Growth When Technology is Changing." *Review of Economic Studies* 34: 95–124.

344

Mirrlees, James A., and N. H. Stern [1972]. "Fairly Good Plans." *Journal of Economic Theory* 4: 268–88.

Moore, Frederick T. [1959]. "Economies of Scale: Some Statistical Evidence." *Quarterly Journal of Economics* 73: 232–45.

Morgenstern, Oskar [1963]. *On the Accuracy of Economic Observations.* 2nd edition. Princeton, N.J.: Princeton University Press.

Morley, Samuel A., and Jeffrey G. Williamson [1973]. "The Impact of Demand on Labor Absorption and the Distribution of Earnings: The Case of Brazil." Paper no. 39, Program of Development Studies, Rice University.

Morva, T. and G. Bager [1972]. "Principal Features of the Mathematical Model of the Fourth Five-Year Plan of Hungary, and the Most Important Experiences." In *First Seminar on Mathematical Methods and Computer Techniques,* United Nations, Economic Commission for Europe, proceedings of a conference held at Varna, Bulgaria, September 28–October 10, 1970. Geneva (ST/ECE/MATHECO/2).

Moses, Leon N. [1955]. "The Stability of Interregional Trading Patterns and Input-Output Analysis." *American Economic Review* 45: 803–32.

Murukami, Y.; K. Tokoyama; and J. Tsukui [1970]. "Efficient Rates of Accumulation and the Turnpike for the Japanese Economy." In A. Carter and A. Brody, eds. *Applications of Input-Output Analysis.* Amsterdam: North-Holland.

Myrdal, Gunnar [1968]. *Asian Drama: An Inquiry Into the Poverty of Nations.* New York: Pantheon.

Nam, Joon Woo; Yung Whee Rhee; and Larry E. Westphal [1973]. "Data Development for a Study of the Scope for Capital-Labor Substitution in the Mechanical Engineering Industries." Mimeographed. Development Research Center, International Bank for Reconstruction and Development.

National Planning Association [1966]. *Capacity Expansion Planning Factors.* Washington, D.C.

Negishi, Takashi [1972]. *General Equilibrium Theory and International Trade.* Amsterdam: North-Holland.

Nelson, Richard R. [1970]. "The Effective Exchange Rate: Employment and Growth in a Foreign Exchange Constrained Economy." *Journal of Political Economy* 78: 546–64.

Nelson, Richard R.; T. Paul Schultz; and Robert L. Slighton [1971]. *Structural Change in Developing Economy.* Princeton, N.J.: Princeton University Press.

Netherlands, Government of, Central Planning Bureau [1956]. *Scope and Methods of the Central Planning Bureau.* The Hague.

Newbery, David M. G. [1972]. "Public Policy in the Dual Economy." *Economic Journal* 82: 567–90.

Nove, Alec [1964]. *The Soviet Economy.* New York: Praeger.

Nugent, Jeffrey B. [1970]. "Linear Programming Models for National Planning: Demonstration of a Testing Procedure." *Econometrica* 38: 831–55.

Nurkse, Ragnar [1953]. *Problems of Capital Formation in Underdeveloped Countries.* New York: Oxford University Press.

—— [1961]. *Equilibrium and Growth in the World Economy.* Cambridge, Mass.: Harvard University Press.

Oakford, R. V. [1970]. *Capital Budgeting.* New York: Ronald Press.

Oort, C. J. [1958]. *Decreasing Costs as a Problem of Welfare Economics.* Amsterdam: Drukkerij Holland N.V.

Organization for Economic Cooperation and Development [1965]. *Econometric Models of Education.* Paris.

—— [1967]. *Mathematical Models in Educational Planning.* Paris.

345

Parnes, Herbert S. [1962]. *Forecasting Educational Needs for Economic and Social Development*. The Mediterranean Regional Project, OECD.

Pekelman, Dov, and Subratak Sen [1974]. "Mathematical Programming Models for the Determination of Attribute Weights." *Management Science* 20: 1217–29.

Perry R., Guillermo E. [1972]. "Los Modelos de Coeficientes Fijos y los Posibles Conflictos Entre Metas de Producción y Empleo." Centro de Estudios Sobre Desarrollo Económico, Universidad de los Andes.

Phelps, Edmund S. [1961]. "The Golden Rule of Accumulation: A Fable for Growthmen." *American Economic Review* 51: 638–43.

Polenske, Karen R. [1972]. "The Implementation of a Multiregional Input-Output Model of the United States." In A. Brody and A. P. Carter, eds. *Input-Output Techniques*. Amsterdam: North-Holland.

Pontryagin, L. S.; V. G. Bolyanskii; R. V. Gamkrelidze; and E. F. Mishchenko [1962]. *The Mathematical Theory of Optimal Processes*. New York: Interscience.

Pratten, C., and R. M. Dean [1965]. *The Economies of Large-Scale Production in British Industry*. Occasional Papers no. 3, Department of Applied Economics. Cambridge: At the University Press.

Psacharopoulos, George, and Keith Hinchliffe [1972]. "Further Evidence on the Elasticity of Substitution Among Different Types of Educated Labor." *Journal of Political Economy* 80: 786–93.

Pyatt, Graham, et al. [1974]. "A Framework for Economic Statistics in Sri Lanka: With Special Reference to Employment and Income Distribution for 1970." Mimeographed. Population and Employment Project, World Employment Programme International Labour Office. Geneva.

Pyatt, G.; with J. Bharier; R. Lindley; R. Mabro; and Y. Sabolo [1973]. "Employment and Income Policies for Iran." Mission Working Paper no. 12, Methodology for Macro-Economic Projections. International Labour Organisation. Geneva.

Pyatt, G., and E. Thorbecke [1973]. "Principles of Planning." Mimeographed. International Labour Organisation. Geneva.

Radner, Roy, and Santiago Friedmann [1965]. "An Algorithm for Dynamic Programming of Economic Growth." Mimeographed. Center for Research in Management Science, University of California at Berkeley.

Raduchel, William J. [1972]. "A General Equilibrium Model for Development Planning." Ph.D. dissertation, Harvard University.

Raiffa, Howard [1968]. *Decision Analysis*. Reading, Mass.: Addison-Wesley.

——— [1969]. "References for Multi-Attributed Alternatives." Memorandum RM–5868–DOT. Rand Corporation.

Ramaswami, V. K., and T. N. Srinivasan [1968]. "Optimal Subsidies and Taxes When Some Factors Are Traded." *Journal of Political Economy* 76: 569–82.

Ramsey, Frank P. [1928]. "A Mathematical Theory of Savings." *Economic Journal* 38: 543–59.

Rhee, Yung Whee, and Larry E. Westphal [1973a]. "A Model for Evaluating Investment Projects in the Mechanical Engineering Sector." Mimeographed. Development Research Center, International Bank for Reconstruction and Development.

——— [1973b]. "The Specification of Process Analysis Models with Economies of Scale." Mimeographed. Development Research Center, International Bank for Reconstruction and Development.

Richardson, Harry W. [1972]. *Input-Output and Regional Economics*. New York: John Wiley.

van Rijckeghem, Willy [1969]. "An Intersectoral Consistency Model for Economic Planning in Brazil." In H. S. Ellis, ed. *The Economy of Brazil*. Berkeley: University of California Press.

Rimler, J.; Zs. Daniel; and J. Kornai [1972]. "Macrofunctions Computed on the Basis of Plan Models." *Acta Oeconomica* 8: 375–406.

Robinson, E. A. G., ed. [1963]. *The Economic Consequences of the Size of Nations*. London: Macmillan.

Robinson, Sherman, and Byung-Nak Song [1972]. "A Dynamic Input-Output Model of the Korean Economy." Discussion Paper no. 30, Research Program in Economic Development, Woodrow Wilson School, Princeton University.

Rosenstein-Rodan, Paul [1943]. "Problems of Industrialization in Eastern and South-Eastern Europe." *Economic Journal* 53: 202–11.

—— [1961]. "Notes on the Theory of the 'Big Push'." In H. S. Ellis and H. C. Wallich, eds. *Economic Development for Latin America*. New York: St. Martin's Press.

Rothenberg, Jerome [1960]. "Non-Convexity, Aggregation, and Pareto Optimality." *Journal of Political Economy* 68: 435–68.

Roy, B. [1971]. "Problems and Methods with Multiple Objective Function." *Mathematical Programming* 1: 239–66.

Ruggles, Nancy D. and Richard Ruggles [1956]. *National Income Accounts and Income Analysis*. New York: McGraw-Hill.

—— [1970]. *The Design of Economic Accounts*. New York: Columbia University Press.

Russell, C. S.; W. O. Spofford, Jr.; and E. T. Haefele [1972]. "Environmental Quality Management in Metropolitan Areas." Mimeographed. Resources for the Future.

Ryder, Harl E., Jr. [1969]. "Optimal Accumulation in a Two-Sector Neoclassical Economy with Non-Shiftable Capital." *Journal of Political Economy* 77: 665–83.

Samuelson, Paul A. [1953]. "Prices of Factors and Goods in General Equilibrium." *Review of Economic Studies* 21: 1–20.

Sandee, Jan [1960]. *A Demonstration Planning Model for India*. Bombay: Asia Publishing House.

Sapit, D. [1966]. "Multi-Objective Linear Programming." Mimeographed. Operations Research Center, University of California at Berkeley.

Sato, K. [1967]. "A Two-Level Constant Elasticity-of-Substitution Production Function." *Review of Economic Studies* 34: 201–18.

Savage, L. J. [1954]. *Foundations of Statistics*. New York: John Wiley and Sons.

Scarf, Herbert E. [1969]. "An Example of an Algorithm for Calculating General Equilbrium Prices." *American Economic Review* 59: 669–77.

Schultz, Theodore W. [1964]. *Transforming Traditional Agriculture*. New Haven: Yale University Press.

Scitovsky, Tibor [1959]. "Growth—Balanced or Unbalanced." In M. Abramovitz et al. *The Allocation of Economic Resources*. Stanford: Stanford University Press.

Selowsky, Marcelo [1969]. "On the Measurement of Education's Contribution to Economic Growth." *Quarterly Journal of Economics* 85: 449–63.

Sen, Amartya K. [1967]. "Terminal Capital and Optimum Savings." In G. H. Feinstein, ed. *Socialism, Capitalism and Economic Growth: Essays Presented to Maurice Dobb*. London: Cambridge University Press.

—— [1970]. "Models of Educational Planning and Their Applications." *Journal of Development Planning* 2: United Nations (ST/ECA/129). New York.

—— [1972]. "Accounting Prices and Control Areas: An Approach to Project Evaluation." *Economic Journal* 82: 486–501.

Sengupta, Jati K. [1972]. *Stochastic Programming: Methods and Applications*. Amsterdam: North-Holland.

Shoven, J. B., and J. Whalley [1972]. "A General Equilibrium Calculation of the Effects of Differential Taxation on Income from Capital in the U.S." *Journal of Public Economics* 1: 281–321.

347

Silberston, Aubrey [1972]. "Economies of Scale in Theory and Practice." *Economic Journal* 82: 369–91.

Simon, H. A. [1955]. "A Behavioral Model of Rational Choice." *Quarterly Journal of Economics* 69: 99–118.

Solow, Robert M. [1959]. "Competitive Valuation in a Dynamic Input-Output System." *Econometrica* 27: 20–53.

Sreedharen, V. P. and J. H. Wein [1967]. "A Stochastic, Multistage, Multiproduct Investment Model." *SIAM Journal of Applied Mathematics* 15: 347–58.

Srinivasan, T. N.; M. R. Saluja; and V. C. Sabherwal [1965]. "Structure of the Indian Economy: 1975–76." Discussion Paper no. 4, Indian Statistical Institute.

Stankard, Martin F., Jr.; C. Maier-Rothe; and S. K. Gupta [1968]. "Choosing Between Multiple Objective Alternatives: A Linear Programming Approach." Mimeographed. Management Science Center, Wharton School of Finance and Commerce, University of Pennsylvania.

Stilwell, F. J. B., and B. D. Boatwright [1971]. "A Method of Estimating Interregional Trade Flows." *Regional and Urban Economics* 1: 77–87.

Stolper, Wolfgang F. [1966]. *Planning Without Facts: Lessons in Resource Allocation from Nigeria's Development*. Cambridge, Mass.: Harvard University Press.

Stone, Richard [1964]. *The Model in Its Environment: A Progress Report*. no. 5 in *A Programme for Growth*. London: Chapman and Hall.

—— [1966]. "Simple Financial Models Based on the New SNA." *Review of Income and Wealth*, series 12 no. 1; reprinted in R. Stone, *Mathematical Models of the Economy and Other Essays*. London: Chapman and Hall [1970].

—— [1967]. "The Use of Social Accounting Matrices in Building Planning Models." Presented at the Conference of the International Association for Research in Income and Wealth, Maymouth Ireland; reprinted in R. Stone, *Mathematical Models of the Economy and Other Essays*. London: Chapman and Hall [1970].

—— [1968a]. "The Generation, Distribution and Use of Income." *Review of the International Statistical Institute*, 36; reprinted in R. Stone, *Mathematical Models of the Economy and Other Essays*. London: Chapman and Hall [1970].

—— [1968b]. "The Revision of the SNA: An Outline of the New Structure." *Bilanse Gospodarki Narodowej*, Central Statistical Office of Poland; reprinted in R. Stone, *Mathematical Models of the Economy and Other Essays*. London: Chapman and Hall [1970].

Stone, Richard and Giovanna Croft-Murry [1959]. *Social Accounting and Economic Models*. London: Bowes and Bowes.

Stone, Richard and Giovanna [1972]. *National Income and Expenditure*. 7th edition. London: Bowes and Bowes.

Stoutjesdijk, Ardy; Charles R. Frank; and Alex Meeraus [1973]. "Planning in the Chemical Sector." Mimeograph. Development Research Center, International Bank for Reconstruction and Development.

Streeten, Paul [1959]. "Unbalanced Growth." *Oxford Economic Papers* 11: 167–90.

Sutcliffe, R. B. [1964]. "Balanced and Unbalanced Growth." *Quarterly Journal of Economics* 78: 621–40.

Sydsaeter, Knut [1970]. "Remarks on Some Methods of Choosing Terminal Conditions in One-Sector, Finite Horizon, Optimal Growth Models." *Economics of Planning* 10: 171–6.

Takayama, Takashi and George G. Judge [1971]. *Spatial and Temporal Price and Allocation Models*. Amsterdam: North-Holland.

Taylor, Lance [1971]. "Investment Timing in Two-Gap Models." In H. B. Chenery, ed. *Studies in Development Planning*. Cambridge, Mass.: Harvard University Press.

—— [1973]. "Calculation of Shadow Prices from Models of Optimal Growth: The Case

of Chile." In R. S. Eckaus and P. N. Rosenstein-Rodan, eds. *Analysis of Development Problems: Studies of the Chilean Economy*. Amsterdam: North-Holland.

Taylor, Lance and Stephen L. Black [1974]. "Practical General Equilibrium Estimation of Resource Pulls Under Trade Liberalization." *Journal of International Economics* 4: 37–58.

Taylor, Lance; Paul Ide; and Ruth Sheshinski [1971]. "System Manual for a Forecasting Model of the Chilean Economy." Mimeographed. Project for Quantitative Research in Economic Development, Harvard University.

Tendulkar, Suresh D. [1971]. "Interaction Between Domestic and Foreign Resources in Economic Growth: Some Experiments for India." In H. B. Chenery, ed. *Studies in Development Planning*. Cambridge, Mass.: Harvard University Press.

Theil, Henri [1964]. *Optimal Decision Rules for Government and Industry*. Amsterdam: North-Holland.

——— [1965]. "Linear Decision Rules for Macrodynamic Policy Problems." In Bert G. Hickman, ed. *Quantitative Planning of Economic Policy*. Washington, D.C.: The Brookings Institution.

Thias, H. H., and Martin Carnoy [1969]. "Cost-Benefit Analysis in Education: A Case Study on Kenya." Report EC–173, Economics Department, International Bank for Reconstruction and Development.

Thorbecke, Erik, and Jati K. Sengupta [1972]. "A Consistency Framework for Employment, Output and Income Distribution Projections Applied to Colombia." Mimeographed. Development Research Center, International Bank for Reconstruction and Development.

Thurow, Lester C., and R. E. B. Lucas [1972]. "The American Distribution of Income: A Structural Problem." Joint Economic Committee, United States Congress, Washington, D.C.: U.S. Government Printing Office.

Tilanus, C. B. [1966]. *Input-Output Experiments: The Netherlands 1948–61*. Rotterdam: Rotterdam University Press.

Tims, Wouter [1968]. "A Growth Model and its Application—Pakistan." In G. F. Papanek, ed. *Development Policy—Theory and Practice*. Cambridge, Mass.: Harvard University Press.

Tinbergen, Jan [1958]. *The Design of Development*. Baltimore: Johns Hopkins University Press.

——— [1964]. *Economic Policy: Principles and Design*. Amsterdam: North-Holland.

——— [1967]. *Development Planning*. New York: McGraw-Hill.

Tinbergen, Jan, and Hendricus C. Bos [1962]. *Mathematical Models of Economic Growth*. New York: McGraw-Hill.

Todaro, Michael P. [1971]. *Development Planning: Models and Methods*. Nairobi: Oxford University Press.

Tomlin, J. A. [1970]. "Branch and Bound Methods for Integer and Non-Convex Programming." In J. Abadie, ed. *Integer and Nonlinear Programming*. Amsterdam: North-Holland.

Tsukui, Jinkichi [1968]. "Application of a Turnpike Theorem to Planning for Efficient Accumulation: An Example for Japan." *Econometrica* 36: 172–86.

Turkey, Government of, State Planning Organization [1972]. *Third Five Year Development Plan (1973–1977): Growth Model and Its Solution*. Ankara.

Turnham, David and Ingelies Jaeger [1971]. *The Employment Problem in Less Developed Countries: A Review of Evidence*. Paris: The Development Centre, Organization for Economic Cooperation and Development.

Ullman, E., and M. F. Darcey [1960]. "The Minimum Requirements Approach to the Urban Economic Base." *Papers and Proceedings of the Regional Science Association* 6: 175–94.

United Nations [1966]. *Problems of Input-Output Tables and Analyses* (ST/STAT.SER.F/14). New York.

349

———— [1968]. *A System of National Accounts* (ST/STAT.SER.F/2/Rev.3). New York.

United Nations, Committee for Development Planning [1972]. *Attack on Mass Poverty and Unemployment: Views and Recommendations of the Committee for Development Planning.* New York (ST/ECA/162).

———— [1973]. *Renewing the Development Priority.* New York (ST/ECA/184).

United Nations Industrial Development Organization (UNIDO) [1972]. *Guidelines for Project Evaluation.* New York (ID/SER.4/2).

Uzawa, Hirofumi [1969]. "Time Preference and the Penrose Effect in a Two-Class Model of Economic Growth." *Journal of Political Economy* 77: 628–52.

van Wickeren, Alfred C., and Hans Smit [1971]. "The Dynamic Attraction Model." *Regional and Urban Economics* 1: 89–105.

Varsavsky, Oscar, and Alfredo Eric Calcagno [1971]. *America Latina: Modelos Mathematicos.* Santiago de Chile: Editorial Universitaria.

Verdoorn, P. J. [1956]. "Complementarity and Long Range Projections." *Econometrica* 24: 429–50.

Vernon, Raymond, ed. [1970]. *The Technology Factor in International Trade.* New York: Columbia University Press.

Vietorisz, Thomas [1963]. "Sector Studies in Economic Development Planning by Means of Process Analysis Models." In A. S. Manne and H. M. Markowitz, eds. *Studies in Process Analysis.* New York: John Wiley and Sons.

———— [1967]. "Locational Choices in Planning." In Max Millikan, ed. *National Economic Planning.* New York: Columbia University Press.

———— [1968a]. *Data Requirements for Industry Analysis and Programming.* Vienna: United Nations Industrial Development Organization (IC/WG.23/4).

———— [1968b]. "Decentralization and Project Evaluation under Economies of Scale and Indivisibilities." *Industrialization and Productivity*, Bulletin 12. New York: United Nations.

———— [1973]. "Planning at the Micro Level: The Heavy Electrical Equipment Industry in Mexico." Mimeographed. Development Research Center, International Bank for Reconstruction and Development.

Vietorisz, Thomas, and Alan S. Manne [1963]. "Chemical Processes, Plant Location, and Economies of Scale." In A. S. Manne and H. M. Markowitz, eds. *Studies in Process Analysis.* New York: John Wiley and Sons.

von Neumann, John [1945]. "A Model of General Economic Equilibrium." *Review of Economic Studies* 13: 1–9.

Watanabe, Tsunehiko [1961]. "A Test of the Constancy of Input-Output Coefficients Among Countries." *International Economic Review* 2: 340–50.

———— [1965]. "National Planning and Economic Growth in Japan." In B. G. Hickman, ed. *Quantitative Planning of Economic Policy.* Washington, D.C.: The Brookings Institution.

———— [1970]. "National Planning and Economic Development—A Critical Review of the Japanese Experience." Economic Development Report no. 166, Project for Quantitative Research in Economic Development, Harvard University.

Watanabe, Tsunehiko, and Shuntaro Shishido [1970]. "Planning Applications of the Leontief Model in Japan." In A. Carter and A. Brody, eds. *Applications of Input-Output Analysis.* Amsterdam: North-Holland.

Waterston, Albert [1965]. *Development Planning: Lessons of Experience.* Baltimore: Johns Hopkins University Press.

Wein, Harold H., and V. P. Sreedharen [1968]. *The Optimal Staging and Phasing of Multi-Product Capacity.* MSU Studies in Comparative and Technological Planning. East Lansing, Mich.: Michigan State University.

Weisskoff, Richard [1971]. "Demand Elasticities for a Developing Economy: An Inter-

national Comparison of Consumption Patterns." In H. B. Chenery, ed. *Studies in Development Planning*. Cambridge, Mass.: Harvard University Press.

—— [1972]. "A Multi-sector Simulation Model of Employment, Growth, and Income Distribution in Puerto Rico: A Re-Evaluation of 'Successful' Development Strategy." Mimeographed. Economic Growth Center, Yale University.

Weisskopf, Thomas E. [1967]. "A Programming Model for Import Substitution in India." *Sankhya* 29: 257–306.

—— [1971]. "Alternative Patterns of Import Substitution in India." In H. B. Chenery, ed. *Studies in Development Planning*. Cambridge, Mass.: Harvard University Press.

Weitzman, Martin L. [1971]. "Shiftable Versus Non-Shiftable Capital: A Synthesis." *Econometrica* 39: 511–29.

Westphal, Larry E. [1969]. "Multisectoral Project Analysis Employing Mixed Integer Programming." In I. Adelman, ed. *Practical Approaches to Development Planning: Korea's Second Five-Year Plan*. Baltimore: Johns Hopkins University Press.

—— [1971]. *Planning Investments with Economies of Scale*. Amsterdam: North-Holland.

Yotopoulos, Pan S. [1965]. "The 'Wage-Productivity' Theory of Underemployment: a Refinement." *Review of Economic Studies* 32: 59–66.

—— [1968]. *Allocative Efficiency in Economic Development: A Cross Section Analysis of Epirus Farming*. Athens: Center of Planning and Economic Research.

# SUBJECT INDEX

# AUTHOR INDEX

## A

Adelman, Irma, 53n, 57n, 63n, 76n, 102n, 119n, 130n, 150n, 183, 185n, 196n, 315, 327
Ahamad, B., 329
Almon, Clopper, 57
Anderson, D., 259n, 298
Arrow, Kenneth J., 58, 84n, 97n, 120n, 329
Atkinson, A. B., 74

## B

Bacha, Edmar, 147n, 170n, 210n
Bacharach, M., 45n, 124n
Bager, G., 24n
Bain, J. S., 259n, 261n, 302n
Balassa, Bela, 118n
Baldwin, Robert E., 2n
Balinski, M. L., 287, 329
Ball, R. J., 6n, 124n
Barr, James K., 90
Bassoco, Luz María, 314n
Bauchet, Pierre, 4n
Beckmann, Martin J., 240n
Baumol, William J., 329
Beeson, R. M., 219
Behrman, Jere, R., 103
Benard, Jean, 329
Benayoun, R., 225
Bergendorff, Hans, 54n, 82n, 84n, 93n, 147n, 149n, 152n, 153
Bergsman, Joel, 57, 130n, 147, 149, 165–66, 183n
Bergson, Abram, 4n
Bhagwati, Jagdish N., 40n, 174n, 328
Black, Stephen L., 98n, 101n, 173, 205n
Blaug, Mark, 180, 182n, 187n, 329
Blitzer, Charles R., 1, 8n, 29n, 54n, 76n, 84n, 87n, 93n, 177, 182n, 185, 187n, 190n, 196n, 315
Boatwright, B. D., 247
Boon, Gerard K., 264n
Bos, Hendricus C., 327
Bowles, Samuel, 178n, 180, 182n, 188n
Brody, A., 44n
Brown, A. J., 320n, 329
Bruno, Michael, 40, 41, 65, 77, 78n, 80n, 84n, 90n, 94, 108n, 156n, 163n, 166, 167n, 182n, 183n, 185, 197, 200n, 202n, 208n, 318
Buffa, E. S., 261n
Burmeister, Edwin, 54n, 83n, 95
Byung-Nak Song, 150n

## C

Calcagno, Alfred Eric, 101n
Cao-Pinna, Vera, 58
Cardwell, Lucy, A., 74n, 160n
Carnoy, Martin, 188n
Carter, Anne, 44–45, 90
Carter, Nicholas G., 320, 324
Cauas, Jorge, 47
Celasun, Merih, 149n
CELP, see Subject Index
Cetin, Hikmet, 87n
Chakravarti, A., 330
Chakravarty, Sukhamoy, 40n, 52, 54n, 64n, 83n, 89n, 91n, 130n, 160n, 239–40, 328, see also CELP
Charnes, A., 222, 223
Cheetham, R. J., 8n, 40n, 102
Chenery, Hollis B., 8n, 9n, 27n, 41, 58, 65, 77n, 78n, 80n, 91, 97, 102, 107, 119n, 120n, 138n, 158n, 165–66, 183n, 249–51, 257n, 265–66, 272–73, 307, 310n, 314, 327
Chipman, John S., 328
Çilingiroğlu, Ayhan, 305n
Clark, Peter Bentley, 24n, 58, 77n, 78, 82n, 120n, 129, 147n, 149n, 151, 152n, 153, 163n, 328, 329
Clark, Paul G., 327
Cline, William R., 145
Cohen, S. C., 113n
Colcough, C., 179n
Cole, David C., 53n, 57n, 130n, 150n
Condos, Apostolos, 26n, 29n, 188n
Coombs, Philip H., 329
Corden, Max, 156n, 172
Correa, Hector, 329
Costello, Timothy W., 231n
Croft-Murry, Giovanna (Mrs. Richard Stone), 328

## D

Daniel, Zs., 36n
Dantzig, George B., 59n, 74n, 268n, 270n, 316

# AUTHOR INDEX

Psacharopoulos, George, 180
Pyatt, Graham, 139, 142–45

## R

Radner, Roy, 93n
Raduchel, William J., 77n, 97, 99, 307, 310n, 314
Raiffa, Howard, 231
Ramaswami, V. K., 173
Ramsey, Frank P., 320
Ranis, Gustav, 183
Ray, T. L., 288n
Rendón, Teresa, 314n
Rhee, Yung Whee, 274n, 279n, 283n, 290n, 298, 301n, 314n
Richardson, Harry W., 329
Rimler, J., 36n
Ringstad, V., 45n
Robinson, Sherman, 102n, 150n, 156n
Rosenstein-Rodan, Paul, 257
Rothenberg, Jerome, 301n
Roy, B., 222n, 223n
Rudra, Ashok, 130n, 135, 136n, 137, 147, 148
Ruggles, Nancy D., 328
Ruggles, Richard, 328
Russell, C. S., 231n
Ryder, Harl E., Jr., 89n

## S

Sabherwal, V. C., 130n, 145n, 148
Saluja, M. R., 130n, 145n, 148
Samuelson, Paul A., 59n, 76n
Sandee, Jan, 318, 320
Sapit, D., 231n
Sato, K., 51n
Savage, L. J., 231
Scarf, Herbert E., 97
Schooler, Eugene W., 240n
Schultz, T. Paul, 130n
Schultz, Theodore W., 184n
Scitovsky, Tibor, 257
Selowsky, Marcelo, 40
Sen, Amartya K., 105, 170n, 204n, 329
Sen, Subratak, 329
Sengupta, Jati K., 82, 130n, 305n
Sheshinski, Ruth, 149n
Shishido, Shuntaro, 47n, 102
Shoven, J. B., 97
Silberston, Aubrey, 261n, 263n
Simon, Herbert, 225
Slighton, Robert L., 130n

Smit, Hans, 251–52
Solow, Robert, 55n, 59n
Sparrow, Frederick T., 63n, 183n, 185n
Spofford, W. O., Jr., 231n
Sreedharen, V. P., 296n, 297
Srinivasan, T. N., 130n, 145n, 148, 155, 173
Stankard, Martin F., Jr., 231n
Stern, N. H., 108
Stiglitz, J. E., 74, 173, 206
Stilwell, F. J. B., 247
Stolper, Wolfgang F., 328
Stone, Giovanna (née Croft-Murry), 328
Stone, Richard, 45, 102n, 124, 328
Stoutjesdijk, E. J., 269n, 278n, 290n, 295, 296n, 298
Streeten, Paul, 257
Sutcliffe, R. B., 257
Sydsaeter, Knut, 106
Syrquin, Moises, 9n

## T

Takayama, Takashi, 330
Taubert, W. H., 261n
Taylor, Lance, 9n, 33, 58, 80n, 82n, 91, 93n, 94, 98n, 99n, 101n, 147n, 149n, 151, 152n, 153, 170n, 173, 205n, 210n
Tendulkar, Suresh D., 81n, 163–64
Theil, Henri, 222
Thias, H. H., 188n
Thomas, H. A., Jr., 218n
Thorbecke, Erik, 130n, 183
Thoreson, Richard, 91
Thurow, Lester C., 178n
Tilanus, C. B., 45n
Tims, Wouter, 45n, 80n, 151
Tinbergen, Jan, 2n, 5n, 6, 114n, 127n, 240, 327, 329
Todaro, Michael P., 327
Tokoyama, K., 84n, 90n, 108
Tomlin, J. A., 270n
Tsukui, Jinkichi, 84n, 90n, 108
Turnham, David, 180
Turnovsky, Stephen J., 83n
Tyson, Laura D'Andrea, 102n

## U

Ullman, E., 247
Uzawa, Hirofumi, 91, 158n

## V

van Rijckeghem, Willy, 45n
van Wickeren, Alfred C., 251–52

368